EMIRS IN LONDON

Subaltern Travel and Nigeria's Modernity

Moses E. Ochonu

INDIANA UNIVERSITY PRESS

This book is a publication of

Indiana University Press
Office of Scholarly Publishing
Herman B Wells Library 350
1320 East 10th Street
Bloomington, Indiana 47405 USA

iupress.org

© 2022 by Moses E. Ochonu

All rights reserved
No part of this book may be reproduced or utilized in any form or by any means, electronic or mechanical, including photocopying and recording, or by any information storage and retrieval system, without permission in writing from the publisher. The paper used in this publication meets the minimum requirements of the American National Standard for Information Sciences—Permanence of Paper for Printed Library Materials, ANSI Z39.48-1992.

Manufactured in the United States of America

First printing 2022

Cataloging information is available from the Library of Congress.

ISBN 978-0-253-05916-1 (hardback)
ISBN 978-0-253-05915-4 (paperback)
ISBN 978-0-253-05914-7 (ebook)

CONTENTS

Acknowledgments ix

Introduction: Traveling and Writing the Metropole in the Age of Modernity *1*

1 Literacy, Narrative, and the Colonial Ideational Space *50*

2 Emir Dikko's Metropolitan Adventures *91*

3 Emirs in Britain: Mapping Aristocratic Colonial Itineraries *133*

4 The Dikko-Nagogo British Connection *181*

5 Metropolitan Travel and Utilitarian Literacy *233*

6 Deepening Imperial Exploration, Imagining the Postcolony *273*

Epilogue: The Persistent, Evolving Fraternities of Empire *313*

Bibliography 343

Index 355

ACKNOWLEDGMENTS

So many people contributed to this book in ways both tangible and inspirational.

The research process benefitted from the generosity of many colleagues and interlocutors. Staff of the Nigerian National Archive, Kaduna, and the Arewa House Center for Historical Documentation were exceptionally helpful in locating materials and making them available.

At the outset, Dr. Shehu Tijjani Yusuf and Dr. Samaila Suleiman Yandaki of Bayero University, Kano, Nigeria, helped with pilot research at the two aforementioned archives.

I appreciate the late professor Philip Shea, my undergraduate adviser at Bayero University, who helped facilitate and coordinate this preliminary archival exploration. Vincent Akpakwu was part of my intellectual journey from its beginning in Kano, Nigeria, and I am grateful to him.

At the British National Archive and the Rhodes House Archive, Oxford University, staff filled requests and helped find materials I did not even know were in their collections.

Saheed Aderinto generously sent me relevant files, products of his explorations in the British archives.

As I made multiple trips to archives and fieldwork sites in Nigeria, many individuals provided various kinds of assistance. This research entailed the translation of many Hausa language materials, which I undertook during the early stages of the research. However, when vernacular materials accumulated beyond my capacity to keep up, I turned to Abdulrahman Abdullahi, on the recommendation of Dr. Carmen McCain, to help translate a cache of Hausa newspaper materials.

In Katsina, Dr. Rabe Gambo of Umaru Musa Yar'Adua University (UMYU) was instrumental in arranging interviews and access to the palace and its trophy/memorabilia room.

Dr. Musa Jibril, also of UMYU, helped with interviews in and around the Katsina palace. He also arranged for photographs and, most important, brokered my access to the M. T. Safana Archives, a private collection owned by Alhaji Mohammed Ibrahim Safana.

Over the several years of writing this book, personal conversations with colleagues and friends inspired, confirmed, dispelled, and deepened several of my arguments: Murray Last, Steven Pierce, Abdulbasit Kassim, Farooq Kperogi, Jose Cossa, Ibrahim Hamza, Mairo Mandara, Ja'afar Ja'afar, Munir Mustapha, Aliyu Iliyasu Ma'aji, Adebayo Oyebade, Douglas Anthony, Ibrahim Hamza, Muktar Aliyu, Jonathan Reynolds, and others too numerous to name.

Dianna Bell read the first version of the manuscript and offered both comments and supportive words. Chad Attenborough was a proofreader and sounding board at various stages. He read at least two early versions of the chapters. He also helped me retrieve an important file from the British Archive while conducting his own research there.

Other colleagues, including Tasha Rijke-Epstein and Elisha Renne, listened patiently as I explained my inchoate ideas and politely asked questions that planted seeds of inspiration or caused me to reflect more critically.

Dr. Aliyah Adamu Ahmad of Sokoto State University, Nigeria, generously sent me a copy of her unpublished paper on Dadasare Abdullahi, a precursor to her introduction and afterword in Dadasare's posthumously published autobiography. Her paper helped me flesh out many of my own findings on Dadasare.

Professor Okpeh Ochayi Okpeh is a never-ceasing wellspring of collegiality and support. His intellectual fingerprints are on this book.

I thank the anonymous reviewers of the manuscript for suggesting pathways for strengthening my contentions and the organizational architecture of the book.

Judith Byfield read the manuscript and penned a strong and humbling blurb for the book, as did Lisa Lindsay, Toyin Falola, Stephanie Newell, Adéléke Adéèkó, Mohammed Bashir Salau, and Olufemi Vaughan.

I presented excerpts and aspects of this work at various institutions and conferences—Duke University, the University of Pennsylvania, the University of Michigan, the University of Florida, Northwestern University, and Johns Hopkins University. I appreciate the comments and critiques of colleagues at these institutions, who can see their comments and my responses to them implemented on the pages of this book. I want to single out Derek Peterson of the University of Michigan for special mention. His years-long, thoughtful engagement with this work helped me to strengthen its framing.

The editorial and production staff at Indiana University Press were a delight to work with as the manuscript made its convoluted way from rough draft to a clean, in-press document.

I owe a special gratitude to the emir of Dutse, Dr. Muhammad Sanusi. My first research experience in Northern Nigerian Muslim aristocratic culture occurred through the emir generously granting me access to the royal museum and palace in Dutse, the two repositories of the emirate's history, material culture, and institutional memory. During that visit, the emir generously designated Turakin Dutse and district head of Dutse, Jamilu Basiru Sanusi, to cater to my research needs and to facilitate my travels within the emirate. Jamilu Basiru Sanusi was the perfect research host and interlocutor. That research experience in Dutse helped crystallize my current focus on the nexus of aristocratic metropolitan travel and modernity in Northern Nigeria.

Finally, I thank my wife, Margaret, and our daughters, Ene and Agbenu, for their support, patience, and understanding as I worked on this book.

EMIRS in LONDON

INTRODUCTION

Traveling and Writing the Metropole in the Age of Modernity

> London is more than a city;
> it is a complete country compressed into a single place.
>
> —Abubakar Imam

MUSLIM ARISTOCRATS IN COLONIAL NORTHERN NIGERIA EXPERIENCED the tragedy of submitting to a white, Christian imperial power, suffering racial and religious humiliation in the process. Colonial cultural whiteness and the neo-Christian values of the British colonizers symbolically supplanted the racial and religious dignity of traditional rulers and aristocrats in Northern Nigeria. British colonial hierarchies of race and culture modulated the African and Muslim identities of these colonized African actors. As the cradle of colonial cultural erasure and political subordination, Britain represented the source of this indignity.

Logically, Britain should not have been a magnet for Northern Nigerian Muslim aristocrats seeking the pleasures of travel and adventure, but colonization often confounded conventional logics of affinity and enmity. Imperial itineraries rarely conformed to the teleology and binary oppositions suggested by the initial animosities of colonial conquest. The fact that British colonizers co-opted colonized African elites into colonial administrative business paved the way for less adversarial relationships between African elites, Muslim or not, and British imperials. In this context of convenient alliance between colonizers and colonized aristocrats, it was possible for the elites of Northern Nigeria, like those of other colonial domains in Africa and elsewhere, to reimagine Britain as a place for tourism, sightseeing, and immersion in modernity and colonial culture. It was possible, in this complex relational context, for the aristocratic subaltern to imagine travel to the imperial metropole not as a contradictory, ironic infatuation with the spatial reminder of subjugation but rather as an understandable, profitable mobility as a stakeholder and self-interested actor in the orbit of an empire.

The emirs and aristocrats of Northern Nigeria, simultaneously subalterns and men of status, were explorers in a way both analogous and contrapuntal to the repertoires of white colonial explorers. Overwhelmingly Muslim, the aristocrats were purveyors of colonial modernity. They were enthusiastic participants in colonial modernization initiatives in a region stereotyped in Nigerian popular and journalistic narratives as a site of Islamic conservatism resistant to modernist schemes. This book contends that metropolitan travel was critical to the making of modernity in Northern Nigeria. This twining of travel and modernity mapped onto a vibrant culture of literacy and literary production as well as onto the politics of colonial mediation. Metropolitan tours enabled emirs and aristocrats to translate metropolitan cultures, symbols, infrastructures, and commodities into a Hausa vernacular idiom that their subjects and local interlocutors could relate to. In this way, the tours conferred on the aristocrats social capital with which to mediate between metropolitan colonial cultures and Hausa Muslim ones.

The central argument of this book is that this vernacularized colonial modernity was enabled and sustained by a culture of travel to Britain and the material and textual practices and processes spawned by this type of travel. The logistical, literary, political, and economic products and aftermaths of this metropolitan travel were the fulcrum of a uniquely Northern Nigerian iteration of colonial modernity. *Emirs in London* analyzes this imbrication of mobility and modernity, its history, its evolution, and its implications for the epistemology of colonization, Islam, and subaltern literary culture. In analyzing the movement of African Muslims to and within the metropole, this book contributes to the growing literature on black Muslims' mobility and life in imperial and Atlantic spaces.[1] The colonial mobility of Nigerian Muslim aristocrats, their toing and froing in the geographical and cultural orbit of empire, was sustained by curiosity and the imperative of colonial legitimacy, as well as by new patterns of consumption and their centrality in subaltern self-making.

Emirs in London recounts how Northern Nigerian Muslim aristocrats who traveled to Britain between 1920 and 1960 portrayed the imperial metropole to Northern Nigerian people. It tells how the aristocrats leveraged metropolitan travel to negotiate their roles in the empire, reinforce their positions as imperial cultural brokers, and translate and domesticate imperial modernity in a predominantly Muslim society. In this analysis, the travelers' management of relationships built with metropolitan interlocutors, institutions, and goods is as important as the trips and their narratives. In some cases, these connections found expression in epistolary exchanges before, between, and after visits, illuminating the efforts of the traveling aristocrats to replicate and domesticate metropolitan phenomena, and to repurpose metropolitan goods.

Given the popular, contemporary, and undeservedly overblown reputation of Northern Nigeria as a hotbed of Islamist radicalization and anti-Western rhetoric, it may seem counterintuitive that Britain consistently played host to visitors from Northern Nigeria during the colonial period (1900–60) and beyond and that these visitors enthusiastically embraced imperial adventure and the narrative practice it produced as part of their broader repertoire of colonial mediation and self-fashioning. However, for decades, travel to the metropole was the capstone of the aristocrats' efforts to strategically navigate the imperial system for their own ends. Subaltern travel to the metropole seems well within the norm of mobility that occurred between the colonial center and the periphery. Such mobility was the conduit for imperial cultural interaction and an avenue for the consolidation of a common symbolic imperial loyalty centered on the English monarchy and other metropolitan institutions.

The negotiable, incorporative character of colonization lends logic to the metropolitan adventures analyzed in the chapters of this book. Travel to the imperial center was a logical undertaking full of cognitive possibilities, its cognate being the itineraries and archives of British travel to and writings on the societies of the colonized. Much of this book is informed by an interpretive reading of Hausa- and English-language travel narratives written by Northern Nigerian emirs and aristocrats about their travel to Britain. The analysis culminates in a set of perspectives that approximate Northern Nigerian aristocratic travelers' unique gaze on Britain. The travelers' accounts, rhetoric, and claims provide crucial insights into the ways subaltern elites used the technologies and avenues offered by colonialism to construct complex discourses on empire and refashion themselves as modern aristocrats. Read alongside European travelers' writings on Africa, African elite travel narratives on Britain open an illuminating vista onto a complex and dialectical picture of empire. These narratives offer insights into the colonial politics of imperial travel and the aristocratic kinships and protocols that indexed metropolitan adventures. Additionally, they reveal African eyewitness representations of the imperial metropole and the narrators' negotiation of imperial culture at its metropolitan command post.

This book corrects a major oversight in African colonial historiography—namely, the reluctance to accord analytical significance to the perspectives of African subaltern aristocrats and privileged elites.[2] The voices of aristocrats have been marginalized in African colonial studies as the compromised texts of colonial collaborators. Colonized elites with footholds in imperial cultures and institutions, no matter how ambivalent such entanglements might have been, became "associated with reactionary politics."[3] As Simon Gikandi puts it, in the canonical polemics of decolonization, there was "clearly no sympathy for texts or authors which saw their role as mediating the delicate relationship between colonizer and colonized."[4] This book restores an objective reception to the writings and metropolitan adventures of privileged African colonial mediators. I contend that the travelogues of Northern Nigerian aristocrats, the metropolitan itineraries that informed them, and the ways these elites leveraged their metropolitan experiences to (re)define themselves reveal a unique sensibility that complements rather than contradicts the responses of less privileged African subalterns to colonization. These elite subjectivities should thus be read both along and against the grain of the perspectives of nonaristocratic Africans—long privileged in the literature as embodying an authentic African subaltern experience.

It is important to recognize the epistemological inspiration of works that profile a diverse cast of Africans who lived permanently or quasi-permanently in imperial Britain. Hakim Adi and David Killingray have written African migrant subjectivities and engagements into the historiography of Victorian, Edwardian, and Elizabethan Britain in ways that recognize the African migrants' catalytic humanity in the shadow of metropolitan colonial racism.[5] More recently, this literature has taken an insightful biographical turn with Danell Jones's *An African in Imperial London*, which tells the fascinating story of A.B.C. Merriman-Labor, who immigrated to England from Sierra Leone at the turn of the twentieth century and became a journalist, a publisher, a writer, a socialite, and eventually a forgotten destitute.[6] In these stories we see the remarkable range of African metropolitan adventures and the struggles and triumphs of Africans who navigated the imperial metropolitan space on a permanent or quasi-permanent basis.

A major oversight in these works is the absence of an African comparative frame or foil for understanding the metropolitan struggles and perspectives of the African immigrants. Another is that, in several cases, the authors could not recover the archive of representations the migrants produced, constraining the extent to which the perspectives of the migrants on Britain could be reconstructed. Moreover, the emphasis on permanent and semi-permanent African migrants to Britain excludes the equally instructive metropolitan experiences of African tourists and visitors entering and leaving Britain regularly from the late nineteenth through the twentieth century.

Emirs in London is one of two recent works to focus on the imperial adventures of African tourists and sightseers in Britain—visitors to the metropole who had finite, temporary business to transact and spent no more than weeks or months there at a time. The other work is Neil Parsons's *King Khama*. It is a rich narrative of the visit of three Tswana kings to Britain in 1895 and tries to remedy the aforementioned African voice deficit by reproducing some of the daily itineraries of the kings while analytically contextualizing them in metropolitan imperial politics.[7] Although this approach humanizes the kings and enables readers to see the monarchs acting and being acted upon by imperial spaces, institutions, and personalities, the voices of the kings are heavily redacted through the archived recollections of metropolitan interlocutors. *Emirs in London* combines the biographical narrative approach of the aforementioned works with the analytical contextualization Parsons brings to bear on the metropolitan adventures of the three Tswana aristocratic visitors to Britain. However, unlike the aforementioned works, which deal with Christian or traditionalist Africans, *Emirs in London* highlights an African Muslim perspective on Britain.

Another way this book extends the insights of previous works in this broad genre is that it analyzes the vast, evolving imperial networks, discourses, and logistical infrastructures that facilitated and shaped the trips of the Northern Nigerian aristocrats, taking travel not as an event but as an entire universe of bureaucratic and political practices linking vast temporal and spatial formations. Balancing the biographical, the logistical, and the analytical is the challenge of this type of work.

Emirs in London contributes an additional angle to the existing approaches by letting the traveling aristocrats themselves speak about their metropolitan experiences as much as possible; in so doing, it remains faithful to the idioms, metaphors, and techniques they invoked to make sense of Britain, Britons, and British culture. The narrative scripts of the traveling aristocrats contained both adulatory and critical commentary on Britain. For this reason, and for the fact that the aristocrats sometimes asserted predilections that confounded expressed colonial wishes for the trips, my analysis departs from the popular framing of privileged, similarly conservative subaltern elites as men steeped in mimicry.[8] There were elements of mimesis in the way the aristocrats engaged with metropolitan commodities and symbols, but their overall interaction with British metropolitan interlocutors, British symbols, and material cultures was nuanced, informed as much by their own instrumental, pragmatic, and utilitarian agendas as by the pull and allure of metropolitan phenomena.

Imperial Experience and the Ethnography of Wonder

Scholars of empire recognize the scholarly value of the writings of European colonial traveler-ethnographers on African societies for their embodiment of the so-called imperial gaze, a set of scribal, aesthetic, literary, and rhetorical representations of African peoples by a diverse group of European actors. This book advances a counterpoint to the vast corpus of European portrayals and understandings of African peoples and societies, a body of intellectual production analogous to what Edward Said calls Orientalism.[9] The following analysis reveals what emerges when we flip the inquiry to consider how colonized African elites who traveled to European colonial countries for sightseeing portrayed metropolitan cultures and peoples in their writings. The book's chapters show the ambivalent contents and contexts of a unique and powerful, if colonially constrained, discursive endeavor in which the society and culture of the colonizer, not the colonized, became the subject of intense observational inquiry carried out by colonized elites visiting the colonial metropole.

As Juan Cole posits, a blind spot of Said's *Orientalism* is its effacement of the ways the textual, material, and scribal properties that make up the Orientalist corpus were coproduced, interactively informed, and shaped by the osmotic confluence of European and non-European discourses and initiatives.[10] Moreover, Said's tome is only one side of the mutual constructions of Europeans and those they regarded as their Other in colonially dominated non-European worlds. European observers, travelers, and writers constructed an Africa of benighted humans and untamed flora and fauna, all of which purportedly demanded the interventionist mediation of European actors to unleash their potential and value. African subalterns who returned the gaze did so not merely to reject the Eurocentric characterizations of their societies and affirm that their humanity was already fully realized and needed no external validation. They also wrote to posit a robust ethnographic image of Europe and Europeans—what Cole calls Occidentalism.[11] This African traveler-ethnographer imagination lays claim to knowledge production through experiencing and observing the ways of the white man in the same way European actors established an epistemological genre on colonized societies through the instrumentality of observation, travel, and claims to experiential recall. The important difference of course was that European observational texts paved the way for and legitimized conquest and domination while African traveler-ethnographer discourses were driven by curiosity and adventure.

The connection between travel and ethnography, and thus between experiential observation and the modern practice of anthropology, is often taken for granted,[12] but this is mainly because this association is made for Europeans only, who are posited as those who travel for ethnographic observation, as opposed to those in the non-Western world, who supposedly travel by happenstance or for trade. This perspective persists despite Bernard Lewis's insistence that the West also was the object of ethnographic travel inquiries conducted by non-Western, Muslim actors and despite the painstaking documentation, beginning in medieval times, of Africans adventurously exploring and recording Europe through an observational ethnographic lens.[13]

In the nineteenth century, a travel- and observation-based ethnography of the Other, which had evolved to encompass the travel literary productions of some non-Western peoples,[14] developed further as European imperial maneuvers in Africa and the Middle East intensified. This new imperial moment produced and in some cases was preceded by the development of the epistemological apparatuses of what we now call fieldwork—all-purpose encyclopedic diary recordings, note-taking based on observations, and commentaries informed by the observer's own cognitive predilections, and, in the case of hegemonic actors, the desire to "civilize" and dominate. Travel to supposedly exotic lands was repurposed as an explicit imperial endeavor—a quest to master the ways of life, landscapes, cultures, and languages of those subjected or about to be subjected to European rule.

The invention of mass touristic travel and guided overseas tours, pioneered by Thomas Cook in the 1840s and engendered by the development of geographic, cartographic, and navigational guidebooks, all came to define the new spirit of imperial adventure, but the veneration of travel as an epistemological undertaking persisted in Britain. The powerful epistemic claim of knowing a distant culture and people because of one's personal, intimate experience in that society continued to underpin the institution of travel within the broader configuration of imperial interaction.

It is my contention that the Northern Nigerian aristocrats who traveled to the metropole similarly engaged in an epistemic enterprise utilizing ethnography, which was, in turn, sustained by the power of experience, observation, studious probing, and commentary. In respect to the development of British imperial overseas travel, Nile Green argues that beginning in the nineteenth century, there was a shift from the travel account as a perspectival discourse to one in which it was consecrated as established knowledge to be textually transmitted as a baseline for further epistemological inquiry.[15] In the travelogues of the subaltern travelers analyzed in this book, this distinction is of little analytical utility. These travelers transitioned smoothly between descriptive empiricism and evaluative interpretation. Commentary and chronicle coexisted awkwardly but insightfully in their narratives.

Although foregrounded by empire, the business of curating the Other in the context of imperial travel was not an exclusively imperial affair underwritten solely by British imperatives. Aristocratic travelers from Northern Nigeria were nominated or approved by British colonial overlords to explore the metropole, but their explorations were not entirely determined by the power architecture of colonialism. Rather, the travelers primarily explored the Occident through the twin stimuli that drove European imperial traveler-ethnographers: the possibility of acquiring new cultural capital through the experience of foreign travel[16] and the magical appeal of wonder.[17]

In this context wonder functioned "as a goad to inquiry" rather than as a post-Enlightenment idiom for the implausible inventions of the human mind: myths, mysteries, legends, folkloric fairy tales, and other titillating but immaterial phenomena.[18] The curiosity of Northern Nigerian aristocratic travelers was framed by this expansive notion of wonder as a precursor to concrete, tangible discovery. The materiality of wonder as an object of imperial travel and exploration inheres in the existence of actual metropolitan technological wonders and the fact that the subaltern's wonder was often satisfied by the material culture of utilitarian imperial modernity.

Colonial travelers to the metropole could give concrete expression to their wonder, transforming it into an object of value by purchasing and handling goods and symbols whose stories and fantasies animated their wondrous longing in the first place. In this sense, travel to the metropole enabled the travelers to access a modernity at once sensory, emotive, and material. Travelers encountered metropolitan modernity as a sensory, emotional object of wonder.[19] Thus, abstract, distant wonder became an object once it was projected onto the awesome physicality of metropolitan spaces, edifices, and sights. In wonder as a cognitive stimulus, we find the platform of inquiry that united the travel ethnographies of both the colonizers and the colonized.

Literacy and the Vernacular Aesthetic of Adventure

The growth of mass literacy in Northern Nigeria provided pathways into certain modes of understanding and interpreting the world and certain forms of aesthetic and cultural engagements. It also engendered a cognitive universe that enabled the flourishing of a literary culture of storytelling and story reading in the Roman script. Romanized literacy promoted a shared literary sensibility attuned to certain kinds of stories—stories of adventure, travel and triumph, and discovery and daring.

The extensive acquisition and publishing functions and mediatory literary undertakings of Northern Nigeria's colonial publishing firm, Gaskiya Corporation, and its affiliated agency, the Northern Nigerian Literature Agency (NORLA), were instrumental in forging this culture of literacy. A regionwide colonial mass literacy campaign helped complete this intersection of literacy and literature. Analyzing the evolution of this colonial literary scene in Northern Nigeria is critical to understanding the development of the institution of metropolitan travel and its documentation in various mediums of mass communication. Gaskiya and the NORLA were instrumental to the Romanization of the Hausa folkloric tradition. These colonial organs of ideational dissemination funded and encouraged the textual recording and translation of numerous Hausa folk stories and legends into Romanized Hausa and English forms, and these stories were published with expressive and supplementary illustrations commissioned by the two sister agencies of vernacular literacy.

The intellectual world Gaskiya created was supported by the colonial government's policy of promoting mass literacy founded on the acquisition of basic reading and writing skills outside the formal schooling infrastructure. As discussed in chapter 1, this literacy campaign created an audience for metropolitan travel stories. Gaskiya Corporation—along with its closely affiliated organ, the *Gaskiya ta fi Kwabo* newspaper—became the publisher of choice for Northern Nigerian metropolitan travelers wishing to convey their experiences as visitors in Britain to this new, growing audience of Romanized Hausa readers. Given the vernacular publishing pedigree of Gaskiya Corporation and its niche area of adventure and travel folktales, the new genre of metropolitan travel narratives was a natural fit for its book-publishing endeavor. As analyzed in chapter 5, *Gaskiya ta fi Kwabo* was a dialogic space where a Hausa-speaking audience, already curious about the metropole, nudged both travelers and the newspaper's editors to satisfy their informational curiosities about how the white man lived in Britain. This preexisting appetite for fantastical and factual stories about the metropole helped sustain the genre of metropolitan travel narratives and the dialogue that ensued around them among travelers, editors, and newspaper readers.

This vernacular world of writing, reading, and experiential sharing, which was managed by a bilingual colonial elite, instantiates two catalytic factors Benedict Anderson identifies in relation to the emergence of national and protonational solidarity in colonies.[20] The caveat here is that this new reading Northern Nigerian public did not forge a nationalist consciousness in the traditional sense. Its continued invocation of metropolitan idioms of modernity as guiding motifs must be seen not as the simple adoption of a nationalist model but as a local aesthetic and cultural project imbricated in metropolitan tastes and symbols.

The world birthed by the Gaskiya family of vernacular institutions was thus similar in ideological content to those created in colonial India by a similar admixture of vernacularized literacy and the paradigmatic ubiquity of European signs and symbols of modernity. In India, the subaltern's "desire to be modern" meant he wanted to be culturally "European" while staking out niches and realms that expressed and satiated vernacular aesthetics, sensibilities, and anxieties.[21] *Emirs in London* reiterates this duality by analyzing the popularity of metropolitan travel narratives that circulated in the Gaskiya vernacular literary universe.

The cognitive avenues opened by expanded Romanized Hausa literacy and small pockets of English-language literacy ensured a familiarity with and even appetite for metropolitan cultures and other markers of colonial modernity. To be literate in English or Romanized Hausa was to enter into a world of mutual intelligibility between tradition and modernity, between colonizer and colonized. Romanized literacy helped Northern Nigerians access a world in which colonial ideas and cultural forms became legible, relatable, and sometimes even desirable as paradigmatic standards of the unfolding colonial cultural economy.

Travel, Mobility, and Colonial Aristocratic Courtship

Subaltern aristocratic travel to the metropole was grounded in the larger politics of imperial courtship. Courting aristocrats in African colonies relied on significations rooted in the hierarchies of British society. British colonizers saw subaltern societies possessing traditions of centralized kingships through the lens of their own society as "a seamless web of layered gradations, which were hallowed by time and precedent [and] sanctioned by tradition and religion" in a "great chain of being" connecting kings to subjects.[22] This British imperial attitude, David Cannadine argues, enabled colonizers to imagine an "extra-metropolitan world" of aristocratic class solidarity that sublimated racial otherness in the relationship between metropolitan colonizers and upper-class subalterns of aristocratic pedigree.[23] Subaltern aristocratic subjectivity, in this sense, was constituted as an aspirational copy of the metropolitan privileged classes. My analysis aligns in part with Cannadine's characterization.

This vision of empire as an idealized continuum of shared symbols among men of privilege on both sides of the imperial divide thrived on reinforcing hierarchy in both the metropole and the colony as a pragmatic idiom of rule. If, as Cannadine posits, the British saw subaltern lower classes as the overseas equivalents of the metropolitan poor, aristocratic subalterns logically became aspirational extensions of metropolitan aristocrats.[24] This imperial understanding was fraught with, and often disrupted by, the overarching ideological subtext of race. Nonetheless, for both utilitarian and symbolic purposes, imperial aristocratic solidarity underwrote an elaborate "honors system" that "homogenized the heterogeneity of empire" through the elaborate ritual of courtship extended to aristocratic imperial allies in certain colonies.[25] Courtship took many forms, but a favored medium was exposure, through travel, to the awesome industrial and cultural materialities of the metropole. Controlled and scripted travel by favored subalterns was a particularly powerful organ of colonial courtship.

One of the sociopolitical bedrocks of colonization was the sophisticated art of controlling and monitoring the freedoms of the colonized, one of which was freedom of movement. Colonizers sometimes measured the success of their enterprise on their ability to restrict or monitor colonial subjects' mobility.[26] Several colonial policies, especially those dealing with labor, whether migrant or stable, fetishized the value of stasis when it came to African colonial subjects.[27] These policies conveyed the notion that Africans would be better off if they did not move to or within unfamiliar urban settings and instead remained in their natal villages. Colonizers sought to keep Africans quarantined to the supposed stability of rural, ancestral areas, believing that traditional country settings and institutions were agents of sociopolitical restraint and control. British colonizers believed that travel and migration to new colonial urban areas could denude Africans of their alleged propensity for subservience and deference to established authorities and institutions.[28]

Subaltern travel within and outside the empire, if not planned or monitored by colonizers, signaled to colonialists a desire to be free of colonial control. Unregimented travel disrupted the economic and social rhythms of life as imagined by colonizers. Allowing colonial subjects to move freely threatened the political economy of colonization since mobile Africans could drive up wages and unsettle colonial urban markets, infrastructures, and social arrangements. If done according to colonial dictates, subaltern travel provided colonizers with opportunities for mind management and control. However, colonizers worried about subaltern travel going awry and mobile subaltern bodies slipping away from the brittle grip of official minders, in which case such travel could backfire and produce traveling subjects who were either overly enamored with modernity or disdainful of it. Unauthorized mobility, within and outside the colonial territory, was a significant concern because the subaltern could exercise independent subjectivities that undermined the colonial obsession with documenting and shaping every facet of a subject's life.

African colonial subjects' travel to the metropole for private business outside the orbit of official logistics and protocols intensified colonizers' anxiety about colonial bodies moving independently through colonial space. Because colonially sponsored travelers with predetermined itineraries could veer off scripted paths, approved travel to the metropole by the colonized was fraught with the potential for subversion. Such travel could lead to what colonizers considered dangerous self-discovery on the part of the subaltern travelers, not to mention a consciousness-awakening demystification of the colonizer.

Travel is an intimate experiential endeavor beyond the deterministic reach of powerful planners. Only the travelers know how they truly feel about what they are observing and experiencing. Metropolitan travel itineraries could be bureaucratized and organized to give colonizers some control, but traveling African colonial subjects could obey their inner curiosity and sidestep the organized program of tours and sightseeing, opening up a space for independent exploration of the metropole and its cultures and in turn producing an unpredictably complex economy of knowledge and ethnological inquiry.

Traveling African aristocratic subalterns posed a particular risk for colonizers who saw metropolitan travel as a tool of imperial courtship. Rulers who were imbued with "popular legitimacy" conferred by both tradition and their centrality to colonial administration, such as emirs from the defunct Sokoto Caliphate, proved to be "most difficult and independent-minded."[29] When such rulers traveled to the metropole, colonizers constructed a discursive and bureaucratic universe through which their metropolitan observations could be expressed—imperial institutional superstructures that Ann Stoler calls "colonial common sense."[30] Nonetheless, traveling emirs and aristocrats found ample space to observe and narrate the metropole in unexpected ways.

It is precisely because travel by colonized people within and across imperial jurisdictions was such a charged, potentially destabilizing endeavor that its payoff for the traveler and his kinsfolk was significant and worth the risk. A successfully completed trip indicated the ability to evade or negotiate the multiple jurisdictional apparatuses of colonial and neocolonial state entities. To travel to the world of the white man and return to tell the story was to lay claim to that which the white man had sought to render exclusive to his race: the ability to understand far-flung lands and peoples through adventure and exploration.

In colonial Nigeria, the cachet of metropolitan travel was not restricted to the aristocrats of the North. The trope of the "been-to" had a powerful resonance across the entire colonial territory of Nigeria. It was a pan-Nigerian shorthand for recognizing the accomplishment of those who had gone to observe the white man in his "habitat." The most famous Nigerian traveler of the colonial period was not a Northern Nigerian aristocrat; rather, it was Olabisi Ajala, a Yoruba from Nigeria's western region who toured eighty-seven countries, including several in North America and western Europe, between 1957 and 1958. Ajala used his observations, notes, experiences, and reconstituted memories to pen his acclaimed travel memoir, *An African Abroad*.[31] Ajala's adventures became the stuff of popular

Nigerian legend, further mystifying the image of the been-to as a restless, subversive, and daring adventurer who could not be held down by colonial strictures and whose desire to see the white man's world was stronger than the white man's desire to keep him confined to the assigned social spaces of colonial society.[32]

The Conceptual Context

In an age of accelerated human mobility, how can we understand African mobilities in Western spaces outside the reductive frames of displacement, economic refuge, and the search for a better life? How can scholarship on African mobility posit Africa as the origin as well as the destination of colonial exploratory travel?[33] Without posing the question directly, this study intervenes in the growing scholarly interest in African mobilities.[34] I argue that focusing exclusively on the political economy of African travel is a reductive frame and that a more robust accounting for African itineraries must reckon with the emotional economy of African mobilities—the range of affective resources and quests at stake when Africans leave their ancestral lands for other locales.

The frame of exile and escape dominates popular theorizations of African travel. The circulation of people and goods examined in this book, admittedly set in different temporal and political dynamics than those of today, challenges this popular understanding and provides a historical baseline for making sense of African mobilities in the twenty-first century. The African subaltern itineraries analyzed in the following chapters were based on a search for the pleasure, leisure, and affective rewards of travel and adventure. They were not produced by the pressures and adversities of political economy. African aristocratic subalterns, traveling to and within the metropole, were savvy travelers motivated by the emotional economies and psychic yearnings satiated by travel and exploration.

The overbearing presence and influence of European textual claims on the art and politics of geographical discovery, consequential mobility, and the knowledge that emanates from them have constrained scholarly inquiry into African exploratory activities. The vast corpus of European travelers' writings on Africa constitutes an archive of representation that provides a reference for deciphering how various groups of European colonial actors—missionaries, explorers, travelers, geographers, ethnographers, and others—produced knowledge about African societies and the topographies, flora, and fauna of Africa.[35] Much less scholarly attention has been devoted to the works of Africans who traveled to Europe within and outside the protective and restrictive ambience of colonization and returned to pen their impressions.

Some of this inattention stems from the assumption that such travelers were little more than preselected and sponsored native imperial propagandists—props and puppets in imperial schemes to conceal and humanize the harm of colonial oppression. That may be true of some travelers, but two points undermine this contention. Many African travelers to the colonial metropole, including most of those whose itineraries and narratives are featured in this book, funded their own trips. Second, if external sponsorship in and of itself is a mark of irrelevance, then the vast pool of European travel writers who were sponsored, controlled, and directed by a diverse set of European state and private interests and groups should not be accorded the analytical attention it enjoys.

The travelogues analyzed here are texts deserving serious scholarly attention on their own terms. They mainly targeted a Hausa-speaking, largely Muslim audience that relied on the authoritative voices of aristocrats to make sense of British policies, goods, and ideas in relation to their own Muslim sensibilities. Some African travelers paired visits to London with the Muslim hajj, combining a religious pilgrimage with a political one. Given the complexity of this travel endeavor and the circuits of imperial cultural mobility in which travelers immersed themselves, the trips cannot simply be described or theorized as British hegemonic projects; they entailed the active participatory agency of the traveling aristocrats. Metropolitan travel also enabled the emergence of a vibrant space of discourse that, while sympathetic to colonial idioms, became a robust platform for interrogating the broader relationship between Northern Nigerian Muslim modes of life and the culture of colonialism embodied by metropolitan institutions.

Africans who traveled to the colonial center can be theorized in two ways: as those who wrote back to the European representational corpus on Africa and those who wrote *into* that representational epistemology. Africans who used the instruments of literacy to speak to and about the metropole were entering the colonial representational space and attempting to upend "the terms of representation."[36] They were writing into an imperial cultural space saturated by the distorted representational valences of European writers on Africa. This subaltern writing endeavor offered colonized audiences and eventually European readers, once the texts were translated from the vernacular, the unique and at times contrarian perspectives of colonized elites on metropolitan imperial culture.[37] In cleverly speaking to a second audience of colonial officials through their narratives, Northern Nigerian traveler-narrators were able to inscribe their perspectives in the colonial cultural and political conversation, even if they did not consciously set out to do that.

In this travel-writing enterprise, the interaction between writers and audiences was critical since the author's perspectives and reconstructions of the author's experiences in the metropole had to "meet some kind of authentic recognition in the reader," as Ilan Stavans and Joshua Ellison argue in *Reclaiming Travel*.[38] In other words, Northern Nigerian readers of these narratives first had to trust the traveler's narrative fidelity to the metropolitan events and conditions being described before the material would be favorably received. The mere existence of a Roman-literate community of Northern Nigerians hungry for stories of the metropole told by their own kind does not fully explain the persistent appetite for such stories. Ultimately, an audience coalesced and remained loyal to such writers because that audience trusted the writer-travelers to transcend colonial entanglements and write a relatively independent experiential account of the metropole.

Although travelers were not required to write about the metropole upon their return, a close reading of the sources indicates the existence of an unwritten expectation: the narratives emanating from the trips should help promote the glories and splendors of the Crown and other observed metropolitan political and cultural symbols. This hidden but powerful expectational economy inflected the writings of the travelers. Many Northern Nigerian aristocrats paid their way to Britain, but their income still depended on colonial patronage or at least on the material reward of performing assigned colonial tasks. Dependence on the revenue nodes of colonialism wrought unconscious ideological restraint on Northern Nigerian metropolitan tourists and dulled their critical edge. Nonetheless, to the extent that "we are responsible for the content and consequences of our experiences"[39] and the travel experience is shaped by the traveler's own desires and not by the external scripts that undergird such travel, the writings of the aristocratic travelers proclaim their ownership of their travel experiences and the structures within which the experiences were narrated.

The Katikiro Effect and Its Limits

The imperial epistemological space was suffused in multiple textual and representational practices and products, including the most well-known—the European travel ethnography genre. However, African narratives and discourses on the empire and its various facets and iterations proliferated in obscure, undocumented forms. The African oral corpus, for instance, is a rich depository of African reactions to, and engagements with, colonial institutions in that it contains cryptic notes on subaltern conditions and the banality of colonial subjugation.

Some African narratives on empire were not oral, cryptic, or obscure. Arguably, the most notable of these assertive African narratives on the British imperial metropole and on colonization is Ham Mukasa's *Uganda's Katikiro in England*, which was first published in English in 1904.[40] In 1902, the katikiro (or chief minister) of the Buganda kingdom, Apollo Kagwa, traveled to Britain for the coronation of King Edward VII. Accompanying the katikiro were his official interpreter and a missionary of the Church Missionary Society in Uganda, the Reverend Ernest Millar, as well as the katikiro's secretary, Ham Mukasa, who took copious notes during the visit and then used them to author the published account. For his part, Reverend Millar translated the text from the original Luganda to English.[41]

There is no evidence that the traveling aristocrats of Northern Nigeria read or even knew about Ham Mukasa's book on the katikiro's visit to Britain, yet there is no escaping the disarming similarity between the katikiro's itinerary in Britain and their own and between Mukasa's account of Britain and the accounts of the traveler-narrators of Northern Nigeria. Mukasa's account can be seen as having pioneered a genre of African commentary on the British imperial center that, consciously or not, the aristocrats of Nigeria replicated in their own travel accounts of Britain. This connection is not simply a matter of temporal or chronological precedence but is eerily etched in the themes, idioms, rhetoric, and narrative strategies employed by both Mukasa and the travel-narrators of Northern Nigeria.

The katikiro's trip was logistically organized by colonial authorities and guided by a colonial official, as were most of the trips discussed in the following chapters. Like the katikiro, Northern Nigeria's emirs traveled to Britain with a retinue of aides, including the obligatory secretary who painstakingly recorded observations and impressions. Both narratives were written in African languages—Luganda and Hausa—in their initial iterations, indicating that the imagined audience was local and that the primary purpose of the narrative was to construct a certain imaginary of Britain in conjunction with a coterminous perceptual economy of modernity in which the narrator was deeply imbricated. In that sense both Mukasa and the aristocrats discussed in this book occupied the same position in the British imperial system: they inscribed themselves as intercessors in the business of colonization and as translators of metropolitan culture to regular colonial subjects in their African domains.[42]

The similarities extend to the rhetorical field. The katikiro's narrative indicates that his alliance with the British and his highfalutin adulatory comments on Britain and British imperial institutions were codes for a more nuanced engagement with Britain. The katikiro saw his liminal niche within the empire as a liberating space enabling him to carry out the modernization of his own kingdom. Similarly, several of the aristocrats discussed in the following chapters—notably the emir of Katsina, Muhammadu Dikko—regarded their relationship with the metropole, lubricated by travel, as a source of the resources needed to modernize their domains.

Both the katikiro and the Northern Nigerian aristocrats were steered to the same sets of sites—mostly regal and official political institutions and spaces of Britain. These included Windsor Castle and Buckingham Palace, museums and other spaces that displayed the legacies and histories of imperial greatness, factories and other centers of technological operations and commodity manufacturing, military institutions, and centers of recreation and contrived hospitality. Both texts placed colonial culture on a pedestal as a paradigm of modernity that could determine the trajectory of their own societies. Both valorized the metropolitan symbols of English civilization, seeing them as capable of being adopted or domesticated for projects of development and modernization or at least serving as a reference for analogizing the processes of cultural evolution in their own societies.

Two main narrative devices are integral to Ham Mukasa's text. The first is the refrain that the British metropolitan center contained many wonders. The second is the difficulty of faithfully representing observed British marvels and the inadequacy of the narrator's language and vernacular vocabulary to convey a full sense of these marvels. These two interrelated themes similarly dominate the prefatory and concluding schemes of the travel accounts of Northern Nigerian emirs and aristocrats. Like Mukasa, they posited a claim of metropolitan modernity as an entity so vast, so wondrous, and so exotic that the lexical and idiomatic resources at their disposal were inadequate to capture it. The notion that metropolitan sights were too wondrous to be communicated by African indigenous lexicon was a recurring feature in African narratives on Britain. When three Tswana kings, Bathoen, Sebele, and Khama, visited Britain in 1895, their effusive portrayal of British metropolitan objects included claims such as "It will be difficult to make our people understand how iron and wood can move without being pulled by someone" and "We cannot explain these new ideas, because we have no [Tswana] words to correspond."[43] Like the claims of the Tswana kings, both Mukasa's narrative and those of Northern Nigerian aristocrats demarcated a zone of experience and observed culture that only the privilege of metropolitan travel could reveal and only a technological upgrade could tangibly replicate but that African speech was ill-equipped to describe.

Despite these similarities, there are marked differences and divergences in Mukasa's textual practice and that of the aristocrats discussed in the following chapters. The most obvious of these differences is religion. Mukasa and his subject, the katikiro, were proud Protestant Christians who identified self-consciously with metropolitan Anglicanism. As a result, they sought to establish and consolidate a religious and cultural affinity with the metropole. Much of their book "strenuously refuses to provide a critique of Englishness"[44] and thus stresses aspirational sameness over difference. Most of the aristocrats whose texts animate this book at different junctures were proud Muslims. While their narratives indicate they saw no contradiction between their Islamic identity or Muslim devotion and their conscious immersion in neo-Christian colonial culture, these same texts seem preoccupied with the politics of difference and distance and routinely highlighted the ways of the exotic metropolitan Other. The politics of contrast and difference emerges with much sharper clarity in the texts of these writers than in *Uganda's Katikiro in England*.

Although many of these Muslim aristocrats strategically embraced colonial modernity and the prestige it conferred, unlike Mukasa and the katikiro, they never sought to supplant their Hausa Muslim identity with the toga of Englishness, aspirational or otherwise. This difference stems partly from temporal factors, since Buganda's connection to English Anglicanism predated and arguably catalyzed the colonial annexation of the kingdom.[45] Mukasa drew on Buganda's traditions and English Christian lore as structuring devices for his narrative on the imperial center. Northern Nigerian aristocrats considered the category of customs and traditions *jahilci* (pre-Islamic ignorance), and, of course, as Muslims they could not have unquestioningly adopted the neo-Christian customs of the metropole. Thus, while Mukasa was reluctant to "produce a knowledge of Britain as the radical other,"[46] Northern Nigerian traveler-narrators wanted to precisely demarcate metropolitan culture from a Northern Hausa Islamic one. Contrast and radical divergence were thus the fundamental elements in their narrative craft even if, as my analysis demonstrates, many narrators advanced radical contrast merely as a prelude to establishing the importance of shrinking the cultural chasm between center and periphery and as a way of bolstering their claimed authority as interpreters of the mystery and magic of Britain.

In his introduction to the 1998 edition of *Uganda's Katikiro in England*, Simon Gikandi correctly states that the authorial voice of the text is self-effacing because Mukasa wanted to simply juxtapose Buganda and Britain in a culturally differentiated continuum of Protestant Englishness and did not want the traveler or the writer to disrupt this higher objective.[47] Northern Nigerian metropolitan travel texts were anything but self-effacing. The narrator often blended into his own narrative, in some cases becoming his own subject. In this narrative corpus, the very fact that the narrator was central to the metropolitan event he describes confers authority on the enterprise.

The claim of the writers was that they had witnessed and even participated in the programmatic enactments of metropolitan modernity. It is this intimately personal experiential agency, this perspective of the been-to, that attracted and sustained the audience for their writings. Self-effacement would have undermined this relationship between writer and audience and between writer-observer and the observed. Moreover, unlike Mukasa, who seemed intent on placing Buganda in the ideological universe of the metropole, the Northern Nigerian travel writers were not burdened by such anxieties. As I argue in chapters 2 and 4, and less explicitly in other chapters, the aristocrats had successfully compartmentalized the world of Englishness from the world of caliphate Islam. Thus, they did not aspire to an ideological kinship with the colonizer but only desired a kinship founded on mutual interests and the transformative capacity of certain carefully selected aspects of colonial culture.[48]

Subaltern Metropolitan Travel as Colonial Translation

Yahaya Ibn Haliru, the respected Muslim emir of Gwandu, penned a travelogue on his sightseeing trip to England in 1934, concluding his piece with a memorable summarizing punch line: "Duniya na birnin London" (The world begins and ends in London). Haliru's multivalent commentary on imperial Britain is fully analyzed in chapter 3. For now, it should be noted that while Haliru's rhetoric was uniquely melodramatic, the sentiment was hardly exclusive to him. Haliru's statement said as much about Britain as it did about a desire to posit the center of empire and its tropes of cultural and technological advancement as a paradigm of aspirational debates and conversations in Northern Nigeria's Muslim elite colonial circles.

The aristocrats' perch in the middle of the colonial hierarchy offered them a unique position as the cultural and administrative middlemen of colonialism. This book's analysis of mediation and translation builds on and extends the growing literature on colonial intermediaries by positing imperial sightseeing trips as pivotal to colonial mediation. These trips were made possible by the ethos and grammar of patronage inscribed in the relationship between British colonial officials and Hausa colonial mediators. Valued intermediaries who had been to England fancied themselves partakers and interpreters of British colonial culture. Describing the awe-inspiring majesty of Britain to regular colonial subjects was the very essence of colonial mediation. The travelers' ability to recount to their readers what they saw, did, and were told in Britain underscored their claimed intimate connection to this modernity. Their capacity to command the attention of their audience and persuade them on matters concerning metropolitan Britain was critical to their role as colonial intermediaries.

The aforementioned Haliru belonged to a colonial culture in which patronage was an unwritten but expected aspect of colonial business. African colonial allies had to be cultivated and nurtured to be effective interpreters of empire. This culture of mediation in turn generated a shared concept of modernity represented by the physical and cultural spaces of London and other British cities. Emir Haliru and his fellow travelers used the travelogues to underscore their membership in imperial circuits of power and prestige. They used the piercing power of imagery, mastery of Hausa storytelling aesthetics, and deft rhetorical techniques to enthrall an audience of Hausa readers. The traveler-writers' glamorization of metropolitan modernity and the promotion of their own privileged membership in this modernity were entwined in their narratives.

Clearly, there was a class undercurrent in the metropolitan adventures of the aristocrats, and the ornamental, sartorial, and technological outcomes and products of the trips reinforced existing class hierarchies.

The criticism of the trips by NEPU-affiliated Northern radical intellectuals (chap. 5) bears out these tensions. The accusation of the influential Sheikh Abubakar Gumi that the Northern aristocrats had abandoned their Muslim subjects to court neo-Christian British honors underscored the disruptive resonance of the trips among the region's Hausaphone Muslim population.[49] Such class frictions were, however, mitigated by the status of the emirs as inheritors and custodians of the Sokoto Caliphate's religious authority. An additional factor that regulated the class divides that the trips and their optics highlighted was the fact that regular Muslims looked to the emirs for guidance and direction in their engagement with colonialism.

In an Islamic society where emirs functioned as custodians of Islamic culture and human referents for Muslims who wanted to navigate colonial processes without violating Islamic precepts, the traveling aristocrats were treasured for their firsthand insight into imperial culture. As a result, their travel narratives routinely elicited letters, queries, and feedback from readers. The travelers were respected arbiters of what constituted acceptable Muslim engagement with imperial goods and cultures.

Mediation is an important and evolving object of inquiry in modern African history. Scholars have sought to understand the diverse arrangements that allowed certain Africans, whether in groups or as individuals, to occupy the middle position in colonization and translate colonial instructions into actions or colonial culture and ideas into terms intelligible to Africans.[50] Colonial middlemen were not simply conduits of imperial projects or mere interpreters of colonial ideas, however. Scholars have shown that African middlemen intervened vigorously and robustly in the colonial situation and, in some cases, stamped the imprimatur of their interests on important encounters and exchanges. African intermediaries expanded the dictionary of colonial communication by inventing a new lexicon through which the speeches, idioms, and predilections of the colonizer could be translated to the colonized and vice versa. This capacious definition of the role and importance of mediators and translators captures the discursive gamut and itinerary of the aristocratic travelers of Northern Nigeria.

As illuminating as it is, however, the current literature of colonial mediation hardly accommodates the ways travel, mobility, and the ability to traverse colonial space facilitated and expanded the task of mediation. Northern Nigerian traveler-narrators used the institutions of travel, participant observation, and travel narration to enrich their mediatory repertoires.

Travel to the metropole supplied more empirical material, context, and epistemological resources with which to translate colonial cultures, institutions, and practices for Africans who could not travel themselves. Travel to Britain alternately concretized, consolidated, or dispelled impressions forged in the crucible of colonial power relations. Travel enabled colonial mediators such as the Muslim aristocrats of Northern Nigeria to enter momentarily into the circuits of imperial cultural and political power and to more intensely study and scrutinize the ways of the white man. This metropolitan reverse ethnography enabled the aristocrats to evolve in their relatively privileged positions in colonization and develop additional approaches to colonial interpretation.

A Critical Admiration

Britain and its capital city, London, are often represented in colonial and postcolonial studies as incubators for oppressive and at times Islamophobic policies that harken back to Muslim encounters with Britain in the heydays of imperial conquest and colonial rule.[51] Britain was the site where the imperial subjugation of the Sokoto Caliphate was hatched and coordinated; it was the space from which the caliphate's formal annexation to the empire was directed. Moreover, Britain symbolized a marauding ideology that, while allowing African Muslim traditions to functionally exist in colonial governing and cultural practices, emasculated those traditions and brought them into ideological conformity with Victorian British practices and mores.

In light of this representation of Britain, a construct with its own blind spots, the question of why African Muslim tourists found Britain and its symbols appealing is intriguing. We need to consider the colonial logistical support for the trips, the broader Cold War geopolitical underpinnings of British courtship of African colonial elites, and the colonial imperative of maintaining commodity capitalism wherein colonial officials courted and prompted African rulers to help promote the production of certain cash crops in their domains. Nonetheless, the allure of London is discernible in the travel adventures and repertoires analyzed in the chapters ahead because the push and pull of travel to the metropole depended largely on vernacularized discourses and curiosities about the metropole. The travelers were eager translators of metropolitan modernity, but they were not starry-eyed African colonial subjects seduced by the charm and razzmatazz of metropolitan culture. In fact, they were also polite critics of that culture, and their travel accounts reflect this subtle critical engagement.

A representative example will suffice to illustrate this ambivalent disposition toward the metropole. After a tour of British warships in Portsmouth, one emir praised the impressive naval power of the British but then remarked that he would never want war to come to his country, especially a war in which such weapons of mass devastation would be used. It was an underhanded commentary on Britain's perpetuation of the nexus of warmongering adventures and arms buildup and an incipient critique of what we now call the military industrial complex and its symbiotic connection to warmongering imperialism.

When the Etsu Nupe (paramount ruler of the Nupe people) Muhammadu Ndayako returned from a six-week sightseeing trip with the emir of Ilorin in 1954 and penned a book on his experiences in England titled *Tafiyan Etsu Nupe Ingila* (Etsu Nupe's travel to England), he provided a robust glimpse into the subtle but powerful mix of admiration and critique that characterizes the perspectives of the traveling aristocrats. The relevant sections of Ndayako's text are discussed in greater detail in chapter 5, but a brief analysis of his observations points to the delicate rhetorical dance of traveler-writers when they expressed their views on the material and symbolic realities of the metropole.

Writing on British urban architecture, Ndayako states that British cities "have good structures" lined up in rows and that the interior beauty of such buildings eclipsed their outer attraction. This positive portrayal is consistent with the overall tenor of imperially mediated travel accounts of Britain from other parts of the British imperial world, which tend to romanticize British institutions and societal norms in relation to those of the narrators' societies.[52] In the Indo-Persian context, the connection between imperial mediation and positive portrayal is even clearer, since Europeans often conscripted local notables to author commentaries "from a point of view that flattered the British."[53] Ndayako's polite homage to British greatness was thus part of a transnational and transtemporal imperial protocol.

However, much like subaltern commenters on Britain elsewhere, Ndayako transitioned fluently into a critique of the same urban architecture. One flaw in British architecture, Ndayako noted, was that British houses had a bland uniformity to them.[54] This subtly critical comment bookends a narrative dripping with general reverence for the aristocratic trappings of Britain, the technological repositories of British modernity, and the quaint ways of the British aristocracy. Thus, as in other texts, there was a stubborn ambivalence in Ndayako's seemingly unreflective adulation for Britain.

Ndayako was, in fact, critiquing the colonial obsession with order, organization, and disciplined, replicable norms. The critique, stripped of its contextual specificity, also reveals a fundamental contradiction in metropolitan sociological evolution: as a metropolitan phenomenon, modernity had not resulted in creative freedom or a free-will pursuit of individual and group interest; instead, it seemed to have catalyzed a seemingly arbitrary commitment to order and synchronized living.

Other Northern Nigerian aristocratic travelers extended this critique, suggesting, however subtly, that British metropolitan work discipline and the mechanized rhythm of life it produced contrasted sharply with the relaxed, less regimented pace of life in Northern Nigeria. They criticized metropolitan life as devoid of laughter and spontaneity, and as a life captive to machines, industrial technologies, and capitalist rhythms of work and productivity. The traveling aristocrats juxtaposed this regimen with life in their Northern Nigerian emirates, which they claimed was more flexible. They then leveraged this observation to critique the fundamental logic of modernity—or, more precisely, modernization—which invokes freedom from regimentation and the luxury of choice as cognates to modern life.[55]

In analyzing observed British phenomena in relation to their analogues in Northern Nigerian society, the travelers were acting consistently within the classic tradition of ethnography as a self-reflexive, subjective observational practice. The European ethnographic production of a library of knowledge on Africa was skewed—perhaps even shaped—by the "self-image of their [African] informants,"[56] leading Lyn Schumaker to posit the concept of the coproduction of Africanist anthropological knowledge.[57] That epistemic corpus was also shaped, of course, by the Europeans' own imported prejudices and frames of reference. Similarly, the ethnographic and curatorial commentaries on British society by Ndayako and other traveling aristocrats were inflected by their own self-image and cultural inclinations. This ethnographic propensity to interpret Others using the tools supplied by one's own social milieu was the subtext of the travelers' commentaries.

Knowing the Colonizer, Knowing Oneself

Narratives of travel to the metropole intersected poignantly with a widespread desire to know the colonizer. Africans who claimed to know the metropole through their travel commanded respect among their kinfolk as knowledgeable interlocutors and interpreters of imperial culture. Moreover, metropolitan travel narratives had an immediate and practical utility in two ways. They served the didactic purpose of instructing would-be visitors to Britain on the social boundaries of the permissible, on social faux pas, on etiquettes, and on the mores of a distant colonial world. Second, the narratives functioned as educational guides to the unfamiliar ways and worlds of the colonizer. To many Northern Nigerians, there was something distant and mysterious about colonial officials who worked in Nigeria, many of whom were given Hausa nicknames that crystallized these perceptions. Colonizers' individual and group predilections were seemingly inscrutable enigmas. This led to curiosity about why these officials acted the way they did, what informed their strange idiosyncrasies, and why they had esoteric expectations of Africans. Travel to the metropole to bear witness to the metropolitan everyday was seen as a way of unlocking the mysteries of colonizers' habits. Unraveling the mystique of the metropole entailed perpetuating a paradox, however: the mythology of metropolitan society in the eyes of Northern Nigerian subalterns had to be restated, even exaggerated, to make the work of decoding it both important and necessary.

The traveling aristocrats were writing into a receptive cultural space since a certain mystique already framed the image of the white man in Northern Nigeria. The idea of Europeans as men of mystery and magic had a long genealogy in the minds of Africans. The idiom of magic and whiteness dates back to West Africans' first encounters with Portuguese sailors in the fifteenth and sixteenth centuries, when the "strange visitors" were regarded as "great wizards . . . whose marvelous [technological] possessions came through the use of evil magic"[58] and who possessed "diabolical powers and magical properties."[59] In colonial times, circulating rumors attributed magical and supernatural powers to white colonial officials.[60]

Throughout the colonial period, Africans struggled to understand and master colonial practices and goods they considered magical. This quest extended to the "magical language of the foreign ruler," a form of expression considered necessary for unraveling imperial mysteries and presenting a successful challenge to colonialism.[61] In his autobiography, anthropologist and Mozambican nationalist leader Eduardo Mondlane recalls his mother telling him to go and learn the white man's magic in the white man's school.[62] He states that his mother specifically "insisted that I go to school to understand the sorcery of the white man, so I could fight him."[63] From this perspective, knowledge gained through metropolitan experiential observation could be weaponized to enhance one's position in the hierarchies of imperial power and domination and challenge colonization itself. A similar ethos of navigating domination from a position of epistemic empowerment motivated Northern Nigerian tourists in their quest to see and understand the white man's magic at its source in Britain.

This quest can be read another way. Northern Nigerian emirs wanted to fight their inner political and cultural battles of reconciling their inherited traditions with colonial culture by leveraging knowledge of the white man's seemingly magical modernist technologies. It was only fitting that the acquisition of such a mystical arsenal of knowledge occurred at its source: in the metropole, where the sounds, smells, and other sensory elements of metropolitan life amplified the formal rituals of colonial education. For emirs not interested in Western education, travel to the metropole was the primary gateway to acquire the white man's vaunted magic. Not only did the travelers seek out the metropolitan sources of the white man's most wondrous technological inventions, but their colonial minders also shepherded them toward this magic, ensuring that the curiosities of the colonized sometimes converged on the same sights as the preferred itineraries of chaperones. Sightseeing, then, was the very essence of managed imperial tours. Everything else complemented this visual spectacle that established certain memories and images in the minds of visitors.

The resulting colonial touristic imagination was animated and sustained by the "human and pan-cultural" provenance of sightseeing as "tourism's default" and as a vector of new, exotic experiences.[64] Moreover, as indicated earlier, knowledge of the colonizing Other had practical applications to the quotidian vagaries of colonial relations. Subaltern groups versed in the ways of the colonizer could better negotiate the instabilities of colonial life and the unfamiliar predilections and expectations of colonial officials. If the colonizer had to know the colonized or master their cultural, political, and economic worlds to become effective in the business of domination and exploitation, the colonized, too, could use knowledge of the colonizer's culture and socialization processes to either thwart or escape unpalatable colonial circumstances.

Going to the metropole freed the aristocratic traveler from the inhibitions and stifling traditional protocols of the colony. Metropolitan hospitality, authentic or not, conferred freedom on the African aristocratic traveler, who could leverage it to pursue personal interests unavailable to him or incompatible with colonial or traditional social ethos in Northern Nigeria. The metropolitan space was thus not only a place for knowing the colonizer but also a catalyst for self-knowledge. Furthermore, it was a place of refuge from the burdens and scrutiny that came with the role of religious custodianship performed by aristocrats. For example, in the judgment-free space of London and other British cities—and, in one case, in Paris—some emirs engaged in sports betting (see chaps. 2, 3, and 4)—an activity outlawed in Islam.

Touristic Imagination and "Staged Authenticity"

Like modern-day tourists removed from the strictures of empire and colonization, the Northern Nigerian visitors to Britain were attracted to "exotic" localities by the generic human "desire for a new experience, an experience different from one's own."[65] In short, they were "attracted to difference" and the opportunity to "break free of routine, to have an adventure, to change scenes and think new thoughts . . . and to have something to say."[66] I contend that travel to the metropole by the colonized was a form of ethnography: a survey of the colonial Other, whether or not it was self-consciously understood in those terms.

Sightseeing was the most important methodology in this ethnographic project.[67]

The colonial politics of regulated and managed international mobility obviously intruded into the economy of curiosity and desire that drove aristocratic subaltern visitors to the metropole. The convergence of the authorities' manipulation of adventure and sightseeing on one hand and the desires and yearnings of the visitors on the other added to the drama of the metropolitan trips. It is important to stretch this point even further to accommodate the ways the programmed sightseeing of the visitors was part of the elaborate effort of colonial authorities to manipulate the emotions of the visitors and shape their attitude toward the empire and its symbols. As an entity of might and majesty, the empire was, in effect, staged for the African visitors.

This process of "staged authenticity," as Dean MacCannell calls it,[68] required the generic touristic expectations of the visitors to be managed and channeled into certain avenues and diverted from others, a process of jaundiced gazing that was seductive in its own scripted way. The staged metropolitan sites not only produced instant reactions but also inflected the tone and texture of written accounts about the sites, in which melodramatic and theatrical textual reenactments purporting to display fidelity to observed metropolitan events and things only superficially reflected the rhythms of what the tour was "designed to reveal."[69]

Bringing Home Metropolitan Modernity

The materiality of empire, modernity, and consumption can best be understood through a study of imperial technological interactions. Such a study cannot conceive of subalterns as passive consumers of imperial technologies but rather as active agents in the process of making and remaking imperial technological goods and ideas.

Travel to the metropole afforded subaltern aristocrats an opportunity to indulge an appetite for imperial technology that was honed by a conscious, creative appropriation of machines and mechanical objects into their social repertoires and infrastructures of mobility. This process of recalibrating awesome imperial technologies into everyday utilitarian objects,[70] and activating related consumerist curiosities, usually preceded and foregrounded the trip to Britain. In investing in imperial technology, the travelers were also participating in a rather universal, xenophilic phenomenon: the captivating allure of the foreign and exotic and the ascription of value to cultural and physical distance.

Shopping was the favorite pastime of the emirs in Britain, and they navigated programmed sightseeing tours strategically to free up time for shopping expeditions. The emirs found high-end shopping particularly appealing. Repeated visits to Harrods, Maple's, Hampton's, Liberty's, Goldsmith's, and Silversmith's featured prominently in the emirs' itineraries.[71] When the sultan of Sokoto, the emir of Gwandu, and the emir of Kano visited Britain in 1934 (chap. 3), they all purchased perambulators, an apparent symbol of aristocratic exclusivity popularized and modeled by the British aristocracy.

Some emirs and chiefs, such as Och'Idoma Ogiri Oko, used their trips to enhance the regal aesthetics of their courts by purchasing royal accessories for their palaces (chap. 6). Others, such as Usman Nagogo, sought to embellish the sartorial prestige of royal processions by importing designs and fabrics from Britain for emirate princely robes (chap. 4). Other travelers worked to transplant the procedural and scientific elements of metropolitan agriculture into their domains as a way of modernizing the agricultural practice of farmers. Some travelers purchased fragrances and cars (chaps. 3 and 4); others bought beds, jewelry, gramophones, and other commodities associated with metropolitan modernity and convenience (chap. 4).

These shopping expeditions can be partly attributed to the touristic inclination to memorialize one's leisurely mobility through the experiential reminders of concrete objects and utilitarian indulgence in new forms of consumption. Consuming or using goods from the metropole long after the completion of the travel prolonged the experience and extended the sensory enjoyment of metropolitan offerings. Moreover, the visitors engaged these metropolitan commodities not simply from a position of material need but also from a position of what these items and their metropolitan provenance symbolized.

These goods were important because of the social meanings and myths constructed around them in Northern Nigeria. This was a classic instance of Marxian commodity fetishism.[72] Once in Nigeria, the commodities so fetishized satiated new desires, illustrating the ways travel to the metropole enabled commodities to move and acquire new utilitarian and symbolic identities. Luxury metropolitan goods such as perambulators piqued the interest of Northern Nigerian visitors to Britain because they could be adapted to multiple uses in Nigeria and because of their association with privilege and aristocratic exclusivity. In such goods, and in the various ways they were repurposed by Northern Nigerian travelers, we see the dual trajectories of imperial consumption. One suggests the persistence of self-interested mimicry as a form of imperial cultural reception; the other showcases the adaptive and creative consumption of imperial cultures and goods.[73]

Some emirs who visited Britain sought to literally recreate aspects of metropolitan culture and practices in their domains. After visiting agricultural fairs in England, the emir of Kano instituted an annual agricultural show at Karaye, making it clear that metropolitan agricultural shows were the model for his new enterprise. The emir of Katsina, Muhammadu Dikko, remodeled the front facade of his palace after Buckingham Palace (chap. 4). More than any other emir, Dikko sought to bring the metropole back with him and recreate its technological ensemble in his domain. He famously bought five Morris trucks during his trip to England in 1933 and declared, after flying on a plane at the North Weald Airfield, that he would like to be the first person to own an aircraft in Nigeria.

Dikko and his son and successor, Usman Nagogo, were avid players of polo, the English aristocratic sport, and Dikko helped build a polo ground and financed the establishment of the Katsina Polo Club in 1921. Katsina subsequently became a famous polo town in Nigeria, routinely hosting tournaments and matches, and it is reasonable to assume that these tournaments were modeled after those Dikko and Nagogo witnessed in Britain (chap. 4). Moreover, Nagogo played polo on some of Britain's most prestigious polo grounds and may have sought to import some of the features he saw in these venues into Katsina. The premier of Northern Nigeria and the most powerful aristocrat of all, Ahmadu Bello, returned from the United Kingdom in June 1960 and introduced the game of Eton Fives, an aristocratic sport played by students at the elite Eton College in England. He became a passionate player and succeeded in converting many of his friends, aides, and associates to the sport. Through his influence and followership, the game spread in Northern Nigeria and even became known in Hausa as the sardauna's game (chap. 4).

Aristocratic Culture and Colonial Kinship

The notion of an aristocratic kinship that connected the emirs of Northern Nigeria to British officials may seem at odds with conventional interpretations of colonialism as a consistently adversarial struggle between colonizers and the colonized. However, if one sets aside the obvious oppressions and foundational brutality of colonization, it is possible to look at the colonial encounter as a moment animated by elaborate rules of conduct. In this context, it is possible to appreciate the dexterity with which certain privileged groups of Africans navigated the imperial system.

When focusing specifically on interactions between British colonial officials and their African aristocratic allies, it is useful to imagine colonialism as a vast political chessboard; playing the game requires skill and mastery over certain idioms, languages, protocols, and modes of expression. The emirs and aristocrats of Northern Nigeria were masters of this colonial game of mutual patronage and ritualized courtesies. Like most high-stakes political games, colonialism entailed both risks and rewards. One's exposure and access to these two consequences corresponded to one's degree of mastery over the protocols governing colonial relations.

I suggest that scholars regard connections that carried over to the metropole as a manifestation of a particular kind of colonial kinship. When Northern Nigerian aristocrats bonded with their British interlocutors over aristocratic pastimes and objects, the result was a symbolic and unequal brotherhood that was instrumental to the emirs fulfilling their roles as mediators of imperial culture. Tapping into these metropolitan personal networks gave the emirs access to the spaces and objects of imperial power and culture. The emirs brought these markers of imperial culture back to Northern Nigeria and incorporated them into their own modernist repertoires and claims. In retelling their interactions with retired and serving colonial officials in Britain, the emirs gave substance to their claim that they were intimately connected to the networks of British colonization—a claim that carried immense cultural purchase in Northern Nigeria.

The kinship posited here was interpersonal, not structural, a function of connections forged in the quotidian interactions of colonial life in Northern Nigeria and Britain. However, some of the affinity was predicated on the foundational assumptions of the British about Hausa-Fulani aristocrats with ties to the defunct Sokoto Caliphate. Frederick Lugard, the most important figure in the British colonization of Northern Nigeria, authored a colonial administrative manual that posited Hausa-Fulani Muslims, especially aristocrats, as superior "natives" whose temperament, prior political activities, and monotheism qualified and prepared them for British patronage and partnership and made them natural political allies of the British. In *The Dual Mandate*, the most important text of colonial administrative practice in Northern Nigeria, Lugard went to elaborate lengths to justify privileging the Hausa-Fulani as logical, if convenient, political allies of the British.[74]

To be sure, Lugard was a racist ideologue; he subscribed to and helped enunciate the social Darwinist evolutionary theories of race and civilization of his day. Lugard elevated Hausa-Fulani ethnoreligious identity to a sociopolitical standard for Africans in Northern Nigeria and recommended an administrative system that sought to instill a so-called Hausa-Fulani mode of conduct and temperament into other peoples in the region. In the same breath, Lugard expressed an undifferentiated devaluation of the humanity of all Africans in the territory of Northern Nigeria, regardless of ethnic or religious identity.[75] Lugard thus believed in a monolithic notion of African civilizational and evolutionary lag. Nonetheless, for purely functional, instrumental purposes and to satisfy his own social Darwinist racial and civilizational taxonomies, Lugard carved out a discursive space in which Hausa-Fulani aristocrats emerged as subalterns who possessed personal and group attributes that put them in civilizational proximity to their

British overlords and thus made transracial kinships, friendships, and partnerships possible.

Lugard's racialized theories on colonization left ample room for—and, in fact, anticipated—a sociopolitical tutelage that he hoped would culminate in the emergence of a non-Muslim aristocracy considered deserving of British colonial patronage and kinship.[76] Lugard's ideological enterprise thus envisaged a robust kinship between colonizers and their Northern Nigerian aristocratic allies, a kind of ritualized and instrumental imperial brotherhood that would purportedly benefit both groups. This influential foundational endorsement of cultivating ties with Northern Nigerian aristocrats authorized and sustained the rituals of mutual courtship and the ethos of aristocratic kinship posited here.

Colonial kinship did not mechanically translate to subservience or docility on the part of Northern Nigerian travelers. This is why these trips triggered colonial anxiety and panic. There was no telling what tangents travelers would pursue or what their impressions would be. Colonial officials sometimes worried about whether the visits would elicit the hoped-for feedback from the visitors and eagerly awaited the perfunctory letters of gratitude expected to follow upon the visitors' return to Nigeria (chaps. 3 and 4). They welcomed the feedback because the retrospective reflections in them provided a window into the impressions left on the visitors.

Metropolitan Travel and Empire Loyalism

In several respects, colonial travel programs that entailed interactions with British royalty, copious entertainment, and visits to British landmarks represented a reward for the emirs' loyalty to Britain and thus seem to fit into new histories of empire loyalism emerging insightfully in the works of Daniel Branch, Hilary Sapire, and Christopher Lee.[77] Scholars of imperial loyalism as a broad category, and of royalism as a narrower empathy for the English monarchy and its regal symbols, have moved beyond the simplistic notion that colonized subjects who expressed any level of affection for the Crown or the metropolitan glories of empire were uncritically enamored with imperial institutions. Even longer-span studies set in the larger geographical context of the British world that stretched across several continents and a diverse array of imperial arrangements have arrived at a similar consensus: loyalism was a diverse, multifaceted, and differently motivated expression of sympathetic feelings toward the empire.[78]

The itineraries and narratives analyzed here extend this contention. Northern Nigerian aristocratic travelers to the metropole expressed admiration for the pageantries and ceremonial practices associated with the English Crown. The traveling subalterns were also fascinated by the defining institutions of English culture and the visual and performative elements of British aristocratic life. This positive reception of metropolitan society was often mitigated and mediated by subtle critique and an overarching desire on the part of the traveler-narrators to promote their roles as firsthand observers of metropolitan phenomena. Moreover, the question of motive is as inscrutable as it is complicated. Empire loyalists and royalists in India, the United States, Canada, and Africa were motivated by multiple convictions, ranging from sentimental admiration for the Crown to belief in its capacity to guarantee rights and privileges within a just imperial framework, faith that the Crown was a counterbalancing force against despised local power formations, the pull of familial connections, desire to draw on royal and metropolitan social and political capital for domestic purposes, disillusionment with a waning nationalist cause, and desire to escape the excess, retribution, or undisciplined violence of popular revolutionary forces.[79] Daniel Branch further suggests that in addition to recognizing a spectrum of loyalist sentiments, there is a need to track the instability of such commitments to identify how colonized people alternately embraced and abandoned loyalism as circumstances demanded.[80]

These perspectives provide the epistemological foundation for my analysis. From their writings, Northern Nigeria's aristocratic travelers to Britain seem to be consistently loyalist in their epistemological engagements, but to read their expressions solely in this way is reductive. Scripted travel to the metropole may seem to be the ultimate demonstration of loyalist instincts, but the travelers also saw it as an opportunity to enhance their prestige in Nigeria—not as demonstrating loyalty to colonial ideals but as restating their legitimacy by immersing themselves in *zamani*, or modernity, which could endear them to their constituents. Their travels and metropolitan engagements were more about them than about metropolitan institutions of power and culture, despite the ample perfunctory praise of these institutions in their writings.

Imperial nostalgia and loyalism rarely manifested as total surrender to colonial forces. Nor were they products of an unquestioning reaction to the seduction of prestigious imperial sites. Theoretically, it may be important to recognize the seductive power of the English monarchy, its guardianship over the British Empire, and its professed commitment to imperial solidarity and justice. However, a more productive inquiry—one that is faithful to the complexity of African engagements with metropolitan culture—must recognize that engagement was dictated by colonial domination and that the decision to engage and immerse oneself in metropolitan institutions was often strategic and self-interested, calculated to mitigate the harm of domination and to open up spaces for personal socioeconomic advancement. Some African groups certainly appealed strategically to these aspects of empire, expressing their total submission to and belief in the organs of imperial redress and protection as a way of working the system and accessing its circumscribed ameliorative possibilities.[81] Northern Nigerian aristocratic travelers, even those who seemed so enamored with colonial modernity, should be understood within this framing.

The stories in the following chapters advance a more nuanced understanding of Africans who enjoyed imperial patronage and wrote with both adulation and subtle critique about metropolitan institutions and cultures. A simplistic framework of loyalism that flattens the range of attitudes exhibited by privileged African subalterns toward the empire—attitudes such as admiration, aspirational identification, sarcasm, critique, strategic flattery, mimicry, and curiosity—is inadequate for unpacking the lives of Africans who reversed the imperial gaze and, unlike most European colonial travel writers, expressed sympathetic and adulatory thoughts toward the colonial Other. By highlighting the complex and shifting strategies and gestures of Northern Nigeria's aristocrats toward British metropolitan culture, my analysis deepens the useful category of loyalism. I show specifically that notions of loyalism were complicated by the multivalent attitudes and impulses exhibited by African travelers toward the imperial center.

The Subaltern as Colonial Explorer and Reverse Ethnographer

Traveling Nigerians in the metropole were engaged in reverse colonial exploration and ethnography, whether or not it occurred to them in those terms. The connections between the Nigerian explorers and British imperial institutions were deep and variegated. These connections were consolidated through subaltern curiosities about the metropole that were in turn satiated when the visitors to Britain carefully observed, recorded, and made sense of metropolitan phenomena.

Positing traveling Nigerian subalterns—or any other subalterns, for that matter—as colonial explorers and ethnologists may seem problematic given the negative reputation of European colonial explorers as imperial precursors who established the ideological tone for representing Africans and their societies. However, the observational and narrative methodologies of Northern Nigerian metropolitan travel writers bear an eerily instructive resemblance to those of European colonial travelers and ethnographers who explored and wrote about African societies for European audiences. Both groups utilized contrast, self-referential idioms, hyperbole, and cultural distancing to understand their subjects.

The ethnography of European explorers, administrators, and official ethnographers was sustained by the usefulness of such ethnographic renderings in colonial policy making and colonial administration. The reversed ethnographic gaze of African colonial subjects was honed, in the case of Northern Nigerian aristocrats, in the crucible of metropolitan travel. However, both ethnographic imaginations thrived on the attraction of the different, on the idea of the exotic and fascinating but enigmatic Other.[82] Both ethnographies strategically deployed the idioms of homogenization, generalization, self-referencing, contrast, similitude, and distancing to render the subject of such ethnographic gaze intelligible to a particular audience or to reinforce a subsisting set of understandings and suppositions.

There are, however, two important distinctions to note. The first concerns the power and purpose of texts that purport to explain or decipher the Other. According to Mary Pratt, colonial travel and exploratory writing has two interlinked features. The first is that such texts functioned within "European forms and relations of power."[83] In other words, they were texts empowered and legitimized by the fact of colonial conquest or the force of post-Enlightenment European claims to cultural and political superiority. These texts were thus animated by European domination, even when they were produced prior to formal European colonial occupation. They were implicated in and empowered by European claims to a universal, replicable modernity. This is precisely why such texts were instrumental to or repurposed for the work of "preparing" the ground for encountering and subduing African peoples.

The second feature of the imperial travel-writing genre turns on the recurring idiom of heroism. The standard template of colonial travel writing is one in which the tale, no matter the context or characters, devolves into a predictably linear narrative of the difficulties of the colonial space and the triumph of the European colonial masculine hero over them.[84] The European colonial travel imagination is thus informed—and hamstrung—by the imperative of conquest and domination.

Northern Nigerian aristocratic travelers' narratives illustrate an alternative traveler imagination in which subjugation and domination are not the drivers of curiosities. This does not mean that the metropolitan adventures and the texts they spawned were apolitical or devoid of the perspectival proclivities of autobiographical memories and experiential narration. The contention here is simply that narratives produced out of these reverse imperial ethnographic adventures did not enter the colonial discursive and epistemological arena with power. African colonial travel writers and visitors to the metropole depended on the mechanics of imperial knowledge production to get their narratives published and their voices heard. The mediatory intrusions of colonial minders, guides, interlocutors, and "staged" metropolitan scenes converged to rob the African travel narrator of the intellectual power of his European counterpart. The text of the African colonial travel writer is thus ambivalent and seeks to affirm the writer's membership in and dependence on a protocol of intellectual exchange while subtly challenging it—and while pretending to map the metropole in a gesture similar to the exploratory travel narratives of influential European men and women of colonial ethnography.

The second point of distinction between African travel narratives of the type analyzed in this book and European travel accounts is that the former—however vigorously they spawned the discourse of difference, contrast, and lack or lag—ultimately sought to collapse the cultural space between colony and metropole by making the metropole more intelligible to African audiences who, without the physical ability to observe Britain, constructed myths and fantasies about the imperial center. Even if the African travel writers did not intend to do so, they were satisfying a taste for the metropole and helping clarify and thus make relatable a seemingly unapproachably distant Britain. In doing so, the African elite subalterns swam against the tide of European representations of Africa, which self-consciously sought to expand the cultural gap between metropole and periphery by manufacturing and replenishing difference, the lifeblood of colonial hierarchy and colonization itself. Northern Nigerian travel narrators had to first widen the cultural chasm between Britain and the colony by confirming and even expanding the space of difference before intentionally shrinking that space and rendering the metropole legible and familiar to their audiences.

Subaltern Travel Writing and the Weight of Minutia

The travel narratives analyzed in the preceding chapters were inspired by different experiences and itineraries, written in different styles and registers, and suffused in different rhetorical flavors. Despite these differences, the narratives share a common attribute: they devolve into detailed narrative denseness and seemingly pointless prioritizing of the minutia of quotidian metropolitan realities. Why were the travelers so insistent on conveying the minute details of what they observed in a painstakingly fastidious effort to capture every aspect? Why the preoccupation with narrating, in boring, technical details, the workings of niche metropolitan industries and machines? The answer to this question is complex. To our contemporary predilections, excessive narrative detail induces boredom and disinterest and goes against our desire for large, easily digestible narrative themes.

However, to the Northern Nigerian audiences of the travel narratives, detail was precisely the marker of the exotic. The greater the detail, the easier it was for narrators to establish the claim that metropolitan culture was different and distant. The claim that Britons in their "natural" habitat of the United Kingdom were driven by certain sensibilities different from those that drove African colonial subjects in Northern Nigeria had to be substantiated and proved. The weight of detail in the narration of observed events proved that the metropole was a distinct society and that knowing it was truly a difficult and commendable endeavor. Moreover, the overarching reality of mutual imperial curiosities between colonizers and the colonized determined how subaltern readers received narratives on the metropole. The preexistence of intense curiosity about the metropolitan world of British colonizers among Romanized Northern Nigerian readers altered the dynamic of reception. This economy of curiosity transformed boring minutia and esoteric details of obscure metropolitan phenomena into objects of fascination, enabling them to be received and consumed as such by Northern Nigerian audiences.

Details and minutia performed another function. They were markers of authority. They authenticated authorial credibility. A traveling aristocrat who returned to Nigeria to give lectures, publish a travelogue in *Gaskiya ta fi Kwabo*, or write a book about his metropolitan adventures was invariably claiming authority as an expert on the affairs of Britain in a local milieu functionally ignorant of the metropole. Such claims lacked credibility unless demonstrated through details of how Britons lived, farmed, worked, parented, relaxed, and governed. The volume of detail in these narrative endeavors was proportional to the credibility of the narrator's claim of being an authority on the metropole by virtue of his travel there. In short, details formed the contours of the traveler-narrator's claimed expertise and authority.

Minutia was not a digressive detour into irrelevances or merely the product of fecund ethnographic imaginations, although those elements are discernible in the travel texts. Minutia and detail embodied the encyclopedic character of the travelogues discussed in this book. When travelers recounted their experiences of the colonial metropole, they were positioning themselves in much the same way that colonial anthropological attachés positioned themselves as experts on all things African. The topical versatility of the narratives, the informational indiscipline of the texts, and the narrative promiscuity of the traveler-narrators all point to the importance of detail in the claims of those who sought to inscribe themselves in popular consciousness as encyclopedic authorities on metropolitan society.

Chapter Sequence

Chapter 1 analyzes the emergence and growth of a Northern Nigerian intellectual culture of reading and writing that developed between 1930 and 1950 and provided a vibrant, actively engaged audience to aristocratic travel writers returning from Britain and writing about their experiences there. The travelers wrote into the space created by this culture of literacy and literary flourish and sated intellectual curiosities about the metropole.

This story of literary ferment in the orbit of colonial domination has three aspects, each encompassing a realm of programs and actions that fed into an inchoate world of lively intellectual transactions between writers and readers, between producers of ideas and stories and consumers of those stories, and between those purporting to have experiential resources for storytelling and those eager to access these stories through Romanized Hausa language literacy. The first aspect of this intellectual history of the early Northern Nigerian Romanized literary scene is the development of a colonial infrastructure of story writing, publishing, and literary production enabled by the Gaskiya Corporation. The second is the vigorous promotion of adult literacy by the Northern Nigerian colonial education bureaucracy, mainly in rural areas but also in some urban centers. The third is the evolution of a secular school culture in Northern Nigeria, which developed simultaneously with the growth of literary practices for which travel and adventure provided material and inspiration. Finally, chapter 1 analyzes Abubakar Imam's *Tafiya Mabudin Ilimi* as a seminal metropolitan travelogue in Northern Nigeria, a text that established and anticipated many of the narrative techniques that other traveler-narrators adopted, and that several travel writers referenced for inspiration and example.

Chapter 2 analyzes the early metropolitan adventures of Emir Muhammadu Dikko of Katsina. Dikko pioneered a particular Northern Nigerian aristocratic engagement with the institutions, cultures, and symbols of the colonial metropole. He was the first among his aristocratic peers to visit Britain. Dikko was not an accidental pioneer, however. His entanglement with Britain and his intimate cultural and personal connections to local and metropolitan colonial institutions and personnel began in the first decade of the twentieth century, during which the British appointed him emir to reward him for his loyalty. Given the longevity and profundity of Dikko's subsequent immersion in colonial culture, his biography is a lens through which to understand the colonial kinships and travel-enabled cultural appropriations discussed throughout this book.

Chapter 2 demonstrates that Dikko, as emir, was an admirer of British symbols and institutions. He sought to give Katsina a modernist identity through a makeover underwritten by colonial patronage and cultural investments. Through his cultivation of British recreational and educational institutions, among other projects of modernization, and through his adventures in Britain, Dikko demonstrated the possibilities of leveraging connections to colonial power to remake the emirate space and refashion the image of the emir as a modern aristocratic subaltern. By embracing British high culture and profusely proclaiming his admiration for British aristocratic symbols during his visit to metropolitan sites, Dikko also demonstrated a mastery of imperial protocols and ritualized hospitality.

Chapter 3 focuses on Northern Nigerian aristocratic explorations of Britain in the 1930s. In particular, it analyzes the touristic adventures of four Muslim chiefs in Britain—the sultan of Sokoto, the emir of Gwandu, the emir of Kano, and the Muslim chief of Ebira. The importance of the 1930s—and of aristocratic journeys to Britain in this period—lies in the persistence of subaltern travel to the metropole in a difficult economic period. From the colonizer's perspective, the visits were important because Northern Nigeria, like other colonies, was reeling from the aftershocks of the Great Depression, but the visiting aristocrats saw an imperial center that seemed unshaken and seemingly remained functional and grandiose. This projection of the spectacle of order and imperial stability was central to how British colonial trip planners imagined the aristocrats' metropolitan tours in this period. It was a visual counternarrative to the economic turmoil in the colonies.

Returning Northern Nigerian Muslim aristocratic travelers wrote about Britain and British modernity in generally complementary terms, and emirs such as Yahaya Ibn Haliru viewed the British monarchy and its figurehead, the king of England, as models of power, dignity, and sartorial elegance. However, a closer reading of their travel narratives also reveals instrumental calculation and strategic intent on their part. One prominent, recurring theme is how they sought to strategically parlay their physical and symbolic connections to the British monarchy and the accoutrements of British metropolitan modernity into local prestige for themselves.

Chapter 4 analyzes the conscious, polyvalent metropolitan cultural appropriations of Dikko and his son Usman Nagogo, who succeeded him as the emir of Katsina. This father-son aristocratic endeavor was subsidized by their travels to Britain in the 1930s and 1940s. In particular, I highlight the duo's modernization of Katsina Emirate using Britain as a visual and cultural referent. They drew consciously on the symbolic and material cultures of Britain. This landscape of inspiration and modernist replication defined much of the cultural and physical changes in Katsina during the reigns of both Dikko and Nagogo. Furthermore, they appropriated and promoted the British aristocratic sport of polo in their domain, domesticating it as an extension of the emirate's equestrian traditions. Being an avid polo player opened up additional metropolitan spaces to Dikko but especially to Nagogo, who accompanied his father to Britain on all five of his trips. Regular participation in metropolitan polo circuits was unique to Nagogo and added another layer to the Dikko dynasty's British connection.

In the polo fields of Britain, as during the guided tours of metropolitan sites, the hierarchies of colonialism became subordinated to the imperatives of imperial hospitality. This caused British guides and officials to observe a ritualized deference to their valued guests from Nigeria, which empowered Dikko and his entourage to claim social liberties that were absent in their interactions with colonial officialdom in Katsina. Finally, the chapter explores the afterlives of Dikko's travels to and within the vast metropolitan world of Britain. In the aftermath of his travels to Britain, Dikko, more than any other Northern Nigerian aristocratic traveler to the metropole, sought to replicate the architectural preferences and symbolic accoutrements of the British aristocracy. His son Nagogo continued in that mold, implementing a set of modernist reforms inspired by and derived from institutions and governmental practices he had observed during his multiple trips to Britain.

Chapter 5 takes up the dialogic newspaper public that sustained robust vernacular discourses on metropolitan Britain, in particular the central position of *Gaskiya ta fi Kwabo* and the new platform of public lectures. Northern Nigerian travelers positioned themselves to demystify the colonizers by translating the metropole and its cultures into relatable Hausa vernacular idioms. By giving their readers a metropolitan cultural referent against which to understand and evaluate the conduct of on-ground colonizers, the travelers were leveraging travel to further their work as colonial mediators. The veracity of their portrayal, its fidelity to metropolitan life, and its completeness as a reflection of British metropolitan culture are, of course, robustly debatable. Nonetheless, these narratives functioned in the mutually unintelligible world of cultural relations as primers for Northern Nigerians seeking a deeper understanding of the colonial oppressor.

In addition, chapter 5 focuses on three varieties of metropolitan travelogues: those published in the Hausa newspaper, *Gaskiya ta fi Kwabo*, by the travelers themselves; those written and published by the newspaper's editors using notes and diaries supplied by the travelers and supplemented by widely available print and broadcast resources on Britain; and travel memoirs written and published by travelers. Gaskiya and its metropolitan travel writers were creating, from afar, knowledge about the colonizer's society—a new ethnographic archive on the ways of the colonizer. It is not clear that they intended to do so, but they were inventing a new vernacular vocabulary for making sense of Britain and its inhabitants. This epistemological database satiated local curiosities about Britain but also legitimized the writers and travelers who sought to position themselves as ethnographers and experts on British society.

Chapter 6 maps the evolution of overseas colonial touring. I consider the ways travelers helped institutionalize the practice of traveling to Britain and, more crucially, the tradition of returning to publish travel memoirs. Between the 1940s and 1960s, the trips morphed into an expected ritual for Muslim elites craving recognition, visibility, and further colonial patronage through a self-referential narration of Britain. Furthermore, in this period, colonial authorities opened the trips to non-Muslim chiefs from the Middle Belt, as well as to women. The chapter highlights and distills the epistemological insights of this evolved institution of metropolitan travel. I consider the impact of this travel on the changing cultural ecology of Northern Nigeria, the self-fashioning of Northern Nigerian elites in the late colonial period, and the reverse imperial courtship that required Northern Nigerian aristocrats and bureaucrats to actively seek out British travel, technocratic expertise, and cultural goods.

This chapter analyzes how trips to Britain and the motivation for such travels evolved in the late colonial period of the late 1950s to include quasi-diplomatic tours and visits. Northern Nigeria's ruling elites, led by Ahmadu Bello, the prime minister of the self-governing Northern Nigerian government in the mid- to late 1950s, repurposed the visits to Britain as educational and diplomatic outreaches. In this period, many Northern Nigerians found themselves in Britain as educational visitors and on official missions to recruit British experts for the government. The visits were thus recalibrated to enable the Northern Nigerian government to acquire British expertise and training to replace Southern Nigerian workers in the civil service, education, and industry—a policy called northernization.

In the epilogue, I map the cultural and symbolic residues of Northern Nigerian aristocrats' decades-long explorations of metropolitan Britain. I analyze the persistence of certain court and aristocratic symbols of authority traceable to connections between some emirates and Britain that were forged or consolidated through travel to the metropole in colonial times. The epilogue also teases out the tension between the contemporary reputation of Northern Nigeria as a hotbed of anti-Western, antimodern Islamist political awakening and the intimate political kinship that bound the region's aristocrats and elites to Britain and later the United States from the 1920s through the 1960s. I highlight and explain how the relationship between Northern Nigeria's Muslim elites and Western modernity has evolved.

Finally, the epilogue tells the story of Hajiya Dadasare Abdullahi, a Muslim Fulani woman who experienced trauma at the hands of a British colonial official but ended up marrying another British colonial official, thus inserting herself into a vast British colonial network in Nigeria and Britain. This story demonstrates that colonial kinship, one of the overarching conceptual frames of this book, manifested in multiple arenas through unlikely avenues, including colonial trauma. This extreme, seemingly improbable story of Dadasare's transition from colonial victimhood to active, self-consciously strategic cultivation of colonial human connections illustrates a central contention of this book regarding the possibilities of aristocratic and nonaristocratic pragmatic connections between colonizers and the colonized. Such affinities were unequal and, on the side of the subaltern, largely aspirational. Nonetheless, they demonstrate that the capacious frame of colonial kinship is a powerful, if context-limited, analytical category for understanding the complex relationship that developed between colonizing British officials and African aristocratic subalterns, a connection enhanced by transnational mobility and the cultural exchanges it catalyzed.

Notes

1. Michael A. Gomez, *Black Crescent: The Experience and Legacy of African Muslims in the Americas* (Cambridge: Cambridge University Press, 2005); Sylviane Diouf, *Servants of Allah: African Muslims Enslaved in the Americas* (New York: New York University Press, 2013).

2. The work of Frantz Fanon set the tone and direction for this epistemic devaluation of African elite voices. See, for instance, Frantz Fanon, *The Wretched of the Earth*, trans. C. Farrington (London: MacGibbon and Key, 1965), chap. 3. The chapter is titled "The Pitfalls of National Consciousness" and represents a forceful, canonical polemical denunciation of African colonial elites—elites that morphed into the vanguard of the anticolonial nationalist movements and then became the national bourgeoisie after independence.

3. Simon Gikandi, introduction to *Uganda's Katikiro in England*, ed. Ham Mukasa, 1–35, 30 (Manchester, UK: University of Manchester Press, 1998).

4. Gikandi, introduction, 30.

5. Hakim Adi, *West Africans in Britain 1900–1960: Nationalism, Pan-Africanism and Communism* (London: Lawrence and Wishart, 1998); David Killingray, ed., *Africans in Britain* (London: Frank Cass, 1994).

6. Danell Jones, *An African in Imperial London: The Indomitable Life of A.B.C. Merriman-Labor* (London: Hurst, 2018).

7. Neil Parsons, *King Khama, Emperor Joe, and the Great White Queen: Victorian Britain through African Eyes* (Chicago: University of Chicago Press, 1998).

8. Homi Bhabha, *Of Mimcry and Man: The Ambivalence of Colonial Discourse*, October Vol. 28, Discipleship: A Special Issue on Psychoanalysis (Spring, 1984).

9. Edward Said, *Orientalism* (New York: Vintage Books, 1979).

10. Juan Cole, "Invisible Occidentalism: Eighteenth-Century Indo-Persian Constructions of the West," *Iranian Studies* 25, no. 3/4 (1992): 3–16.

11. Cole, "Invisible Occidentalism."

12. See Claude Levi-Strauss, *Tristes Tropiques* (Paris: Librairie Plon, 1955), translated into English by John Russell (London: Hutchinson, 1961).

13. See Bernard Lewis, *The Muslim Discovery of Europe* (Cambridge: Cambridge University Press, 1957) and David Northrup, *Africa's Discovery of Europe, 1450–1850* (Oxford:

Oxford University Press, 2002). The association of Europe with an ethnographic travel imagination and the silencing of analogous imaginations among Africans and other non-Western peoples is illustrated in the Eurocentric focus of recent, iconic publications on travel writing. See, for instance, Peter Hulme and Tim Youngs, eds., *The Cambridge Companion to Travel Writing* (Cambridge: Cambridge University Press, 2002). For a critique of the neglect of non-Western travelers' accounts and ethnographic records, see Cole, "Invisible Occidentalism," and Nile Green, "Among the Dissenters: Reciprocal Ethnography in Nineteenth Century Inglistan," *Journal of Global History* 4, no. 2 (2009): 293–315.

14. See Muzaffar Alam and Sanjay Subrahmanyam, *Indo-Persian Travels in the Age of Discoveries, 1400–1800* (Cambridge: Cambridge University Press, 2007).

15. Green, "Among the Dissenters."

16. Green, "Among the Dissenters," 1.

17. Loraine Daston and Katherine Park, *Wonders and the Order of Nature, 1150–1750* (New York: Zone Books, 1997).

18. Daston and Park, *Wonders and the Order of Nature*, 14–15.

19. For an insightful discussion of the entwinement of modernity and emotions, see Margrit Pernau, "Emotions and Modernity in Colonial India," seminar paper, Vanderbilt History Seminar, Vanderbilt University, February 13, 2017.

20. Benedict Anderson, *Imagined Communities: Reflections on the Origin and Spread of Nationalism* (London: Verso, 2003), 40–41.

21. Dipesh Chakrabarty, "Postcoloniality and the Artifice of Hsitory: Who Speaks for 'Indian' Pasts?" *Representations* 37, Special Issue: Imperial Fantasies and Postcolonial Histories (winter 1992): 1–26, 7, 10.

22. David Cannadine, *Ornamentalism: How the British Saw Their Empire* (Oxford: Oxford University Press, 2001), 4.

23. Cannadine, *Ornamentalism*, 8–9.

24. Cannadine, *Ornamentalism*, 6.

25. Cannadine, *Ornamentalism*, 85.

26. South Africa's colonial and apartheid regimes were notorious for developing a vast apparatus of surveillance and restriction whose ultimate purpose was to curtail the ability of nonwhites, mostly blacks, to move freely. The logic and intent were clear. Unregulated movement would disturb the segregationist infrastructures of the state and would, of course, threaten the availability of black labor, whose cheapness depended on placing and enforcing restrictions on the migratory impulses and mobility of blacks. See Leonard Thompson, *A History of South Africa* (New Haven, CT: Yale University Press, 2014), chaps. 5 and 6. For an insightful treatment of South Africa's vast surveillance state system, see Keith Breckenridge, *The Biometric State: The Global Politics of Identification and Surveillance, 1850 to the Present* (Cambridge: Cambridge University Press, 2014).

27. See Jacob Dlamini, *Native Nostalgia* (Auckland Park, South Africa: Jacana Media, 2009), 45–46. For a discussion of an extreme case of colonial surveillance methods, see Brekenridge, *The Biometric State*.

28. Several working colonial anthropologists made this belief into an orthodoxy within the colonial bureaucracy, and colonial policymakers acted accordingly, passing laws against vagrancy, discouraging rural-urban migration, allowing migrant labor in colonial enterprises but only in the context of time-limited labor contracts, and harassing young men and women who had migrated from their ancestral villages to new colonial urban areas. See, for instance, David M. Goodfellow, *Principles of Economic Sociology: The Economics of*

Primitive Life as Illustrated by the Bantu Peoples of South and East Africa (London: G. Routledge & Sons, 1939); Max Gluckman, *Custom and Conflict in Africa* (London: The Free Press, 1955); J. Clyde Mitchell, Elizabeth Colson, and Max Gluckman, eds., *Human Problems in British Central Africa: The Rhodes-Livingstone Journal* 19 (1955). The studies conducted by the anthropologists hired and funded by the Rhodes-Livingstone Institute (RLI), which began operations in 1937, proved particularly useful to British colonial authorities in South-Central and Southern Africa. These studies became the bedrock of policies whose point of departure was the notion that migration out of rural traditional settings was bad for Africans, destabilized families and household economies, produced urban vagrancy and vices, and created a so-called floating population of rootless Africans. For a critical review of the connections between colonial policies and the works of the institute and how the anthropological studies produced by the institute shaped colonial economic policies regarding labor and urbanization, see Lynette Schumaker, "'A Tent with a View': Colonial Officers, Anthropologists, and the Making of the Field in Northern Rhodesia, 1937–1960," *Osiris* 11, 2nd series (1996): 237–58.

29. Cannadine, *Ornamentalism*, 143.

30. Ann Laura Stoler, *Along the Archival Grain: Epistemic Anxieties and Colonial Common Sense* (Princeton, NJ: Princeton University Press, 2009).

31. Olabisi Ajala, *An African Abroad* (London: Jarrolds, 1963).

32. Yoruba highlife musician Ebenezer Obey would immortalize Ajala's world tour in his 1975 album *Boardmembers*, further establishing metropolitan travel in the social imagination of Nigeria as a cultural idiom of transcendental yearning and adventure.

33. Janet Remmington and Nickals Hallen, "Africa Travels, Africa Writes: Notes on African Intellectual Mobilities," Africa in Words, February 26, 2015, https://africainwords.com/2015/02/26/africa-travels-africa-writes-notes-on-african-intellectual-mobilities/.

34. See, for instance, the June 2016 issue of the journal *Transfers*, which contains a special feature on African mobilities. The Nordic Africa Institute at Uppsala organized an international conference on African mobilities, September 19–21, 2018.

35. See F.R.N. Denham, Hugh Clapperton, and Walter Oudney, *Narratives of Travels and Discoveries in Northern and Central Africa in the Years 1822, 1823, and 1824*, 3rd ed. (London: John Murray, 1831); Richard Lander, *Records of Captain Clapperton's Last Expedition to Africa*, vol. 2 (London: Henry Colburn and Richard Bentley, 1830); MacGreggor Laird and R.A.K. Oldfield, *Narrative of an Expedition into the Interior of Africa by the River Niger in the Steam-Vessels Quorra and Alburka in 1832, 1833, and 1834* (London: Richard Bentley, 1837); May H. Kingsley, *Travels in West Africa: Congo Francais, Corisco, and Cameroons* (London: MacMillan, 1897); David Livingstone, *The Last Journals of David Livingstone, in Central Africa, from Eighteen Hundred and Sixty-Five to His Death, Continued by a Narrative of His Last Moments and Sufferings, Obtained from His Faithful Servants, Chuma and Susi, by Horace Waller, F.R.G.S., Rector of Twywell, Northampton* (New York: Harper and Brothers, 1875); John Speke, *Journal of the Discovery of the Source of the Nile* (New York: Harper and Brothers, 1964); Richard Burton, *Lake Regions of Central Africa: A Picture of Exploration*, vols. 1 and 2 (London: Longman, Green, Longman, and Roberts, 1860); Henry Morton Stanley, *In Darkest Africa*, vols. 1 and 2 (New York: Charles Scribner's Sons, 1890).

36. Gikandi, introduction, 20.

37. Gikandi, introduction, 16.

38. Ilan Stavans and Joshua Ellison, *Reclaiming Travel* (Durham, NC: Duke University Press), 5.

39. Stavans and Ellison, *Reclaiming Travel*, 142.

40. Ham Mukasa, *Uganda's Katikiro in England: Being the Official Account of His Visit to the Coronation of His Majesty King Edward VII* (London: Hutchinson, 1904).

41. Mukasa, *Uganda's Katikiro in England*, preliminary pages.

42. Gikandi, introduction, 4.

43. Parsons, *King Khama*, 5–6.

44. Gikandi, introduction, 28.

45. For a succinct discussion of the incorporation of Buganda into the British Empire, see Jonas Fossli Gjerso, "The Scramble for East Africa: British Motives Reconsidered, 1884–95," *Journal of Imperial and Commonwealth History* 43, no. 5 (2015): 831–60, 839–50.

46. Gikandi, introduction, 5.

47. Gikandi, introduction, 19.

48. For Florence Bernault, colonial convergencies, transactions, and strange affective expressions, whether deliberate or accidental, were a necessary, logical outcome in a colonial situation fraught with both mutual ignorance and mutual curiosities between colonizers and colonized Africans. See Florence Bernault, *Colonial Transactions: Imaginaries, Bodies, and Histories in Gabon* (Durham, NC: Duke University Press, 2019).

49. In the 1940s, Sheikh Abubakar Gumi, one of the north's most influential clerics, criticized emirs for traveling to Britain and seeking the approval of, and accepting awards and honors from, the King, the Colonial Office, and other metropolitan British entities. He described it as a betrayal of Muslim commoners, who looked up to the aristocrats in religious matters. See Abubakar Gumi (with Ismaila Abubakar Tsiga), *Where I Stand* (Ibadan, Owerri, Kaduna, Lagos: Spectrum Books Limited, 1992), 47.

50. Benjamin Nicholas Lawrance, Emily Osborne, and Richard Roberts, eds., *Intermediaries, Interpreters, and Clerks: African Employees in the Making of Colonial Africa* (Madison: University of Wisconsin Press, 2006); Amadou Hampate Ba, *The Fortunes of Wangrin* (Bloomington: Indiana University Press, 1999); Philip Afeadie, *Brokering Colonial Rule: Political Agents in Northern Nigeria, 1886–1914* (Saarbrücken, Germany: VDM Verlag Dr. Müller, 2008); Emily Lynn Osborn, "'Circle of Iron': African Colonial Employees and the Interpretation of Colonial Rule in French West Africa," *Journal of African History* 44, no. 1 (2003): 29–50; Ralph Austen, "Colonialism from the Middle: African Clerks as Historical Actors and Discursive Subjects," *History in Africa* 38 (2011): 21–33; Ralph Austen, "Who Was Wangrin and Why Does It Matter?," *Mande Studies* 9 (1997): 149–64; Tamba E. M'bayo, "African Interpreters, Mediation, and the Production of Knowledge in Colonial Senegal: The Low Land Middle Senegal Valley, ca. 1850s to ca. 1920s" (PhD dissertation, Michigan State University, 2009); Femi Kolapo and Kwabena Akurang-Parry, eds., *African Agency and European Colonialism: Latitudes of Negotiation* (Lanham, MD: University Press of America, 2007).

51. For representative examples of explorations of Britain's history of tense reception of Muslims and its difficult entanglement with Islam, see Scott Poynting and Victoria Mason, "The Resistible Rise of Islamophobia: Anti-Muslim Racism in the UK and Australia Before 11 September 2001," *Journal of Sociology* 43, no. 1 (2013: 61–86); and Deepa Kumar, *Islamophobia and the Politics of Empire* (Chicago: Haymarket Books, 2012). More broadly, Edward Said's canonical works have explicated the fraught relationship between post-Enlightenment Euro-American constructions of the self and the Other on one hand and the vast lands of Islam on the other. See Edward Said, *Culture and Imperialism* (New York: Vintage Books, 1993), and Said, *Orientalism*.

52. See, for instance, Cole, "Invisible Occidentalism," 6–7.
53. Cole, "Invisible Occidentalism," 6.
54. Muhammadu Ndayako, *Tafiyan Etsu Nupe Ingila* [Etsu Nupe's Travel to England] (Zaria, Nigeria: Gaskiya Corporation, 1954), 70.
55. Dean MacCannell, *The Tourist: A New Theory of the Leisure Class* (Berkeley: University of California Press, 2013), 5–6.
56. Cole, "Invisible Occidentalism," 6.
57. Lyn Schumaker, *Africanizing Anthropology: Fieldwork, Networks, and the Making of Cultural Knowledge in Central Africa* (Durham, NC: Duke University Press, 2001).
58. Northrup, *Africa's Discovery of Europe*, 11–13.
59. Michal Tymowski, "African Perceptions of Europeans in the Early Period of Portuguese Expeditions to West Africa," *Itinerario* 39, no. 2 (2015): 221–46, 227.
60. See Luise White, "Cars Out of Place: Vampires, Technology, and Labor in East and Central Africa," *Representations* 43 (1993): 27–50.
61. Thomas Hodgkins, *Nationalism in Colonial Africa* (New York: New York University Press, 1957), 140.
62. João Reis and Armando Pedro Muiuane (org.), *Datas e documentos da história da FRELIMO* (Lourenço Marques: Imprensa Nacional de Moçambique, 1975). This document contains the original recollection from Mondlane. I thank Jose Cossa for pointing me to this reference and source, supplying the original Portuguese passage, and helping with translation.
63. Reis and Muiuane, *Datas e documentos*.
64. Dean MacCannell, *The Ethics of Sightseeing* (Berkeley: University of California Press, 2011), 42.
65. MacCannell, *The Tourist*, xix.
66. MacCannell, *The Tourist*, xix, xxii.
67. MacCannell, *The Ethics of Sightseeing*, 42–43.
68. MacCannell, *The Tourist*, chap. 5.
69. MacCannell, *The Tourist*, 98.
70. A model of such a study is David Arnold's *Everyday Technology: Machines and the Making of India's Modernity* (Chicago: University of Chicago Press, 2013).
71. Arnold, *Everyday Technology*, 3.
72. See Karl Marx, *Capital*, vol. 1 (Moscow: Progress, 1965), 74–75.
73. For colonial mimicry, see Homi Bhabba, "Of Mimicry and Man: The Ambivalence of Colonial Discourse," *October*, Discipleship: A Special Issue on Psychoanalysis 28 (1984): 125–33.
74. Frederick Lugard, *The Dual Mandate in British Tropical Africa* (Oxford: Frank Cass, 1926). For a critical analysis of Lugard's ethnoracial, historical, and religious justifications for recommending Hausa-Fulani aristocrats as candidates for British imperial partnership, see Moses Ochonu, *Colonialism by Proxy* (Bloomington: Indiana University Press, 2014), chap. 1, and Moses Ochonu, "Protection by Proxy: The Hausa-Fulani as Agents of British Colonial Rule in Northern Nigeria," in *Protection and Empire: A Global History*, ed. Lauren Benton, Adam Clulow, and Bain Attwood, 228–44 (Cambridge: Cambridge University Press, 2017).
75. Lugard, *The Dual Mandate*, 70.
76. Ochonu, *Colonialism by Proxy*.
77. Daniel Branch, "The Enemy Within: Loyalists and the War Against Mau Mau in Kenya," *Journal of African History* 48 (2007): 291–315; Hilary Sapire, "African Loyalism and

Its Discontents: The Royal Tour of South Africa, 1947," *Historical Journal* 54, no. 1 (2011): 215–40; Hilary Sapire, "Ambiguities of Loyalism: The Prince of Wales in India and Africa, 1921–22 and 25," *History Workshop Journal* 73, no. 1 (2012): 37–65; Christopher J. Lee, *Unreasonable Histories: Nativism, Multiracial Lives, and the Genealogical Imagination in British Africa* (Durham, NC: Duke University Press, 2014).

78. See, for instance, Allan Blackstock and Frank O'Gorman, eds., *Loyalism and the Formation of the British World, 1775–1914* (Suffolk, UK: Boydell, 2014).

79. Branch, "The Enemy Within," 292–93.

80. Branch, "The Enemy Within," 292–93.

81. See Bonny Ibhawoh, *Imperial Justice: Africans in Empire's Court* (New York: Oxford University Press, 2013).

82. MacCannell, *The Tourist*, xix.

83. Mary Luise Pratt, *Travel Writing and Transculturation* (London: Routledge 1992), 203.

84. Pratt, *Travel Writing and Transculturation*, 203. See also Graham Dawson, *Soldier Heroes: British Adventure, Empire, and the Imagining of Masculinities* (London: Routledge, 1994).

1

LITERACY, NARRATIVE, AND THE COLONIAL IDEATIONAL SPACE

> My hope is for [this book] to serve as a catalyst for
> the modernization of Northern Nigeria.
> —Abubakar Imam

Northern Nigeria's aristocratic travelers, the subjects of this book, wrote their metropolitan experiences into an emergent colonial literacy culture. In several respects, the aristocrats were part of a fast-evolving intellectual culture in which reading and writing acquired a social allure for Western-educated young men and women and for an older generation socialized into a colonial world of adult literacy. In the intellectual and literary space in which metropolitan travel narratives were written and read, writing and reading had moved from the sacred spaces of religion and morality to one marked largely by the production and consumption of stories and ideas as aesthetic forms. In this space, the writing and reading of secular texts and their associated practices were thriving and evolving, underwritten by a slew of colonial initiatives designed to promote Romanized literacy. The ensuing literary production was dominated by fictional and nonfictional stories whose overarching motifs harkened back to local folkloric traditions.

This chapter analyzes the emergence and evolution of a Northern Nigerian intellectual and literary culture that developed between 1930 and 1960 and provided a vibrant, engaged audience for aristocratic travel writers who returned from Britain and wrote about their experiences there. This story of literary ferment in the context of colonial domination—the backdrop to the travel-writing endeavor analyzed in this book—has three aspects, each encompassing a realm of programs and actions that fed into an inchoate world of lively intellectual transactions between writers and readers, between those purporting to possess experiential resources for storytelling and those eager to vicariously access these stories through the medium of Romanized Hausa literacy. The first aspect of this intellectual history was the development of a colonial infrastructure of story writing, publishing, and literary production. The second was a vigorous colonial promotion of adult literacy, mainly in rural areas but also in some urban centers. The third was the evolution of a school culture of secular, modern education in Northern Nigeria that developed simultaneously with the growth of literary practices, for which travel and adventure provided material and inspiration.

The last section of the chapter analyzes the metropolitan travel memoir of Abubakar Imam. It highlights the literary and discursive techniques and modes of critical commentary deployed by Imam to make sense of Britain, capture his experiences there, recall his encounters with British acquaintances and interlocutors, and translate many aspects of metropolitan life for his Hausaphone Northern Nigerian audience.

In 1906, shortly after the departure of Frederick Lugard, the first governor of colonial Northern Nigeria, colonial administrators banned Christian missionary educators from opening mission stations and schools in the Muslim-majority districts of colonial Northern Nigeria.[1] Lugard had initiated the ban, claiming he was honoring the religious and intellectual heritage of these Muslim-majority districts. As part of his initial outreach to the Muslim rulers after the military conquest of the region, Lugard had assured them that he would not undermine their religious heritage and practices. British missionaries, such as Hans Vischer and Walter Miller, disagreed with Lugard and believed that the British colonial administrator was pandering to Muslim emirs and aristocrats because he needed their cooperation and partnership to administer the vast region.

Whatever Lugard's motive, he found a ready, credible alibi in the precolonial Islamic intellectual heritage of emirate Northern Nigeria. Here, in the vast Muslim region to the far north of the Benue and Niger Rivers, there was a "long-established world of Arabic and Hausa *Ajami* literature and learning."[2] Some secular writing in the precolonial Hausaphone world had been done in *Ajami*, a modified Arabic script configured to convey Hausa speech and phonological systems. In the nineteenth-century Sokoto Caliphate, much of the literature produced in *Ajami* was religious in nature, focusing on "the tenets of a Sunni way of life for Muslims in the region."[3]

The literary and intellectual corpus of the precolonial world of the caliphate and Muslim Bornu consisted of religious and moral writings, with secular poetry, philosophy, and other types of nonreligious thought accounting for only a small portion of this intellectual heritage.[4]

The increased engagement of the caliphate with a succession of European actors, a mid- to late nineteenth-century process that culminated in the British colonial conquest between 1900 and 1903, "signaled a turn toward secular concerns in Hausa [literature]."[5] Much of this literature followed the traditions of Islamic verse pioneered by the Dan Fodio ruling family of the Sokoto Caliphate. Hausa secular writings in *Ajami* mainly consisted of expressions of the quotidian realities and vagaries of everyday life in relatable verse, in contrast to esoteric Islamic verse. Some of this poetry creatively transcribed Hausa oral folklore, legends, and folk histories into versified prose for popular enjoyment. Others grafted the language of religion and moral instruction onto a tradition of storytelling and poetic production and vice versa. The development of this incipient literary culture was discernible by the time of the colonial conquest, even if it was subsumed in the broader universe of Islamic literary production.

Notwithstanding this growing secular Hausa literary culture, colonial bureaucracies superintending the cultural aspects of colonization contended with persistent tropes that saw literature, literacy, writing, and reading as bound up with religious devotion and other rituals of piety. Moreover, whatever appeal the emergent colonial modernity of secular book learning may have held for Northern Nigerian youth, British officials did not capitalize on it to promote colonial culture through secular popular literature. Instead, in the first decade of colonial rule, officers in the education bureaucracy of the colonial government sought to excavate and publish a latent trove of Hausa tales, traditions, and folk histories as a way of countering and diluting the feared intellectual influence of Christian missionaries, who were disseminating religious and secular materials in defiance of and outside the official colonial system.[6] These early investments in literacy and literature were circumscribed by the colonial conflation of literature and moral character and by excessive pandering to legends, traditions, and folklore to the exclusion of current affairs, contemporary realities, and creative storytelling. Colonial attempts to cultivate a Romanized literary culture rooted in the caliphal *Ajami* literary tradition foundered because the Roman script did not have the ethical and religious resonance of *Ajami*.

It was understandable, then, given the preceding literary muddle, that in the early 1930s, when colonial authorities began to actively try to nurture and satiate the literary sensibilities of their Northern Nigerian subjects, officials had to contend with an ambivalent intellectual culture. This literacy was secularizing in response to the ideational currents of colonialism and the instrumental imperatives of colonial learning, but it was still haunted by the notion that writing and reading had to be informed by a moral quest and a social commitment to character development and not by a secular economy of aesthetic literary pleasure. The contemporary observation of a colonial official regarding this intellectual scene and the challenge it posed to the emergence of a full-fledged intelligentsia of secular readers and writers is apt:

> The first difficulty was to persuade these *Malams* [in this context, Western-educated teachers] that the thing was worth doing. The influence of Islam produces an extremely serious-minded type of person. The art of writing, moreover, being intimately connected in his mind with his religion, is not to be treated lightly. Since the religious revival at the beginning of the last century, nearly all the original work produced by the Northern Nigerian authors has been either purely religious or written with a strong religious motive. Most of it is written in Arabic, which ... was considered a more worthy medium for any work of importance than the mother tongue.[7]

Given this backdrop, the evolution of a Romanized culture of secular literacy seemed improbable. The major challenge was how to engender interest in a new Romanized literature, whose linguistic medium and content were considered secular, mundane, and unmoored to piety and morality, in a conservative Muslim region. The seduction of Arabic and *Ajami* was their function as conduits for scripture. There was a coextensive understanding that texts written in these scripts were sacralized by the scripts themselves, even if the texts tackled mundane, quotidian, and secular matters. In colonial times, Romanized literacy enjoyed no such perceptual advantage and was, to compound its fate, associated with the epistemic violence of, and anxieties sparked by, colonization.

Considering this disadvantage vis-à-vis *Ajami* literature, the challenge for colonial officials seeking to promote Romanized literacy and an associated reading and writing culture was to forge interest in the production and reception of aesthetic texts. The production and circulation of materials capable of enthralling the new Western-educated men and women of Northern Nigeria were critical to overcoming this challenge. Additionally, these materials had to come wrapped in indigenous idioms and methods of narration relatable to potential readers. Colonial educators sought to promote the production of "a substantial amount of interesting material" for the lettered young people of Northern Nigeria to read.[8] The envisaged corpus needed to be "texts that Hausa-speakers could take pleasure in reading," not turgid colonial or Islamic manuals or instructions.[9] Colonial officials surmised that didactic texts with no explicit moral content or sacred vernacular would not be received well. The mediatory voice of the trusted local emir, aristocrat, religious authority, or Western-educated man considered knowledgeable in colonial affairs was "particularly necessary when writing for Moslems."[10]

Forging a Reading Culture

No colonial or postcolonial literary and intellectual history of Northern Nigeria would be complete without exploring two entities whose biographies and histories have become entwined. Rupert East—a British colonial educator, vernacular literature connoisseur, and publisher—and the Northern Nigerian Literature Bureau, which he headed from 1932 to 1953, were critical to the development of a colonially mediated and funded culture of writing, reading, and public intellectual life in Northern Nigeria. Rupert East transformed the bureau from an obscure bureaucratic afterthought in the colonial system to a visible organ for promoting vernacular literary expression and engendering a literary public sphere.

East joined the Northern Nigerian Colonial Service in the early 1920s and served as a colonial officer in multiple districts. His appointment as an education officer in the Colonial Service transformed the trajectory of his colonial career and brought him into contact with the emergent class of Northern Nigerian aristocratic scions being educated in the premier government-run school in Northern Nigeria, Katsina College. Established in 1921 to train sons of emirs and Muslim aristocrats to replace their parents in the Native Authority or take up careers as teachers and clerks, Katsina College was a fledgling intellectual and educational oasis where young men received the quality secondary education denied to millions of their non-aristocratic Muslim kinsmen. East, posted there in 1929, taught several subjects and built teacher-student mentorship relationships with future figures of Northern Nigerian intellectual life, such as Abubakar Imam and Nuhu Bamali.

East's work at Katsina College activated his interest in vernacular literature. His experience at the school also alerted him to the need for a larger community of Romanized writing and reading to keep pace with the rise of secular, liberal education among the privileged aristocratic young men of the region. In 1931, East was posted to the colonial government's Translation Bureau, a branch of the educational department that translated government pamphlets and other public documents into Hausa and helped produce manuals for the mandatory Hausa-language exams for British colonial officials. The bureau had been established in 1929 but did little beyond the translation of educational and public information material. As head of the bureau, East dedicated himself to engineering a Romanized vernacular reading culture in Northern Nigeria.

Reading required writers, and writers, in turn, had to cater to the reading palates of readers. For writers, the challenge was how to produce texts that Northern Nigerians literate in the Romanized script could read for aesthetic and educational value. East set out to repurpose the Translation Bureau to perform this role of forging a symbiotic community of readers and writers. The bureau was thus transformed from a simple bureaucratic organ serving the translation needs of colonization to one invested in promoting writing and reading without insisting on these activities being explicitly connected to colonial priorities.

In 1935, East renamed the bureau the Northern Nigerian Literature Bureau to reflect its expanded focus. Headquartered in the village of Tukur Tukur just outside the ancient emirate city of Zaria, the bureau sent personnel to schools "to solicit examples of imaginative writing that [East] could publish" for the reading pleasure of literate Northern Nigerians.[11] East tapped into his Katsina College network of Western-educated young aristocrats to acquire his first five works of creative storytelling—works he hoped would both showcase and prefigure his vision for publishing vernacular stories for a local Hausa-speaking readership.

The bureau's new role included promoting not just vernacular fiction but also newspaper articles on current affairs, travel, adventure, culture, and other mundane topics that budding Nigerian writers deemed newsworthy or of interest to the growing community of Romanized Hausa-language readers. For East and other colonial officials, the local writers would perform instrumentally mediatory roles, translating "our ideas on education, hygiene, science, husbandry, social reform, and so forth" and ensuring these markers of colonial modernity were "made intelligible to [their] own people."[12] Thus, East envisioned his commissioned writers using their storytelling skills to promote the "modernizing" projects of colonialism. This robust remit prefigured and was consistent with the scribal venture of traveler-writers. From the colonial perspective, travel to Britain to observe the prototypes of the aforementioned colonial ideas and practices was the ideal inspiration for fictional and nonfictional stories of the type East was promoting.

Rupert East's efforts to cultivate an indigenous reading public pivoted partly on guiding the embryonic Northern Nigerian educated class to develop a standard, replicable orthographic tool kit, with "a recognized spelling and grammar," that could be preserved in the literary imaginaries of Northern Nigerians.[13] A related aspect of this effort found expression in the chicken-and-egg dilemma of whether publishing folktales and adventure books for a small, commercially insignificant readership should precede or follow the forging of a Northern Nigerian literacy culture. In other words, East wondered whether establishing the infrastructure of mass publishing and mass literacy should take precedence over promoting the literary output of a select group of privileged aristocratic men who could end up writing for each other in an incestuous community of writers and readers.[14]

The early intellectual and literary scene in Northern Nigeria was inchoate and in constant flux, but the region's Western-educated class was growing. Along with this growth came heightened intellectual restlessness and adventurism. Teaching in the region's schools, working in the local Native Authorities, and clerking in the colonial bureaucracy were respectable professional endeavors for secularly educated young men, but these positions proved inadequate to fulfill their intellectual and political yearnings. Teaching was particularly restrictive; the evidence suggests that students in government-funded schools, who were being trained and groomed to become teachers, increasingly saw teaching as a constraint on their intellectual ambitions.[15]

These young men wanted to express their own ideas, tell their own stories, and cultivate their own readership among the growing population of Northern Nigerians literate in Romanized Hausa. Northern Nigeria's colonially educated young men, such as Sa'adu Zungur and Aminu Kano, had already become prolific newspaper intellectuals, and their letters and public commentaries appeared regularly in Southern Nigerian newspapers such as the *West African Pilot*.[16] This substantial scribal and intellectual engagement of the Northern Nigerian intelligentsia belied the absence of a local medium of public expression. In the eyes of colonial officials, these intellectuals were advertising the colonial problems of the North and amplifying their criticism of Northern Nigerian colonial policy in the Southern Nigerian press. Colonial officials regarded this as a potentially subversive activity. Leveraging the reach and influence of Southern Nigerian newspapers, which had long been regarded with anxiety and suspicion by Northern Nigerian colonial officials, Northern Nigerian intellectuals inadvertently provoked a paradigm shift in the ideational space of colonization in Northern Nigeria. Colonial officials in Northern Nigeria sought to counter the emergence of independent Northern Nigerian intellectual activity by regimenting the intellectual energies of writers. A consensus soon began to form around the idea of establishing a tightly controlled Northern Nigerian print media outlet.

Colonial authorities developed a heightened sensitivity to the intellectual aspirations of Northern Nigeria's educated young men. It was hard to ignore the underground economy of writing, engagement, and reading that had developed among the graduates of colonial schools in the region. As East stated in a postwar note to Nigeria's then governor, Sir Arthur Richards, there was "a growing restlessness among the young educated Northerners" that necessitated "an outlet for reasonable self-expression."[17] The implicit anxiety encapsulated by this recognition was that if the colonial government did not invest in the infrastructure of mass literacy, mass media, publishing, and public intellection, the emergent Northern Nigerian Romanized intelligentsia might embrace alternative, independent, and thus potentially subversive forms of intellectual and literary self-expression. East argued that it was necessary to channel the scribal impulses of Northern Nigeria's emerging intelligentsia into a quasi-official print medium where political writings would be disciplined or replaced by aesthetic and, from the perspective of the colonizers, apologetic ones.

Abubakar Imam

Rupert East initially acquired five short novels for publication, one of which was written by his prized pupil at Katsina College, Abubakar Imam. In the years to come, Abubakar Imam would become one of the most beloved Romanized Hausa fiction and travel writers in Northern Nigeria. Imam also came to epitomize East's vision of literary mentorship and intellectual coproduction in which European mentors would tutor and shepherd local writers through the gamut and vagaries of the creative and publishing processes. As East himself put it, the "plan is, therefore, to collect together from all parts of the Northern Provinces a body of educated young men, the best that can be found in character and ability, and set them down in close contact with a carefully selected European staff. All books and important newspaper articles will for the present be produced by Africans and Europeans working together in close collaboration. As long as the work is done in the native language the writing will be done entirely by Africans, though the European may help with the arrangement and editing."[18]

Even before the establishment of a formal publishing infrastructure for popular books and newspapers in colonial Northern Nigeria, the collaborative vision of intellectual production East was trying to forge was materializing. Imam was a teacher in the Katsina Native Authority school when East invited him to the Literature Bureau as one of the initial group of Northern Nigerian apprentice writers. Imam quickly distinguished himself by what he himself described as his "writing skill."[19] Imam was precocious in learning the storytelling templates being taught to the cohort, but he needed to adapt these narrative styles to a new Romanized Hausa storytelling form.

What followed was an intense literary mentorship that saw Imam studiously engaging with a cache of "books on European fables and Arabian Nights stories . . . as background material."[20] The mimetic and adaptive style of early Romanized Hausa prose owes its existence to the tutelage of East,[21] but Imam was a creative genius who invented a new genre of Romanized Hausa storytelling that became popular among a growing audience of Northern Nigerians who could read Hausa in Roman script. Imam's crucial role in this literary culture unfolded over the next few years and crystallized in several important developments, but in the early to mid-1930s, he made it possible to imagine the realization of a Northern Nigerian intellectual culture in which writers and readers symbiotically sustained one another through the exchange and consumption of ideas and stories.

Imam was a prolific writer. His stories were eclectic, drawing on Hausa folkloric traditions, metropolitan English prose, and experiences in colonial society. In 1934, Imam's unpublished play, *Ruwan Bagaja*,[22] caught the attention of East, who was reviewing it as a judge in a literary competition. East facilitated its publication in 1935. In 1937, Imam published his seminal work, *Magana Jari Ce*, a collection of Hausa folktales written with remarkable literary license as a pastiche of Hausa narrative styles and marked by stories and motifs adapted from foreign, mostly Middle Eastern, narrative conventions. *Magana Jari Ce* was a work of masterful storytelling whose effectiveness was enhanced by the relatable cultural quality and settings of the stories. The text was a literary if not commercial success among Northern Nigeria's Romanized Hausa reading public.

Magana Jari Ce was the stylistic standard-bearer of the Romanized Hausa narrative style. The text was generously laced with proverbs (*karin magana*) and strategic embellishment. It was marked by the subtle exploration of morality and the interface between normative and insurgent cultures. As a collection of stories, *Magana Jari Ce* inaugurated an intellectual public sphere of Romanized Hausa writers assuming the role of cultural interpreters and connoisseurs of both indigenous Hausa culture and metropolitan imperial culture. Imam and other writers in this Romanized Hausa storytelling tradition found themselves increasingly functioning as interpreters of empire, translators of colonial modernity, and mediums for circulating the factual and mythical imaginaries of British metropolitan peoples and cultures. *Magana Jari Ce* became a classic and a stylistic referent for other Hausa writers, whether they were creating fictional stories, retelling stories from the Hausa oral folktale corpus, or writing nonfictional biographical and travel accounts. The deployment of Hausa exaggerative techniques, the clever use of binary oppositions for enhanced effect, and the advancement of proverbs and allegories to convey deep thought and meaning were all aspects that would be imitated by traveler-writers.

Magana Jari Ce established adventure as a veritable theme in Romanized Hausa public storytelling, carving out a vast expressive territory for experimenting with imaginative renderings of distant colonial phenomena. Exploring the foreign and the unfamiliar through contrast with the banal, familiar, local, and comfortable culture of home became a motif of Romanized Hausa writing and increasingly defined the appetite of Romanized Hausa readers. It was not enough to simply write about adventures undertaken in unfamiliar lands and implicitly highlight the moral significations in the story; writers also developed elaborate literary techniques that invited readers to vicariously participate in the exotic adventures.

Romanized Hausa travel writing was birthed in the crucible of this interaction between writers and readers. The success of Imam's *Magana Jari Ce* was critical to the emergence of a Northern Nigerian intellectual space that meshed literary and adventure writing into a rich and eclectic genre that captivated a growing audience of readers. This audience hungered for local stories that explored unfamiliar themes and places in familiar idioms as well as stories that presented unfamiliar topics in familiar, intelligible Hausa narrative and thought frames. This underlying literary appetite proved invaluable for sustaining the popularity of metropolitan travel narratives.

Gaskiya Corporation and the New Public Sphere

The emergence of a Northern Nigerian community of Romanized Hausa writers and readers portended the emergence of an indigenous, albeit colonially funded, publishing industry. Rupert East's vision had been to eventually transform the Northern Nigerian Literature Bureau into a publisher of vernacular fiction, nonfiction, and newspapers. He wanted to give members of the emerging regional intelligentsia an outlet to air their thoughts on the colonial situation in a controlled, disciplined mass medium. It was an expansive and potentially expensive plan that required colonial financial subsidy given the fact that even the most optimistic estimation at the time could not have predicted the emergence of a self-sustaining publishing industry in a nascent market for books, pamphlets, and other Romanized Hausa texts. Thus, the realization of this publishing vision through the establishment of the Gaskiya Corporation and its aggressively wide-ranging foray into the collection and publishing of Hausa texts should be understood as evidence of the mutual interests of Northern Nigeria's Western-educated class and the colonial government in creating a semi-official space for intellectual and literary engagements. The structure was simple: the colonial government would provide the technology and technical expertise while Northern Nigeria's intellectuals and writers would supply publishable materials.

The 1939 establishment of the Hausa-language newspaper *Gaskiya ta fi Kwabo* under the auspices of the Literature Bureau laid the groundwork for the formation of the Gaskiya Corporation publishing company. The newspaper was set up primarily to counter German propaganda in the months preceding World War II in September of that year. Once the war started, the British sought to mobilize the Hausa-speaking populations of Northern Nigeria for the British war effort. *Gaskiya* became the most potent propaganda instrument in Northern Nigeria during the war.[23]

The intellectual restlessness of the Northern Nigerian educated class, already a source of colonial concern, came into sharper relief after the start of World War II as German radio broadcasts and other materials filtered into Northern Nigeria and threatened, colonial officials feared, to seduce young Northern Nigerian colonial subjects away from "the right way of thinking and writing."[24] *Gaskiya ta fi Kwabo* and the larger Gaskiya Corporation publishing project, of which it became a part, were needed to constrain, manage, and properly channel the intellectual ferment among the Western-educated class into a culture of edifying, aesthetic public intellection and away from one the British colonizers understood to be rooted in dissent and subversion.

The first few months of *Gaskiya* proved a watershed in the intellectual history of colonial Northern Nigeria. The Western-educated class of the North shifted radically away from Southern Nigerian newspapers and began to redirect their prolific public intellection to the Hausa-language newspaper. This was a seminal, paradigmatic shift—a vernacular newspaper funded by the colonial government became the preferred medium of ideational exchange among the Western-educated Northern Nigerian intelligentsia. Many *mallams* (lit. teachers), a reverential name for a broad array of Western-educated Northern Nigerians in the colonial system, began to dominate the letters-to-the-editor section of the paper, inundating the editor with correspondence on a variety of sociopolitical and economic issues and criticizing "the weaknesses in native administration."[25] *Gaskiya* quickly became the platform of public thought in Northern Nigeria, even though it was funded, edited, and presumably filtered by government censors to keep out ideas and perspectives deemed too radical.

Gaskiya was an arena as well as a catalyst for public literary and political expression. Although this public sphere was mediated and moderated by colonial bureaucratic oversight, it birthed secondary, perhaps tertiary, public spheres in which Hausa-speaking lettered and unlettered subjects were participants. Maimunatu Dadasare Abdullahi,[26] the Fulani female companion of Rupert East whose biography and work are discussed in chapter 5 and the epilogue, played an important role in the intellectual world created by *Gaskiya*. Dadasare began as an engaged reader who consistently wrote letters to the editor on burning issues of the day, often under a pseudonym.[27] She also wrote occasional pseudonymous opinion editorials in which she raised issues of concern to her immediate constituencies—women and Zaria residents. On one occasion Dadasare "complained bitterly" about the absence of clinics "in Zaria City or its densely populated suburb, Tudun Wada."[28] This op-ed rattled the colonial authorities, and they sought to identify the writer, but to no avail. The thrust of the op-ed clearly registered because the colonial authorities eventually established clinics in Zaria and Tudun Wada. This is just one example of the early influence and unintended reach of the newspaper and its tight-knit community of activist writers. Through

Dadasare's unpublished memoir, we get a glimpse into the inner workings and influence of *Gaskiya* and its network of readers and writers.

Within a few years of operation, the newspaper's sphere of influence expanded rapidly, instantiated most tellingly by the large number of letters to the editor that poured in from all parts of Northern Nigeria. So heavy was the volume of these dialogic missives that Rupert East and the management of the newspaper employed Dadasare full time as an editor and sifter of reader contributions. It was her job to "read these letters and make a selection for printing."[29] Dadasare also responded to the letters and answered the writers' questions, an intellectual interaction that sometimes took on the character of debate and disputation. This eager public engagement with the newspaper and its stories points to the emergence of a vibrant community of intellectual interlocutors who considered *Gaskiya* an arena of sociopolitical discourse. Dadasare, writing about this early expressive fervor, asserts that "readers certainly did not hesitate to express their feelings" about a variety of contemporary social and political topics.[30] The newspaper was a constrained space for public intellection, but Northern Nigeria's Romanized Hausa intellectual community repurposed it into an organic platform of vernacular communication and ideational exchange.

The newspaper successfully constructed a sense of free expression, no matter how constrained. As Dadasare puts it, *Gaskiya* "helped to show . . . that the public was free to express its needs, opinions, and criticisms in print." The newspaper offered a space for Northern Nigerians to sound off on the familiar anxieties of reconciling colonial social and gender roles and traditional expectations. Men wrote to complain about the rising rate of divorce due to "the modern wife's inability to cook." Women, for their part, wrote to decry the disproportionate empowerment of men in the colonial economy and the impunity and "meanness" this bred in husbands.[31] *Gaskiya* was instrumental in building a Northern Nigerian literary and intellectual imaginary. It was a site where readers and writers, both anonymous and self-identifying, shared stories and perspectives on an evolving colonial society where views on modernity, tradition, colonial culture, and socialization found narrative expression.

Consolidating an Intellectual Space

In 1944, five years after *Gaskiya ta fi Kwabo* began publishing its twice-monthly editions, Rupert East requested funding from the Colonial Welfare and Development Fund to help establish a full-fledged publishing house. This press would encompass *Gaskiya ta fi Kwabo* but would expand to publish a variety of vernacular literary and nonliterary materials for the Roman-literate, Hausa-speaking populations of Northern Nigeria. The request, which enjoyed the strong support of Governor Arthur Richardson and retired former governor Frederick Lugard, received Whitehall's approval in 1945. Gaskiya Corporation was incorporated in the United Kingdom as a publishing firm dedicated to the promotion of Hausa vernacular writings. The company's broad mission was the development of a public intellectual sphere populated by readers and writers connected by a shared realm of ideational exchange and aesthetic transactions.

East was appointed chairman, and Abubakar Imam's previously informal appointment as the editor of *Gaskiya ta fi Kwabo* was ratified. In addition, Imam was East's de facto deputy—an understudy unofficially in training for the eventual assumption of the corporation's leadership. The corporation's operational hub, Tukur Tukur, would later become a laboratory for a program of mass literacy designed to sustain the company by creating more Romanized Hausa readers. A slew of new hires followed the formal establishment of the corporation. The new staff were expected to quickly learn the entire gamut of the technical and editorial processes of publishing—from generating ideas and stories to refining them into publishable materials to producing them in printed physical materials.

In 1946, Gaskiya Corporation launched *Jakadiyya*, a newspaper targeted to women. Because most of Northern Nigeria's Roman-literate women spoke a first language other than Hausa, *Jakadiyya*'s stories and articles were written in "very simple Hausa."[32] Like *Gaskiya*, *Jakadiyya* was "successful beyond expectation," as Dadasare describes it in her memoir.[33] This success stemmed in part from the expansion of the newspaper's readership beyond the original targeted audience. Many Hausa and Fulani women who lacked the ability to read in the Roman script but craved participation in this new world of current-affairs literacy and literary aesthetics had their "literate husband" read the newspaper's stories and articles to them "aloud."[34] Another reason for the newspaper's popularity was Dadasare's decision to establish a women's page, where she wrote biographical articles on successful English women, such as Elizabeth Fry and Florence Nightingale, as well as essays on relatable Victorian "feminine" subjects such as hygiene and childcare.[35] Yet another reason for the newspaper's success was that, unlike in her writings for *Gaskiya*, Dadasare used her real name in the byline of her column, creating for many female readers a composite of their own lives as urban, Roman-literate women burdened by both Victorian colonial ethos and traditional expectations.

The public sphere created by and on the pages of *Gaskiya* and *Jakadiyya* endured and intensified through a type of replicative literacy common in environments of limited scribal intelligibility. As with the secondary transmission of *Jakadiyya* from husbands to wives, *Gaskiya* was consumed in replicative gradations that gave the newspaper much more valence than it would have had if its reception had been confined to those who could read Romanized Hausa themselves. An expanding network of vicarious, communal literacy carried the newspaper's stories to remote spaces where the Roman script was unintelligible. As Dadasare writes in her memoir, "Even in a little village if there was one literate person he would give public readings of these papers."[36] Public readings of *Gaskiya* expanded the web of intellectual exchange and deepened a discursive space that merged formal and informal traditions of literacy. Public readings were also spectacular mediums of intellectual transmission that mapped neatly onto the apparatuses of colonial public enlightenment that utilized public-address systems mounted on vans to disseminate messages and propaganda to unlettered rural folk.[37] In the 1940s, the Northern Nigerian public sphere of literary production and intellectual exchange was consolidated through the appropriation of books and newspapers for purposes of self-edification and engagement with colonial realities.

For the next three decades, Gaskiya Corporation, despite its perpetual financial struggles, became the infrastructural backbone of Northern Nigerian intellectual life, not only publishing the newspaper that would become its capstone project but also most works of fiction, folklore, autobiography, travel accounts, and colonial educational texts produced and read in Northern Nigeria. Crucially, for our purpose, Gaskiya Corporation pioneered and sustained the genre of the metropolitan travel memoir, including two major metropolitan travelogues published as books: Abubakar Imam's *Tafiya Mabudin Ilimi* and Muhammadu Ndayako's *Tafiyan Etsu Nupe Ingila*, both of which are discussed later. At its peak, the corporation's orbit was intellectually inhabited by a large community of writers, journalists, actively engaged letter-writing readers, and, vicariously, many other Nigerians who consumed the newspaper's stories indirectly through proximate readers.

The corporation's work was crucial for the emergence of a community of readers and interlocutors who were the target audience of the travel narratives analyzed in several chapters of this book. The promotion of mass literacy was critical to the cultivation of a mass audience of newspaper readers. The literacy acquired by young aristocratic men in the formal setting of the regimented and restricted colonial school was a narrow, class-based enterprise. This kind of literacy sparked an intellectual ferment in Northern Nigeria and provided the first, compact community of writers and readers, but it was limited in scope. The newspaper-reading culture revolving around *Gaskiya ta fi Kwabo* coalesced gradually but discernibly around the expansion of mass, class-neutral Romanized literacy.

Literacy and the Creation of a Mass Audience

Mass Romanized literacy was desirable for a variety of colonial purposes. The most obvious was the need to convey messages demanding compliance and the fulfillment of obligations to the state to the urban and rural mass of colonial subjects. Colonial propaganda, whether instructional and didactic or designed for orientation and manipulation, required a variety of mass communication strategies. These included the classic public-messaging tour van equipped with a public-address system and loudspeakers as well as the deployment of cinematic technology and the distribution of Hausa-language posters and flyers, methods of colonial messaging that worked more through pictorial associations and graphic illustrations than through textual readability.[38]

These methods were sufficient for the purposes of colonial message dissemination. For the more ambitious purpose of engineering the emergence of a functional and aesthetic reading culture, however, mass literacy was essential. The Northern Regional Literature Agency (NORLA), which inherited the intellectual capital of the Northern Nigerian Literature Bureau along with a more robust mandate for undertaking a regionwide literacy campaign, was established in 1950 and revamped in 1953. Mass literacy was, of course, imagined as a vehicle for turning Northern Nigeria into a vast society of readers whose love of the written word would make expensive colonial propaganda unnecessary while producing colonial subjects with disciplined political, aesthetic, and cultural consciousness rooted in Hausa culture and colonial modernity.

The colonial sources written by the officials who superintended NORLA and its campaigns provide an unreliably effusive portrayal of the outcomes of the literacy campaigns. Statements claiming that Northern Nigerians were expressing "the desire to explore new horizons through literacy"[39] in the postwar years were clearly the familiar exaggerative bluster of colonial officialese and should be read with caution. In the analysis that follows, I read these sources on the literacy campaigns both along and against the grain because the history of the literacy campaign is as much a history of the colonial hopes invested in it as about its actual unfolding and outcome.

The literacy campaign was tagged *Yaki da Jahilci* (war against ignorance/illiteracy) and was launched with the establishment of NORLA in 1950 and its mandate to produce materials for adult education in 1953. In 1958, officials decided to take stock of the campaign in an elaborate report, which claimed that two million of Northern Nigeria's population of roughly twelve million were participating in the program. The campaign hinged on adult literacy. Although poor residents of some urban centers came under the campaign's influence, *Yaki da Jahilci* was essentially a rural project, targeting rural farmers and herdsmen who were more likely to have been untouched by colonial education and modernist influences and were thus removed from the government's message loop. The literacy campaign, the report states, "is generally aimed at rural areas, where the country folk, as everywhere, [view] themselves to be less favored than townsmen."[40] The report tells us that even nomadic Fulani herdsmen were so eager to read and write that they were "risk[ing] family censure, ostracism or even severe chastisement to give vent to this urge."[41]

It is possible and indeed likely that rural Northern Nigerians and nomadic herdsmen enthusiastically desired entrance into colonial literacy, with the reward of access to a vast, emerging world of ideational exchange and edifying storytelling. Nonetheless, this likely hyperbolic claim about nomads leaving family, vocation, and clan behind to pursue literacy dovetails with two claims officials made regarding literacy in postwar Northern Nigeria. The first was that yearnings for literacy expressed an "eagerness to become better acquainted with those things which fit man everywhere for a more dignified role [in society]." Here we see a conflation of literacy and dignity—indeed, of literacy and modernity, if modernity is read from the colonizer's perspective as a set of transformations and tastes that confer dignity on the subaltern. From the perspective of the colonial officials leading the literacy campaign, those who read Romanized texts were dignified and those who could not read were not. Investments in literacy and the production of a mass community of readers—and writers—were thus reflective of a colonial commitment to producing dignified "natives."

The second point was that literacy was understood as a commodity desirable for everyone "everywhere," as the report put it.[42] For colonial officials, mass literacy was a desirable egalitarian offering of colonialism that equalized the inherited and acquired status hierarchies of colonial society. Colonial officials argued that democratized access to information, ideas, and stories mitigated social hierarchies. The promise of ideational equality and unmediated access to colonial modernity through the written Romanized word was irresistibly alluring and led to the claimed popular embrace of the literacy campaign and its lynchpin of rural adult education. In truth, Northern Nigerians had been socialized by either their religious observances or their gerontocratic cultures to accept the informational and interpretive musings and outputs of authoritative intellectual figures, learned men, and people considered intellectual and social superiors.

Many Northern Nigerians did not enthusiastically gravitate toward Romanized book learning, not least because they were content to rely on the literary expertise of learned men when it was important for them to cognitively engage with colonial ideas and stories. Unless one's vocation required a consistent deployment of Romanized literacy, there was little practical reason for a rural-dwelling colonial subject to enroll in the mass literacy program. However, the colonial report was correct about the aesthetic allure of reading and writing. Literacy opened the door to the growing body of literary, travel, and biographical writings in Romanized Hausa to anyone possessing the ability to make sense of them. The pleasures of direct readership were no doubt appealing, but the "mass urge to know"[43]—as the report characterizes the positive response to the literacy campaign—was situated in a primal appreciation of the everyday functionality of literacy rather than in a disdain for intellectual hierarchy and the mediation of secularly educated men.

Adult Education and a Culture of Literacy

The work of NORLA involved many actors and a variety of engagements. Staffers of NORLA in Zaria provided training to local volunteer adult literacy organizers and then sold organizers instructional materials, including textbooks and teaching aids. The organizers would return to their districts and acquire land or secure buildings from the local Native Authority and local government administrations for outdoor and indoor classes. Once these logistics were completed, the colonial government and the local government authorities shared the financial cost of running the classes while NORLA staffers continued to provide guidance and supervision.

Working with the Gaskiya Corporation, NORLA published special textbooks and storybooks designed for adult aptitude training and reading predilections.[44] Writers of these texts consciously crafted the materials to depart from the curricular script and learning methods of formal schools for adolescents, reckoning that additional motivation was necessary for adults learning to read and write and should include the aesthetic pleasure of literary discovery. Instructors were trained to not treat enrollees in the classes as students or pupils. The instructors were not teachers, the NORLA officials insisted; rather, they were assistants to the adult enrollees. NORLA educationists felt that the budding adult readers must be left to independently explore the joy of reading and the sense of pleasure and knowledge that come with it.

In some cases, communities would raise money from their own people to build classrooms. With no fees charged for the classes and only minimal payments for textbooks, the classes proved quite popular. The standard six-month adult literacy program ran from March to September and ended with a test. Passing the test secured a certificate of literacy; more important, it announced one's passage into the coveted rank of literate people and into the community of readers. It secured membership in an esoteric assemblage of those capable of accessing the white man's secrets tucked away in written texts. Once literacy was achieved, one could become a reader and translator of newspapers, pamphlets, and other materials for one's village or family, and for added social prestige, one could read and write letters for those without Romanized literacy.

In an Islamic culture of gender segregation and purdah (the seclusion of adult females in separate quarters closed off to male nonrelatives), the challenge was how to give women access to the functional colonial modernity that literacy stood in for. The social cachet of literacy filtered through to women in secluded domestic spaces and single girls who, although prevented from participating in the outdoor and indoor classes populated by men, desired entrance into the burgeoning reading economy of Northern Nigeria. NORLA found a solution for married and single women craving the instrumental literacy of Romanized script. In 1957, overwhelmed by requests for women's adult classes, the agency persuaded some emirs to open up the secluded spaces of their palaces to be used for literacy instruction.[45] Here, female instructors, some of them Christian Northern Nigerian women who had been exposed to missionary education in the non-Muslim areas of the region and missionary enclaves in Muslim-majority areas, instructed female students on the rudiments of reading and writing, teaching them to comprehend the written word in Roman script.

Over the next year and half, a group of female African organizers emerged to mobilize personnel and resources for promoting a distinctly female reading and writing culture. NORLA's documents state that these organizers were married and that being married was "essential status for such work."[46] Whether marriage was an enforced prerequisite for volunteer female literacy activists is not entirely clear. One possibility is that married women whose husbands had embraced the formalized literacy of school culture or basic adult literacy were better positioned to appreciate the utilitarian value and aesthetic pleasure that literacy could bestow on readers and writers.

A snapshot of the profiles of a few of these female instructors and organizers indicate that the "wife of a Christian clergyman, wives of Native Authority councilors in Muslim Emirates and the sister of the Region's Minister of Education [Alhaji Isa Kaita]" were active participants in this new female adult literacy initiative.[47] Women's adult education classes rounded out the expanding repertoire of literacy and reading in Northern Nigeria and helped broaden the "nation of readers" that Rupert East had envisaged two decades earlier, a literary community that was now big enough to sustain a culture of writing, including travel writing.

Travel Writing as Experiential Literacy

The growth of Northern Nigeria's reading culture produced a discernible divergence of preferences and genres. It produced scribal specialization. A preference for certain styles of storytelling and certain types of stories emerged. Apart from fiction and folktales, travel and adventure accounts that translated foreign objects, practices, and cultures to the Hausa-speaking readers of Northern Nigeria emerged as a popular genre. *Gaskiya ta fi Kwabo* regularly published accounts, even secondhand narratives, of travel to foreign lands. These stories proved very popular and elicited active audience interlocution. Many of the popular local writers quickly identified this preference for travel stories and catered to it by writing up their own foreign travel experiences for *Gaskiya* and as pamphlets and booklets.

The most popular writer in Hausaphone Northern Nigeria between the 1930s and 1950s was Abubakar Imam, the one-time editor of *Gaskiya* and the deputy director of Gaskiya Corporation. As he had done with folktales, Imam pioneered a genre that combined biographical travel narratives with wide-ranging cultural commentary that sought to translate a distant, seemingly unfathomable set of foreign cultural artifacts into cultural semiotics intelligible to his Hausa-speaking audience in Northern Nigeria. The reading public particularly craved stories about travel to the imperial metropole, Britain, seeking a deeper understanding of the colonizers' cultural roots as well as vicarious participation in a colonial modernity often posited as a remote, elusive commodity. Imam understood this yearning and provided an outlet for such travel narratives in *Gaskiya*. He also embraced the genre in his own personal writings. The highlight of Imam's sustained foray into travel and adventure writing, and especially into the translation of British imperial culture through the lens of travel, was his 1944 metropolitan travel memoir, *Tafiya Mabudin Ilimi* (Travel is the gateway to knowledge).

Tafiya is an account of Imam's trip to and experiences in England in 1943 and is based on a diary he kept throughout the trip. The British Council, founded in 1934 and granted a royal charter in 1940 to promote British culture overseas and encourage cultural and educational exchange between Britain and other countries, sponsored Imam's trip.[48] He embarked on a guided wartime tour of England with Southern Nigerian journalist Nnamdi Azikiwe and six other newspaper editors from Britain's other West African colonies (map 1.1). Upon his return, he penned *Tafiya*.

Tafiya is a profound cultural project carefully designed to satisfy the growing aesthetic and cultural appetites of Northern Nigeria's Romanized Hausa readership. As Imam himself states in his prefatory remarks, he consciously focused on themes, sights, and experiences that "would be most interesting to readers [in Northern Nigeria]." He also elected to write his travel account in "a humorous manner to make it more interesting to readers."[49] Imam's casual, folksy narrative style appropriates the folkloric template of Hausa storytelling, wedding a Hausa literary form to eclectic content drawn from British metropolitan material and symbolic subjects.

Given that Imam's experiences in Britain would not, on their own, have transparent semiotic resonance in Northern Nigeria, the writer did what professional ethnographers do. He extracted meaning from observed facts of metropolitan life that have no meaning outside the interpretative and analytical regimes of those seeking to make them accessible to a distant audience. Imam appealed to his audience's culture of telling and consuming stories. This narrative exercise is analogous to the ways anthropologists

Map 1.1. Itinerary of Abubakar Imam's journey to Britain in 1943.

interpret the world of the Other to their audience by using mediatory and interpretive techniques intelligible to their audience or consistent with the protocols established by a professional community.

Given the centrality of the audience to the story, *Tafiya* was a work coproduced by Imam and his absent putative readers, whose literary appetites exerted much pressure in shaping the trajectory and thematic preoccupation of the account. Additionally, *Tafiya* should be read as a didactic text dedicated to inspiring a Northern Nigerian modernist imagination. As Imam declares in the preface, "My hope is for [this book] to serve as a catalyst for the modernization of Northern Nigeria."[50] The modernity that foregrounded Imam's imagined project was British colonial modernity. Thus, *Tafiya* not only intended to satiate the curiosities and aesthetic tastes of Northern Nigeria's reading public but also had the ambitious goal of nudging them toward a certain calculus of modernity—a vision of progress purportedly modeled on the British imperial metropole.

Imam traveled by sea, stopping over in Takoradi in the Gold Coast, Sierra Leone, and then Gibraltar before making his way to the English port city of Liverpool. Imam's narrative begins with commentaries on the events of the meandering voyage, setting the tone for some of the narrative techniques he deploys later in the text to discuss Britain as he saw it. One strategy Imam utilizes early on is that of positioning himself both as a colonial insider familiar with the workings of colonial culture and also as an outsider unable to comprehend or participate in some quaint social rituals because of his proud connection to the Hausa Islamic culture of Northern Nigeria. On his encounter with European table manners and eating traditions on the ship, he writes:

> The first thing that irritated me in the ship was the mode of eating. Here in Northern Nigeria we are used to eating food with our hands. Europeans do not do that. They use knives and forks to eat. Fortunately I was quite used to the cutlery as several Europeans had invited me to dinner before. However, there was one rule that I was not aware of: When you strike the knife on the fork you signal that you are through with the dish. One day we were eating meat when unknown to me I struck my fork with the knife. I was chatting to the person next to me when the steward removed the dish. I stared at him thinking he was going to bring me more meat but he didn't return. I looked at my neighbors but nobody took away their dishes. They were busily eating and I pretended as if I didn't care. The next day the same thing happened.[51]

This passage illustrates Imam's silent communion with his audience. He presents himself as familiar with European cutlery and its use at European tables because of his Western education, close association with the colonial bureaucracy, contact with colonial educators, and work with European officials of the Literature Bureau. He was thus a member of a colonial culture of fine dining and dinner-table etiquette. But Imam was also careful to portray himself to his readers as an outsider alienated from his natal culture by virtue of assimilation to British colonial social norms.

Imam was telling his readers that even he, with all his intimate connections to the personnel and cultures of colonialism, was an imperfect colonial modern. Late Victorian British culture, he seems to be suggesting, was knowable only to a limit, and his experiential immersion in this British culture was necessarily circumscribed by his rootedness in Hausa culture. Imam was marking his intellectual authority as a credible translator of colonial culture but was also positing British culture as a distant, unfathomable, and exotic set of practices. He was familiar enough with British culture to mediate and interpret it for his readers but not enough to claim full membership in it.

This conundrum of Britain and its culture being simultaneously near and far has a parallel in the effort of colonial ethnographers to reeducate a largely Western audience about seemingly familiar but distant and exotic African cultures—cultures that westerners presume to know by virtue of their stereotypical representations in popular consciousness but that, according to the ethnographer, remain largely unknown to metropolitan audiences. For Imam, travel to the metropole was capable of either resolving or deepening this ambivalence of simultaneous nearness and distance, familiarity and ignorance. The rhetorical prelude to rendering the metropole familiar was to magnify its physical and cultural distance from the colonial precinct of Northern Nigeria. For Imam, confessing that there was so much about British culture that he, a Western-educated colonial insider, did not know was a deft way of priming his audience for the metropolitan stories that awaited them in the rest of the text.

Imam repeats this insider-outsider dyadic positioning elsewhere in *Tafiya*. On the journey from Gibraltar to England, their ship came under bombardment by German warplanes, and Imam's gesture of membership in a British colonial cultural and political realm is completely realized with this statement: "When we turned our eyes there, we saw a huge warship belonging to *us* coming at our heels."[52] The use of the phrase "belonging to us" indicates Imam's acceptance of a British political and cultural community of citizens and subjects, a unit of solidarity that he embraced and that was under threat from German military aggression. Here he positions himself to his readers once again as a colonial insider and perhaps hopes to co-opt them into this wartime imperial solidarity. At the same time, in the same encounter, he tells of how he defied an order to wear a life jacket and hunker down in the ship's deck, instead engaging in his Islamic religious rituals of prayer and Qur'an recitation: "I went down to our cabin, performed ablution, removed the life jacket and performed some prayers. I then took out my prayer book and recited some portions. After I was done, I sought God's forgiveness for my sins and prayed for the prophet of Islam, Muhammad, peace be upon him, as bombs continue to fall above me. I felt reinvigorated as I wore the life jacket again and went back on deck amid the raging battle."[53] In these passages Imam modeled how to embrace and claim membership in a British culture and political solidarity while remaining rooted in and loyal to Hausa Islamic culture. Whether he was conscious of this is uncertain, but he demonstrated that one could reconcile the rituals of imperial modernity and move between imperial spaces and those of one's natal origins.

Translating Imperial Modernity

The theme of translation, which encompasses the gestures of mediation and interpretation, is appropriate for describing what Imam's text did for his Northern Nigerian readers. I use the term *translation* here in the expansive sense in which Susan Bassnett and Andre Lefevere articulate it—that is, as a transfer of semiotic properties from one context to another using not just linguistic tools but also cultural signifiers and idioms.[54] Following these scholars, I suggest that Imam was a cultural translator and that *Tafiya* is a work that translated the material, symbolic, and intellectual markers of colonial modernity into intelligible cultural idioms for Imam's Northern Nigerian readers. The following analysis reveals the variety of translation techniques Imam used to render metropolitan cultures and objects comprehensible to his audience.

Once Imam and the other visitors arrived in Liverpool, they were received by a retinue of colonial handlers and driven to the Hyde Park Hotel in London, their home for the entirety of their stay in England. Imam's ethnographic observation of British society then began. Imam translates England to his audience using several rhetorical devices—the power of imagery, evocative description, and the occasional conversational language of a tour guide—to bring Britain to his readers. His diary entries sought to render British sights and landscapes in lexicons and idiomatic language that he thought would be intelligible to Northern Nigerian Hausa speakers. For example, when explaining the high-rise architecture of London, Imam uses the graphic visual idiom of one house "built atop another." The roof of the top house is then covered "and another house [is] built above it . . . and it goes on and on until the government feels it is too much and stops any further development."[55]

Colonial handlers guided Imam and his fellow visitors on a tour of the Colonial Office and various historical churches, including Westminster Abbey. In the following passage, we see Imam unfurling yet another device in his repertoire of cultural translation: the literary technique of similitude to communicate parallels.[56] Imam combines this rendition of the unfamiliar through familiar cultural idioms with the poetics of contrast so that metropolitan sights and objects are both similar to and different from the Northern Nigerian parallels Imam constructs for his readers: "Westminster Abbey. This is a very beautiful church. I don't think white people have more impressive buildings than their churches. Every church is full of adornments in different fabulous styles as if they are built by djinns. However there is a striking difference between churches and mosques. Christian churches serve as burial grounds for important personalities like kings, inventors, explorers, artists, war heroes, and other famous persons."[57] Here Imam references the supernatural powers of djinns to emplace an Islamic mental and abstract referent for his audience, which enabled them to imagine the grandeur of a cathedral from far away in Northern Nigeria. Imam tells his readers that the cathedrals are similar to mosques in style, conception, and possible supernatural guidance. Imam translates the English church into an Islamic frame and constructs instructional parallels for his readers. However, he transitions from this deployment of similitude to a complementary explanation located in contrast. The church may be similar in conception to our mosque, he says, but it is also different from a mosque because *we* Muslims do not bury our dead in the mosque. Similitude is an easily exhaustible frame and wears out quickly, generating redundancy, so the use of both parallel and contrast in the same descriptive scheme helps maintain the seduction of Britain's distant allure as a strangely different habitat for an exotic culture.

Contrast and parallels are complementary. The former sharpens the alterity of the metropole and its distinction from the material and symbolic landscape of Northern Nigeria; the latter forges a kinship foregrounded through intimate sameness. Imam wanted his audience to see England through these two intertwined lenses. When he says "the English parliament is totally different from our traditional councils," for instance, he quickly follows it up with the balancing, equalizing comment about how the speaker sits "in the center [of parliament] like an imam [sits in the mosque]."[58] Here the invocation of the parallel positions and moderating roles of the imam (Islamic prayer leader) and the speaker substitutes a familiar, revered religious and clerical motif for a secular one. This technique helped Imam's readers visualize the speaker's position, role, and relationship to parliamentarians through the familiar visual of how an Imam relates with worshippers in a mosque. This translation involves a deliberate cultural and religious gesture of semiotic transference, a type of transculturation.

In *Tafiya*, the construction and deployment of familiar referents sometimes serve as a device for enunciating contrast and difference. Imam gives his readers a visual window into a racecourse in the English town of Epsom by referencing the racecourses in the Northern Nigerian cities of Zaria, Kano, Kaduna, Katsina, and Jos. Once familiarity is established through references to similar sights in colony and metropole, Imam shifts to a register of contrast: the Epsom racecourse measures one and a half square miles while those in Northern Nigerian cities measure one square mile. Moreover, the prize monies for tournaments on the Epsom course were much larger than those in Northern Nigerian horse-racing contests.[59]

This explanatory brew of contrast and similitude is carried over to other narrations. Imam likens the technological efforts and accomplishments of the people of Birmingham, the "ancient blacksmiths of Birmingham," to the early nineteenth-century jihad of Othman dan Fodio in Northern Nigeria. Both, Imam surmises, were "waging a war for the glory of their country." Transposing a familiar local religious history on a secular, technological metropolitan one was a clever narrative move to signal or construct parallels where none seemed to exist, but this was also a springboard to reiterate the ecology of difference between colony and metropole since "while Dan Fodio was using spears the people of Birmingham were using their intellect."[60]

Tafiya is packed with similar transcultural maneuvers. When trying to give his readers in Northern Nigeria a visual, geometric image of the expanse of London Bridge, Imam first sets the stage by referencing the Thames. He then presents London's affinity with coastal Lagos in terms of access to the sea and ports before invoking the weight of numbers: the number of pedestrians and vehicles crossing the bridge daily, 100,000 and 20,000 respectively, according to him. Imam goes even further, reaching for a decidedly local metaphor, a key quotidian referent in the transactional and monetary literacy of traditional Northern Nigerian societies dating back to precolonial times: designating large monetary volume with bags. This harkened to precolonial monetary systems in which various currencies—cowries and other commodities used as measures and instruments of value and exchange—were carried and measured in bags for large transactional and revenue-recording purposes. Accordingly, Imam told his readers that "about 25 bags of money were spent on [London Bridge's] construction."[61] London's underground rail tunnels "resemble squirrel burrows," a wildlife and subterranean metaphor that would have conjured up a familiar image and aided his readers' comprehension of London's underground railway system.

A complement to this device of translation is Imam's use of familiar local objects, referents, and metaphors to illustrate the metropolitan objects of his narrative. Describing the British Parliament, which the visiting West African journalists toured, Imam illustrates the 320-foot height of the building by stating that "53 tall men will have to climb on top of one another before they can equal its height!" The building houses a clock on its tower whose minute hand he describes as "equal to the height of two men and a boy."[62] Describing a tour of the margarine factory at Purfleet, Imam has this to say:

> From there, we were driven to Purfleet, a margarine factory about 20 miles from London. We went there to see how the groundnut we grow is processed in England. Margarine is made from groundnut and taken as a substitute for cheese. The moment our groundnut arrives, engines extract its oil and pack it in reservoirs the way that water from Challawa River is stored in Gwauron Dutse reservoir before distribution to Kano city. From there, the oil is piped to the factory like water is piped from Gwauron Dutse to Kano city homes. Inside the factory, different types of machines await the arrival of the oil. It is processed in stages and then pumped to the next machine. After processing, the groundnut oil turns to margarine. It is then pumped to another machine that pours it into tins. As you watch, you'll see margarine-filled cans streaming out of the machine. Each is tightly sealed and branded. From there it is taken to the market where cooks buy it and use in preparing food.[63]

This passage contains several gestures and homages to the experiential and visual surroundings of Imam's readers. Narrating the process of transforming groundnut into margarine in a metropolitan factory, Imam first invokes the familiar local farming object of the "groundnut we grow." Second, there is a reference to the groundnut being exported from Northern Nigeria to England ("The moment our groundnut arrives"). The production process is then rendered relatable and technically proximate with the reference to the Challawa Water Works of Kano as a parallel process of extraction, storage, pumping, and piping.

Translation as Pedagogy

In some passages Imam's account reads like a pedagogical manual written by a teacher to educate pupils lacking familiarity with a certain phenomenon. However, this pedagogy is not simply informational. Instead, we see the interplay of translation and pedagogy where translation serves as an instrument of instruction; "modernization," to use Imam's own prefatory bromide; and persuasion. Nowhere is this continuum of translation and pedagogy more apparent than in the section of Imam's travelogue dealing with the city of Birmingham. Here he positions himself as a teacher introducing his pupils to a subject:

> Birmingham is the industrial center of England. It is the second-largest city in the country. The city is 50,000 acres wide. This is where the people of the city have their houses and factories. It is said that more than 1,500 trades are practiced in Birmingham. . . . Birmingham is now an industrial center producing anything from airplanes to needles. If you want to see the fastest motorcycle in the world, go to Birmingham. If you want to see the best bicycle factory in the world, go to Birmingham. If you want to see the best car factory in the world, go to Birmingham. It is the industries of Birmingham that elevated human beings from walking on the bare ground to travelling in vehicles.[64]

Imam seems concerned with giving his readers a vicarious visual and mental tour of industrial Birmingham. He mediates metropolitan technology for his readers. Some of this technology had made its way to Northern Nigeria but retained a mystery associated with colonial mechanical objects. He situates the origins of British technological prowess by using his narrative technique of choice: a pedagogical, instructional tone.

Later in the narrative, Imam explains to his readers that "Birmingham is the birthplace of engines." He proceeds to recount how Birmingham's chief blacksmith, Matthew Boulton, invented a water-fueled engine while another Birmingham native, James Watt, took it a step further to develop the rudiments of the steam engine. Imam then tells the story of how James

Watt was inspired to invent the steam engine by "watching his mother boil water in a pot as a child."[65] This story uses an extensive cultural dictionary of referents and images to establish familiarity, from the "blacksmith" reference to the image of the boiling water to the assertion that "people used to travel on horses and donkeys" and horse carriages before "pensioned-off horse and donkeys [gave] their work to engines."[66] These gestures of translation are then hoisted on an overarching utilitarian declaration: "It is the product of James Watt's brain that takes you from Kano to technological Lagos in just two days." The translation works because it is conveyed in a pedagogically methodical style. Pedagogy is effective here because it is suffused in a set of cultural, utilitarian, and technological registers familiar to Imam's readers.

Imam's narrative enterprise relied on a translational and mediatory voice that interceded between Northern Nigerian Romanized Hausa readers and a vast complex of metropolitan modernity represented by objects, practices, monuments, and cultures. Imam's commentaries on the English economy of recycling—in which "no refuse is thrown away," "human feces is processed by machines and piped to farms as manure," "used papers are taken back to factories to be recycled into new papers," and "remnants of decayed foodstuff is used as pig feed"—all inhabit a spectrum of translation that is concerned with making sense of British material and industrial infrastructures for Northern Nigerians.[67] Translation begins where the familiar—feces, refuse, paper, decayed foodstuff—morphs into unfamiliar technological processes.

Imam provides a detailed description of English urban planning as a model of the built space interspersed with "green fields reserved for citizens to relax when they are bored of their houses."[68] The English town, Imam tells his readers, "has public places such as sports centers, swimming pools, laundries, and libraries full of books for the benefit of students."[69] British urbanity is allowed to stand on its own without the mediatory work of advancing familiar local parallels and idioms. Absence and difference are the operative devices in the text. They illustrate for Northern Nigerians how the British live in their towns and how those towns differ from those of Northern Nigeria.

Imam also waxes pedagogical when discussing his visit to Oxford: "We also visited Oxford, the city of knowledge. You know that there are two main centers of knowledge in England; Oxford and Cambridge. Most of the colonial officers you see, of whatever specialization, must have been to study at one of these centers before coming to serve overseas."[70]

He invokes the familiar human figures of "colonial officers" as a way of helping his readers appreciate the far-reaching educational influence of Oxford. In Northern Nigeria, colonial officers exuded a certain aura of learnedness and were seen to embody a certain acquired, if sometimes ritualized, wisdom. Imam's association of British colonial officers in Northern Nigeria with the citadels of English learning such as Oxford University supplies a context for understanding the assumed sagacity of colonizers.

In *Tafiya*, Imam sometimes uses the power of hyperbole and sensation to enhance the pedagogical effect of his descriptions. For instance, his rhetorical description of London is riddled with the usual invocation of local geographical, material, and symbolic referents, but it is also strategically sensational: "London is more than a city; it is rather a complete country compressed into a single place. London is the biggest city in the whole wide world. Where is your region in Northern Nigeria; East, West, South or North? If you are in the east, if you take the whole of Potiskum province and divide it into four that is equal to the size of London. Or if you belong to the tin mining area, if you take the whole of Jos province or Jema'a and divide it into two you'll get the size of London."[71]

Like other narratives analyzed in this book, Imam's descriptive repertoire shifts and expands to accommodate his narrative instincts and objectives. For him and other Northern Nigerian travelers discussed in other chapters, London was the ultimate cultural, geographic, and aesthetic symbol of British imperial modernity. Accordingly, Imam, like other traveler-writers, deployed hyperbole and enhanced his narrative with a rhetorical gesture toward a set of resonant geographical registers to approximate for his readers the greatness of London as an imperial city.

Mobile Colonial Kinship

In England, Imam reunited with several colonial officials he knew from Northern Nigeria, notably Frederick Lugard, who had retired to his home in Abinger, and Hans Vischer, a colonial educator in Northern Nigeria and Imam's former teacher. These encounters provided Imam with ample material to enrich his narrative and construct for his readers a certain notion of the kinship between colonizers and the colonized. Imam writes about his serendipitous meeting with a certain Mr. Waterfield, who had been his teacher at Katsina College. Waterfield was on leave in Britain and was moonlighting for the British Council as a cinematographer filming Imam and his group of West African visitors to produce a film on their visit to be "shown in colonial cinemas."[72]

Narratives of metropolitan encounters with colonial officers who were serving or had served in Northern Nigeria proved popular with the Northern Nigerian reading public for two related reasons. First, colonial officials occupied certain mythical positions in the popular imagination of Northern Nigerian subalterns. Their individual habits, eccentricity, and predilections, which usually earned them corresponding nicknames, were known across the region.[73] These officials were familiar yet esoteric figures, and so narratives of personal encounters with them outside the official circuit of the colonial bureaucracy intrigued Northern Nigerians who knew them by reputation. Second, such stories humanized the powerful human symbols of colonial authority, giving readers a glimpse into the inner, nonofficial lives of these mythical figures who embodied British imperial might.

Imam understood this appetite for stories of metropolitan meetings and interactions with members of the colonial bureaucratic oligarchy. His encounter with Waterfield, fleeting and conversational, was followed by extended engagements with Hans Vischer and Frederick Lugard. Perfunctory visits to Lugard's retirement home in Abinger and extensive recreational outings with him were by now established staples of Northern Nigerian elite travelers' itineraries. By the 1940s, it would have been unusual for a visible Northern Nigerian intellectual figure, a product of aristocratic colonial education such as Imam, to visit Britain without paying homage to Lugard. For a writer like Imam, consciously seeking to bring unexpected metropolitan stories to his readers, meeting Lugard would have been a priority whether or not it was on the official itinerary.

Imam's first visit to Lugard was in the company of four of his traveling companions. The interaction on that day was necessarily shallow, he would later tell his readers, because both he and Lugard were inhibited by the presence of the other West African editors. Imam returned to Lugard's home on a later date, accompanied by Hans Vischer, who was nicknamed "Dan Hausa" by his Northern Nigerian colonial interlocutors because of his proficiency in the Hausa language as well as his facility with the cultural referents and mores of Hausa society. Imam's detailed narrative on this second, more private encounter with Lugard is rich:

> [Lugard's house] is ... surrounded by tall trees. A man that worked as hard as Lord Lugard really deserves such a house. You know that Lord Lugard was

the first governor of Nigeria. When we visited him in 1943 he was 82 years old. But he was still sound. His eyes and ears were focused on Northern Nigeria. He always talked about Northern Nigeria. He also had lots of artifacts from Northern Nigeria such as the gate of Emir of Kano's palace, a sword given to him by the emir of Bida, metal kettles from the Emir of Kontagora.[74]

There are several representational and narrative gestures at work in this passage. Imam seeks to situate Lugard as a sympathetic figure for his readers. Lugard, he states, was thinking about and empathizing with Northern Nigerian interests and causes, even in retirement. He uses Lugard's reputation as both the conqueror and benefactor of the Northern Nigerian emirates as a heuristic medium. Imam's commentary strategically posits Lugard as a former colonial official who remained fond of Northern Nigeria, even adorning his home with material and artistic reminders of Northern Nigeria and its cultural heritage. Because Lugard's military violence against the Sokoto Caliphate had become tempered with a positive narrative of him as a protector of Muslim-majority Northern Nigeria against the encroachment of Christian missionaries, Imam's favorable commentary on the retired colonial official was inscribed in a familiar idiom of popular perception.

Imam constructs a vivid itinerary of his daylong visit to Lugard in a manner that projects his metropolitan interlocutor as an avuncular figure devoted to his former colonial subjects: "I was totally at home in his house, going about like I was visiting my grandparents. I spent the day and ate there."[75] Imam's remaking of Lugard into a welcoming, grandfatherly figure of colonial metropolitan hospitality may have struck some of his more radical readers as odd, but even though he was an intellectual, journalist, and writer, Imam remained rooted in the educational ethos into which he and other young aristocratic Hausa Muslim men had been socialized in a few carefully organized secular schools. It would seem that residual connections to the relationships forged with Europeans in these schools and in the imperial networks that subsequently developed continued to influence him thereafter.

Imam's representations of this encounter strategically aligned with the preexisting tropes and narratives of Northern Nigerian aristocratic affinity with British colonial officials. Imam's interactions with Lugard had, in fact, not only been marked by cordiality, hospitality, and warmth, but there were tense elements to the interactions as well. In their conversation, Imam had critiqued in compellingly substantive detail the workings of British indirect rule in Northern Nigeria, Lugard's signature colonial administrative invention, but this extensive conversation about Lugard's troubled administrative legacy in Northern Nigeria and how the crisis of indirect rule was creating an ominous restiveness among the Northern Nigerian educated class was excluded from *Tafiya*.[76]

Imam met with an unceasing stream of former colonial officials. Upon finding out through their Northern Nigerian Colonial Service network that Imam was visiting, they thronged to see one of their star pupils, who, in their estimation, had leveraged his colonial education to come into his own intellectually.[77] Imam's sense of kinship with these colonial officers ran deep. He tries to convey this intimacy of colonial connections in a language that is deeply personal, even emotive: "The most wonderful thing is when you meet colonial officers who had worked in your country. When I started meeting those that had worked in Northern Nigeria, I felt I was among my family. This one would visit me today while another would visit me the next day. We used to think that the officers that worked in our country forget us when they get back home but I found out it was not true."[78]

Imam's familial reference is the culmination of a rhetorical and pedagogical refashioning of former colonial officials as people intimately connected and committed to Northern Nigeria. More important, it was a personal statement of an unspoken but powerful aristocratic kinship between colonial official mentors and their Western-educated mentees. Many of Imam's Romanized Hausa readers, themselves products of this kind of colonial tutelage, would have appreciated and grasped Imam's enunciation of this kinship in a manner that appears to be a celebratory narrative gesture of gratitude.

Sensation and Narration

Abubakar Imam's narrative of his metropolitan travel and experiences is peppered with humor and is largely written in a folksy, conversational style. This choice appears to be a repurposing of Hausa popular storytelling technique. It is a style he self-consciously embraced as a method of sustaining the interest of his audience, as he declares in the preface. The symbiotic interaction of humor, narration, and pedagogical commentary constitutes the stylistic signature of Imam's narrative. The overarching outcome of these techniques is a narrative steeped in sensationalism. Other contemporaneous narratives of metropolitan travel similarly employed the exaggerated tone of sensationalizing the objects and cultures being narrated, but no other text mines the terrain of humor to complement sensation as consistently as that of Imam. Two passages, one from *Tafiya* and the other from his memoirs, illustrate Imam's conscious appropriation of humor and sensation for maximum narrative effect.

The first passage was analyzed earlier in this chapter—the story of how Imam was embarrassed into an awareness of the dinner-table culture of Englishmen. In this story, Imam's dramatization of his awakening to the subtle rules of English dining culture dovetails with the overarching tenor of his narrative style. As elsewhere, he is enunciating the unfamiliarity of British culture through a self-deprecatingly humorous narrative. The distance of empire, a prerequisite for his subsequent descriptions of and commentaries on metropolitan British life, is rendered in humorously sensational stories that appropriate extant stereotypes of the insular African Muslim colonial subject stepping awkwardly into the unfamiliar realm of imperial high culture.

The second passage comes from Imam's memoirs, specifically from the long section dealing with his trip to Britain. Imam tells a story that uses sarcasm and other techniques rooted in humor to illustrate the theme of metropolitan ignorance of and distance from African Muslim cultures: "So a reporter, an Englishman, who probably wanted to show that he knew a lot of everything approached Dr. Azikiwe, and pointing a finger toward me, he asked, 'Which Maharaja is this?' Dr. Azikiwe replied, 'It is His Highness the Maharaja of Poona Poona!' The reporter put that down. Next morning our photograph appeared with the title of 'His Highness the Maharaja of Poona Poona arrived yesterday together with seven of his followers!' We laughed. I asked Dr. Azikiwe, 'Please, where is Poona Poona?' He said, 'Who knows?'"[79] It is telling that Imam, in his flowing aristocratic Muslim gown, would be interpellated into a South Asian construct of identity and understood in a sartorial frame that was already familiar to British people from their Asian colonial adventures but was not faithful to who Imam was. In the British popular imagination of the time, an obstinate, residual Orientalist register shaped how African Muslims—dressed, British people thought, in the robes of the East—were defined in metropolitan spaces by British interlocutors. In this perceptual universe, Muslim aristocracy was an Eastern phenomenon steeped in Orientalist constructs.

The sight of Muslim aristocrats who were unmistakably black and African did not fit the discourses of aristocratic otherness circulating in early to mid-twentieth century Britain, hence the struggle of Imam's metropolitan interlocutors to define and understand him. Imam and other Northern Nigerian Muslim visitors disrupted the extant racial-evolutionary hierarchies in which Africans were understood as lacking coherent sociopolitical institutions, let alone the transferable, transhistorical status gradations aristocracy represents. Imam and other Northern Nigerian Muslim visitors to Britain embodied both blackness and dignified aristocracy in ways that unsettled their metropolitan acquaintances and the latter's assumptions about race, honor, and class.

The Poona Poona story and similar ones stretched the credulity of Imam's Northern Nigerian readers, who already believed, to varying extents, that the white man was epistemologically removed from the cultures and traditions of Northern Nigeria and that Northern Nigerians were likewise ignorant of a confusing assemblage of metropolitan imperial cultures. Humorous stories like this that poked fun at metropolitan ignorance helped confirm and solidify assumptions about the seemingly irreconcilable cultural distance between colony and metropole; Imam stepped into this distance and sought to bridge the gap by bringing a distant Britain closer to his readers textually, aesthetically, and dramatically.

Colonial discourses tended to extend the cultural space between colony and metropole; the civilizing mission of colonization turned on this construct of cultural distance and the claimed capacity of colonialism to shrink that chasm. Imam's narrative tempered that enunciation of cultural distance between colony and metropole with a more complicated script in which distance is acknowledged but then mitigated by the invocation of experiences and forms of knowing that only travel to the metropole was considered capable of conferring. In this contrapuntal exercise, Imam not only collapsed the space between Northern Nigeria and Britain by translating and rendering metropolitan culture familiar and proximate, but the rhetorical trajectory is much more complex, sustained by the nexus of distancing and shrinkage. For Imam to succeed in bringing the sights, objects, and cultures of England to his readers in Northern Nigeria, he first had to reinstate the colonial discourse of civilizational difference by reiterating Britain's distant, modern, awe-inspiring, and even inscrutable allure. Then, like a literal interpreter or translator, he decoded this culture, brought it closer, and made it relatable through a variety of narrative and literary techniques.

The sophistication of Imam's scribal craft and the power of his narrative subjectivity inhere in this ability to render metropolitan culture both distant and near, to both expand and shrink the cultural and material divide between Britain and Northern Nigeria. Unraveling the mystique of the metropole required the development of certain rhetorical and narrative tools. It also entailed the perpetuation of a paradox: the unfathomable mysteries of metropolitan society in the eyes of a Northern Nigerian subaltern had to be restated, even reinforced, to make the work of cracking the code, as it were, both important and necessary. However, the allure of the metropole lay in its intractability, its epistemological distance.

The most enduring legacy of Imam and *Tafiya* is that they engendered the fusion of travel, writing, reading, cultural translation, and modernity—the five main narrative themes of this book. With Imam playing a prominent part in the establishment of *Gaskiya* and the emergence of a Northern Nigerian public sphere of writing, reading, and storytelling and then traveling to the metropole and writing about his experiences there, he embodied the convergence of literacy and literary ferment on one side and travel and experiential writing on the other.

Conclusion

A reading and writing culture evolved in colonial Northern Nigeria out of several related developments: the advent of secular, modern education, albeit with tight limits; the emergence of a colonial publishing infrastructure; the founding of the *Gaskiya ta fi Kwabo* newspaper in 1939; the promotion of mass literacy in the Roman alphabet; and the evolution of Hausa literary, adventure, and travel writing. All these developments produced a community of reading and writing that incentivized those with stories to tell and the ability to tell them in Romanized Hausa script, whether such stories were fictional or experiential, to write and publish them for popular consumption.

As the culture of Hausa writing evolved out of the aforementioned developments and out of the networks of literary mentorships created by colonial educators, a unique storytelling template emerged that blended Hausa storytelling folkloric traditions and techniques with a new imperative to translate the distant realities, sights, cultures, and technologies of imperial Britain for a growing Northern Nigerian reading public. In the crucible of this new intellectual space, metropolitan travel and the new practice of adventure writing meshed. Western-educated Romanized Hausa writers, such as Abubakar Imam, subsequently wrote about their metropolitan adventures, using such narratives as a touchstone to culturally translate a plethora of metropolitan phenomena for Northern Nigerian readers. They wrote into a literary space in which readers looked to writers imbued with a repertoire of experiential resources to draw from, especially travelers to Britain, to give them a glimpse into metropolitan life and modernity.

The adventure- and travel-writing craft that grew in this literary ferment utilized a publishing infrastructure and print medium composed of *Gaskiya ta fi Kwabo*, a regional newspaper, and Gaskiya Corporation, a publisher of fiction and nonfiction as well as government texts. The organizing motif of this new genre of travel and adventure memoirs was a preoccupation with both alikeness and alterity, with similitude and difference. Writers like Abubakar Imam portrayed the imperial metropole as both similar to Northern Nigeria and starkly different from it, both distant and proximate, familiar and unfamiliar, a rhetorical move meant to render the metropole intimate but at the same time underscore its legendary, mysterious inscrutability. If metropolitan travelers were to maintain their relationship of epistemic and mediatory trust with their readers, narratives purporting to explain British society and British ways of life to Northern Nigerians had to necessarily participate in mystifying the metropole even as they claimed to clarify metropolitan life and culture for their audience. This duality of mystifying and demystifying the metropole defined the early travel narratives written about Britain. Many of the metropolitan travel endeavors analyzed in the following chapters of the book are fraught with this paradox.

Notes

1. Emmanuel Ayankanmi Ayandele, *Missionary Impact on Modern Nigeria, 1842–1914: A Political and Social Analysis* (London: Longman, 1966), 517–18; E.P.T. Crampton, *Christianity in Northern Nigeria* (London: Chapman, 1979), 45–61; C. N. Ubah, "Problems of Christian Missionaries in the Muslim Emirates of Nigeria," *Journal of African Studies* 3 (1967): 351–71. These works offer a comprehensive discussion of colonial efforts to keep Christian missionaries out of the Muslim-majority areas of Northern Nigeria and the reasoning behind these efforts.

2. Graham Furniss, "On Engendering Liberal Values in the Nigerian Colonial State: The Idea behind the Gaskiya Corporation," paper presented at the School of Oriental and African Studies, Commonwealth History Seminar, October 19, 2007, 15. Housed in Rhodes House Archives, MSS. Afr. s. 8839.

3. Beverly Mark, *Hausa Women Sing: Hausa Popular Song* (Bloomington: Indiana University Press, 2004), 29.

4. The poetic and prosaic writings of Othman dan Fodio are overwhelmingly religious in character and concern; the poetry of Nana Asma'u, one of the caliphate's most prolific writers, was semi-secular but had a didactic moral quality rooted in Islamic learning. See Ibraheem Sulaiman, *The African Caliphate: The Life, Works, and Teaching of Shaykh Usman dan Fodio* (Norwich, UK: Diwan, 1999); see also Jean Boyd, *Collected Works of Nana Asma'u, Daughter of Usman 'dan Fodiyo (1793 to 1864)*, African Historical Studies 9 (East Lansing: Michigan State University Press, 1997).

5. Mark, *Hausa Women Sing*, 29.
6. Mark, *Hausa Women Sing*.
7. Rupert East, "A First Essay in Imaginative African Literature," *Africa* 9 (1936): 351–52.
8. East, "A First Essay."
9. Furniss, "On Engendering Liberal Values," 3, 15.
10. Rupert East, "An Experiment in Colonial Journalism," *African Affairs* 45 (1946): 85.
11. Furniss, "On Engendering Liberal Values," 3.
12. East, "An Experiment in Colonial Journalism," 85.
13. Rhodes House, MSS. Afr. s. 1838, "H. P. Elliot's Reminiscences of Nigeria."
14. Graham Furniss, "Hausa Popular Literature and Video Film: The Rapid Rise of Cultural Productions in Times of Economic Decline," working paper 27, Institut fur ethnologie und Afrikastudien, Johannes Gutenberg-Universitat, Mainz, Germany, 1.
15. "Education in Northern Nigeria: From the Old to the New," *Times Literary Supplement*, September 4, 1943, 8.
16. Trevor Clark, *A Right Honourable Gentleman: Abubakar from the Black Rock* (London: Edward Arnold, 1991), 51.
17. Rhodes House MSS. Afr. s. 597, Rupert East to Sir Arthur Richards.
18. East, "An Experiment in Colonial Journalism," 85.
19. Abdulrahman Mora, *Abubakar Imam Memoirs* (Zaria, Nigeria: Northern Nigerian Publishing Company, 1989), 26.
20. Mora, *Abubakar Imam Memoirs*.
21. Abadallah Uba Adamu, "Divergent Similarities: Culture, Globalization and Hausa Creative and Performing Arts," a lead paper presented at the International Conference on Literature in Northern Nigeria, Department of English and French, Bayero University, Kano, December 5–6, 2005, 1. Adamu argues that Imam's seminal work pioneered the phenomena of adapting, appropriating, and domesticating foreign cultural tropes and idioms in Hausa creative productions.
22. Abubakar Imam, *Ruwan Bagaja* (Zaria, Nigeria: NORLA, 1935, 1957).
23. Rupert East alluded to this when he stated the newspaper was important "for itself and in political management of what was happening in the war years." See Rhodes House MSS. Afr. s. 597. See also Mack, *Hausa Women Sing*, 30.
24. Rhodes House MSS. Afr. s. 597; Annual Report of the Gaskiya Corporation 1947–49; Rupert East's papers.
25. Clark, *A Right Honorable Gentleman*, 48.
26. Hereafter Dadasare.
27. Dadasare Abdullahi, *Memoir*, 24.
28. Ibid.
29. Ibid., 25
30. Ibid.
31. Ibid.

32. Ibid., 24
33. Ibid.
34. Ibid.
35. Ibid.
36. Ibid.
37. See Brian Larkin, *Signal and Noise: Media, Infrastructure, and Urban Culture in Nigeria* (Durham, NC: Duke University Press, 2008), chap. 3.
38. See Larkin, *Signal and Noise*, 75–77, 84–104.
39. Rhodes House Archives, MSS. Afr. s. 8839. Warner Vanter, "Nearly Two Million Northern Nigerians Have Joined Up for War Against Ignorance."
40. Rhodes House Archives, MSS. Afr. s. 8839. Vanter, "Nearly Two Million."
41. Rhodes House Archives, MSS. Afr. s. 8839. Vanter, "Nearly Two Million."
42. Rhodes House Archives, MSS. Afr. s. 8839. Vanter, "Nearly Two Million."
43. Rhodes House Archives, MSS. Afr. s. 8839. Vanter, "Nearly Two Million."
44. NORLA merged with Gaskiya Corporation in 1960; the resulting company retained the NORLA name. The company would later become the Northern Nigerian Publishing Company in partnership with MacMillan Publishers. It then mutated until it was dissolved in 1991.
45. Rhodes House Archives, MSS. Afr. s. 8839. Vanter, "Nearly Two Million."
46. Rhodes House Archives, MSS. Afr. s. 8839. Vanter, "Nearly Two Million."
47. Rhodes House Archives, MSS. Afr. s. 8839. Vanter, "Nearly Two Million."
48. For a historical snapshot of the British Council, see Frances Donaldson, *The British Council: The First Fifty Years* (London: J. Cape, 1984).
49. Abubakar Imam, *Tafiya Mabudin Ilimi* [Travel is the gateway to knowledge] (Zaria, Nigeria: Gaskiya Corporation, 1944), 2.
50. Imam, *Tafiya Mabudin Ilimi*, 2.
51. Imam, *Tafiya Mabudin Ilimi*, 7.
52. Imam, *Tafiya Mabudin Ilimi*, 16. Italics mine.
53. Imam, *Tafiya Mabudin Ilimi*, 16.
54. See Susan Bassnett and Andre Lefevere, *Constructing Cultures: Essays on Literary Translation* (Clevedon, UK: Multilingual Matters, 1998); see also Susan Bassnett-McGuire, *Translation Studies* (London: Routledge, 1991).
55. Imam, *Tafiya Mabudin Ilimi*, 19.
56. In Foucault's *The Order of Things: An Archaelogy of the Human Sciences* (London: Routledge, 1979), he explains the human urge to see parallels between objects in nature that do not share similar properties. This investment in the discourse of parallels is a strategic method of rendering things familiar and beyond their immediate context. It is also a way to construct intelligibility between and among objects.
57. Imam, *Tafiya Mabudin Ilimi*, 21.
58. Imam, *Tafiya Mabudin Ilimi*, 21.
59. Imam, *Tafiya Mabudin Ilimi*, 30.
60. Imam, *Tafiya Mabudin Ilimi*, 29.
61. Imam, *Tafiya Mabudin Ilimi*, 25.
62. Imam, *Tafiya Mabudin Ilimi*, 24.
63. Imam, *Tafiya Mabudin Ilimi*, 22.
64. Imam, *Tafiya Mabudin Ilimi*, 28.
65. Imam, *Tafiya Mabudin Ilimi*, 29.

66. Imam, *Tafiya Mabudin Ilimi*, 29.
67. Imam, *Tafiya Mabudin Ilimi*, 29.
68. Imam, *Tafiya Mabudin Ilimi*, 30.
69. Imam, *Tafiya Mabudin Ilimi*, 30.
70. Imam, *Tafiya Mabudin Ilimi*, 31.
71. Imam, *Tafiya Mabudin Ilimi*, 33.
72. Imam, *Tafiya Mabudin Ilimi*, 18.
73. Notable nicknames include "Karen Giya" (lit. a dog of alcohol), presumably because just as a dog in heat cannot control its urge, the colonial official so named had an uncontrollable desire for alcohol. One colonial officer was nicknamed "Langa Langa." *Langa langa* is an onomatopoeic name for a cutlass used to clear bushes. It is perhaps a metaphorical appelation suggesting the said officer was as harsh on Nigerian colonial subjects as the *langa langa* is on grass.
74. Imam, *Tafiya Mabudin Ilimi*, 31.
75. Imam, *Tafiya Mabudin Ilimi*, 32.
76. Upon his return to Nigeria, Imam wrote a lengthy report/summary of the conversation he had with Lugard and sent it to both Lugard and Hans Vischer. This letter/report has now been published in a collection of Imam's papers edited by Abdurrahman Mora and published in 1989. See Mora, *Abubakar Imam Memoirs*. See also MSS. Afr. s. 8839, Hans Vischer to E. L. Mort, August 27, 1943. Vischer confirms the substance of Imam's account of the conversations as contained in the report/letter.
77. In Vischer's letter cited prior, he is effusive in taking credit for and giving the same to a variety of colonial educational officials for the man Imam had become—"the excellent English with which he expressed himself and the perfect manners."
78. Imam, *Tafiya Mabudin Ilimi*, 38.
79. Mora, *Abubakar Imam Memoirs*, 62.

2

EMIR DIKKO'S METROPOLITAN ADVENTURES

> We read that London is the city of cities; we had no idea it was like this.
> —Muhammadu Dikko

IN 1951, THE RESIDENT OF KATSINA PROVINCE, R.L.B. Maiden, authored a circular to fellow residents and other high-ranking colleagues in the Northern Nigerian colonial bureaucracy pitching the recently published biography of the late emir of Katsina, Muhammadu Dikko. Authored by Mallam Bello Kagara, the alkalin alkalai (chief judge) of Katsina's Islamic court, the biography was a Hausa-language publication of the Northern Nigerian Literature Agency, a subsidiary of Gaskiya Corporation. In his endorsement of the biography, the resident described Emir Dikko as "one of the most striking figures in the history of the Northern Provinces of Nigeria since the British advent."[1] Maiden echoed the prevailing sentiment about Dikko in colonial officialdom.

Indeed, Dikko was a near-mythical figure of colonial reverence—a model, from the British perspective, of African Muslim aristocratic accommodation of the colonial modernist ethos. In his foreword to the biography, H. R. Palmer, who served as resident in Katsina between 1906 and 1911 and became Dikko's lifelong friend, describes the late emir as "an icon among his peers because of his outstanding qualities . . . qualities [that] distinguished him from others and made him stand out from the rest."[2] British officers who encountered and thereafter commented on Dikko tended to be effusive with praise. Because British colonizers were typically economical in their praise for African interlocutors, these words were uniquely

Figure 2.1. The Emir of Katsina locomotive.

significant indicators of the unusual esteem Dikko commanded. It was, of course, not entirely sincere praise; Palmer and Maiden were taking credit for Dikko's aristocratic polish and his mastery of colonial political and social etiquette. Their praise of Dikko was thus as much about their own sense of accomplishment as it was about the late emir's perceived assimilation to or accommodation of British modernity. The late emir was supposedly their model subaltern aristocratic pupil who, more than any of his peers, internalized and practiced his assigned symbolic and political role with panache and verve. Dikko was clearly the British colonizers' favorite emir and aristocratic interlocutor. An indication of the esteem with which colonizers in Nigeria held Dikko was the Nigerian colonial railways naming a locomotive after Dikko, a distinction unparalleled in colonial Nigeria (see fig. 2.1). Dikko (pictured in fig. 2.2) was something of an exemplary "native" king in British eyes. In their characterization, he was dignified, self-assured, and assertive, but he was also sufficiently beholden and loyal to the colonial system.

Additionally, in the heady post–World War II period of anticolonial nationalism, figures such as Dikko reemerged as nostalgic reminders of a more pragmatic, some might say docile, response to colonization. Dikko was a counterpoint to the nationalist figures positioning themselves for the imminent political and bureaucratic configurations of independence. Whether out of a romantic reinterpretation and recalling of a purportedly harmonious

Emir Dikko's Metropolitan Adventures | 93

Figure 2.2. Emir Muhammadu Dikko wearing the medal presented to him in Buckingham Palace in 1921. Credit: Kagara, *Sarkin Katsina*, front matter.

time of mutually beneficial alliance between British rulers and their Northern Nigerian aristocratic allies or out of sincere respect for a fallen ally, Maiden and other colonial officials upheld Dikko as an exemplar of a productive aristocratic kinship that connected colonizers to privileged subalterns in Northern Nigeria.

When he reigned as the emir of Katsina (1906–44), Dikko acquired a reputation for being favored by British colonizers in both Nigeria and Britain. This reputation translated to rare metropolitan honors, patronage, and access. Dikko traveled to the United Kingdom five times during his reign, in 1921, 1924, 1933, 1937, and 1939—more times than any other contemporary emir. On each occasion, he enjoyed the metropolitan hospitality reserved for the most treasured African aristocratic partners of British colonialism. Dikko became a fixture in metropolitan diplomatic, political, and bureaucratic circles, moving with ease within the British imperial world and treating Britain as a vacation and recreation site. He established a comfortable personal connection to Britain—a sense of being at home that enabled him to appropriate the symbolic and concrete instruments of British imperial modernity.

Like other Northern Nigerian aristocrats, Dikko courted and cultivated British imperial patronage as much as the British courted and cultivated him as an ally. While other Northern Nigerian emirs and noblemen merely seized on the British desire for reliable imperial middlemen and enforcers to ingratiate themselves with British officials, Dikko seemed more self-consciously committed to making his way within the empire and within the highest interpersonal networks of the imperial system. He seemed intent on inserting himself into consequential precincts of imperial culture so he could, within the allowable limits of the imperial hierarchy, dictate and shape his participation and interests in the colonial system.

To understand the relative deliberateness of Dikko's uniquely intimate relationship with British colonial culture and modes of political governance, one must understand the ways Dikko became entangled with the British colonial power structure, the circumstances of his appointment as emir of Katsina in 1906, the mutual political dependence that developed between him and his British benefactors, and his shrewd maneuvers within the imperial system through a sustained engagement with metropolitan institutions, personalities, objects, and cultures. The story of how the British made Dikko emir in 1906 and how he owed his ascension to the good graces of the British was well-known in imperial circles and became an occasional footnote to stories of his visits to Britain. For instance, in August 1939, while reporting on the departure of Emir Dikko and his retinue from Britain after a six-week visit, the *Edinburgh Evening News* concluded the story with the following words: "The Emir of Katsina received his emirate as a result of the support given by his troops to Lord Lugard in 1900."[3] Metropolitan sources highlighted the theme of the emir enthroned by the British and now firmly within the orbit of the British colonial system. The story that Dikko was, politically speaking, a creation of the British—a beneficiary of British largesse in return for his loyalty to the empire—was the underlying factor that shaped British opinion about Dikko. Dikko's story was one of imperial reciprocity. For that reason, it rang positively in metropolitan circles, where feel-good tales of mutual imperial appreciation and colonial amity were the currency of self-congratulatory discourse.

However, it is not only in metropolitan sources that Dikko is presented as a political beneficiary of British imperial favor. Dikko's own family oral history attests to the late emir's career being boosted by the British as a reward for his early demonstration of loyalty to the colonizers during the initial occupation in 1900. In interviews, Dikko's descendants fondly recall a family history peppered with tales of his connections to and friendship with successive colonial officials in Katsina. They also remember how his logistical assistance and loyalty to occupying British forces convinced the British he was a competent and loyal leader, which prompted his installation as emir.[4]

Dikko's career trajectory illustrates the arc of mobile and complex imperial relationships that is at the heart of this book. He embodied a successful imperial courtship that was then sustained and expanded over several decades through the institution of metropolitan travel. However, Dikko's precolonial life harbored few clues about his later colonial itinerary. When the British declared a protectorate over Nigeria in January 1900, Dikko was the durbi of Katsina, just one of several aristocratic titleholders in the Katsina Emirate. Moreover, he had obtained the title not by personal distinction but by inheritance on the death of his father, who had held the title before him. Yet British colonizers made him emir in 1906, effectively overthrowing the Dallazawa dynasty and establishing a new one beginning with Dikko. British colonizers were rewarding Dikko for his loyalty.[5] A colonial report made this clear several decades after the fact: "[Dikko] was appointed for courageous loyalty at a time when the political situation was critical owing to British troops suffering a serious reverse."[6] Dikko's twentieth-century biography was entwined with the British colonial enterprise in his native Katsina.

As emir, Dikko remained indifferent to how his role in the colonial enterprise was perceived and interpreted by his subjects. His appointment was the realization of a long-held personal ambition and a seminal change of fortune for his clan, but he appeared to want more for both himself and his emirate. He seemed to view his emirship as leverage he could deploy to attract the symbolic and infrastructural indicators of modernity to his emirate. As emir, Dikko proved himself to be committed to a set of ideals: he wanted Katsina to become a model of a modern, Northern Nigerian emirate, unabashedly remade to respond to and absorb colonial modernist influences. Years later, when Dikko's biography was being published posthumously, Palmer wrote in the foreword that Dikko was a great modernizer and that the establishment of a treasury—a gesture signaling a radical embrace of colonial governmental rationality—was initiated by Dikko without prompting.[7]

Colonial admiration for Dikko's purported administrative skills, loyalty, and reformist instinct was not only a posthumous adulatory exercise. British colonial officials praised Dikko contemporaneously for initiating progressive reforms in the Native Authority judiciary, pioneering the Beit-el-Mal treasury system, giving a "free hand" to the "native police" (the Dogarai) building "a good court house and gaol," and "support[ing] a school of his own."[8] In a biographical report enclosed in correspondence relating to one of his visits to England, officials lavished praise on Dikko: "[Dikko] has amply justified his choice [as emir] as he has proved to be the most progressive Chief of the Northern Provinces. He was the first Chief to visit England, own a car, and make an ascent in an aeroplane. His Emirate has always led the way in supporting the schemes of the Education, medical, Agricultural and Veterinary Departments and in the establishment of a Native Treasury. He was the first Emir to open a school for girls and his wife . . . takes a keen interest in it."[9]

Colonial and local vernacular praise aside, Dikko was not a halfhearted ally; as emir he engaged in the most robust outreach to Britain and the most self-conscious appropriation of material and symbolic goods associated with British colonial modernity. Unlike his predecessors, who initially embraced the British only to later scoff at colonial political and cultural changes and reforms, Dikko was the driver of colonial modernist reform and a restless modernizer who leveraged his imperial connections and friendships to transform Katsina into a modern province. He seemed to have decided that his privileged membership in the colonial system should be fully mined for all its benefits. His repeated travels to Britain later concretized this belief. As new emir, Dikko sought to give Katsina a head start in colonial modernist transformation.

Colonial Associational Leverage and Modernization

Dikko initiated a process of bureaucratizing the traditional institutions of emirate administration to complement his modernization goals. In consultation with the British, Dikko established a colonial court system and set up the treasury bureaucracy—the first of its kind in the emirate zone of Northern Nigeria. The treasury kept the province's accounts and revenue and paid the salaries of the Native Authority staff, a departure from the past practice of the emir appropriating all revenue, keeping only a percentage, and remitting the remainder to the colonial government.

Dikko's early efforts to "modernize" his emirate focused on peasant agriculture, the mainstay of majority of his subjects. Dikko borrowed a script from metropolitan agricultural shows used as avenues to improve farming and animal production techniques and showcase the latest agricultural techniques and technologies. In 1911, with the help of colonial authorities, Dikko organized what the *Illustrated Sporting and Dramatic News* described as "the first agricultural show in West Central Africa."[10] It is clear from the tone of the magazine's report that Dikko was showcasing the agricultural potential of his district not only for a local audience but also for a metropolitan British one and that the story helped the emir accomplish that goal.

The magazine printed a set of illustrative photos to go along with the story of the show and primed its British audience by stating that while "the British public is apt to associate the name West Africa with swamp, crocodiles, and mosquitoes," Katsina, located "inland in our latest Protectorate," was "governed by an exceptionally enterprising and intelligent Emir, who, advised by the British resident, is adopting measures to improve the condition of his country, whilst eschewing all those customs which are likely to debase instead of improving his people."[11] The reputation of Dikko as a modernizer and as an emir uniquely receptive to colonial modernist ideas, practices, and reforms was being disseminated in metropolitan colonial circles through similar publications. Dikko's eagerness to open his emirate to British cultural and technological influence converged with the desire of British colonial actors and publications to locate and celebrate their "civilizing" work in self-congratulatory rhetoric.

Dikko was unlettered in Roman script and relied on interpreters and scribes in his official functions, but he sought to remake Katsina into a center of colonial secular education. Dikko wanted a school for the province, and colonial authorities obliged, establishing Katsina Provincial School in 1914. Although the establishment of the school was part of a broader but heavily regulated expansion of schooling culture in Northern Nigeria,[12] Emir Dikko was instrumental in efforts to make Katsina a colonial education city.

Dikko's personal and official investment in and enthusiasm for the markers of imperial modernity did not go unnoticed in the colonial bureaucracy. British officials sought to reward him by complementing his efforts. In 1920, the colonial government selected Katsina to host the newly conceived school for sons of emirs and aristocrats; this educational pipeline was designed to produce the next generation of enlightened aristocratic allies, teachers, and workers in the Native Authority bureaucracies. The choice of Katsina indexed its rising profile in the Northern Nigerian colonial system synchronous with the favored status of Emir Dikko as a model aristocratic ally.[13] Moreover, the force of Dikko's charismatic personality, as well as his influence in the colonial system, likely helped recruit British teachers to the new school. Katsina Training College, as it was called, quickly became the preeminent center of secular education in Northern Nigeria. The first principal of the school and several teachers were British. The congregation of so many British educational officers in Katsina, a relatively obscure emirate town, gave it immediate sociopolitical visibility. Katsina became associated with Western education, British educational culture, and the inculcation of British mannerisms and modes of sartorial carriage. The disproportionately heavy presence of whites in Katsina conferred an aura of colonial prestige; the city's resulting social reputation was rooted in colonial codes of whiteness as a marker of civility and superiority.

The establishment of Katsina College was a crystallization of Dikko's modernization efforts—part of his strategic attempt to inscribe Katsina firmly within the nodes of imperial cultural transmission. Dikko's courtship of colonial modernist signifiers was extensive, but it was Dikko's educational efforts that made Katsina a destination for several groups of stakeholders, both European and African, in the business of colonial cultural exchange. Dikko envisaged a colonial educational enterprise that gave Muslim men, especially those from aristocratic backgrounds, access to a vast imperial world of knowledge, commodities, technologies, and sartorial innovations without undermining their commitment to the ethos of Islam and tradition. The proclaimed ideals of Katsina College dovetailed with Dikko's vision. The most compelling evidence for this convergence is a speech given by the governor of Nigeria, Sir Hugh Clifford, during the formal opening of the college on March 5, 1922.

Governor Clifford stated that Katsina Training College was rooted in the ideal of educating "young-men . . . from every part of the Muhammedan

States" without turning them into radicals who would challenge traditional aristocratic authority or British lordship:

> It too often happens, however, that when foreign learning is acquired, evil lessons are learned with it, that when men who become possessed of knowledge which is not commonly available to all their countrymen become pompous by pride in themselves, and imbued with contempt for their own customs and traditions, to neglect their religion and to lose respect for those who are older and wiser, even though they be less learned than themselves. These are very great evils and it would have been better if the people of the Muhammedan Emirates were left without foreign learning and knowledge than those who acquire those things should thereby be made unworthy members of the community. It is the special design of this Training College that it should be so conducted that those who pass through it should enjoy all the advantages of a wider knowledge while avoiding the evils to which I have referred. The young man who shows that he is unable to acquire knowledge without becoming arrogant to his fellows, impertinent to his superiors, neglectful of his religion, or scornful of the customs and traditions of his forefathers will not be allowed to remain in this institution.[14]

Katsina College was one of the high points of Dikko's efforts to modernize Katsina and connect the emirate more intimately to British colonial cultural and epistemological currents and institutions. With its teeming population of British educational officers and its metropolitan-inspired curriculum, disciplinary ethos, etiquette, and codes of honor and conduct, the college was a pipeline for cultural transmission.

Dikko wanted Katsina to draw cultural patronage from the imperial metropole and function as an outpost of British imperial modernity. It was a self-conscious cultivation of various infrastructures of British modernity. Dikko's broad vision included the vigorous embrace of other markers of British high culture, such as the game of polo, discussed shortly. The emir saw no contradiction between his Muslim identity and devotion on the one hand and his cultivation of imperial patronage on the other. As Mohammed Sani Umar correctly contends, Dikko compartmentalized Islam and colonialism into separate zones in his political and personal life, at times even relying on imperial logistical resources to perform religious obligations.[15]

Polo and Katsina's Cultural Identity

Dikko's modernist repertoire was boosted by his embrace of, investment in, and domestication of the British aristocratic sport of polo. The transformation of Katsina Emirate into a famous polo destination is one of the greatest testaments to Dikko's aggressive modernization project. Katsina was not on the railway system or a major trading route and had no other distinction, prior to the establishment of Katsina College, that would make it attractive for polo players in colonial Nigeria. What Katsina did possess was Dikko, a charismatic emir who saw the promotion of polo as part of a larger project of connecting Katsina to metropolitan high culture and as a platform for forging cross-racial fraternities between British colonial officials and the Hausa-Fulani elites of the emirate. Because Dikko saw no conflict between colonialism and authentic performances of Islamic and Hausa identity, his interpretation of the colonial encounter was not adversarial. Polo's recreational quality, social exclusivity, and metropolitan origins made it the perfect instrument for achieving Dikko's vision of transracial aristocratic connections in the Nigerian colonial system.

Prior to Dikko's conscious courting of colonial institutions and symbols, the little polo played in Katsina was played by British colonial officials in a casual, unorganized format. It was a way for colonial officials to unwind and enjoy a recreational interlude between and after bureaucratic duties in a colonial backwater with little else to do. This changed in June 1924; in that year, the assistant district officer, Captain Sheridan, suggested that polo be formally introduced in Katsina.[16] Sidney Hogben, one of the colonial officials who had played polo in Sokoto while serving there, "welcomed the suggestion enthusiastically."[17] The district officer, Mr. Hamlyn, also "lent his support."[18] Other British colonial officials, including Mr. Norwood, the principal of the Katsina Provincial School, joined this core group in the first organized polo game in Katsina. The Katsina Polo Club emerged with these British officials as its founding members.

Almost immediately, Emir Dikko "entered the scheme with zest," corralling his two sons—Usman Nagogo and Yusuf Lamba, who were already skilled horsemen—into the nascent polo scene. Mallam Ibrahim Nagwamatse, a Katsina College teacher who had previously played some polo and had a rudimentary familiarity with its rules, joined this initial group of "native" players. This European and African nucleus of the Katsina polo community worked hard to overcome initial challenges; for instance, they needed to devise good saddles for the horses and protect their hoofs from frequent injuries on the hard playing surfaces. The polo community cobbled together enough European saddles and horseshoes to solve these challenges and began to have regular "knockabouts," especially during the rainy season, when there was greenery on the improvised polo field.[19] At the end of the rainy season in 1924, the Katsina Polo Club took over the old golf course in the city and leveled it to make a new, standardized polo ground. An alternative site was then turned into a new golf course. In October, regular polo matches were held on the new ground, with the game approaching the "standard of station polo."[20] The emir, his sons, and other African players, most of them beginners, improved rapidly.

Emir Dikko was instrumental in this early growth of the game in Katsina. He approved the conversion of the golf course to a polo ground, invested his own money to buy equipment needed for the game,[21] and continued to encourage his sons to become better players. As part of their training, the young princes received written polo instructions on the blackboard of the Katsina Provincial School, which both attended. Norwood, himself an avid player, also routinely provided the princes with sticks and saddles to practice on the school grounds.[22]

In April 1926, the Katsina Polo Club entered a team in the Commandant's Cup, its first competitive tournament. Although this team was all European, subsequent polo teams representing Katsina were racially mixed. Dikko's sons, Nagogo and Lamba, became fixtures on the polo circuit, and they teamed up with Hogben and Norwood to represent the Katsina Polo Club at multiple tournaments across Nigeria. Katsina Club then began to play regularly in the major polo tournaments in Nigeria, including the Georgian Cup, named in honor of King George V. The highpoint of the Katsina Polo Club's tournament history came in 1932, when a team that included Nagogo and Lamba beat the Zaria polo team to win the Nigerian Cup.[23]

In November 1926, Dikko provided the Katsina Polo Club with land to build a new polo ground in the Kofar Yandaka area of Katsina. Through the Katsina Native Authority treasury, Dikko continued to support the club and its activities financially and logistically until the end of 1927, when the club became an independent, paid membership entity separate from the Katsina Games Club. The Katsina Polo Club began to charge a subscription fee in 1928 and used the money to fund its own activities and tournament travels.[24]

Usman Nagogo, who succeeded Dikko as emir, became a legendary polo player known in polo circuits in both Nigeria and Britain. Dikko himself was never as good a player as his sons, but his investment in the game went beyond a personal recreational hobby. Katsina's polo revolution was critical to Dikko's self-fashioning and his consolidation of his own intimate relationship, and that of Katsina, with colonial aristocratic culture.

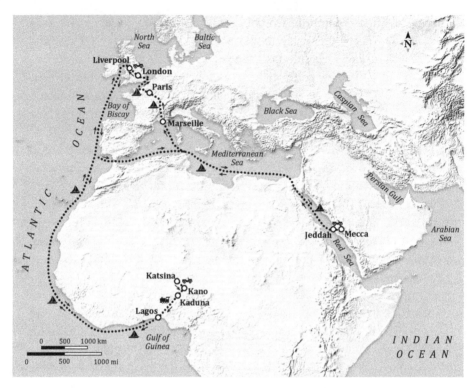

Map 2.1. Itinerary of the journey of Emir of Katsina, Muhammadu Dikko, and his entourage to Britain and the Hejaz in 1921.

Imperial Pilgrimage

The center of the imperial culture that encompassed polo was Britain, which Dikko visited multiple times during his reign for vacations, sightseeing, shopping, cultural excursions, and immersion in metropolitan rituals of power and recognition. Dikko's first visit to Britain occurred in 1921 and was combined with the Muslim pilgrimage to Mecca. Dikko left Katsina on May 29 with a party of ten—seven men and three women (see map 2.1 for itinerary).

The emir traveled with his son Usman Nagogo, his brother Nuhu Kankiya and his brother's wife, his scribe Mallam Barmo, one of his wives, and others. The party first made their way to Kaduna through Kano and then traveled by rail to Lagos, where they boarded the England-bound ship *Appam*, accompanied by Mr. F. G. Webster, the resident of Sokoto Province,

Figure 2.3. Dikko and his two sons in London, 1939. Credit: Kagara, *Sarkin Katsina*, 61.

whom Governor Hugh Clifford had designated as the official guide for Dikko and his contingent.[25] The party arrived in Liverpool on June 27, where arrangements had been made for cars, accommodations, and sightseeing in the city before their departure for London (see fig. 2.3).

With the help of his scribe, Mallam Barmo, Dikko kept a detailed journal of his experiences and the things he saw and did in Britain. This journal allows historians to retrace his itinerary and provides an illuminating glimpse into Dikko's interpretations of and perspectives on what he experienced in Britain. The sections of his posthumously published biography dealing with his travels to Britain faithfully reproduce the journal entries from those trips. Relying on these journal entries and metropolitan newspaper accounts and coverage, in the following I reconstruct the range of Dikko's reactions to the sights, sounds, and cultures of the British imperial metropole, unearthing the unique perspective of an African Muslim aristocratic visitor.

Accessing a Subaltern Ethnographic Notebook

If Dikko was a subaltern colonial ethnographer exploring and observing the metropole, his initial descriptions both confirm and confound that appellation. Dikko's first few journal entries are giddy descriptions of his hotel accommodations. Dikko describes in glamorous but redundantly mundane details his suite on the seventh floor. He depicts the seven-story hotel as a "house on top of a house on top of a house," a vernacular rendering of multistory buildings that would have been the only way to make this architecture intelligible to his Hausa readers. Dikko then describes his first encounter with an elevator and its workings and wonderous mobility. As for his suite, he declares that it could comfortably accommodate fifty guests and discusses in great detail the decor, bedding, bathrooms, and other features.[26]

This preoccupation with detail and minutia in Dikko's account may appear too dense and trivial for our postcolonial reading appetite, but such detail helped confer credibility and authority on travel writers like Dikko, who wanted to give their subjects, clients, and readers in Nigeria vicarious access to their metropolitan experiences. The more seemingly trivial the details in the narration, the greater the authorial credibility accorded the traveler-writer and the wider the vicarious participatory vista. Those, like Dikko, who claimed to know the metropole through their travels there had to demonstrate this knowledge by giving as vivid and detailed an account as possible. Without these details, their claims of metropolitan knowledge might be questioned. Since narrators of the metropole sought to portray Britain as starkly different from Northern Nigeria, detail served to underscore that argument about an exotic, distant, and elusive Britain.

Dikko's narratives are peppered with a great deal of detail both central and tangential to his accounts of life in Britain. There was deliberateness to the choice, for even seemingly tangential details helped make the metropole more concrete for those who read the accounts and sought to populate and reify their fantasies about Britain. During his first two days in Liverpool, Dikko participated in an eclectic itinerary. On June 28, he toured the Tropical School of Medicine and thereafter described seeing different therapeutic products as well as a demonstration of the workings of the human body.[27] A certain Professor Stephens took Dikko and his team around the school's museum, explaining to them "the life histories of various parasites."[28] The following day, Dikko and his entourage visited the offices of the *Echo* newspaper, where they watched as the "the evening edition [was] set up and printed with the photograph of the emir."[29]

On July 2, Dikko, Webster, Nuhu Kankiya, and Usman Nagogo traveled by car to the town of Derby, where they toured the Derby Cattle Show and saw a variety of breeds, as Dikko relates in this passage from his journal:

> We saw very big cattle and very fat. Each one of them was as large as four of those in our country. We saw the milk of a single cow, as much as that of ten of ours. We saw sheep with horns, without, and horses, very fat and exceedingly large far more so than in our country. Then again we saw splendid, large . . . fat horses. We saw many different breeds. Some were like horses of our land. Others were three times the size of ours in height and size altogether, they had a great deal of horses. . . . We saw horses only six months old like our six year old horses. . . . Each single bird was ten times the size of one of ours.[30]

Like other accounts of the metropole, Dikko's narrative thrives on hyperbole and exaggerative similitude to underscore the wonders of Britain. The notion that a British cow was as large as four Northern Nigerian ones, or that a British cow produced ten times the amount of milk as its Northern Nigerian counterpart, was a calculated, strategic narrative idiom. Dikko wanted his readers to imagine metropolitan animals and the methods used to breed and nurture them as vastly superior to and different from Northern Nigerian livestock and breeding techniques. This rhetorical maneuver is similar to his portrayal of metropolitan technologies, which he presented as infinitely wondrous aspects of imperial modernity that had no equivalent in Northern Nigerian society.

We also learn from Dikko's recorded observations that as he and his entourage toured the show and beheld different breeds of domestic animals, they themselves became objects of amazement, attracting a crowd of curious English people even as the emir and his group expressed their own curiosity about what they were observing. Dikko's articulation of this layered gaze is instructive: "We gazed at the animals. We admired what we came to see, and the people there followed and gazed at us. We marveled at what we saw, while they marveled at seeing us—they gazed at our rigas, our colour, and our turbans and shoes. Many people followed us and surrounded us."[31] Whether Dikko intended it or not, he was signaling a double ethnological gaze: the travelers from Northern Nigeria were observing the metropole but were in turn being ethnologically observed by the metropole. Even as Dikko and his entourage inverted traditional colonial ethnological scrutiny by conducting a reverse ethnography of the metropole, their presence in Britain and their exotic alterity in that imperial space reproduced and prolonged the colonial gaze they were attempting to reverse. The result was a complex landscape of colonial ethnography in which visiting subalterns, such as Dikko and his entourage, and metropolitan colonial actors sought to satiate curiosities whetted by decades of imperial contact.

Dikko described a tour of a car manufacturing plant, where the entourage saw "different parts" of a car being assembled to produce a car "all in one building."[32] Next, Dikko's journal records a visit to a newspaper publishing company. To his amazement, the emir saw published news of his arrival in Liverpool, including information on "my colour and the type of clothes I was wearing."[33] This encounter further heightened his awareness of his exposure to metropolitan curiosity. He, an observer of the metropole, was being intensely observed and reported in Britain's mass media. The emir and his party toured the newsroom of the newspaper company, where, by his account, they saw more than fifteen "girls" typing very fast on a "wonderful machine which struck the letters according to what one wanted to write."[34]

Dikko and his fellow tourists visited a telephone exchange, and they were allowed to make mock telephone calls to one another—a system of communication Dikko described as "a marvelous thing." The visitors then toured a museum, where they saw many statues of "great men of old and many different kinds . . . some soldiers, some men who had done something wonderful . . . all carved in stone."[35] The party then went to a cinema in the basement of their hotel and viewed a movie of the Duke of Connaught's tour of India.[36] Dikko recounts the experience thus:

> We saw the land of India, all of it, what it was like and what its inhabitants were like—the kings and the soldiers of India, and some games of that country.

All of this we saw without understanding the magic. We saw also the great seas. . . . We saw many great ships and we saw some unloading their cargoes and passengers and others loading; after this we saw horses and soldiers on them, many of them, they were galloping, raising the dust as they went. All this we saw without understanding how it came about. We saw many horses and horsemen about a thousand in number. They were making play in their gathering as if on a journey of the king and his chiefs in India. We saw also camelmen loading their camels as though . . . just about to start. We saw monkeys fighting each other—all of them magnificent animals. We saw charcoal humans and smiths in iron and copper and silver.[37]

Dikko's journal included even more detailed descriptions of the film, as though he was trying to recall the entire audiovisual experience for his readers. While in Britain, Dikko and his entourage also saw the movie *A Yankee at the Court of King Arthur*, which was specially released for the emir and his team for a private viewing at the Liverpool cinema.[38]

It is no narrative accident that Dikko describes the cinematographic display as magic. Magic is the ultimate denotation of mystery, elusiveness, and indescribability. Magic provides a handy idiom for describing what one does not fully understand, what titillates and mystifies the senses precisely because one does not understand its workings. When Dikko stated that they saw the moving pictures "without understanding how it came about," this was a textual gesture of surrender to the seductive power of mystery and magic. Dikko's invocation of magic is a culmination of his repeated use of the words *wonderment* and *marvel* to describe his party's emotive reactions to the sights they saw across Britain. Later in his journal, Dikko reiterates this sense of wonderment and the necessary incompleteness of narrative coverage—the sense that one could never quite capture the wonders on display in text: "All the things that we saw in this wonderful house of pictures, without understanding the marvelous magic . . . is very difficult to describe to one who has not seen it by the very reason of its wonders."[39] Dikko sought to make two interrelated points: the impossibility of full narrative accounting and the necessity and uniqueness of personal observation. Essentially, Dikko was saying that nothing written in text was adequate to describe what he and his entourage had seen and that there was no faithful correspondence between what was seen and what was written. Writing, he suggests, is an inadequate conveyor of audiovisual experience, an inferior medium for reenacting in-person experience. In saying this, Dikko granted himself the discretion to invoke mystery and magic to describe the unfathomable aspects of British life.

Like other travelers discussed in this book, Dikko returns often in his journal to the "difficult to describe" narrative motif discussed in other chapters. Earlier in the journal, Dikko concluded his description of the tour of domestic animals by stating that "we cannot adequately describe [the animals'] quality [and] size." Similarly, in his description of the car factory, he writes about "wonderful things that we cannot describe."[40] The hook of a travel narrative designed to evoke wonder in readers would leave the readers wishing they had witnessed the objects of the narrative for themselves. There had to be a zone of knowing that only physical proximity and seeing could achieve so the traveler himself could retain his authority as the one who has truly seen and truly knows what he is trying, with modest success, to describe. The phrase "difficult to describe" put Dikko and his fellow travelers above the readers in the hierarchy of metropolitan knowledge. Dikko preserved a zone of mystery—a zone of indescribability wherein readers of the narrative wondered what details and depths they were missing because of their physical distance from Britain.

Suspense and wishful wonderment are rewarding responses to a travel narrative. Dikko clearly knew that and used multiple idioms to elicit these responses. This technique of underlining the inadequacy of textual description helps preserve the exclusive privilege of metropolitan travel. Carving out a zone of textual descriptive limitation or a zone of narrative suspension had the effect of leaving potential readers imagining what was lost in narration, in the spatial constraints of text, and in the fog of memory, all of which could only be recovered through exclusive, expensive travel to the metropole, thus preserving the prestige of aristocrats who embarked on the trip.

The Allure of London

On July 5, Dikko and his party, accompanied by another guide, William Gowers, arrived in London and was reported to have noted during the trip that the roads of Britain were "as smooth as the floors of their own houses" in Katsina.[41] Dikko and his team marveled at the size of London, remarking that although they had "read it was the city of cities," they "had no idea it was like this."[42] The next day they paid a visit to the home of the governor of Nigeria, Sir Hugh Clifford. During their discussion, the governor asked Dikko what he had seen, and Dikko responded that he had seen wonderful things. Governor Clifford responded that he was delighted the emir was enjoying his trip, and he continued, "When I come to Katsina, you must

Figure 2.4. Dikko and his entourage admiring a bear at the London Zoological Gardens in 1921. Credit: Kagara, *Sarkin Katsina*, 41.

gather your people together and get them to make play before me there—the wrestlers, boxers, and camel races and foot races too."[43] The governor then offered to personally take Dikko and his party to see any sport they wanted to see in Britain. After leaving the governor's home, Dikko and his entourage headed to the Colonial Office, the most powerful citadel of British colonial policy making, where they were received by officials.[44] Later that day, the visitors were given a tour of horse-racing tracks, a sight Dikko described as "magnificent." Dikko and the group then shopped at a store that sold "woolen and silken high-priced gowns."[45]

The next few days were packed with tours. The group visited the London Zoological Gardens (fig. 2.4), where the visitors likened the rhinoceros to the kakanda, a legendary beast of Hausa folklore said to have fought "with the great snake that surrounded the world."[46] Dikko and his entourage swooned over the peacocks and were told a pair would be given to them as a gift.[47] The visitors attended a reception in their honor organized by the lord mayor of London at his home. In his journal, Dikko goes to great narrative lengths to describe the decor of the mayor's residence: "We saw ... very beautiful rugs and carpets everywhere in the house, and many chairs worked in gold and silken coverings."[48] At one point during the tour, the emir sat "dignified and stately in the Lord Mayor's chair in the Guest Hall."[49] Dikko was photographed seated on the lord mayor's chair surrounded by members of his entourage and the mayor, an iconic photograph in Dikko's

110 | Emirs in London

Figure 2.5. Dikko (seated) and his entourage in the residence of the lord mayor of London. Credit: Kagara, *Sarkin Katsina*, 16.

metropolitan visual archive that was printed in Bello Kagara's biography of the emir and reproduced here (see fig. 2.5). The *Dundee Courier* reported that a member of Dikko's entourage was so taken by the uniformed footmen that he fixed his gaze on one of them, although "both men were wondering whose clothes seemed the stranger."[50] The group then toured the Royal Mint and witnessed the process of turning gold and other precious metals into coinage.[51] The deputy-master of the Mint, Sir John Cawston, explained to the tourists how money was made, after which Dikko reportedly exclaimed, "It is the house of the world."[52]

The party set out on a forty-mile drive to visit the home of an English aristocrat, Lord Wilma. On their way, they stopped to visit the home of Colonel Miacke, the resident of Katsina Province. After a brief reception and a conversation between Dikko and Miacke, the latter joined the party; along with Gowers, they visited the Bank of England, where Dikko purchased souvenir coins of some foreign lands.[53] The party then proceeded to Wilma's home. Later that day, Dikko and his entourage proceeded to the Lingfield horse race, where the emir, a horse breeder and avid fan and promoter of traditional horse racing in Northern Nigeria, enjoyed several races and watched as bettors picked horses prior to each race.[54] In the fifth race, Dikko joined in the betting, choosing "a lay mare" that won and netted him a modest, undisclosed winning. Dikko's scribe reports in his journal that he and his entourage were "very pleased" and that "the Europeans were astonished at the emir's knowledge of horses though he was a stranger [to the sport]."[55] Dikko and his party attended the interregimental polo match at Hurlingham and a horse-racing event at Newmarket.[56] The visitors then retired to the serenity of Hyde Park "to take in the air" before returning to their hotel.[57]

On another day, the visitors attended a Russian ballet, where they wondered whether the dancers in the performance of *Les Papillons* "were human." Dikko's wives attended this show, guided by Maud Gowers, the wife of their guide. Maud Gowers subsequently took the wives to the London Zoological Gardens, but their attempt to take a walk in Regent's Park "proved impossible owing to mobbing" by members of the press and park users.[58] On July 11, Dikko and his group visited a private stock farm owned by Major Morrison, where the emir purchased a "Red Poll Bull and Heifer" for his farm in Nigeria.[59] Visits to a bath club and a squash racquets game preceded a lavish shopping spree at Harrods.[60]

Buckingham Palace

The high point of Dikko's 1921 tour of Britain was a meeting with the king at Buckingham Palace. Accompanied by Webster, Dikko and his party arrived at the gate of the palace, showed their permission forms, and were ushered inside. There, in a large reception hall, they saw Governor Hugh Clifford, Lieutenant Governor Gowers, and Lord Hamilton, the guardian of the palace gate, waiting for them. Lord Hamilton provided chairs for Dikko and his party while they waited to be called into the king's chamber.

As they waited, Dikko surveyed the palace's inner features. He apparently recorded a vivid mental picture of the decorations and artistic features of the reception hall, remarking in his journal thus: "We saw that the whole of the hall was decorated with gold . . . [and] there were lamps above, amongst them some splendid ones."[61] A few moments later, Governor Clifford entered, and Dikko was ushered into the king's waiting chamber by "three gentlemen." Clifford then invited Gowers, who joined Dikko. A few more moments of suspenseful waiting passed before Gowers ushered Dikko into the king's presence.

Dikko's scribe, Mallam Barmo, recorded the moment in the emir's journal: "Mr. Gowers called the Emir; they entered together and he took him into the presence of the King. Then the Emir greeted the mighty King,

God give him victory—and rejoiced to see him. They conversed with him for about twenty minutes—then the King gave him a medal of honor of gold; with his own hand he gave it into the hand of the Emir."[62] The twenty-minute chat between Dikko and the king was a typical aristocratic conversation and covered elite pastimes. The king is reported to have said to Dikko, "I understand you are a good judge of horses, and at Lingfield races picked out several winners."[63] The *Dundee Evening Telegraph* reported that "the Emir's eyes sparkled with pleasure and he enthusiastically explained to His Majesty that Nigerians were magnificent horsemen"[64] and that if he was shown a parade of horses, he could instinctively pick out the winner most of the time.[65]

The king presented Dikko with the King's Medal for African Chiefs, the highest imperial honor accorded to African chiefs in British Africa. Dikko made sure to say in his journal that the king personally gave the medal to him "with his own hands" as a way of signaling to his readers that he made bodily contact with the mystical head of the British Empire. As Dikko chatted with the king in the chamber, Gowers called Prince Nagogo in to greet the king. He then brought the rest of the party in. The emir's scribe recorded the group's collective reaction to meeting the king: "We greeted the mighty King and beheld his face with joy; we saw him clearly—we rejoiced to behold him and at the gift which he bestowed on the Emir, and we returned grateful thanks. Then the emir spoke with the great King of England, and Gowers interpreted what was said."[66]

When they left the king's inner chamber, Dikko and his party, accompanied by Governor Clifford, Gowers, and Webster, were taken on an extensive tour of the palace. They saw "different reception rooms" and entered a section with fourteen rooms between the north and south walls of the building. Dikko reports that "each single room [was] beyond comparison on account of the beauty of its furniture and decoration and the many wonderful things" it contained. He describes seeing "golden chairs," "rugs of beautiful colours," beds and pillows of multiple colors, three portraits of queen Victoria at different stages of her life, and "the likeness of beautiful maidens."[67] After the tour, reporters covering the visit asked Dikko what he thought of Buckingham Palace. The *Leeds Mercury* reported that the emir responded: "It is the house of houses. I used to think the Governor's residence in Lagos was magnificent, but it is a hut compared with the great king's palace."[68] Upon leaving Buckingham, Gowers drove the party to a stream behind the palace, where they saw "water fowl and marveled greatly to see them." Dikko and his party then returned to their hotel "greatly pleased to have seen the King, to have the great gift from him, and to have seen his palace and the great portrait of the great powerful Queen [Victoria]."[69]

Dikko's visit to the king of England had gone well. He had made history as the first emir or chief from Northern Nigeria to be awarded the King's Medal for African Chiefs (First Class) by the king, and this honor gave him entry into a network of symbolic prestige reaching from London to all corners of the British Empire. As David Cannadine notes, the tradition of awarding medals to chiefs and aristocrats in British colonial domains began in colonial India and quickly spread to other parts of the British Empire as its use as a tool for cultivating and rewarding loyal allies became established. The invention of an elaborate honorific system followed in which medals, awards, and honors of various gradations and nomenclatures proliferated across the empire.[70] Gestures of this nature gave subaltern aristocrats a symbolic stake in the exclusive honor system of British metropolitan society. A medal award was a confirmation of membership in a transcolonial community of honor and shared imperial prestige.

For Muslims like Dikko, however, such medal awards were fraught with risk. Some had neo-Christian names, such as Companion of the Order of St. Michael, a clear reference to Christian sainthood. Most of Dikko's subjects would not have known about this, but some members of the clerical establishment took notice and criticized Dikko and other emirs for, in their rhetoric, compromising their Islamic identity by coveting honors endowed with Christian symbolism. One such critic was the reformist Sheikh Abubukar Gumi, who argued that if one could not see "the [British] Resident in Sokoto accepting to be made the Companion of the Order of Sheikh Uthman and Abdullahi," then it was wrong for Muslim leaders to accept awards steeped in the symbols and iconographies of Protestant England.[71]

Metropolitan Encounters

Metropolitan newspapers covering Dikko's tour of Britain pressed the emir to explain why his wives, who had accompanied him to Britain, were not part of the tours and sightseeing. The *Dundee Evening Telegraph* speculated about why the women were "left behind at the hotel,"[72] and the *Diss Express and Norfolk and Suffolk Journal* declared outright that Dikko's wives did not go along for the sightseeing tours because "custom demand[ed] that they should live a secluded life."[73] These inquiries compelled Gowers to organize a "press presentation" on Dikko's behalf, at which he informed reporters that "the Emir did not intend to allow [the wives] to go shopping in the city."[74] The conspicuous absence of the women of the entourage from the public touring itinerary was fodder for the British press, who saw it as evidence of a fundamental cultural difference between Northern Nigeria and imperial Britain. One newspaper even mocked Dikko by writing that the emir, after seeing the movie *A Yankee at the Court of King Arthur*, "went to his hotel and told his wives all about it."[75] The newspaper then concluded on a note of sarcastic pity with the words, "poor old wives!"

Even in the imperial space of London, Dikko did not upend the gender dynamics of traditional Hausa Muslim patriarchy. His curt response on the question of the women's public invisibility was a way to once again express his compartmentalization of devotion to Hausa/Islamic tradition and commitment to colonial modernity. Nonetheless, whether as a response to the press inquiries or as part of the planned program of sightseeing, Dikko, accompanied by Gowers, Webster, and Prince Nagogo, took the women to the London Zoological Garden on July 10. The women, Dikko writes, spent several hours looking at the animals and "marveled just as we did."[76] The women returned to the hotel in the afternoon while the men continued touring sights in London.

In the evening, Dikko and his entourage visited a public pool and water park, where they observed men bathing and diving into the pool from "a very high place like a tall tower." At the same park, Dikko and his group got on a ride that, from his description, may have been a Ferris wheel. Dikko's description captures the thrill and wonder the group felt on the ride: "We got into a thing that took us up about thirty two cubic feet aloft. We marveled at this magnificent house and this wonderful thing. Then this thing descended with us on its own power to the ground."[77]

Dikko's itinerary for the rest of the day included a tour of a cattle-breeding farm owned by Major Moore; a brief visit to a boxing club; and a tour of the home of Lord Wyfold, a famed hunter who had hunted across the British Empire in Africa. He and Dikko had befriended each other years earlier when the aristocrat had visited Northern Nigeria on an expedition that included a team hunt with Dikko. The emir reported seeing the stuffed heads of a variety of African "wild beasts" in Lord Wyfold's estate and commented in his journal about many other aristocratic trappings, including "many magnificent rugs." On the instruction of his father, Lord Wyfold's son presented Dikko with a "large beautiful sword in a silver sheath with a gold hilt and a sling of rich embroidery."[78] After Dikko posed for a photograph with Lord Wyfold, the tourists left the estate "with exceedingly great joy."

Back in London that night, Dikko and his group visited a boxing club, where they paid to watch a fight between an Englishman and an American. It was the first boxing match Dikko and members of his entourage had seen. The emir described the match in a detailed play-by-play manner analogous to modern sports commentary,[79] underscoring the previously discussed importance of narrative detail and minutia in the process of recording and transmitting the metropole for the consumption of Northern Nigerian readers.

On July 12, Dikko and his entourage toured Kew Royal Botanical Gardens, where the curator lectured them on the garden's collection of trees, plants, and flowers from all over the world. Upon seeing the pelargonia plant and flower, Dikko was smitten by its beauty and asked if it would grow in Nigeria because "he would like some to take with him."[80] Outside Kew Gardens, the group toured the temperate glasshouse—a vast nursery for plant species from all over the world—that was "built on the former bed of the river Thames."[81] At the conclusion of the tour, the officer in charge of the glasshouse nursery autographed a catalogue of the plants housed therein for Dikko.[82] The *Diss Express and Norfolk and Suffolk Journal* reported that Dikko, a lover of flowers, planned to take "some English rose-trees back with him, as he intends to 'make the desert bloom like a rose.'"[83]

On July 13, Dikko and his group embarked on their wildest metropolitan adventure yet: visiting the Hendon Aerodrome, where they were entertained by an air display and maneuver by Royal Air Force (RAF) pilots in three Bristol fighter jets. Air Marshall Sir Hugh Trenchard, who had commanded the British army of conquest in Southern Nigeria, went on to help found the Royal Air Force, and was now the chief of air staff, arranged the flight exhibition. The exhibition went as planned, dazzling Dikko and his party and prompting the remark that the planes were "more wonderful than hawks for even a hawk cannot fly upside down."[84] When a fourth jet appeared and prepared to take to the skies, Dikko surprised his hosts by requesting to get on board, a request granted by the RAF authorities. Dikko then requested that his flight avoid the "stunts . . . they had just seen."[85] He and Prince Nagogo put on the appropriate gear and climbed aboard the aircraft, sitting behind the pilot.[86]

What happened next was captured in all its marvelous detail by a story in the *Leeds Mercury*: "Earlier in the day, the Emir had been out at

Hendon for an aeroplane flight and the novelty of the outing seems to have impressed him tremendously. When the propeller started 'roaring' his first thought was that the engine was ill, and that it might be advisable to wait until it was better. After a ten minute spin, his comment was that it was 'very pleasant to be a bird.'"[87]

After the flight, the emir and his entourage were photographed with some officers of the aerodrome. They also toured the hanger, where Dikko reported seeing several "big aeroplanes" in the various sheds. He also relayed seeing planes being assembled and repaired.[88]

Dikko and his group visited the Royal Air Force Station at Kenley and the House of Commons, where the group sat in on debates and observed the House in session.[89] On the evening of their departure from London, the group entertained themselves at Euston Train Station by watching "trains arriving and . . . leaving," and they observed as each train "filled with people and luggage."[90] Asked by the British press about his experiences in and around London as he left for Liverpool, Dikko was effusive: "It is a city of cities, and very much bigger than I ever imagined it would be. There is nothing to compare with it. There is no rest here. It is all movement, bustle, and hurry."[91]

On July 16, Dikko and his entourage sailed from Liverpool to Jeddah in the Holy Land to perform the Muslim pilgrimage. Even in this religious endeavor, Dikko's imperial connections enabled him to gain passage and mobility in logistical spaces that would otherwise have posed challenges to his pilgrimage. British diplomatic and colonial institutions and the reciprocal niceties activated by a vast, global British imperial infrastructure helped Dikko navigate the journey to the Hejaz and, once there, go smoothly through the pilgrimage rituals, his mobility in Arabia aided by British consular support. Imperial and Islamic obligations tend to be analyzed as separate zones in the life of a Muslim subaltern. As argued earlier in this chapter, Dikko, managed, however imperfectly, to carve out separate mental spaces for his colonial and religious endeavors. Nonetheless, there was no denying that the colonial seeped into the religious and vice versa. Given the constraints on subaltern mobility in an early twentieth-century world of inchoate, fluid sovereignties and territorial nationalism, religious mobility inevitably relied on colonial instruments and practices. The opposite was also sometimes true. Perhaps it was this reality that caused Dikko to refuse to see any contradiction between his colonial subalternity and his Muslim identity.

Dikko reconciled himself to the inevitability of osmotic convergence between his subaltern and Muslim selves. His ability to compartmentalize his participation in colonial protocols and his commitment to traditional Muslim obligations reflected the working pragmatism of his colonial engagements. This self-interested pragmatism enabled him to go so far as to express gratitude to British authorities for facilitating the performance of his religious obligations, a remarkably counterintuitive gesture with profound analytical import for how colonization and Muslim subjectivities are posited and analyzed. When the Reuters news agency interviewed Dikko after his return from London and Mecca, the emir reportedly said that the "British administration in Nigeria had enabled [him and his entourage] more thoroughly to carry out the teachings of the Koran."[92] Rather than being a hindrance to a Muslim's expression of religious devotion and obligations, Dikko posited British colonial rule as a catalyst for Muslim religious revival, stating, "I am fully confirmed there is nothing like British rule to help Moslems to carry out their own religion, and even to make clear what the teachings of that faith mean."[93] Where other Muslims might have seen hostility or been suspicious of scripted metropolitan hospitality, Dikko saw empathy and acceptance. He reportedly stated that he encountered "an amount of humanness in England that surprised me," and he claimed that "even in Mecca and among my co-religionists in Arabia," he had not encountered the "sympathetic treatment" that was accorded him in Britain.[94]

By his own account, Dikko was enamored with Britain. Such was the seduction of the metropole that on his way back from the pilgrimage, he detoured to England, where he is reported to have toured a pottery and even descended into the pit at the Fenton Colliery. At a luncheon there, Dikko "was presented with a pair of silver-plated safety lamps suitably described as a souvenir."[95] During the same detour, Dikko visited a weapons manufacturing factory at Erith in Kent; after being shown how to fire a machine gun, he remarked, "It is the most terrible weapon I have ever seen."[96] Here, Dikko was both glorifying the military might of Britain and expressing discomfort with the deadly capacity of Britain's war arsenal. Dikko deployed this double entendre to express his reactions in other encounters with metropolitan interlocutors and objects, but in this instance, it is particularly illuminating because of its articulation of the subaltern's ambiguous understanding of colonial power, which was rooted in the emotional economy of both fear and awe. Like other subalterns who had to make sense of the empire's greatness as well as its fearsome capacity to inflict harm, Dikko had his own theory on the might and power of the empire. When the vacationing Lord Leverhulme, a fellow passenger on the West Africa–bound Elder Dempster liner *Appam*, asked Dikko what impressed him the most about Britain, Dikko simply said "coal," adding that "it was, in his opinion, the source of Britain's power."[97]

The certitude of Dikko's answer to Lord Leverhulme bespeaks an important outcome of metropolitan trips that will become clearer as it is amplified in the subsequent chapters of this book. Nigerian aristocrats who completed an excursion to Britain felt confident that they now understood or had unraveled the mystery at the heart of Britain's might and that propelled and helped maintain her imperial sovereignty. Accordingly, they emphatically formulated their own explanations for why Britain was a powerful imperial force in the world, why her empire had endured turmoil of different kinds, and why their own societies lagged behind Britain technologically. Dikko, like other subaltern been-tos, was staking his ground as a newly minted expert on Britain and its imperial might.

The 1921 visit to Britain was Dikko's inaugural exploration of the metropole. The elaborate trip enjoyed wide coverage in British newspapers, which scrutinized, dramatized, and sensationalized the exotic sartorial and cultural cues Dikko and his entourage left in their wake as they toured the different sites. Dikko and his delegation became curios for a British press suffused in a Victorian imperial ethos of othering and difference. They were subjected to the journalistic "mobbing" referenced earlier, which other scholars have discussed in regard to the visits of other African aristocrats to Britain.[98] While some press coverage reveled in the subtle imperial racial condescension of remarking obsessively about the robes and appearances of Dikko and his fellow tourists, others, like the *Diss Express and Norfolk and Suffolk Journal*, blatantly marked the visitors as originating from an inferior culture and civilization. In an example of this tendency, the newspaper published the following excerpt on Dikko's entourage: "The Emiresses, or whatever his wives are called, have never seen a moving picture. In Nigeria, where the Emir holds sway, it is considered highly improper for ladies to attend public meetings or entertainments, their only claim to advanced culture being in the fact that they smoked cigarettes long before English flappers ever tried it."[99]

As the British press exoticized Dikko, the emir's journal indicates he was similarly exoticizing Britain for his audience in Northern Nigeria. The only difference, of course, was that his exoticizing was rooted in adulation and reverence, not in condescension, denigration, and the intent to dominate and devalue. The obvious culture shocks of the visit aside, Dikko clearly enjoyed the sights of Britain. Being in the metropolitan imperial space helped Dikko better understand and define his place in the British imperial system. For a man who had expended so much time and effort cultivating and embracing the symbols and materialities of the empire, touring Britain was analogous to being formally initiated into a British imperial modernist fraternity.[100]

It was not only in matters pertaining to Dikko's wives that the British press deployed a tone of condescension and mockery. Newspaper headlines and stories on Dikko's activities in Britain thrived on the trope of obsessive exoticization that verged on the comical. Dikko's reactions to metropolitan sights were magnified and reported in preordered bromides as the spontaneous, excited, emotional outbursts of a rustic African king discovering modern technologies and practices for the first time and reacting as a child exposed to a new toy. The British press infantilized the emir and his team; their portrayal in the British press as loyal, awestruck children of the empire was as soothing to extant ideas of British self-understanding as it was consistent with the colonial discourse of the time.

Confidential and routine colonial documents on the visits employed snide remarks, mockery, and condescension in discussing visiting emirs. Take the colonial correspondence between the British Residency in Cairo and the Colonial Office on Dikko's impending visit to England in 1933, which referenced his 1921 visit. In one correspondence, Dikko was described as follows: "This potentate performed the pilgrimage . . . after a visit to England during which he made sanitary history in the Khedivial steamer by persistently misapprehending the object of the trash basin; incidentally he stowed his luggage on his bunk [bed] and slept on the floor of his cabin."[101] Such descriptive mockery was often an integral part of the reportorial and scribal repertoires of colonial bureaucrats. It is no surprise that the British press drew on the same discursive register in their representation of Dikko and his group.

A Repeat Excursion

On August 25, 1924, Emir Dikko and a large entourage consisting of his wife and several members of his family, including his brother, Nuhu Kankiya, departed Katsina for England to attend the Wembley British Empire Exhibition. The Colonial Office in Whitehall had extended a special invitation to Dikko to attend the exhibition. The party arrived at the port of Plymouth eighteen days later (map 2.2); the exhibition, which had started on September 6, was already underway. Dikko and his entourage were then driven to London, where they embarked on an elaborate program of sightseeing that culminated in a tour of the exhibition grounds.

The group visited the Madame Tussaud Wax Museum, where they saw wax statues of royal figures and other prominent men and women. Dikko recalled that the statues "looked so real as if they would speak" and that they were "decorated with golden and silver colors" that accentuated their lifelikeness.[102] Dikko and his entourage toured an electricity company and an automobile manufacturing plant and attended a car-racing event the emir described as "very interesting but very risky."[103] During their stay in Britain, Dikko and his group toured courthouses in London and one of the palaces of the king of England, where they saw "the King's horses" and "the King's carts."[104] The entourage visited the London Zoological Gardens, as Dikko and his retinue had done in 1921.[105] On this visit, Dikko donated "a white Oryx antelope" to the zoo authorities.[106] Dikko and the men in his entourage also performed what would become a ritual of metropolitan visits by the Northern Nigerian aristocracy: a visit to Frederick Lugard's home in Abinger.[107] Very little information exists on the interactions between Dikko and Lugard on this occasion.

Adventures and Otherness

The garb and robes of Dikko, his wife, and other members of his entourage gave away their foreignness in the metropolis of London. Even in a city accustomed to visual, sonic, and sartorial markers of exoticism because of the ongoing British Empire Exhibition, Dikko and his group stood out. British newspapers and publications took particular delight in reporting on the itinerary of Dikko's group, but they especially engaged in the visual othering common in imperial Britain. Reporters and press photographers covering the exhibition were enamored with the visiting members of the Northern Nigerian aristocracy, and they took and published photos of them in their newspapers and publications. The September 17 edition of the *Leeds Mercury* displayed a picture of the two women in the delegation. Taken at the exhibition grounds in Wembley, the picture depicts the two women in a blushing,

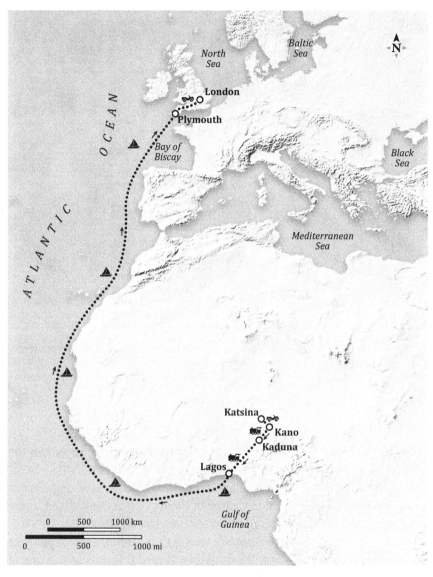

Map 2.2. Itinerary of the journey of Emir of Katsina, Muhammadu Dikko, and his entourage to Britain in 1924.

DONOR OF A WHITE ORYX ANTELOPE TO THE "ZOO": THE EMIR OF KATSINA (THIRD FROM LEFT) WITH HIS SON (EXTREME LEFT) AND NIGERIAN NOTABLES AT WEMBLEY.

Figure 2.6. Dikko and his entourage at the Wembley British Empire Exhibition. Credit: *Illustrated London News*, September 20, 1924, 27.

reluctant pose. One of them is said to have "reluctantly raised her veil for the photographer" while the other "could not be persuaded" to do likewise.[108] The *Illustrated London News* similarly photo-profiled the male members of Dikko's delegation, publishing a picture of them taken at the British Empire Exhibition on its Personalities of the Week page (see fig. 2.6).[109]

Dikko and his delegation began touring the exhibition on September 16, starting with the so-called "West African Walled Compound" section of the "Races in Residence" exhibit. The walls of the compound were a replica of the famous clay walls of Northern Nigeria's largest city, Kano, and a gate "fashioned in Nigeria . . . and specially made for the walled city" mimicked the gates of Kano city.[110] Within the larger compound, the Nigerian Pavilion, as it was called, was designed as an emir's palace compound.[111] In this contrived metropolitan space, Dikko and his party saw a reenactment of a palace very much like his own. This was an awkward ritual of touring a foreign space purporting to represent their own home, "an encounter with a representation of their own otherness."[112]

The Dikko party's experience is analogous to that of Egyptian aristocratic visitors to Europe in the nineteenth century, as described by Timothy Mitchell. Egyptian tourists, human curios in European spaces, often "found themselves something of an exhibit" in an elaborate spectacle of objectification that rendered exotic things, including the thingified visitors, as objects to be "experienced by the dominating European gaze."[113] The Northern Nigerian tourists saw familiar items being exhibited—tin, rubber, and hides and skins—and witnessed familiar sights, such as the inhabitants of the pavilion "weaving, making pottery or working in leather and metals."[114] This was a staged "object-world," to use Mitchell's coinage,[115] designed to enable exhibition goers to experientially enter the supposedly static world of "natives" and to feel, touch, smell, hear, and taste the material and quotidian universe of African colonial subjects. Dikko's presence in that space was meant to authenticate the exhibit. In the process, he and his party became, much like Middle Eastern monarchs visiting European exhibitions in the nineteenth century, "a part of the exhibition,"[116] or, as one colonial correspondence put it, a "naturalistic attraction," at the exhibition's so-called West African compound.[117]

In all, the West African compound "housed seventy African men, women, and children in a village setting."[118] The so-called walled city was designed to showcase the traditional architecture and cultures of several West African peoples, including the Hausa and Fulani of Northern Nigeria. At the exhibit were "residents"—representatives of Hausa, Mendi, and Fulani peoples imported into London for the exhibition. They lived in purportedly authentic West African mud-and-straw huts, cooked their own meals, conducted their daily affairs, did chores, lounged, and interacted as the exhibition's audience, mainly white Britons, walked by or stopped to gaze voyeuristically at them.[119] This ensemble of "authentic" West African culture also included a display of "traditional" handicraft. The Hausa, Fulani, and Mendi peoples selected to animate the "native village" and "native workshops" subsection of the compound showcased a miniaturized version of what organizers understood as a West African compound replete with quotidian objects and chores. This exhibit was a high point of British colonial anthropological othering of African subject peoples to feed the curiosity of metropolitan audiences.

According to Anne Clendinning, the selection of the Hausa and Fulani peoples of Northern Nigeria was deliberate. She posits that the Hausa,

Fulani, and Mendi peoples "embodied the qualities most valued by the British colonial administrators and missionaries, including industriousness, intelligence, the cultivation of community, and conversion to Christianity."[120] The Wembley exhibition, ostensibly a display of imperial diversity and the empire's cultural assets, lasted two years. It was, in truth, a bizarre and intensely racialized spectacle whose "display of foreign peoples" for metropolitan entertainment and the patronizingly racist gaze of Europeans would be apparent to latter-day analysts.[121]

Racism was not a prominent aspect of Dikko's perceptual register. Accordingly, he did not remark in his journal about the portrayal of his own kinsmen and culture in the West African compound because the ideological subtleties underpinning the portrayal would have eluded him or would not have been intelligible to him in those terms. Even if he had perceived the exhibition space and the portrayals as racist, his participation in the ceremonials of this racist pageantry precluded his acknowledgment of them as such. Moreover, even the usually acerbic anticolonial press in West Africa had objected only to the nonrepresentation of Africans in the organizing committee but not to the racialized, othering portrayal of Africans until "several derogatory articles, racist cartoons and misleading descriptions of life in West Africa" were published in the British press during the exhibition, outraging Africans and other blacks living in the United Kingdom.[122]

It is not clear why Dikko had been invited to this exhibit, other than that he was a treasured aristocratic ally in the most populous British colony in Africa and a composite of the treasured, romanticized sensibilities of the Hausa and Fulani peoples of Northern Nigeria, who constituted, along with the Mendi of Sierra Leone, the basis of the display. From the perspective of the colonial organizers, the decision to invite Dikko was vindicated since the emir did not recognize the racial baggage of the West African display, which became magnified when reports of London hoteliers refusing accommodation to African visitors to the exhibition drew protests by black student groups.[123] As an official guest of the Colonial Office, Dikko moved in a semi-enclosed circuit that put him in a colonial diplomatic bubble in which the exhibition was portrayed as a glorious celebration of the greatness of the British Empire, its familial solidarity, and its wondrous diversity.

Dikko's gaze on the Wembley exhibition was constrained and circumscribed by the exhibitionist protocols that underpinned his visit and his officially scripted circumnavigation of the British imperial capital. Thus, rather than see the exhibition in the same light as the radical black student groups who protested its racism, the emir basked in the imperial grandeur of which he and his entourage were now a part. In his biography, *Sarkin Katsina Dikko*, Dikko recalls that he and his group visited the Nigerian (Hausa and Fulani) pavilion within the West African compound, where "we saw houses built with mud, like those in Katsina."[124] Several of the houses on display, Dikko writes, were done in the style of Kano.[125] For Dikko, the point of reference for evaluating the compound and its content was not ideology or polemics but the physical spaces of Northern Nigeria the organizers sought to replicate.

Even though Dikko's visit to the Wembley exhibition sidestepped the racial atmospherics that haunted and plagued the event, two important points suggest themselves to scholars looking back at his participation. First, it is apparent that, from the perspective of the Colonial Office, the exhibition was the ideal event at which to fete a favored aristocratic ally. The gathering exhibited peoples, cultures, and materials from all over the British Empire, presenting a unified but diverse image of the work of empire and colonial modernity in fostering variegated cultural formations in different parts of the world. It was a choreographed visual of imperial harmony and cultural flourishing under the canopy of British imperialism. Second, there was an awkward spectacle to the reality of Dikko, a prominent emir from the Hausa-Fulani world of Northern Nigeria, seeing his own culture and people on display in a strategically curated metropolitan space. It is difficult to fully capture the range of contradictory emotions and perceptions that may have coursed through the emir at the sight of purportedly re-created authentic Hausa and Fulani village settings in London.

What we get from Dikko's own written account of his encounter with the exhibition is a sense of pleasant surprise at seeing in London what he regarded as an accurate architectural depiction of a Kano and Katsina village setting. Whether this reaction conceals another one is a matter of conjecture. What appears clear to us as we examine the awkward encounter is that Dikko essentially went to London to see himself—or, more appropriately, a colonially mediated version of himself—on display. The ethos of metropolitan travel dictated this reality. Dikko and other Northern Nigerian emirs regularly saw their Hausa and Fulani material cultures, sartorial images, and other markers of purportedly authentic emirate Nigerian life on display in metropolitan museums, each time seemingly appreciating the gesture as a display of the white man's valuation of that culture rather than a denigration of it.

On the part of the Colonial Office, the tendency to include tours of familiar cultural sites, objects, and museum displays in the emirs' sightseeing itineraries may suggest that the intent was precisely to enable the visitors to see a bit of themselves in the metropole and thus feel a sense of incorporation, of having been permanently inscribed and accepted in the metropolitan imperial cultural imagination. It appears that these displays were part of the elaborate protocol of courtship and patronage that had an ultimate goal of consolidating ties to aristocratic allies whose very presence at the imperial metropole signified an imagined, and illusory, imperial solidarity.

Conclusion

Emir Muhammadu Dikko was the pioneer of a particular Northern Nigerian aristocratic engagement with the institutions, cultures, and symbols of the metropole. He was the first among his peers to visit Britain. However, as this chapter shows, Dikko was not an accidental pioneer. His entanglement with Britain and his intimate cultural and personal connections to local and metropolitan institutions and personnel ironically began in the moment of the colonial conquest of Katsina, when he was a titled official in the emirate. Given the longevity and profundity of Dikko's subsequent immersion in colonial culture, his biography is a lens through which the transracial colonial kinships and travel-enabled cultural appropriations discussed throughout this book can be understood.

Clearly, Dikko featured in an elaborately scripted metropolitan travel event overseen by colonial planners, minders, and guides, but it would be problematic to consider him a mere prop in a colonial performance of power and courtship. The literature on imperial spectacle and, in particular, royal tours in Africa and the emerging historiography of imperial loyalism posit a rather passive agency for African participants, seeing these rituals largely as events to which African subjects were invited as spectators to be impressed and perhaps terrified.[126]

It is clear from both colonial sources and Dikko's own travel narratives that he was impressed by the visual, sonic, material, and infrastructural symbols of metropolitan modernity. However, the emir was not a naively impressionable colonial tourist who could consistently be used as a disembodied instrument in imperial political exhibitions or relied upon to be an unquestioning consumer of British metropolitan modernity.

Dikko was an active agent, if inconsistently so, in these trips, and he helped shape their itineraries while his preferences inflected the metropolitan tours. He also carefully curated his experiences and perspectives on the metropole in his diary, stamping his discursive imprimatur on representations of the trip and rendering the metropole in language and rhetoric filtered through his own ideological and political leanings and in a vernacular that privileged the idioms and comparative semiotics of his natal Hausa society. The trips discussed in this chapter, like others, should thus be considered in this dual frame as scripted performances of authority and modernity and as excursions animated and shaped in part by Dikko's own predilections and interests.

As emir, Dikko voraciously craved British symbols and institutions, but this desire stemmed from his own strategic vision. He sought to give Katsina a symbolic and modernist identity through a makeover underwritten by colonial cultural patronage and investments. Through his cultivation of British recreational and educational institutions, among other projects of modernization, and through his adventures in Britain, Dikko demonstrated the possibilities of leveraging aristocratic connections to colonial power to remake the emirate space and refashion the image of the emir as a modern aristocratic subaltern. By embracing British high culture and profusely proclaiming his admiration for British aristocratic symbols during his visits to metropolitan sites, Dikko also demonstrated his mastery of imperial protocol and ritualized hospitality. Ironically, this contrived universe of metropolitan imperial diplomatic protocols shielded Dikko from the racism associated with the 1924 empire exhibition to which he was invited and that he unwittingly helped to authenticate.

Dikko's transformation of Katsina through the deployment of imperial resources and connections signaled to his British colonial acquaintances that he was worth their courtship. The robustness of the metropolitan reception accorded Dikko was matched only by the amount of colonial socioeconomic investment he was able to attract to Katsina. The emir's subsequent travels to Britain, which are analyzed in chapter 4, deepened Dikko's imperial entanglements. They also brought his son and successor, Usman Nagogo, into the orbit of this imperial culture, continuing the legacy of Katsina as the Northern Nigerian epicenter of Britain's cultural encounter with emirate traditions.

Finally, Dikko's pioneering example of metropolitan travel established a pipeline for similar aristocratic metropolitan adventures. Other emirs and

Muslim chiefs soon began to use the same logistical networks and affective colonial connections to explore Britain.

Notes

1. NAK/KATPROF 496/Vol. II, Emir of Katsina—General Correspondence 1941–52, Circular Number 496/540.
2. H. R. Palmer, preface to *Sarkin Katsina Muhammadu Dikko, C.B.E., 1865–1944*, by Bello Kagara (Zaria, Nigeria: Gaskiya Corporation, 1951).
3. "The Emir's Stakes," *Edinburgh Evening News*, August 17, 1939, 6.
4. Interview with Hassan Kabir Usman, great-grandson of Emir Dikko, forty-four years, at Kofan Soro, Emir's Palace, February 18, 2015. See also interview with Alhaji Idris, grandson of Emir Dikko, fifty-four years, at Filin Sami Quarters, Katsina, December 29, 2014.
5. Dahiru Rabe, "The British Colonial Occupation and the Christian Missionary Activities in Katsina Emirate C. 1903–1936" (Seminar paper, History Department, Ahmadu Bello University, Zaria, Nigeria, 2011).
6. British National Archives, CO 383/187/11, Nigeria Original Correspondence, Proposed Pilgrimage to Mecca and Visit to England by Emir of Katsina.
7. Palmer, preface to *Sarkin Katsina*.
8. Frederick Lugard, *Collected Annual Reports of Northern Nigeria* (Lagos, Nigeria: His Majesty's Stationary Office), 1910–1911, 33–36; 1907–1908, 38.
9. British National Archives, CO 383/187/11, Emir of Katsina, Proposed Pilgrimage to Mecca and Visit to England by Emir of Katsina.
10. "The First Agricultural Show in West Central Africa," *Illustrated Sporting and Dramatic News*, June 17, 1911, 26.
11. "The First Agricultural Show."
12. See Albert Ozigi and Lawrence Ocho, *Education in Northern Nigeria* (London: Allen and Unwin, 1981); James Patrick Hubbard, *Education Under Colonial Rule: A History of Katsina College, 1921–42* (Lanham, MD: University Press of America, 2000).
13. Kamarudeen Imam and Dahiru Coomasie, *Usman Nagogo: A Biography of the Emir of Katsina, Sir Usman Nagogo* (Kaduna, Nigeria: Today Communications, 1995), 41.
14. Speech by Hugh Clifford, given on the occasion of the formal inauguration of Katsina Training College, March 5, 1922. Reproduced in Imam and Coomasie, *Usman Nagogo*, 44–49.
15. Mohammed Sani Umar, *Islam and Colonialism: Intellectual Responses of Muslims of Northern Nigeria to British Colonial Rule* (Leiden: Brill, 2006), 146–52.
16. NAK/KatProf/HIS/37, A History of Katsina Polo Club 1925–39.
17. NAK/KatProf/HIS/37, A History of Katsina Polo Club.
18. NAK/KatProf/HIS/37, A History of Katsina Polo Club.
19. NAK/KatProf/HIS/37, A History of Katsina Polo Club.
20. NAK/KatProf/HIS/37, A History of Katsina Polo Club.
21. Malam Bello Kagara, *Sarkin Katsina Alhaji Muhammadu Dikko, C.B.E., 1865–1944* (Zaria, Nigeria: Northern Nigerian Publishing Company, 1951), 81.
22. NAK/KatProf/HIS/37, A History of Katsina Polo Club.

23. NAK/KatProf/HIS/37, A History of Katsina Polo Club.
24. NAK/KatProf/HIS/37, A History of Katsina Polo Club.
25. Kagara, *Sarkin Katsina*, 26.
26. Kagara, *Sarkin Katsina*, 28.
27. Kagara, *Sarkin Katsina*, 28.
28. British National Archives, FO 141/699/5, From H. E. the Governor of the Sudan, dispatch # 69 (18-3-1933), Pilgrimage of the Emir of Katsina (of Nigeria) via Sudan, "An extract from the Diary of the Emir of Katsina's Visit to England and Mecca in 1921." Hereafter FO 141/699/5, "An extract from the Diary of the Emir of Katsina's Visit to England and Mecca in 1921."
29. FO 141/699/5, "An extract from the Diary of the Emir of Katsina's Visit to England and Mecca in 1921."
30. NAK/KatProf 1951/Diary of Journey to England and Mecca 1921. Hereafter *Dikko's Journal*. Entry for July 2, 1921.
31. *Dikko's Journal*, entry for July 2.
32. *Dikko's Journal*, entry for July 4.
33. Kagara, *Sarkin Katsina*, 28–29.
34. *Dikko's Journal*, entry for July 4.
35. *Dikko's Journal*, entry for July 4.
36. FO 141/699/5, "An extract from the Diary of the Emir of Katsina's Visit to England and Mecca in 1921."
37. *Dikko's Journal*, entry for July 4.
38. "The Emir at King Arthur's Court," *Diss Express and Norfolk and Suffolk Journal*, August 12, 1921, 2. See also FO 141/699/5, "An extract from the Diary of the Emir of Katsina's Visit to England and Mecca in 1921."
39. *Dikko's Journal*, entry for July 4.
40. *Dikko's Journal*, entry for July 4.
41. FO 141/699/5, "An extract from the Diary of the Emir of Katsina's Visit to England and Mecca in 1921."
42. FO 141/699/5, "An extract from the Diary of the Emir of Katsina's Visit to England and Mecca in 1921."
43. *Dikko's Journal*, entry for July 6.
44. "Wives Not to Be Allowed to Go Shopping; However, He May Take Them to the Zoo," *Dundee Evening Telegraph*, July 7, 1921, 4.
45. "Wives Not to Be Allowed."
46. FO 141/699/5, "An extract from the Diary of the Emir of Katsina's Visit to England and Mecca in 1921."
47. FO 141/699/5, "An extract from the Diary of the Emir of Katsina's Visit to England and Mecca in 1921."
48. *Dikko's Journal*, entry for July 7.
49. "The Emir's Tour Round London," *Dundee Courier*, July 9, 1921, 5.
50. "The Emir's Tour Round London."
51. *Dikko's Journal*, entry for July 7.
52. "The Emir's Tour Round London," *Dundee Courier*, July 9, 1921, 5.
53. *Dikko's Journal*, entry for July 8.
54. *Dikko's Journal*, entry for July 8.

55. *Dikko's Journal*, entry for July 8.
56. FO 141/699/5, "An extract from the Diary of the Emir of Katsina's Visit to England and Mecca in 1921."
57. *Dikko's Journal*, entry for July 8.
58. FO 141/699/5, "An extract from the Diary of the Emir of Katsina's Visit to England and Mecca in 1921."
59. FO 141/699/5, "An extract from the Diary of the Emir of Katsina's Visit to England and Mecca in 1921."
60. FO 141/699/5, "An extract from the Diary of the Emir of Katsina's Visit to England and Mecca in 1921."
61. *Dikko's Journal*, entry for July 9.
62. FO 141/699/5, "An extract from the Diary of the Emir of Katsina's Visit to England and Mecca in 1921."
63. "Emir Talk with the King: Nigerian Ruler's Racing Successes, Wonderful Buckingham Palace," *Dundee Evening Telegraph*, July 11, 1921, 9.
64. "Emir Talk with the King."
65. "Emir Talk with the King."
66. *Dikko's Journal*, entry for July 9.
67. *Dikko's Journal*, entry for July 9.
68. "Emir at the Palace, Amazed at the King's 'House of Houses,'" *Leeds Mercury*, July 11, 1921, 7.
69. *Dikko's Journal*, entry for July 9.
70. See Cannadine, *Ornamentalism*.
71. Sheikh Abubakar Gumi (with Ismaila Abubakar Tsiga), *Where I Stand* (Ibadan, Nigeria: Spectrum Books, 1992), 47.
72. "Wives Not to Be Allowed."
73. "Emir of Katsina: Visit of Dusky Chief to London," *Diss Express and Norfolk and Suffolk Journal*, July 15, 1921, 2.
74. "Wives Not to Be Allowed."
75. "The Emir at King Arthur's Court."
76. *Dikko's Journal*, entry for July 10.
77. *Dikko's Journal*, entry for July 10.
78. *Dikko's Journal*, entry for July 11.
79. *Dikko's Journal*, entry for July 11.
80. *Dikko's Journal*, entry for July 12.
81. *Dikko's Journal*, entry for July 12. The glasshouse now contains over four thousand plant species and has been declared a UNESCO World Heritage site.
82. *Dikko's Journal*, entry for July 12.
83. "Emir of Katsina: Visit of Dusky Chief to London."
84. FO 141/699/5, "An extract from the Diary of the Emir of Katsina's Visit to England and Mecca in 1921."
85. FO 141/699/5, "An extract from the Diary of the Emir of Katsina's Visit to England and Mecca in 1921."
86. *Dikko's Journal*, entry for July 13.
87. "Emir's Flying 'Sensation,'" *Leeds Mercury*, July 4, 1921, 6.
88. *Dikko's Journal*, entry for July 13.
89. "Distinguished Visitors," *Lancashire Daily Post*, July 15, 1921, 4.

90. *Dikko's Journal*, entry for July 14.
91. "Emir's Impression of London," *Scotsman*, July 16, 1921, 9.
92. "The Grateful Emir," *Sheffield Daily Telegraph*, October 21, 1921, 6.
93. "The Grateful Emir."
94. "The Grateful Emir."
95. "Emir Down a Coal Mine," *Lancashire Daily Post*, October 28, 1921.
96. "The Most Terrible Weapon," *Lancashire Evening Post*, October 29, 1921, 2.
97. "Impressed by Coal," *Newcastle Daily Chronicle*, November 3, 1921, 2.
98. See Parsons, *King Khama*, 5.
99. Parsons, *King Khama*.
100. "Emir's Brass Bed," *Lancashire Daily Post*, November 3, 1921, 2.
101. British National Archives, FO 141/699/5, From the Residency in Cairo, "Visit of the Emir of Katsina."
102. Kagara, *Sarkin Katsina*, 55.
103. Kagara, *Sarkin Katsina*, 55.
104. Kagara, *Sarkin Katsina*, 57.
105. "Ancient Visitors to Plymouth," *Western Morning News and Mercury*, December 22, 1924, 3.
106. "Personalities of the Week: People in the Public Eye," *Illustrated London News*, September 20, 1924, 27.
107. Kagara, *Sarkin Katsina*, 57.
108. "Shy Wembley Visitors," *Leeds Mercury*, September 17, 1924. The quoted commentary is from the photo caption.
109. "Personalities of the Week: People in the Public Eye."
110. British Empire Exhibition, Official Guide, 1924 (Special Collections Research Center, Henry Madden Library, California State University, Fresno), 76.
111. British Empire Exhibition, Official Guide.
112. Timothy Mitchell, "Orientalism and the Exhibitionary Order," in *Colonialism and Culture*, ed. Nicholas Dirks, 289–318 (Ann Arbor: University of Michigan Press, 1992), 290.
113. Mitchell, "Orientalism and the Exhibitionary Order," 292–93.
114. Mitchell, "Orientalism and the Exhibitionary Order," 292–93.
115. Mitchell, "Orientalism and the Exhibitionary Order," 294.
116. Mitchell, "Orientalism and the Exhibitionary Order," 293.
117. FO 141/699/5, From the Residency in Cairo, "Visit of the Emir of Katsina."
118. Anne Clendinning, "On the British Empire Exhibition, 1924–25," Branchcollective.org: http://www.branchcollective.org/?ps_articles=anne-clendinning-on-the-british-empire-exhibition-1924-25 (accessed March 18, 2019).
119. Clendinning, "On the British Empire Exhibition."
120. Clendinning, "On the British Empire Exhibition."
121. Clendinning, "On the British Empire Exhibition."
122. Clendinning, "On the British Empire Exhibition."
123. Clendinning, "On the British Empire Exhibition."
124. Kagara, *Sarkin Katsina*, 55.
125. Kagara, *Sarkin Katsina*, 55.
126. Andrew Apter, "On Imperial Spectacle: The Dialectics of Seeing in Colonial Nigeria," *Comparative Studies in Society and History* 44, no. 3 (2002): 564–96, 584–88; Terence Ranger, "The Invention of Tradition in Colonial Africa," in *The Invention of Tradition*,

11th ed., ed. Terence Ranger and Eric Hobsbawn, 211–62 (Cambridge: University of Cambridge Press, 2003); Sapire, "African Loyalism and Its Discontent"; Charles V. Reed, *Royal Tourists, Colonial Subjects, and the Making of a British World, 1860–1911* (Manchester, UK: Manchester University Press, 2017); Philip Buckner, "The Royal Tour of 1901 and the Construction of Imperial Identity in South Africa," *South African Historical Journal* 41, no. 1 (1999): 324–48.

3

EMIRS IN BRITAIN

Mapping Aristocratic Colonial Itineraries

> The world begins and ends in London.
> —Yahaya Ibn Haliru

THIS CHAPTER FOCUSES ON THE 1930S, THE EARLY period of Northern Nigerian aristocratic explorations of Britain. The Northern Nigerian travelers discussed in this chapter were not the first to embark on trips to Britain. That honor, as indicated in the previous chapter, belongs to the emir of Katsina, Muhammadu Dikko. The importance of the 1930s and the journeys to Britain in this period lies in the persistence of the imperial politics of subaltern aristocratic cultivation during a difficult economic period. The economic depression may have provided new relevance to this political courtship since colonial officials needed traditional rulers to keep their restive, suffering subjects under control. The midcolonial period represented a new beginning for British colonialism in Africa—a time to reinvigorate the colonial project and reassure their African allies, even as economic depression undermined colonial ambitions and threatened socioeconomic and political stability.

The chapter analyzes two major aristocratic voyages to Britain undertaken by Northern Nigeria's leading Muslim rulers during this period of colonial instability, the colonial logistics that enabled these trips to occur, and the complex interactions and discourses that accompanied these travels. The chapter also anticipates the contours of subaltern travel to Britain in the 1940s and 1950s, laying out some of the features and exploratory bromides established in the 1930s and carried on to the later periods.

Mapping the Mecca–London Itinerary of Atta Ibrahim

Money was scarce in the 1930s, and the colonial bureaucracy scrambled to sustain its administrative operations amid the financial distress.[1] Travel to the metropole, which required expensive logistical arrangements, was restricted to the most prestigious emirs in Northern Nigeria. In the economic crunch, only politically influential emirs were considered worthy of overseas travel that required official British expenditure. The emirs discussed in this chapter and Muhammadu Dikko, the subject of chapters 2 and 4, constituted the cohort of aristocratic travelers to Britain in this period because of their privileged status in the colonial system. One Muslim ruler from central Nigeria, Atta Ibrahim Onoruoiza, was the rare exception to this Depression-era restriction on overseas travel.

Ibrahim, the attah, or paramount ruler, of the Ebira [Igbirra] ethnic nation in Central Nigeria, was an unlikely political pilgrim to Britain.[2] He was not the most prestigious or influential traditional ruler in Central Nigeria; that status arguably belonged to the attah of Igala. However, Ibrahim had one factor in his favor: he was a Muslim, while the attah of Igala at the time, Obaje Ocheje, was not. Given the familiar bias of British colonizers for Muslim kingship as a preferred medium of indirect rule,[3] officials came to regard Ibrahim as an honorary emir, especially since the majority of his Ebira subjects had embraced Islam by this time. As a result, his court enjoyed more British patronage than that of the attah of Igala.

Ibrahim's Muslim identity alone was not enough to secure a metropolitan travel slot; another factor facilitated his trip to Britain. He was a man of ample financial means, having inherited, as he was eager to tell his subjects and colonial officials alike, a substantial estate from his wealthy mother. This wealth enabled Ibrahim to expand and accessorize his palace. Ibrahim's palace and Native Authority complex in Okene were larger and more aesthetically appealing than the palaces of most emirs in Northern Nigeria. This attracted the attention of British colonial officials since, for them, royal prestige was bound up with the aesthetic grandeur of a ruler's court. Given this imperial attitude, Ibrahim had no competition in terms of other candidates from central Nigeria to be considered for a trip to Britain in this period. His wealth had brought him colonial recognition and some metropolitan attention, a recurring prelude to local aristocrats being invited to Britain. Ibrahim's personal affluence meant that funding was not an obstacle to his plan to visit Britain during the economic crisis.

Like all aristocrats intending to visit Britain, Ibrahim had to formally apply to the Northern Nigerian colonial government for approval. On December 27, 1929, the secretary to the northern provinces approved the request.[4] Under the terms of the approval, the traditional ruler would be accompanied on the trip by his senior wife, Maimuna; his waziri, or chief adviser, Lawal; and his driver, Musa. Ibrahim and his party would first detour to Mecca to perform the Muslim pilgrimage before heading to Britain for a three-week visit. Their departure from Nigeria was scheduled for February 1930. Prior logistical preparations for the complicated itinerary included making elaborate bookings through the British travel agency Thomas Cook.[5] The company would take care of hotel accommodations; paperwork regarding embarkation, transfer, and disembarkation formalities; and other travel logistics. Ibrahim contracted another British firm, Messrs. Horsefield, to handle his transportation, sightseeing, and touring in Britain.[6] The preparations also entailed making deposits for purchases in Britain and logistical expenses. Not being Roman literate, Ibrahim relied on colonial officials in his district to plan his trip. District Officer Effrench, of the Igbirra Division, handled the logistical details on Ibrahim's behalf, paying the total expenses, estimated at 500 pounds, from Ibrahim's own personal funds.

Ibrahim had mapped out his own plans for Britain, making a list of luxury metropolitan goods he wanted to buy. Some of these plans featured prominently in the missive the resident of Kabba Province, H. B. James, sent to guides and travel agents in London apprising them of the trip's details and the expectations of their logistical role.[7] In this memo, James confirmed that Ibrahim had paid the required 500 pounds from "a very considerable fortune." According to James, this money would be sent to the agents to hold for Ibrahim, who would be given whatever balance remained from the deposit after the expenses associated with his long, meandering itinerary. This money was enough, James believed, to satiate Ibrahim's desires for high-end metropolitan goods. In particular, Ibrahim was interested in purchasing a luxury car: "Sunbeam for preference, but he has no objection to a big Humber."[8] Whether to underscore his reputation as a wealthy aristocrat or to preempt and answer local gossip about the funding for the trip,[9] Ibrahim seemed eager to declare that his adventure was independently funded, not only broadcasting this fact to his subjects but also telling the resident in his postvisit report that "the expenses of this journey were all paid by myself and . . . I did not require any assistance from the Igbirra Native Treasury."[10]

Like all Northern Nigerian aristocratic travelers to Britain at this time, Ibrahim had a rotating retinue of British officials shadowing and guiding him throughout his journey. This imperial network of guides, logistical fixers, diplomats, and sociopolitical navigators eased his path as he made his way to and around the metropole. Ibrahim and his fellow tourists were accompanied to Lagos by A. C. Patrick, an assistant treasurer with the Igbirra Native Authority who had been instructed to help the travelers, none of whom spoke English. Their departure for Lagos followed a briefing session with District Officer Effrench, who advised Ibrahim, a first-time overseas traveler, to offer tips to stewards and waiters for their services, insist on the correct exchange rates between the British pound and other currencies, observe proper customs and immigration procedures, and avoid "the hazards of tricksters and such confidence men."[11]

Ibrahim and his entourage would travel by road to Lagos and then sail from there to Marseille. From Marseille they would travel to Port Said, Egypt, and then take a train to Cairo. In Cairo they would obtain a visa from the government of the Hejaz and then depart for Suez, from where they would sail to Jeddah. Upon the completion of the hajj, they would return directly to Marseille from Jeddah and then sail to London via Paris.

Their eventual itinerary differed slightly from the proposed one. The group sailed from Lagos on the SS *Hoggar* on March 1, 1930, to their first stop in Marseille. In Marseille they were accorded the diplomatic protocols facilitated by prior British arrangements. After spending a night in a prebooked hotel in Marseille, the group sailed to the Saudi port city of Jeddah and traveled to Medina and then to Mecca by road to perform the hajj. Their pilgrimage completed, they sailed for Marseille on May 24, with stopovers in Tor and Beirut. Demonstrating the mobilization of British imperial resources and interterritorial bureaucracy in support of this and similar trips, a flurry of triangular telegraphic exchanges between the British representative in Jedda, the consul in Suez, and the consul general in Beirut helped the Colonial Office track Ibrahim's movement as he and his party made their way from the Hejaz to Beirut, and then to Alexandria, before finally transferring to the SS *Champollion* en route to Marseille on June 13.[12] Upon arriving in Marseille on June 18, Ibrahim and his entourage were met by C. A. Woodhouse, the resident of Zaria Province, who had been instructed by the secretary for the northern provinces to welcome the group back to Marseille and attend to their logistical needs there. Woodhouse arranged for hotel accommodations for the party for the night of June 18.

Emirs in Britain | 137

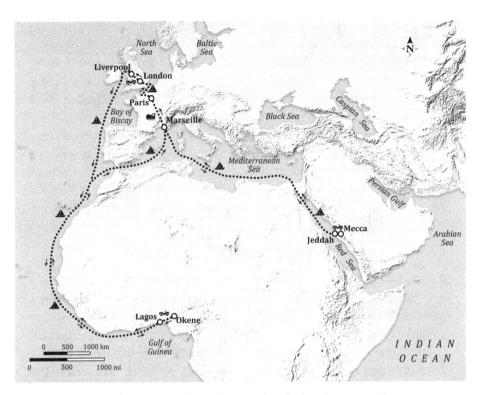

Map 3.1. Itinerary of the journey of Atta of Ebira, Alhaji Ibrahim Onoruoiza Chogudo, to the Hejaz and Britain in 1930.

Together with the representative of Thomas Cook, Woodhouse facilitated Ibrahim's disembarkation and customs procedures. He and the Thomas Cook agent then took the visitors to their prebooked hotel. Later, Woodhouse and Ibrahim visited the local Thomas Cook office to finalize their transportation to London (map 3.1). Afterward, Woodhouse took Ibrahim shopping.

At this stage of the circuitous trip to Britain, Woodhouse's role morphed from logistics coordinator to tour guide and back again. He was an all-purpose imperial facilitator in a complicated itinerary that leveraged the political and diplomatic tentacles of the British Empire. With Woodhouse as a guide, Ibrahim and his fellow travelers toured the Palais de Longchamps and the "miniature Zoological Garden" in Marseille.[13]

The next day the team traveled to Paris by train. In France, Ibrahim and his party experienced some of the exoticizing public gestures that awaited them in Britain. On the train to Paris, several of the French passengers "showed a kindly interest in" the visitors and "brought their children to see and be introduced to [Ibrahim's] wife," Maimuna.[14] By prior arrangement, they were met at the train station by agents of Thomas Cook and driven to the Prince Albert Hotel. Their touristic layover in Paris afforded them an opportunity to immerse themselves in some Parisian adventures. They were driven around Paris in a rented car, touring such iconic Paris landmarks as the Eiffel Tower, the quay, and the shopping district, as well as a race car display that included the first car to cross the Sahara from north to south.[15] Later that day, the group left Paris for London, arriving at Victoria Station at 7:15 p.m., and were promptly driven to the Burnside Hotel.

Beholding Britain, Buying Britain

The archival record indicates that Ibrahim had not envisioned an itinerary in Britain beyond the circuits of shopping and entertainment. The Ebira ruler had apparently expressed to colonial minders only a vague desire to see and experience entertainment-focused sights, but even this expressed desire seemed secondary to his passion for luxury shopping, which became the recurring indulgence of visiting Northern Nigerian aristocrats. The absence of a fixed prior itinerary allowed Woodhouse to cobble together a rough program of sightseeing for the visitors.

Woodhouse designed a touring program that allowed for shopping and entertainment while also accommodating the familiar colonial propaganda of shepherding visiting traditional rulers to factories that refined raw materials from their domains into finished metropolitan goods.[16] The eventual program included "visits to industrial centers, where it was anticipated that a person of [Ibrahim's] intelligence might with profit to himself and his District see something of the great manufacturing organizations of England, especially those connected with the export and import trade of Nigeria."[17] Woodhouse arranged visits to the Dunlop Company and the factories of the United Africa Company, both iconic British imperial brands with much visibility in Nigeria. The official itinerary was just that, however. Everyone involved in the trip recognized that the final decision about what the visitors would see and do rested with Ibrahim. For, as Woodhouse himself stated, the itinerary he designed was "provisional and dependent on what [Ibrahim] himself wished to do, as the tour was being made at his own expense."[18]

Of the three weeks the group spent in Britain, twelve days were spent observing Woodhouse's itinerary, with the rest of the time spent exploring Ibrahim's interests: cars and shopping for luxury goods. The group visited Windsor Castle, touring the grounds of the royal abode and taking a walk in nearby Windsor Park. They also visited Aldershot to watch the Military Tattoo, an entertaining military spectacle that would have satiated Ibrahim's stated desire for metropolitan entertainment and pageantry. The group visited the Zoological Garden in London, with colonial guides obtaining tickets for them ahead of the visit. Ibrahim's entourage was joined at the London Zoo by several former colonial officials who had served in the Nigerian colonial service and were acquainted with the Ebira ruler from administrative stints in Northern Nigeria. The former colonial officials came along to renew their acquaintance with Ibrahim and because they had volunteered to help with logistical details.[19]

A mild drama occurred at the Zoological Garden when Captain Bying-Hall, a former resident of Kabba Province, showed Ibrahim and his party a lion and told them it was from Lokoja, Nigeria. It turned out, much to Ibrahim's amazement, that this was the only surviving member of a set of three lion cubs presented to Ibrahim after their capture in his district. The Ebira ruler had, in turn, presented them as gifts to the Prince of Wales when he visited Nigeria in 1925. The prince had no way of caring for the cubs and so had transferred them to the London Zoological Garden, where two had died. As an avid recreational hunter with several trophies of earlier game kills displayed in his court, the sight of the lion he had last seen five years ago thrilled Ibrahim.

The scene also represented the culmination of a ritual of exchange practiced between Northern Nigerian rulers and British officials, as seen in their masculine fraternity of game hunting. From Ibrahim's perspective, the encounter with the lion recalled the moment of his connection with a visiting English prince. There, in the Zoological Garden of London, was the living, breathing evidence of that imperial kinship. Ibrahim was not the only Northern Nigerian traditional ruler who toured the London zoo at the behest of his British hosts. On the contrary, that site was a constant presence in the itinerary of visiting aristocratic tourists because the zoo, with its tropical, exotic animals from far-flung colonies, was a "product of . . . colonial penetration,"[20] a spatial symbol of domination that simultaneously enabled British minders to pay "symbolic tribute" to colonized Africans "in the form of animals" sourced from colonial domains.[21] In engaging with the zoo as a site of imperial relational nostalgia, a place to remember a moment of aristocratic kinship over game hunting, was Ibrahim blind to the symbolic power of the zoo as a forceful appropriation of the fauna of Nigeria? It is difficult to tell, but it is clear from the story of the cub turned adult lion that the zoo was a more complex space for visiting African colonial subjects than the imperial politics of its emergence would suggest.

June 23 and 24 were set aside in the itinerary for the visiting ruler to purchase his desired metropolitan goods. The colonial records state that Ibrahim had intended to purchase a used Sunbeam car. He changed his mind after taking a test drive in a new six-cylinder Morris-Oxford. He traveled to Hampstead to purchase the vehicle, which cost 299 pounds. Ibrahim subsequently made arrangements at Elder Dempster's London office for the car to be shipped to Lagos through the port of Liverpool on the same vessel scheduled to convey the visitors back to Lagos, the MV *Apapa*.[22] Since the purchase of a car was the most important item on Ibrahim's list of metropolitan touristic activities, the purchase of the Morris probably represented the highlight of the chief's visit to Britain. Ibrahim also purchased an expensive hunting rifle that required a license from the British Board of Trade before it could be exported. The license obtained, Ibrahim arranged for it to be shipped to the Lagos office of Jeffery's, the British rifle company. There, the rifle's range would be upgraded, and it would be fitted with a telescope, as Ibrahim requested. Ibrahim paid the cost of these upgrades along with the shipping cost, ensuring that when he returned to Lagos, the rifle with all the requested improvements would be waiting for him.[23]

Ibrahim and his group toured the Tower of London, where they were shown royal weapons of various kinds as well as the crown jewels and regalia. While there, they witnessed the Tower Bridge opening to allow a ship on the Thames to pass. The visitors toured the British Museum and then visited Halbern Empire to watch a circus with various acts. Other touring destinations included the London office of the Bank of British West Africa, where Ibrahim and his group encountered an escalator for the first time and showed a mix of wonder and excitement at the ability of a staircase to move. Riding the escalator, however, proved a challenge, as Ibrahim—unfamiliar with its workings, with his flowing royal regalia caught in the crevice between the stairs—"nearly came to grief."[24] The paramount ruler and his entourage also secured a rare appointment to visit an aircraft manufacturing plant, the Handley-Page Works at Crichelwood. There, guided by one Mr. Mackenzie, they observed an aircraft being built for addition to the fleet of Imperial Airways.[25]

Birmingham

On June 30, the party left London for Birmingham. Upon their arrival, the local press corralled them into a photo session in which Ibrahim and his entourage were photographed together and individually. During the photo session, Ibrahim resisted attempts by some members of the press, through small talk, to elicit his opinion on whether local English girls should play tennis with stockings. This issue apparently was contentious in Birmingham at that time. Whether the inquiries were a genuine attempt to solicit the opinion of an outsider and foreigner or a calculated attempt to rhetorically entrap the paramount ruler, Ibrahim successfully and politely declined to comment, using humor as an escape.[26]

The press in Birmingham was relentless in bringing what Woodhouse described as "publicity and mild lionising" to Ibrahim and his party. In addition to following Ibrahim and his entourage around, reporters would call Woodhouse for information on the visitors to round out their stories, but they would sensationally mangle the facts he gave them to produce what he described as a "considerable amount of fiction."[27] The unsettling public gaze other Nigerian visitors encountered, which began in France for Ibrahim's entourage, escalated in Birmingham. On one occasion, as the group toured the Hercules Cycle and Motor Company at Aston, a large crowd gathered around the visitors, and the police had to restrain the gawkers. On another occasion, when Ibrahim and his wife went shopping, crowds of Birmingham residents gathered around them, some following them as they entered and exited shops.[28]

In Birmingham the party toured a car assembly factory of the Wolseley Motor Works and watched from the factory floor the process of building a car from start to finish; as Woodhouse explained the various steps in Hausa to Ibrahim, the chief, in turn, explained them to the members of his group in the Ebira language. This was a layered translatory exercise. Aside from the potential for details getting lost, it was also an "exhausting process," especially when information needed to be shouted and passed to different people through different linguistic mediums in "the neighborhood of some particularly high-powered and vociferous machine."[29]

The group also visited the Morris Commercial Car Company, where they observed as various models of Morris trucks and cars were test driven over multiple simulated terrains to determine their endurance and tenacity. After watching cars being put through punishing driving routines, Ibrahim is reported to have remarked that American car models, which were widely sold in colonial Nigeria, would not withstand such tough conditions.[30] He may have been trying to flatter his British hosts or, given his intense interest in cars, may have been exhibiting an educated sentiment derived from his own experiences with different car models. Ibrahim was a mildly obsessive car enthusiast even if he did not view his affection for automobiles as an obsession. At the Morris factory, Ibrahim enthusiastically asked questions about car components, discussed ordering spare parts for Morris cars in Nigeria with factory managers, and engaged his guides in informed car talk.

Ibrahim and his fellow tourists visited the Dunlop factory in Birmingham, where they witnessed the process of making a variety of tires. Ibrahim used his visit to indulge his taste for cars and related automobile products. On June 27, executives of the Hercules Cycle and Motor Company picked up the group and drove them in luxurious Rolls-Royces to the company's car manufacturing plant in Aston.[31] Upon completing the perfunctory photo sessions and welcoming niceties—in which Ibrahim received a gift of a bicycle and his wife was given two motorized scooters for their children—the visitors toured the factory. Later that day, they were taken on a driving tour of Kenilworth, Worcester, Broadway, and Shakespeare's birthplace, Stratford-upon-Avon, as well as other landmarks and historical institutions.[32] As a poignant illustration of the diverging mentalities and interests of the visitors and their colonial minders, on the drive through Stratford, Ibrahim and his entourage were more interested in the size of the English countryside chickens than they were in the town's association with a prominent literary figure. Sensing this, Woodhouse, somewhat deflated, abandoned his plan "to explain the reasons which make Stratford famous."[33] The visitors' preference for chickens over Shakespeare is a compelling signifier of the ways African aristocratic visitors confounded the touristic assumptions and guidebooks of colonial minders and explored Britain in the context of their own predilections and desires. Woodhouse's frustration at not being able to deliver his planned lecture on Shakespeare as they drove through Stratford is another illustration of this divergence.

Metropolitan Explorations

From Birmingham, Ibrahim and his party traveled to Liverpool, with brief sightseeing stops at Birkenhead, Chester, Wolverhampton, and Whitechurch. While in Liverpool, they visited the vast Unilever industrial complex at Port Sunlight, where they were given a tour of the factory in which palm oil imported from Ebiraland and other parts of Nigeria was transformed into soap and other finished products that were then exported to Nigeria. The party visited several parts of the Unilever village, which housed the factories, the employees' living quarters, schools, and recreational amenities for workers and their families. Ibrahim and his group visited one of the schools in the Port Sunlight village. The party then toured the Liverpool dockyard.[34] Also, in Liverpool, Ibrahim and his entourage toured the cotton mills, with the local press describing the chief as "a picturesque figure with his turban head-dress."[35]

On July 1, Ibrahim and his party departed for Manchester to tour textile factories there; the visit was organized by the Calico Printers Association, whose leader, Lennox Lee, received the visitors in his office on Oxford Street. This tour proved particularly resonant for the visitors because Ebiraland in Nigeria was and still is one of Nigeria's main cloth-making regions, where the weaving and dyeing arts had been developed over several centuries. At textile factories in Manchester, the group saw how metropolitan-manufactured textiles, which were exported to Nigeria and other colonies, were made. At the end of the tour, they received printed handkerchiefs as souvenirs. Ibrahim and his party also visited Messrs Bibby's Oil and Cake Mill. There, they observed the process by which groundnuts, palm kernels, and cotton seeds from West Africa were processed into oil and oil cake.

Ibrahim is reported to have stood out in the rainy Manchester weather as his attendant held "a carefully-rolled umbrella for use by [Ibrahim] and his mistress."[36] Metropolitan reportage on the tour of the oil-cake and seed-crushing mill is faithful to Ibrahim's knack for inquiring studiously about observed metropolitan processes:

> By the intelligent questions which he put at intervals to Mr. John Bibby, who acted as guide in the mills, the African visitor showed himself quite at home amongst the raw products of his own country which are utilised in the big mills, and he explained the various processes to Mamouna [*sic*], his wife. The whole party stood entranced before the vast power-hammer, weighing several tons, which was put into action for their benefit; and they gasped with

admiration at an endless-chain, with steps fastened at intervals, by which workmen were ascending from floor to floor. The tour included visits to the oil tanks, the toiler-home—hot enough even for an African chieftain—end the laboratories.[37]

In this passage from the *Liverpool Echo*, the participatory agency of Ibrahim comes across, defying the infantilizing filter of the British journalist who wrote the story. Ibrahim was not only inquisitive about the workings of metropolitan technology, he was also an interrogator of it, not merely accepting to be awed by loud, vast machines but also seeking to know the logic of their functionality. In addition, Ibrahim was an instant interpreter of British factory technology, assuming the position of vernacular expert on and interpreter of metropolitan machines and manufacturing infrastructure to his wife, Maimuna.

Ibrahim's last two days in Britain were largely spent on last-minute shopping in and around Liverpool, their departure city. The colonial report on the paramount ruler's visit describes July 2 as a frantic day of purchases, ending with the Ebira ruler amassing such a high volume of metropolitan goods that he required two taxis to carry them to the dockyard.[38] There, the goods, most of them high-end purchases, were loaded onto the ship MV *Apapa* along with earlier purchases. With its cargo of aristocratic visitors and metropolitan goods, the MV *Apapa* arrived in Lagos on July 16.

Was Ibrahim an impressionable imperial tourist? Was he a blank slate of curiosity and expectation that Britain could indelibly exert itself on, or was he a self-aware participant in a colonial cultural transaction marked by melodrama and mutual performance? Ibrahim's metropolitan shopping list indicates a level of preparation and a prior cognitive familiarity with Britain. As a wealthy chief, Ibrahim was already in the orbit of British colonial modernity, represented most notably in the Northern Nigerian colonial context by machines, infrastructures, and automobiles. He was thus not encountering colonial modernity or its technological representations for the first time. This mitigates the exaggerated reactions he reportedly had to colonial technologies, and yet colonial archival retellings of Ibrahim's itinerary were steeped in the dramatic language of imperial awe.

Material and symbolic repositories of metropolitan modernity, particularly the workings of strange machines, certainly inflected the impressions travelers like Ibrahim developed about Britain. However, to fully appreciate the mobile colonial theater of sightseeing encounters and adventures, one must explore the vernacular renditions of the metropole in local aristocratic and popular imaginations. This world of cognition, narration, and aesthetic performance foregrounded Ibrahim's metropolitan encounters. It also supplied a template for aristocrats who visited Britain after him and sought to rhetorically—and retroactively—reinforce circulating idioms of metropolitan wonder.

In the colonizers' view, the "object [of the trip] was achieved" since the tours encompassed "a certain amount of entertainment with inspection of some of the Works and Businesses, whose operators impinged on the Nigerian trade."[39] This colonial self-congratulation did not take into account the impressions of the visitors or the obvious and subtle problems Ibrahim and his party encountered in Britain—some clearly related to their race and African origin.

Some of the hotels the African tourists stayed in were comfortable and the services satisfactory, but others, such as the Burnside Hotel in London, proved problematic, and the management "seemed at a loss how to deal with the visitors."[40] The hotel booked for the visitors in Liverpool—"a dark, dingy and depressing little hotel"—was so bad that an embarrassed Woodhouse, reacting to the complaints of the tourists, angrily confronted the agent of Thomas Cook, who "said that he fully realized the shortcomings of the Hotel, but that he had great difficulty in securing accommodation anywhere, as the colour question was somewhat acute in Liverpool and none of the big Hotels were willing to receive the party."[41]

Metropolitan racism not only marred the experience of Ibrahim and his party, it also exposed them, despite the seemingly careful choreographing of their visit by colonial planners, to what Woodhouse described as "a variety of welcome," a deceptively elegant way of expressing the at best uneven and at worst inhospitable reception the visitors received in Britain. When colonial epistolary accounts of the visit exited the realm of routine colonial correspondence and entered the more exclusive zone of confidential reporting, the result was a more blunt assessment of failures, missed opportunities, and unflattering representations of the visitors. While Ibrahim and his entourage were portrayed in the regular report as dignified aristocrats who conducted themselves with grace and class in metropolitan spaces, the confidential report Woodhouse sent to the Colonial Office discussed how "their lack of sophistication as regards dealing with English food with the appropriate cutlery sometimes caused them some embarrassment."[42]

In the confidential missives of colonizers, performances of imperial courtesy dissolved into the familiar casual racism of colonialism. In this realm, Ibrahim and his group emerged as little more than bumbling African visitors who would complain that they were cold at night but would neglect the "European custom of getting into bed instead of laying on the top of it" and who preferred to get water with a jug when bathing rather than "pouring water into the basin."[43] In the less guarded space of the confidential report, we also get a direct admission that the trip planners had, in fact, failed to deliver what they promised the visitors—in particular, that "several things, which [Ibrahim] required and which they had promised to have ready, when he visited Manchester, were not forthcoming."[44] Unlike some of the emirs discussed in this book, Ibrahim did not author a journal or a travel memoir, so we have no direct account of his impressions about his visit to Britain. However, given the unusually self-indicting assessment of the trip by Woodhouse in the confidential report, it is safe to assume that some of the problems and logistical blunders referenced would not have been lost on Ibrahim and his entourage.

London in Vernacular

In 1939, Yahaya Ibn Haliru, the respected Muslim ruler and emir of Gwandu,[45] penned a travelogue in the local Hausa-language newspaper *Gaskiya ta fi Kwabo*. Ibn Haliru had accompanied his predecessor, Usman Ibn Haliru, to England in 1934 when the latter—along with the sultan of Sokoto, Hassan dan Mu'azu Ahmadu, and the emir of Kano, Abdullahi Bayero—visited Britain on a sightseeing adventure at the invitation of the Colonial Office. Sokoto, Gwandu, and Kano were the most important states in the loose precolonial Islamic federation of the Sokoto Caliphate. Yahaya Ibn Haliru wrote his travelogue to reminisce about the experience of travel to and around England, seeking to recapture the sights, sounds, and cultures of London as he and the other visitors had experienced them.

After discussing the daily routines of their stay in England, the highlight of which was a visit with King George V in Buckingham Palace, Yahaya concluded his piece with a memorable punch line: "Duniya na birnin London" (The world begins and ends in London).[46] What did Yahaya seek to convey to his readers through his hyperbolic adulation of London as the center of the world? What cultural and political economies authorized such a glowing endorsement of the human, technological, and cultural registers of Britain? Yahaya and other emirs had aspirational and emotive connections to London, but probing the inner meaning of Yahaya's declaration requires an exploration of the colonial arrangements that demanded and rewarded a reverential relationship between African colonial auxiliaries and metropolitan spaces, material culture, and institutions.

I suggest that historians read Yahaya Ibn Haliru's rhetorical and narrative flourishes as indicators of a neglected but fairly common transracial colonial kinship that linked colonies to the metropole. Yahaya's locution signified the seduction of the material modernity of empire—a fetishization of metropolitan objects, infrastructures, and experiences that inspired and informed highfalutin recollections among privileged colonial subjects. Yahaya's travelogue was both a document of self-representation and a commentary on colonial metropolitan life. Perspectival recollections of these phenomena reinforced the narrator's own status claims within Northern Nigerian colonial society.

Yahaya belonged to a colonial culture in which instrumental agency rested with both British colonial officials and trusted African allies. Patronage and protection were expected, if unwritten, aspects of colonial business. This culture, in turn, generated a shared concept of modernity that mapped onto the physical and cultural space of London. Northern Nigeria's Muslim elites and aristocrats enjoyed a mutually beneficial relationship of patronage and clientage with British colonial overlords. British colonizers conferred protection and recognition on a cadre of Muslim Hausa rulers, essentially outsourcing the business of colonization to them in the Muslim rulers' own domains. The British colonizers conscripted the Hausa rulers to replicate this system of protection and obligations in various non-Muslim districts of Northern Nigeria.[47]

British colonial patronage of local Muslim aristocrats came in several forms. The British colonial bureaucracy in Nigeria cultivated Muslim rulers, administrative allies, and intellectuals with elaborate gestures aimed at facilitating and consolidating the ties of protection and obligation between the colonizers and trusted Muslim elites. Gifts and ceremonial recognition from the former to the latter constituted another layer of patronage. These gestures included sightseeing trips to London. The British intended to awe the Muslim loyalists with the grandeur of Britain and reassure them of the technological and aesthetic signs of British imperial protection. Scripted performances of the magnificence of empire and metropolitan hospitality were crucial in this endeavor of impressing and seducing subaltern allies. Visiting Northern Nigerian allies were exposed to the razzmatazz of metropolitan modernity through guided sightseeing tours.

However, the Muslim tourists had their own agendas, their own expectations, and their own purposes for embarking on these trips. Muslim tourists expressed these parallel agendas in strategically written travel narratives published in local Hausa-language newspapers and magazines. Haliru's narrative was one example of this trend. These complex landscapes and palates of reception intersected with the politics of metropolitan visual and performative propaganda to produce travel texts rich in insights and commentary on the subtleties of metropolitan life, the material culture of imperial Britain, and its consumption in the colonies. Travel to Britain was a major sociopolitical event for individual emirs. When a group of emirs traveled there together, the social valence of the occasion was magnified.

The Caliphate Goes to England

In June 1934, the three Muslim rulers of Sokoto, Gwandu, and Kano, along with a party of fifteen servants and aides, arrived in England by ship after more than two weeks at sea (map 3.2). The visitors were elegantly robed in flowing "Muslim" gowns. The *Gloucestershire Echo* prefaced its story on the emirs' visit with the melodramatic words, "The glamour of the East enveloped Plymouth yesterday."[48] Another report described the emirs and their retinue as "tall and dignified [and] wearing high turbans and long flowing robes of blue, gold, and white," stating that they projected "a strange spectacle" as they "walked through the busy docks."[49] The emirs were later treated to a daylight fireworks display organized in their honor at the South Parade Pier.[50]

Other items in the visitors' sartorial ensemble advertised their Muslim and royal pedigrees, including their scepters of office and their attendants' conspicuous clutching of "scores of tin kettles containing the special water with which the party wash their hands and faces before unrolling their prayer mats and making their solemn obeisance five times a day."[51] The party was guided by Captain H. D. Tupper Carey, who saw to their every need during the voyage—a task described in a colonial report on the trip as an "arduous duty."[52]

A large welcome party awaited the emirs and their retinues at London's Paddington train station. The welcome party demonstrated the centrality of pageantry to British imperial cultivation of subaltern elite support, and the ceremonial rituals of hospitality advertised the importance of patronizing allies among the colonized. The caliber of actors who waited

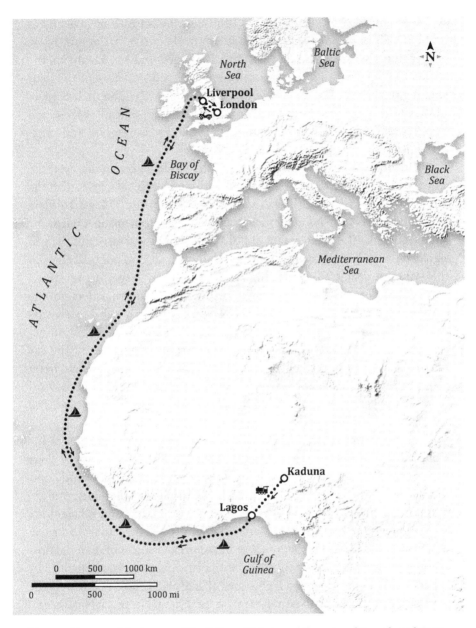

Map 3.2. Itinerary of the journey of the Sultan of Sokoto and the emirs of Gwandu and Kano to Britain in 1934.

at the station to welcome the emirs indicated the breadth of investment in the rituals of colonial patronage and political courtship. Captain E. W. Thompstone, Mr. F. M. Noad, Captain J. D. Symes, and Mr. Elvalwyn, the resident of Sokoto Province who had been assigned to represent the lieutenant governor of Northern Nigeria, greeted the emirs upon their arrival. Admiral Bromley, a high-ranking British government official, represented the Colonial Office, which superintended Britain's vast empire and organized the trip.

With the perfunctory pleasantries of the welcome ceremony over, the emirs and their entourage were ushered to three Morris cars, "placed at the disposal of the chiefs by the kindness of Lord Nuffield."[53] Lord Nuffield pioneered British car manufacturing and had just been made a baron by King George V. The involvement of Lord Nuffield in the logistics of the trip signaled the convergence of Britain's royal, industrial, and political elites in this elaborate drama of imperial courtship. Moreover, the gesture rewarded the loyalty demonstrated by Northern Nigeria's Muslim rulers to the empire, a colonial political and cultural formation for which Morris cars were visible and desirable stand-ins. The Morris automobile was an imperial brand recognizable among subaltern elites, and executives of the car manufacturer leveraged their connections to metropolitan imperial circles to explore and consolidate overseas colonial markets. At the time, several Northern Nigerian emirs and aristocrats already owned Morris cars, and the company was enjoying brisk sales in the region.

The emirs were driven in a convoy to the Hyde Park Hotel, where the Colonial Office had made reservations for them for the duration of their visit. So far, the atmospherics of the trip mimicked a state visit and communicated to the guests both their status as important dignitaries of the empire and the efficient workings of British hospitality and officialdom. It was not simply these arrangements that advertised the rituals of British modernity; equally important in these initial performances of imperial hospitality was what one might call the ethos of efficiency—a set of tangible signifiers of functional order and regimented effectiveness, the very bureaucratic logic at the heart of British administrative rhetoric in Northern Nigeria and other British colonies.

As though to underscore the primary goal of the trip, the British guides drove the emirs to the heart of London for what was described as "their first excursion"[54] into the city. In the sophisticated, if frequently breached, administrative hierarchy of British colonial indirect rule in Northern

Nigeria, colonial officials supervised the work of the emirs and overrode any decisions deemed repugnant to British Victorian mores.[55] In the metropolitan space of London, the same colonial officers, now guides to the visiting emirs, inverted this order and engaged in a ritualized reversal of the status and power imbalances of indirect rule, electing to chauffeur their political inferiors around London. This gesture was part of the dramatized visuals of imperial courtesy put on display for the visiting emirs.

The first sightseeing session over, the emirs returned to the hotel to deal with "the serious tasks of what kind of food they preferred."[56] Special waiters assigned to the emirs helped them navigate the hotel's culinary offerings to determine what foods were free of ingredients considered haram, or forbidden in Islam, and to identify other culinary preferences. The colonial report on the trip states that this process of culinary discovery and experimentation took two days.

Culture shock awaited the visitors everywhere, but their conspicuous presence in England's public spaces also elicited cultural consternation in metropolitan observers. One incident on the first day foreshadowed how the social comportment of the emirs and their servants might be unintelligible to British folk. It was customary for courtiers and servants of Northern Nigeria's Muslim rulers to remain outdoors outside an emir's private quarters as both a mark of respect for the emir's privacy and as a way for the courtiers to rest while being available for errands. The practice is called *shan iska* (lit. taking in air), or relaxing in the soothing outside breeze. On the first evening at the hotel, two personal servants, barefooted as was the norm, sat on the front steps of the hotel in their robes in full view of passersby. This caused "some alarm," and hotel officials and colonial chaperones frantically directed them back into their bosses' hotel suites, "where they resumed their lifelong duty without being disturbed by the gaze of interested Londoners."[57]

The days were packed full of tours and activities. A program of touring London landmarks proved too intense for the emirs in the first three days of the visit. While British officials plotted the next itinerary on their program, it was clear that the emirs desired a more flexible, less scripted schedule that allowed them time to indulge in their own interests and shop for goods that would enhance their status and prestige back home. They wanted to see and hear things that would make an impression on their subjects when reenacted aesthetically in travel stories. The Muslim tourists also wanted to acquire metropolitan objects that would reinforce their claimed connections to British imperial modernity.

This divergence of priorities culminated in the emirs complaining about the pace of the official tours and requesting to exercise greater control over them. After the third day, the program of touristic activities was restructured to accommodate these requests and subtle complaints. Under the new plan, the emirs had intervals between visits to selected sites. These breaks allowed them to pray, rest, and shop outside the logistical strictures and suffocating gaze of official colonial minders. The party subsequently split up; each emir went off on his own adventures and at his own pace. After the emirs expressed their aversion to having their servants accompany them on their daily tours, the servants, two for each emir, stayed behind in the hotel during outings, with officials arranging to take them on separate, less flamboyant tours.

Consuming Britain

The cosmopolitan inclination of Northern Nigerian Muslim emirs who coveted the royal culture of Britain and took sartorial and gestural cues from their English aristocratic counterparts was well established by the 1930s. An eclectic aristocratic taste, forged by a simultaneous fascination with the Islamic cultures of the Near East and the aristocratic cultures introduced by colonialism, was a catalyst for consuming metropolitan commodities.

This sophisticated taste in modern goods caused the emirs to creatively reenact and reconfigure the commodities, consumption, and conduct of the English aristocracy in Northern Nigerian emirate domains. So powerful was this mimetic and cosmopolitan eclecticism in their cultural imagination that some emirs adopted the horse-drawn carriage of English royal processions as part of their own royal ceremonial accoutrement. At the coronation of the emir of Kano, Alhaji Ado Bayero (reigned 1956–2014), in 1956, Queen Elizabeth II famously gifted an English-style horse-drawn carriage known as *keken doki*. Ado Bayero continued to ride in this carriage on special ceremonial occasions until his death in 2014.[58]

Colonial cultural histories of luxury items purchased by the visiting emirs help reveal the ways mimesis and innovative adaptation undergirded and drove the relationship of Northern Nigeria's aristocrats to the goods, gestures, and fads they encountered in British imperial spaces and cultures. Travel to the metropole facilitated this relationship between people and commodities. Shopping preoccupied the emirs in Britain, causing them to negotiate the programmed tours in a manner that left them considerable freedom and time for their shopping expeditions. As men of relatively ample funds who made money from a variety of colonial and traditional sources, high-end shopping at Harrods, Maple's, Hampton's, Liberty's, Goldsmith's, and Silversmith's appealed to the emirs.[59] The three emirs purchased goods that corresponded to their tastes and the requests of their networks of associates in Nigeria. It was customary for traveling aristocrats to take metropolitan presents back to their associates. Coincidentally, all three emirs purchased perambulators, an apparent symbol of exclusivity popularized and modeled by members of the British aristocracy who wheeled their children around in them. Perambulators were familiar items to the Northern Nigerian emirs, who were aware of their use by the British aristocracy and the English royal family.

The popularity of the perambulator as an item of aristocratic consumer culture among Northern Nigeria's emirs raises several possibilities for comprehending the commodity fetishes of British imperial modernity and its convoluted transmission between metropole and colony. Prams traveled to Nigeria with emirs on their return trips from Britain and through the cultural influence of British aristocratic practices. The mechanized logistics of imperial mobility ensured the relative ease of purchase and transportation of this important item of aristocratic status distinction. A popular use of prams in Northern Nigeria mirrored its use in Britain: conveying aristocratic children around in a display that was both utilitarian and status-affirming. In addition, prams were expensive aristocratic baby gifts in both Britain and Northern Nigeria.[60]

One possibility is that the emirs adapted the carriages to an alternative use.[61] This utilitarian adaptation is plausible because early to mid-twentieth-century perambulators were spacious instruments of short-distance mobility. Moreover, perambulators were expensive, effectively ruling them out as essential child-rearing royal accessories in palaces marked by polygyny and a teeming population of royal babies. One interlocutor suggests the remote possibility that perambulators may have allowed emirs to enable their favored wives to avoid the cultural practice of carrying babies on their back.[62] Another source suggests that the perambulators may have been used for two important royal purposes: as a royal domestic decorative substitute for a side table and as a food basket for royal outdoor events.[63]

The multiple stories surrounding the use of perambulators by Northern Nigerian aristocrats suggest that the commodity, once transported to

Nigeria, became a multipurpose item of prestige and was used by different aristocratic households for different purposes. These adaptive uses may have been pioneered by one emir and then adopted by others. Given the friendships between emirs and the frequent visits they paid to one another, an innovative new use for perambulators showcased by one emir would have caught on rapidly and transformed the baby carriage into a desired royal accessory and status enhancer. It is impossible to establish the full range of uses for which perambulators and similar luxury goods were adapted given the capacity of temporal and spatial factors to consistently alter the semiotic properties of goods that travel in imperial circumstances from their place of invention to places where they could be reconstituted and recalibrated.[64] Nonetheless, the chains of transmission regarding modern colonial goods are discernible.

Whatever the multiple uses to which perambulators were put, they were rare commodities whose scarcity and resultant high cost created a peculiar status and political economy around their consumption. Perambulators were low-demand, space-intensive, and delicate items. Thus, colonial merchant shipping lines such as the famed Elder Dempster Lines did not export them to Nigeria. Their unavailability in colonial merchandise stores in Nigeria, the exclusivity of their London provenance, and their new utilitarian and status connotations added to the cultural semiotics of this unlikely emblem of aristocratic commodity culture in Northern Nigeria. We may never know the full story of how and why the curious relationship between emirs and British-manufactured perambulators emerged. However, any trajectory of inquiry for unraveling the Muslim rulers' fascination with expensive British baby carriages should reckon with the circum-colonial circulation of goods imbued with modernist significations.

The business of emirs acquiring and collecting perambulators for whatever purpose points to the uncertain, somewhat-elusive trajectories of new and emergent intraimperial cultures—a cultural ferment in which colonized peoples, as Simon Gikandi suggests, were not mere consumers but also important cocreators.[65] This reading of the making and remaking of colonial cultures defies the familiar dichotomous taxonomies of colonial studies in which African colonial subalterns are portrayed as passive consumers of imperial goods. The perambulator story indicates that in the imperial culture enabled by the movement of people and goods between Nigeria and Britain, Northern Nigerian aristocrats were as much creators as they were consumers.

The Politics and Poetics of Colonial Kinship

Emirs and other visitors used imperial tours to rekindle relationships forged in the quotidian grind of colonial administration. The emir of Gwandu, Usman Ibn Haliru, reconnected with Commander Chaytor, an old British friend who had served as a colonial officer in Nigeria. After their metropolitan reunion, Chaytor assumed the unofficial role of coordinator of the emir's shopping and recreational activities. On certain days when the emir wanted to stay indoors in his hotel suite, Chaytor would arrange to have assorted goods brought in from Harrods. From the comfort of his hotel room, the emir would rummage through the selections and pick out items he liked.[66] Such personal departures from the organized touring itinerary were facilitated by the emirs' personal networks and were illustrative of the deep friendships that had evolved between Northern Nigeria's aristocrats and British colonial officials.

Such personal connections complicated what British organizers of the trip sought to accomplish: a touring regimen they could control and steer in preferred, strategic directions. In this case, the informal arrangement of having goods brought in from Harrods effectively took the emir off the scripted trajectories of the visit. On several occasions as the sultan of Sokoto, the emir of Kano, and their councilors were returning from tours in the evening, Emir Usman of Gwandu, well rested and having fulfilled the day's shopping desires, would demand to "be taken out to see something."[67] This proactively independent exploration of the metropole by the emirs leveraged the enduring connections and networks of colonial rule. Logistically, it meant that impromptu arrangements to racing and rodeo events sometimes had to be made for the emirs when they had exhausted their self-designed itineraries and wanted to resume the official tours. Late-night sightseeing and refreshments and last-minute dinner arrangements had to be made on short notice for both the emirs and their accompanying British officials.

Although theoretically subject to the whims and scripts of the trip's organizers, the emirs brought considerably assertive personal agendas and preferences to bear on their metropolitan itineraries. This assertiveness was circumscribed by the overarching power and racial hierarchies of colonialism. Nonetheless, the emirs' proactive self-navigation of the metropolitan space fed off their determination to use their participation in the imperial ritual of metropolitan tourism to insert themselves more deeply into the interstices of British modernity. The emirs were determined to leverage the opportunities offered by the patronage gestures of colonial officialdom to accomplish their own domestic political and symbolic objectives.

The emirs may have resented the strictures of the programmed tours, but the sights they saw made indelible impressions on them. On that account, the large British colonial investment in the trip proved profitable. Colonial testimonies of the emirs' expressed awe should be measured with a careful eye, but given that the tenor of the emirs' own narratives matches these testimonies, the convergence may indicate a genuine seduction of the emirs through the strategically scripted tours. Certain events appealed to the emirs more than others. Some of the emirs had recreational predilections that were rekindled in the entertainment arenas and spaces of the metropole. For instance, the sultan of Sokoto seemed to have been particularly taken by the greyhound race and the rodeo performance at the International Exhibition grounds in White City, London. The sultan was "delighted at winning twelve and sixpence at dog racing and presented Mr. Noad with half a crown on the way home."[68] The sultan was apparently the only emir in the group to have been engrossed enough to place a bet.

Awe-inspiring metropolitan entertainment satiated curiosity but could potentially overload treasured but easily fatigued guests. When asked in the middle of the visit if there were any sites the visiting party wanted to see, the emir of Gwandu, speaking for the emirs, is quoted as having responded thus: "No, you have shown us an elephant trained to take children for a ride, you have shown us [at a display at Fire Brigade Headquarters] a man climbs up the front of a high burning house on the end of a stick, go through a window and throw out on to the pavement apparently dead people who got up and walked away, and you have shown us a man who galloped standing up on two barebacked horses and jumped over a motorcar. We think we had better not see any more marvels until we come back again."[69] These words offer several interpretive possibilities, the most obvious being the party's overwhelming sense of wonder at successive, stunningly entertaining visual and sonic representations of imperial British society. A less obvious semiotic direction is the possibility that Emir Usman and his colleagues were overloaded by the signifying objects of British modernity and that his melodramatic words betray the overzealous overkill of imperial touring. Yet another possibility is suggested by the words "we think we had better not see any more marvels until we come back again," a rather ironic, seemingly sarcastic mockery of the thinly veiled visual propaganda of the programmed tours. Subtly refusing to be further awed by metropolitan marvels indicates that the emirs saw through the elaborate display of imperial grandeur for the benefit of the visitors.

The emirs were not passive consumers and observers of the displays they encountered in London. They seemed aware of the imperial purposes behind their exposure to these displays, hence their unwillingness to endure further pageantry. The emirs suffered from the inevitable mental exhaustion that comes with excessive exposure to material items of wonder and struggled to cope with the sights, sounds, smells, and textures being thrown at them in rapid, choreographed succession. So palpable was the emirs' sensory exhaustion that the confidential report on the trip indicated that touring fatigue was a problem.

The report invoked the tour of the British Naval Dockyard at Portsmouth as an illustration. The emirs and their minders left the hotel in a noisy convoy at 8:30 in the morning and arrived at the dockyard at 11, a long journey that left the parties physically exhausted and rather unable to enjoy the subsequent tours. A tour of two warships, the *Renown* and the *Victory*; lunch with the lord mayor of Portsmouth, Sir Harold Pink; a visit with the commander-in-chief of the Portsmouth fleet at his residence; a tour of a submarine; watching a "display of daylight fireworks";[70] and a two-hour drive to Lee-on-Solent to see a seaplane flyby were all part of the day's overloaded itinerary.[71] The group did not leave Portsmouth until 7:30 p.m. and arrived in London at 10:00 p.m. This remarkable twelve-hour day of touring tested the patience, energy, and attention of the emirs and left them with little time to rest, pray, and indulge in their own pastimes. Writing retrospectively on the schedule, a colonial official who accompanied the emirs remarked that "each detail [of the tours] was most interesting, but half the programme would have afforded a less difficult and less exhausting day."[72]

According to reports, the emirs had been particualrly fascinated by the workings of metropolitan mechanical things—"mechanism" as one newpaper report put it.[73] At the British military academy in Aldershot, they were shown what their minders regarded as "the militant aspect" of metropolitan "mechanism": a demonstration of the lethal capacity of a machine gun. While visiting the Morris Motor Works at Oxford, they were exposed to metropolitan technology's "peaceful phases" when they observed the "rapid assembly of a car," and the emir of Kano purchased a Morris car for himself.[74]

Colonial minders and organizers were determined to show the emirs two distinct but complementary faces of British modernity: one recreational and entertaining, the other serious, pedagogical, and bureaucratic. On the bureaucratic side, the emirs visited the Mansion House of the Lord Mayor of London. They then traveled to Guildhall in London, where they observed the ritualized election of Sheriffs and its quaint, medieval custom of arranging separate rows of pens with separate doors that let in members of city guilds assigned to them, a strange occasion that "must have puzzled the potentates."[75]

Another bureaucratic tour took the visitors to the Colonial Office, an important symbolic political pilgrimage of sorts for the emirs since the office represented the citadel of colonial policy, the space where the emirs' relationship with and role in the colonial system were shaped. The Colonial Office approximated for the emirs the old, now-diminished position of Sokoto, the seat of the defunct Sokoto Caliphate, where emirs of member emirates went to renew their religious and political ties to the sultan and consequential decrees and policies were developed to guide religious and secular conduct in the Muslim federation. From the perspective of the British organizers, their visit to the Colonial Office was concerned with the imperatives of official colonial kinship, a highlight of the trip. Metropolitan newspaper headlines about the visit to the Colonial Office were correspondingly effusive.[76]

Sir Philip Cunliff Lister, the secretary of state for the colonies, received the emirs at the Colonial Office. Sir Lister discussed with his guests many aspects of the British colonial enterprise in Northern Nigeria.[77] The hour-long discussion was part test of knowledge and part customer survey. Sir Lister gauged the emirs' intellectual investments in and commitments to the proclaimed ideals of the British colonial administration in Northern Nigeria and sought their impressions on their guided visits to sites in and around London. The emirs, a confidential memo claimed, displayed "their intimate knowledge of and personal interest in the detailed [colonial] administration of their territories."[78]

The climax of the official touring was a visit to Buckingham Palace for an audience with the king on July 2. The emirs, described as dressed in "flowing robes," were ushered into the palace in "closed motor cars and went in at the Grand Entrance," two Buckingham gestures reserved for honored guests of the king and the empire.[79] The palace organized an elaborate reception for the emirs, each of whom chatted with the king privately. Afterward, the emirs stated that they were "impressed with the simplicity and friendliness of the king,"[80] a meaningful impression partly because the emirs had been nurtured on a British political rhetoric that mystified the king as a distant, mysterious, and unapproachable symbol of the empire. Given this premise, seeing and chatting with this embodiment of British imperial would have been both anticlimactic and satisfying, a complement to their awe at the grandeur of Buckingham Palace.

Personalities and Power

The three emirs were already familiar with one another as the three most senior rulers in the Sokoto Caliphate hierarchy of power and precedence. Their personalities, temperaments, Muslim devotional practices, and commitments to and immersion in colonial culture diverged from one another, however. The ethos of patronage, protection, and reward for loyalty rarely corresponded to inherited traditional or religious status; instead, it followed gradations dictated by colonial whims and preference. Given this dissonance between the ethos of favoritism and the status hierarchy of the Sokoto Caliphate, hosting three emirs with different, contested claims to caliphal prestige and authority presented practical problems for tour organizers and minders. Different personalities and claims to power cohabiting the same space of patronage in a foreign colonial capital aggravated tensions and required delicate management.

During the trip, some of these diverging interests and claims surfaced in both formal and informal settings. One source of tension between the visiting emirs was the question of the religious and political superiority among the three. There was no question as to the nominal leader of the delegation. That honor, whatever it was worth in a colonial setting of circumscribed sovereignty, belonged to the sultan of Sokoto, traditionally the inheritor and embodiment of the defunct Sokoto Caliphate's political, jurisprudential, and religious prestige and legitimacy.

The question of who came after him was settled in the official religious and foundational political canons of the caliphate in favor of the emir of Gwandu, whose seat was first occupied by Abdullahi, the brother of the first sultan, Othman dan Fodio. However, due to Kano's large population, its long precolonial and colonial chieftaincy history, its prominent status as a cosmopolitan center of trade and Islamic learning in the wider West African world of commerce and Islamic intellection, and its elites' embrace of the Tijaniyya Muslim brotherhood in defiance of the dominant Qadiriyya Muslim orthodoxy of the wider caliphate, the emirs of Kano tended to think of themselves as second only to the sultan.[81] Moreover, Kano was conquered and integrated into the British colonial system a few months earlier than Sokoto, giving it a favored status and thus greater visibility in British engagements with the caliphal world. Given the tradition of Kano emirs asserting their claims to second position in the caliphate's order of precedence, the emir of Gwandu was subtle but emphatic in "insisting on his superiority after the Sultan"[82] in dealings with metropolitan interlocutors. This preemptive maneuver by the emir turned out to be unwarranted since the emir of Kano, unlike his predecessor, had little interest in the politics of caliphal supremacy.[83]

The emirs generally struck a note of unanimity and displayed similar sensibilities. They shied away from unwanted public attention in Britain, and they shunned "numerous people who wanted to visit them."[84] These strangers included some Africans, but most were British journalists who were interested in interviewing the emirs to satiate the metropolitan appetite for African Muslim exotica. The emirs unanimously favored privacy, despite some of them being more comfortable with socialization than others.

All the emirs relished reconnecting with old British officials with whom they had worked in the Northern Nigerian emirates.[85] The emir of Kano, accompanied by Captain Tupper Carrey, traveled to York on June 29 to visit Seebohm Rowntree, an old British friend and renowned industrialist,[86] while the other emirs embarked on a tour of Windsor Castle and Eton College. The next day, the emir of Kano made his way back to London, having spent the night at Rowntree's home while the sultan and the emir of Gwandu toured a pottery works at Ashtead.

The moods, tastes, and interests of the emirs led them to different activities, which often meant a divergence of itineraries. For instance, on June 27, while the sultan of Sokoto and the emir of Gwandu toured Unilever House and Unilever's margarine factory at Purfleet, the emir of Kano shopped for cars and other merchandise at Liberty's and Maple's.[87] The tour of the margarine factory was significant for two reasons. The factory belonged to the United Africa Company, the largest British firm buying raw materials in Nigeria and a colonial conglomerate with a ubiquitous presence there. Northern Nigerian emirs and chiefs mediated the flow of cash crops to produce-buying firms through their regulation of peasant farming and were routinely courted and feted by officials of colonial firms.

Unilever was particularly active in Kano's vast commercial arena, yet the emir of Kano skipped the tour to shop for luxury merchandise to take back to Nigeria. The tour was a form of colonial patronage and courtship and included an audience with Colonel F.H.I. Reddington, the chairman of Unilever; the meeting was replete with a ritualized presentation of "kola nuts in silver bowls symbolic of mutual friendship and regard."[88] The tour was also designed to give the visiting aristocrats a glimpse into the industrial processes by which "their own familiar products [were] transformed into British manufactured goods,"[89] as a newspaper story described such excursions. The emirs watched the very process in which "the ground nuts and other products of the Nigerian Provinces are refined, blended with milk, churned . . . kneaded, and finally transformed into packets of margarine,"[90] a food product popular with Northern Nigerian aristocrats.

The tour walked the emirs from their own indulgence in expensive imperial tastes to the imperial industrial spaces that enabled and satiated these tastes. It was an intimate moment in which the tastes and aromas of the empire and the emirs' indulgence in them crystallized in the mechanical space of the margarine factory. Colonial newspaper accounts of the tour describe the emirs' reactions as "enjoyment" and "bewilderment."[91] The imperial cycle of production—marked by groundnut farming in Nigeria, shipping the produce to metropolitan factories, industrial refinement of the groundnuts into edible margarine, and finally the return of the margarine to Northern Nigerian spaces of luxury consumer goods—displayed the logic of colonial economics and consumption.

From the rooftop of the Unilever bulding, the emirs surveyed London below, focusing on the foot traffic on London's busy streets and on the Blackfriars bridge across the River Thames. Sultan Hassan reportedly remarked to the emir of Gwandu that the houses in London seemed to have been piled up one on top of the other, the recurring vernacular rendering of the multiple storey buildings and skycrapers of London.[92] The Thames, however, was underwhelming for the emirs, who remarked that, compared to the River Niger, it was an insignificant stream.[93]

When the emirs of Kano and Gwandu visited the Lancashire County Council Farm at Hutton, the Sultan remained in London and shopped.[94] Similarly, when the emir of Kano paid a second visit to York to inspect a chocolate factory, he traveled there alone in part because this was a private reciprocal visit to return the gesture of factory owner, Seebohm Rowntree, who had visited Kano a year earlier. Although metropolitan newspaper reports cast his visit to York as a continuation of his and the other emirs' observation of the "culture and development of the West," this was largely a visit inspired by transracial personal connections enabled by colonialism.

Upon arriving in York, the two special coaches in which the emir and his entourage traveled from London to York were drawn by a train to the private railway station of Messrs Rowntree, where an elaborate welcome ceremony awaited the visitors. With trumpets blarring, the emir was welcomed onto a red-carpetted platform where Rowntree personally welcomed the entourage with a bowl of kola nuts.[95] Accompanied by Muhammadu Sanusi, his eldest son and holder of the title of ciroma, and other aides, the emir toured the factory where cocoa beans and gum arabic imported from Nigeria were transformed into chocolate and other confectionary items. The tour was followed by tea with Rowntree and the emir's colonial guides in the company's boardroom.

Colonial guides sometimes struggled to keep the attention of the emirs, and the guides admitted that many activities and sights failed to capture the interest of the visiting rulers. For instance, according to the newspaper report, "A round of tiring visits to noisy factories is of little interest to a Nigerian chief."[96] The utilitarian and instrumental intention behind the trip was not exclusively a British colonial calculation. The emirs themselves seemed to have purposed the trip as relevant to their own practical priorities and the pressing issues in their emirates. The utilitarian avenues opened up by the tours appealed to the emirs. They enjoyed their rendezvous with heads of British companies operating in West Africa since such meetings gave them the opportunity to ask the company leaders many questions about produce prices and product distribution.

The emirs also engaged with personnel at metropolitan educational, medical, and agricultural institutions, indicating that they were more impressed by facilities of instrumental and practical consequence than ones devoted to promoting colonial cultural, symbolic, and aesthetic values.[97] This dissonance between what British guides wanted the emirs to learn from the trip and the emirs' more practical desires was on display on their last day of touring, when officials hurriedly organized a cinema show. Naturally the emirs and their entourage preferred to do last-minute shopping for tangible goods they could use to enhance their status and engage in the tradition of royal gift giving.

Given the personality differences among the emirs, activities that elicited the enthusiastic interest of all three were rare. At times, however, their interests converged. All three emirs were fascinated by the science of flight and aerodynamics. It was thus possible to organize joint touristic itineraries for them around this common curiosity. On July 2, all three emirs

Figure 3.1. The sultan of Sokoto and the emirs of Gwandu and Kano at the Croydon Aerodrome, 1934.

"inspected" the new Imperial Airways aircraft named "spring" at the Croydon Aerodrome, an adventure memorialized by a photo in the Hulton Royals Collection held by Getty Images (see fig. 3.1). Furthermore, the emirs were all enthused about one particular activity: visiting the legendary former colonial governor of Nigeria, Frederick Lugard.[98] By the 1930s, it was already a tradition for visiting dignitaries from Northern Nigeria to pay perfunctory visits to Gwamna Luga, the Hausa rendering of his name. On the second day of the emirs' stay in Britain, Lugard, along with the directors of Barclay's Bank, hosted the Muslim rulers' visit to the Zoological Gardens in London (see fig. 3.2).[99] Six days later, all three rulers visited Lugard at his home in Abinger, fulfilling a ritualistic political pilgrimage to the house of the man many Northern Nigerian traditional rulers regarded affectionately as a protector and conservator of Northern Nigeria's Islamic heritage. This intimate cultural economy of kinship turned on reconstituted political memories of Lugard's pragmatic fondness for the political structures perfected by the defunct caliphate and for the fabled mannerisms, grace, competence, and regal comportment of the Hausa-Fulani Muslim ruling classes of Northern Nigeria.

Figure 3.2. The sultan of Sokoto and the emirs of Gwandu and Kano at the London Zoological Gardens with Frederick Lugard.

There are ongoing debates in contemporary Nigeria on whether Lugard was a preserver of the Muslim political culture of caliphate Northern Nigeria or a functional theorist of British imperial rule for whom the potential utilitarian value of Muslim political and governing institutions was merely an incidental part of a usable administrative postulation. To his numerous Northern Nigerian aristocratic visitors, Lugard's status as a rehabilitative influence on a caliphal culture rendered almost irrelevant by colonial conquest was indisputable. The feeling that Lugard was fond of the emirs and their political institutions and had preserved and in some instances expanded their privileges was the basis of the affection the emirs of Northern Nigeria showed the retired colonial official.

The Complex Logistics of Imperial Travel

Logistically, the task of organizing a trip as elaborate as this and managing three important Muslim rulers from a valued colonial region of Nigeria called for creativity and painstaking coordination. For transatlantic transportation, the colonial government engaged Elder Dempster Lines, the largest British passenger and cargo shipping company operating in West Africa at the time. The company assigned the emirs to what it considered the most comfortable quarters of their ship, selected Hausa-speaking European stewards and European staff for their cabins, and, during their three-night stay in Liverpool, provided them with local transportation.[100]

The guides had to improvise to solve new challenges that arose during the trip. Communication between the emirs and the British officials presented one such challenge. The colonial officials often conscripted three English-speaking councilors in the emirs' entourage as ad hoc interpreters to clarify the ambiguities of metropolitan interpersonal and group communications.[101] Financially, the colonial treasuries and revenues of each of the three emirates paid all expenses related to the trip. The Colonial Office essentially provided each emir with an unlimited escrow account to spend on personal expenses, gifts, and upkeep. Additionally, the emirs were allowed to carry a "reasonable sum in cash" drawn from their own funds. One of the colonial minders, Captain Thompstone, kept records of the emirs' expenses and then sent these to the British residents of their respective emirates and provinces for accounting purposes.[102]

Motivated by imperial hubris and the notion that the British metropole was a magnetic, modernist mecca, the *Western Morning News* claimed the emirs were on a self-funded mission of personal enlightenment. The newspaper reported that "the tour has been undertaken at their expense solely for the purpose of pleasure and education," the idea being that their outlook on life generally would be broadened by "personal contact with England."[103] In truth, as much as the emirs performed and expressed their laudatory reactions to metropolitan phenomena, it is important to note that their expectations for the visit differed from the trope of "enlightenment" advanced as the overarching factor by metropolitan newspapers and colonial officials. The tensions between what colonial officials directed the emirs to and what the visitors wanted to do and see, and the seeming disinterest of the emirs in sights and spectacles designed to "broaden" their "outlook on life," were often awkwardly evident. These tensions are indicators that while the trip was a political initiative of the British colonial government, the organizers struggled to control its contours because the emirs had their own funds and used those funds to finance their own metropolitan indulgences.

Colonial Travel as Pedagogy

Colonial authorities wanted to teach modernity to the visiting emirs and expected the emirs to forge and strengthen a middle ground of accommodation between the cultural world of British colonization and the Islamo-African traditional cultures of Northern Nigeria. The emirs were savvy readers of imperial signals. Their mindset was not simply discerning and following the signals but also shaping the optics and protocols of metropolitan imperial patronage. Trips of this nature were designed to reinforce what were already known to be the desired end points of colonial official intervention. In this respect, and from the colonizers' perspective, a focused evaluation of the trip's impact was as important as the trip itself. On the last day of their stay in London, the emirs sat down with their colonial guides for an informal survey on what they had learned, what was memorable to them about British society, and what elicited comparisons with their own domains in Northern Nigeria.

British accounts purporting to represent African opinions on the logistics and bureaucracy of the trip are suspect because they come to us filtered through colonial ideological and bureaucratic norms. Colonial speech paraphrasing African interlocutors is particularly suspicious. Nonetheless, these accounts can guide scholars into the intricate mechanics of how British actors cultivated the affirmations of African allies in a manner that seemed to fulfill the colonizers' own rhetorical projections. The interactions among the emirs and their guides at the end of the visit seemed analogous to a modern focus group. Colonial guides and organizers intended to retrieve whatever impressions and opinions the emirs had formed regarding what the organizers had carefully exposed them to. Here is how E. Walwyn, who wrote the official report on the trip, remembered the expressed reflections and responses of the emirs:

> After seeing England, they had a better understanding of our insistence on cleanliness and orderly ways and of taking proper care of everything both animate and inanimate. One of the reasons for instance why our animals were better than theirs was because they were given proper attention and were kept clean, well-housed and well fed. Every one's house looked well clean and tidy, even in the "bush"; children looked well cared for, healthy and happy; even the streets were washed and cleaned. They now understood that the ideas of the Health, Veterinary, Education and Agricultural Officers in Nigeria were not merely a nuisance but had an object underlying them which was of practical use.[104]

Given the familiar slippages of colonial translation and the ideological strictures of colonial communication, it is hard to tell if these were the terms in which the emirs couched their impressions of British society or if the sharp contrast posited between Britain and Northern Nigeria was a theme of the emirs' feedback. Even so, these words bear out the ideological premise on which the trip was conceived. The emirs were to travel to the center of the British imperial world and see how a supposedly superior culture and its quotidian components functioned in an organic, symbiotic motion. This imperial project of acculturating Northern Nigerian aristocratic allies in metropolitan ways of life should be understood as stemming from a familiar colonial bemoaning of what officials considered the emirs' "slow assimilation to progress" on account of the "flow of Mohammedan philosophy."[105] The tension between courtship, hospitality, and contemptuous colonial Othering characterized the visits and the ritualized performances of colonial chaperones.

The same report remarked on a contrast in attitude between the people of England whom the emirs encountered and their own Muslim people. The emirs were reportedly "struck by the frankness and friendliness even of complete strangers in England, as contrasted with their own rather distrustful and secretive character,"[106] an alleged African character deficit blamed for "causing much waste of time in their dealing with administrative officers."[107] Interpretive and evaluative commentaries such as this lend support to a reading of the trip as a malleable discursive terrain that could be textually mediated to suit prevailing—and contested—colonial beliefs.

In light of the emirs' own posttravel narratives, remarks about the friendliness of Londoners and the orderly marvels of British society were plausible, but it is equally plausible that the binary of English transparency and Hausa Muslim "secretiveness" and deception was an editorial extrapolation emanating from the report's author. Moreover, there was a British colonial tradition in Northern Nigeria of misreading Muslim rulers' strategic use of silence, self-restraint, and other strategically induced gestures of political self-preservation as deliberate deception emanating from the latter's supposed congenital untrustworthiness. The trope of this alleged "native" deceptiveness in colonial bureaucratic narratives was so rampant that a prominent pioneer British resident in Northern Nigeria, Charles Temple, devoted a chapter of his colonial service memoir to the alleged trickery and deception of Muslim officials in the colonial system.[108]

The construction of a distinct Muslim character and cultural universe in the British colonial imaginary received little input from Muslim aristocrats. The terms and contours of this alleged Muslim character, along with its supposed divergence from an essentialized, paradigmatic British colonial cultural form, was unintelligible to the traveling emirs, whose own narratives, although replete with comparative frames of reference, largely refrained from stark cultural binaries.

Did the emirs tell their British interlocutors what they felt they wanted to hear? In other words, were they aware of the colonial script governing these guided metropolitan tours? Certainly some of the impressions attributed to the emirs in the colonial reports fit well within the narrative that resulted from these colonially mediated travels to the metropole. Less certain is the extent to which the emirs, proud custodians of a rich, historical Muslim culture, blindly participated in the simplistic colonial narrative purporting to show backward, insular, and secretive Muslim cultures and peoples passively learning from a civilized, dynamic, and adventurous metropolitan culture.

In colonial reports, the instrumental function of these trips was conveyed rather transparently in the language of pedagogy and binary contrast. The invocation of Northern Nigeria's Muslim heritage, which the visiting emirs personified, worked to underwrite claims for British cultural interventions in colonial Northern Nigeria. As one illustrative sample from the official reportage of the trip states: "The practical value of secular education on the lines now being followed in Nigeria, as contrasted with their own laborious study of Arabic, was better appreciated."[109] Whether or not the statement is faithful to the expressed comments of the emirs, the objective was clear: to signal that the visit to Britain helped the emirs grasp the visual and intellectual contrast between a "laborious" and impractical Arabic-scripted Muslim education and a superior, Roman-scripted one held up as more "practical" and usable. Like British journalists, colonial minders infantilized, spoke for, and parsed the emirs' words.

British officials courted the Muslim aristocrats of Northern Nigeria, publicly showering them with respectful if backhanded patronage. However, in the confidential confines of official correspondence, a discursive script emerged that devalued the cultures the aristocrats projected. These dual politics of public cultural recognition and private bureaucratic devaluation were not in conflict; rather, they were complementary dimensions of a well-coordinated project in which the constructed deficits of Hausa Muslim culture were the referential staples of official commitments to reeducating and reorienting Muslim allies through the poetics and politics of sponsored metropolitan travel.

In the end, official reportage on the trip contained more colonial wishes than true reflections of what the emirs might have thought of the touristic jamboree because the emirs remain silent in the colonial archive. Their voices were mediated and redacted by colonial officials. Even the authors of the report could not be entirely sure the emirs were not gaming the inquiry, playing to a familiar script and hitting notes they thought would please their colonial minders. For instance, Walwyn, who coordinated the posttravel survey, noted that the emirs returning home would act on their observations but added the conditional phrase, "if these were their real impressions."[110] The thoughts of the emirs remained hidden behind the protocols and silences of British colonial communication rituals. The pedagogy of scripted tours had its limits, and even the colonial organizers of the trip, desirous of certain effects, seemed to recognize these limits.

The Afterlives of Imperial Courtship

The officious rituals and mutual patronage that marked the tours outlived the 1934 trip, continuing even after the rulers had returned to Nigeria. Colonial officials sought and received copies of diaries kept by the visitors, and, in at least one documented case, the postvisit "confidential report" of the superintending colonial official drew on the travel diary of a visiting emir.[111] Postvisit protocols were nearly as elaborate as the visits themselves. Upon their return to Nigeria, the emirs performed epistolary homages of gratitude and appreciation; however genuine or contrived, they demonstrated awe, enlightenment, and a sense of lingering amazement regarding their experiences in Britain. They wrote letters of gratitude to their metropolitan hosts. Following these organized tours, the emirs used these epistolary gestures of appreciation to signal their continuing allegiance to British colonials. As important as the quotidian logistics of the tours were, establishing a feedback loop was of paramount significance to colonial guides and planners. The perfunctory letters of appreciation written by the emirs to their hosts partially fulfilled this postvisit stocktaking.

Colonial officials wondered if the visits had succeeded in communicating the right messages and impressions to the visitors. The officials eagerly awaited the letters of gratitude they expected visiting subaltern aristocrats to send because the retrospective reflections in them provided a window, however unreliable, into the depth and scope of the impressions left on the visitors. Officials could parse the contents of these letters, subjecting them to interpretations that were consistent with the ideological outcomes and dividends the Colonial Office expected the visits to produce. The postvisit letters contained clues about what individual visitors liked, which, in turn, gave colonial officials a point of entry in further courting such visitors.

Within three months of their return to Nigeria, all three emirs had written letters of appreciation to the lord mayor of Portsmouth, who had hosted them on their arrival in England and prior to their departure. In August, the emir of Kano wrote to express "thanks for the hospitality you showed us and the pleasure of seeing the wonderful firework display at the Mansion Home of Portsmouth."[112] Along with his letter, the emir sent "a small present"—a leopard skin—to his metropolitan host.[113]

In October 1934, the emir of Gwandu wrote the following words to his host:

> From the Emir of Gwandu, Usuman, son of Emir of Gwandu Haliru, son of Abdulkadir (God rest their souls amen), to the Lord Mayor of Portsmouth. Greetings of friendship, loyalty, and respect, with inquiries after your health and of your people. If you inquire of us, we here are all in good health and prosperity. After greetings, I write this letter to you in order to let you know we have returned home safely and have found all our people well. I want to thank you again for the welcome you gave us at your house. We shall never forget the visit. As for the kindness you showed us at Portsmouth we tender you our sincere thanks. May God give you increased might and power. May God give us both His aid and His blessing in addition.[114]

The emir's letter conveys ceremonial expressions of loyalty and admiration, as well as a keen awareness of imperial protocol. In a passage that demonstrates that the emir of Gwandu knew the visit was meant to communicate the might of the British Empire, he gestures to what he regards as the providential origin of such power. Thus, he portrays himself, a Muslim leader, as accepting of this divine order of political things, this ordained hierarchy of power. After all, in the Hausa Muslim tradition of Northern Nigeria, *iko* (might) is the property of God, which he bestows on or rescinds from whomever he pleases. Although the emir's letter contains few descriptive references to the actual places, people, and events he encountered during the tour, his affirmation of British imperial might indicates he had beheld the might of the empire. If officials wanted the trip to reinforce the emir's belief in an omnipotent and modern Britain, the letter provided evidence to anchor that belief.

For his part, the sultan of Sokoto wrote this letter of gratitude to his metropolitan hosts:

> From the Sultan of Sokoto Alhassanu son of Sultan Mu'azu upon whom God have mercy, Amen. Best greetings, friendship and nicest goodwill. And increasing honor and respect to the presence of the Lord Mayor of Portsmouth. May God give you more health, power and prosperity, Amen. After this the object of my writing this letter to you is to let you know that we arrived home safely from our long journey. We offer our best gratitude to you for the kindness you showed to us during our visit to your famous town; and the reception of your people to us; we also thank you for the nice lunch with which you entertained us. Surely we saw many interesting and amazing things in your town, especially the warships named H.M Renown and Victory, which we add to our recollection and shall not forget them for ever. We were very much delighted and we thank you very much indeed. . . . Peace.[115]

Unlike the emir of Gwandu's letter, the sultan's missive was substantive, recalling specific events and itineraries of the visit. His assertion that the group saw "many interesting and amazing things" was a generalized homage to the awe-inspiring greatness of Britain, a clichéd idiom of colonial visitors' feedback that officials never tired of hearing. The sultan's more specific reference to the two warships the group toured is another rhetorical move that reinforced the theme of British greatness—a greatness embodied, the sultan suggests, in the extraordinary naval arsenal represented by the two warships. The sultan's statement that the visitors would "not forget [the sights] for ever" is another exaggerated gesture pandering to the familiar penchant of colonial officials—metropolitan and on ground—to revel in African peoples marveling at British technological and modernist objects. The emirs employed flattery in their postvisit missives because it reinforced the preexisting convictions of British interlocutors and guides.

Emir, Traveler, Narrator

So far, the account of the trip analyzed here has relied largely on colonial reports and documents on the processes and itineraries of this historic event. In 1938, the new emir of Gwandu, Yahaya, who had accompanied Emir Usman to Britain five years earlier as one of his councilors, succeeded Usman upon his death. Yahaya subsequently penned the aforementioned *Gaskiya* travelogue, whose contents deserve careful analysis as a semi-independent account of the trip since, at the time of the trip, he was not yet emir but only a member of the emir's entourage.

For Yahaya, the wonders of the trip began on the ship, where he was surprised to find "bedrooms, bathrooms, and even relaxation areas."[116] In 1907, at the age of twelve, Yahaya had accompanied the resident of Sokoto Province, Charles Temple, to Zungeru, then the headquarters of the colonial government in Northern Nigeria. In Zungeru, Yahaya was introduced to the then governor, Percy Girouard. Temple showed Yahaya the grand offices and buildings housing the colonial administration. This visit to Zungeru was an induction for the young prince; Yahaya even enjoyed a ride on a horse-drawn carriage and a train. Twenty-seven years later, and ensconced in the luxury compartment of an England-bound ship, Yahaya saw both continuity and improvement between "the things of wonder" he saw in Zungeru and the "wonderful things on this ship."[117] Yahaya connects the two experiences thus: "Here was I who had been astonished by the horse-drawn carriage and train we rode in Zungeru. Little did I know that God destined that I would ride on something even more wonderful."[118]

Yahaya's sense of incremental wonder, his attribution of these acts of colonial courtship to providential favor, and his fascination with modern technologies of mobility fused into a complex and profound appreciation of the privileged world of favored African colonial allies. Because of the novelty of these privileges and itineraries, Yahaya's descriptions were understandably melodramatic, bordering on giddiness. Yet in their exaggerated tone they offer a glimpse into British investments in instruments of luxury that could cause old allies to recommit and new ones to be inducted: "If you desire food or anything, all you have to do is ring a bell krrrrrr! And here comes a white man immediately ready to satisfy your desire! When we arrived in England, we met many people who welcomed us with a convoy of motor cars and took us to our hotel in the city of London. The hotel itself was a thing of wonder."[119]

Yahaya was not new to privilege. He was an aristocrat and a member of the second-most prestigious Muslim ruling family in the Sokoto hierarchy of Northern Nigeria. From boyhood, Yahaya moved in the privileged circuits of British colonial proxy rule and was thus accustomed to luxury, abundance, and the leisures of colonial modernity, yet even he was clearly seduced by the temporary inversion of imperial racial etiquette he observed and experienced on the Britain-bound ship. He and the emirs he accompanied became, for the duration of their voyage, preeminent recipients of staged British hospitality and deference, able to order white colonial officials and white ship hands and stewards around to satisfy their desires and whims.

Yahaya's narrative notes the continuation of this ritualized white deference to and patronage of Northern Nigerian Muslim aristocracy during metropolitan touring. "Our guides who were in charge of deciding our schedule made sure that what we saw today was not what was shown to us the next day," Yahaya wrote.[120] For Yahaya, the highlights of the trip were, in no particular order, the visit to Frederick Lugard, the house of the mayor of London, and an air show where he saw "many incredible things."[121] Yahaya's rhetoric plays on two familiar idioms of affluence and privilege in colonial Northern Nigeria—social proximity to whiteness and precious metals. "There is no doubt that the white people have it so good in this world; even their cutlery and utensils are made from precious metals," Yahaya wrote.[122]

Yahaya's rendition of the visit to the London Zoo is marked by a narrative flourish worthy of careful unpacking. He mentions several animals and then claims that only a few animals in the world were not housed at the London Zoo. The sight of a young boy petting a trained elephant "which did not harm him," the spectacle of the "Emir of Gwandu [feeding] an elephant with his own hands," and the sights of animal-human interactions at the zoo dominated his recollection. The imagery of these eminent visitors—emirs from the so-called jungle continent of allegedly wild animals and wild humanity—in a metropolitan zoo, petting, feeding, and excitedly interacting with a barely familiar cast of wild animals, is rich in signification.

Yahaya concludes his narrative by inviting his readers to imagine and visualize what he was describing since only a visual encounter could render the subject intelligible or believable to his readers: "Kai! [wow!], the affairs of white people are so fascinating you have to see them to believe! You may be doing your own thing and underneath you, right under the earth are trains moving through tracks, complete with stations. People were in awe while the operators of the train simply went about their business. Kai! There is no doubt that the world begins and ends in London!"[123] Yahaya enhanced the ability of his audience—literate Hausa folk and elites alike—to vicariously enjoy his experiences. He followed the best Hausa storytelling and folkloric tradition in which the storyteller tries to capture the multiple sensory elements of the events and phenomena being narrated. The added melodrama of exclamatory and onomatopoeic speech in this genre functions to further the interactional, participatory enjoyment of shared personal experience.

Yahaya had become a privileged participant in the modernity of Britain, a constellation of symbols and material culture into which he inducted his readers through the interweaving of text and experience. London was not just the end point of modernity in this interpretive frame, it was the center of the modern world—a world so expansive that everyone—colonizer and subaltern, emir and subject—could connect to it. London represented a hyperbolic vision of a shared modernity with many arteries, all of which led to and emanated from the city. London, Yahaya seems to imply, was the place where everyone from every corner of the empire could come and partake in the glories of the empire. These imagined partners in modernity would then return to their homelands with a piece of that modernist world that had no equal or better. Emir Yahaya's effusive representation of London as a place where the world begins and ends should be understood not simply as a generous homage to metropolitan imperial modernity; he also clearly pandered to notions of Britain as a site of awe-inspiring technology, infrastructure, and modernist materiality that were circulating in Northern Nigeria's expanding colonial public sphere.

Conclusion

Northern Nigerian Muslim aristocratic travelers represented Britain and their experiences there in generally complementary terms, and emirs such as Yahaya viewed the British monarchy and its figurehead, the king of England, as a model of power, dignity, and sartorial elegance. Yet a closer reading of the travel narratives reveals subtle and unsubtle calculation. One sees strategic textual efforts on the part of traveling emirs to parlay their physical and symbolic connections to the British monarchy and the accoutrements of British modernity into local prestige for themselves.

For the British, protecting and cultivating the goodwill and support of loyal Northern Nigerian elites entailed exposing the aristocrats to the signifiers and repositories of British modernity. Traditionally, Muslim aristocrats arbitrated in matters where the tension between colonial goods and practices and Islamic observances required interpretive and instructional intervention. Metropolitan interactions with the latest technological and material cultures of empire made this mediatory enterprise less challenging for the aristocrats. In going to great lengths to give the sultan and the emirs of Kano and Gwandu an elaborately organized trip, colonial authorities aimed to gain access to the hearts and minds of the visitors and, through them, their subjects. They hoped that exposure to the impressive and awe-inspiring symbols and objects of metropolitan modernity would thrill the emirs and make them better allies and better mediators of imperial projects who would help mitigate Muslim suspicions about imperial goods and practices.

However, the emirs were not entirely seduced. They possessed and expressed their own agenda and their own purposes for embarking on the trip, and they became assertive in pursuing their own personal and collective quests outside the strictures of the official itinerary. The result was a more complex outcome than that envisaged by the trip's planners. The emirs proved adept at playing the game of contrived courtesy, performed gratitude, dramatized wonder, and formulaic protocols. The visiting emirs leveraged the trips to fulfill personal predilections, desires, and needs, both tangible and symbolic. For the emirs, the domestication of metropolitan symbols and commodities such as the popular perambulator was a complex undertaking that advertised rather than concealed their agency.

Muslim rulers such as Atta Ibrahim of Ebiraland were particularly insistent on shaping both their itinerary and their experience in Britain, showing little interest in Shakespeare and being drawn instead to seemingly mundane attractions like English countryside chickens and luxury goods. Independently wealthy and thus weaned from British colonial nodes of monetary patronage, Ibrahim was able to control the terms of his travel to Britain as well as how the trip was perceived in his domain. His insistence on telling his subjects that his trip and the shopping spree he undertook in Britain were independently financed was one aspect of his determination to free himself from the British attempt to control the optical and narrative aftermaths of his travels. For all his robust agency, however, metropolitan racism, both subtle and brazen, bubbled above contrived imperial hospitality. This racism marred Ibrahim's experiences, causing him and his entourage discomfort and displeasure and triggering rare introspection and self-critique in the confidential colonial reportage of the trip.

These travels were important in themselves as instruments of colonial cultural brokerage. However, their enduring local signification depended on an elaborate narrative economy that grew around stories and legends of African travel to and adventures in Britain. In turn, vernacularized legends of imperial adventures intersected with and fed into efforts by some aristocrats—such as Muhammadu Dikko and his successor, Usman Nagogo—to memorialize their metropolitan travels in tangible edifices, institutions, and bureaucratic logics deemed replicative of their alleged metropolitan archetypes. This complex story of adaptation, appropriation, domestication, and modernization through the instrumentality of aristocratic metropolitan travel is taken up in the next chapter.

Notes

1. For a history of the economic distress caused by the Great Depression, see Moses Ochonu, *Northern Nigeria in the Great Depression* (Athens: Ohio University Press, 2009).

2. The Ebira people, who populated colonial Igbirra Division, prefer the name "Ebira" and refer to themselves as such. In colonial bureaucratic parlance, however, the Ebira were known as "Igbirra," a name culled from how their neighbors and other non-Ebira people refer to them.

3. For a discussion of the privileging of Muslim kingship in the implementation of indirect rule, see P. Chunung Logams, *The Middle Belt Movement in Nigerian Political Development: A Study of Political Identity 1949–1967* (PhD diss., University of Keele, 1985), 98–127.

4. NAK/Lokoprof, File 251/1925/Vol. I. Memo 1143/83, October 21, 1930, from Secretary Northern Provinces to Resident Kabba Province.

5. NAK/Lokoprof Memo 251/1925/Vol. II/93, Report on the Visit to England by Ibrahima the Atta of Igbira on his return from pilgrimage to Mecca and Medina, by Mr. C. A. Woodhouse, Resident Zaria Province.

6. British National Archives, CO 583/174/3, Pilgrimage to Mecca and Visit to England by Attach [sic] of Igbirra, "Visit of the Attah of Igbirra to England," A Confidential Report by Mr. C. A Woodhouse, Resident, Nigeria.

7. NAK/Lokoprof Memo 251/1925/Vol. I/93, Memo on Visit to England by Attah of Igbirra by Resident, Kabba Province, Mr. H. B. James.

8. NAK/Lokoprof Memo 251/1925/Vol. I, Memo on Visit to England by Attah of Igbirra.

9. Habibu Angulu Sani, *Has History Been Fair to the Atta?: Biography of a Powerful Ruler South of the Sahara* (Okene, Nigeria: Desmond Tutu Publishers, 1997), 180. Sani claims there were "dirty speculations" in local circles on the question of who was funding the trip.

10. NAK/Lokoprof Memo 251/1925/Vol. II/93, Report on the Visit to England by Ibrahima the Atta of Igbira.

11. NAK/Lokoprof Memo 251/1925/Vol. II/93, Report on the Visit to England by Ibrahima the Atta of Igbira.

12. CO 583/174/3, Pilgrimage to Mecca and Visit to England by Attach [sic] of Igbirra, "Telegram from H.M Representative Jedda," "Telegram from H.M Consul Suez," and "Telegram from Acting Consul General Beirut."

13. CO 583/174/3, Pilgrimage to Mecca and Visit to England by Attach [sic] of Igbirra, An Account of a Visit to England by Ibrahim the Attah of Igbirra (A District in Kabba Province One of the Northern Provinces in Nigeria) On His Return from the Pilgrimage to Mecca and Medina.

14. CO 583/174/3, Pilgrimage to Mecca and Visit to England by Attach [sic] of Igbirra, An Account of a Visit to England by Ibrahim the Attah of Igbirra.

15. CO 583/174/3, Pilgrimage to Mecca and Visit to England by Attach [sic] of Igbirra, An Account of a Visit to England by Ibrahim the Attah of Igbirra.
16. CO 583/174/3, Pilgrimage to Mecca and Visit to England by Attach [sic] of Igbirra, An Account of a Visit to England by Ibrahim the Attah of Igbirra.
17. NAK/Lokoprof Memo 251/1925/Vol. II/93, Report on the Visit to England by Ibrahima the Atta of Igbira.
18. CO 583/174/3, Pilgrimage to Mecca and Visit to England by Attach [sic] of Igbirra.
19. CO 583/174/3, Pilgrimage to Mecca and Visit to England by Attach [sic] of Igbirra.
20. Mitchell, "Orientalism and the Exhibitionary Order," 295.
21. Theodor Adorno, *Minima Moralia: Reflections from a Damaged Life* (London: Verso, 1978), 116.
22. NAK/Lokoprof Memo 251/1925/Vol. II/93, Report on the Visit to England by Ibrahima the Atta of Igbira.
23. NAK/Lokoprof Memo 251/1925/Vol. II/93, Report on the Visit to England by Ibrahima the Atta of Igbira.
24. CO 583/174/3, Pilgrimage to Mecca and Visit to England by Attach [sic] of Igbirra.
25. NAK/Lokoprof Memo 251/1925/Vol. II/93, Report on the Visit to England by Ibrahima the Atta of Igbira.
26. NAK/Lokoprof Memo 251/1925/Vol. II/93, Report on the Visit to England by Ibrahima the Atta of Igbira.
27. CO 583/174/3, Pilgrimage to Mecca and Visit to England by Attach [sic] of Igbirra.
28. CO 583/174/3, Pilgrimage to Mecca and Visit to England by Attach [sic] of Igbirra.
29. CO 583/174/3, Pilgrimage to Mecca and Visit to England by Attach [sic] of Igbirra; see also "African Visitors," *Birmingham Gazette*, June 27, 1930, 14.
30. NAK/Lokoprof Memo 251/1925/Vol. II/93, Report on the Visit to England by Ibrahima the Atta of Igbira.
31. NAK/Lokoprof Memo 251/1925/Vol. II/93, Report on the Visit to England by Ibrahima the Atta of Igbira.
32. NAK/Lokoprof Memo 251/1925/Vol. II/93, Report on the Visit to England by Ibrahima the Atta of Igbira.
33. CO 583/174/3, Pilgrimage to Mecca and Visit to England by Attach [sic] of Igbirra.
34. NAK/Lokoprof Memo 251/1925/Vol. II/93, Report on the Visit to England by Ibrahima the Atta of Igbira.
35. *Western Mail*, July 3, 1930, 13.
36. "The Attah in a Mill: Entranced by Vast Power Hammer," *Liverpool Echo*, July 2, 1930, 30.
37. "The Attah in a Mill."
38. NAK/Lokoprof Memo 251/1925/Vol. II/93, Report on the Visit to England by Ibrahima the Atta of Igbira.
39. CO 583/174/3, Pilgrimage to Mecca and Visit to England by Attach [sic] of Igbirra.
40. CO 583/174/3, Pilgrimage to Mecca and Visit to England by Attach [sic] of Igbirra.
41. CO 583/174/3, Pilgrimage to Mecca and Visit to England by Attach [sic] of Igbirra.
42. CO 583/174/3, Pilgrimage to Mecca and Visit to England by Attach [sic] of Igbirra, "Visit of the Attah of Igbirra to England," A Confidential Report by Mr. C. A Woodhouse.
43. CO 583/174/3, Pilgrimage to Mecca and Visit to England by Attach [sic] of Igbirra, "Visit of the Attah of Igbirra to England," A Confidential Report by Mr. C. A Woodhouse.
44. CO 583/174/3, Pilgrimage to Mecca and Visit to England by Attach [sic] of Igbirra, "Visit of the Attah of Igbirra to England," A Confidential Report by Mr. C. A Woodhouse.

45. Gwandu was second in the hierarchy of semiautonomous Muslim states that constituted the Sokoto Caliphate in precolonial Nigeria. In colonial and postcolonial times, this hierarchy remained, albeit for the largely symbolic purpose of aristocratic and religious protocol.

46. "Gaskiya Ta Tabbata Ga Allah, Daga Sarkin Gwandu Yahaya," *Gaskiya ta fi Kwabo*, October 29, 1939, 4.

47. Ochonu, *Colonialism by Proxy*. I call this unorthodox colonial system "subcolonialism."

48. "And the Rest of To-Day's News," *Gloucestershire Echo*, June 23, 1934, 1.

49. "With a Score of Tin Kettles, African Chiefs on Visit to England," *The Nottingham Journal*, June 25, 1934, 5.

50. "Display of Daylight Fireworks," *The Evening News*, Saturday, June 23, 1934, 3.

51. "Visit of a Sultan and Two Emirs," *Aberdeen Press and Journal*, June 25, 1934, 6.

52. Arewa House Archive, 1/37/291, *Confidential Report on the Visit of the Sultan of Sokoto and the Emirs of Gwandu and Kano to England*, November 26, 1934.

53. Arewa House Archive, 1/37/291, *Confidential Report on the Visit of the Sultan of Sokoto*, 2

54. Arewa House Archive, 1/37/291, *Confidential Report on the Visit of the Sultan of Sokoto*, 2.

55. Martin Chanock, *Law, Custom, and Social Order: The Colonial Experience in Malawi and Zambia* (Cambridge: Cambridge University Press, 1985); Lugard, *The Dual Mandate*.

56. Arewa House Archive, 1/37/291, *Confidential Report on the Visit of the Sultan of Sokoto*, 2.

57. Arewa House Archive, 1/37/291, *Confidential Report on the Visit of the Sultan of Sokoto*, 2.

58. The emir famously and recently rode in the horse-drawn carriage during the celebration of his fiftieth anniversary on the throne in 2013. See "Pomp, Praises, as Emir Marks 50 Years on the Throne," *Sun*, July 10, 2013, http://sunnewsonline.com/new/pomp-praises-as-emir-of-kano-marks-50-years-on-the-throne/.

59. "Pomp, Praises," 3.

60. Personal communication with Muhammadu Sanusi II, former emir of Kano, February 26, 2021. The conversation was held over WhatsApp and was brokered and mediated by Dr. Mohammed Dahiru Aminu.

61. See Arjun Appadurai, ed., *The Social Life of Things: Commodities in Cultural Perspective* (Cambridge: Cambridge University Press, 1988). Appadurai contends that commodities have no inherent, immutable utilitarian value and meanings of their own but are empty, malleable objects whose uses, meanings, and cultural significance shift as the items travel through space and time. I find Appadurai's influential theory on commodities and consumption instructive for the way that perambulators emerged across the colonial Atlantic as objects of high status among Northern Nigeria's royalty.

62. I owe this point to Dr. Musa A. Jibril, personal communication, September 5, 2015.

63. Munir Mustapha, personal communication, September 3, 2015.

64. See Appadurai, *The Social Life of Things*.

65. Simon Gikandi, *Maps of Englishness: Writing Identity in the Culture of Colonialism* (New York: Columbia University Press, 1996).

66. Arewa House Archive, 1/37/291, *Confidential Report on the Visit of the Sultan of Sokoto*, 3.

67. Arewa House Archive, 1/37/291, *Confidential Report on the Visit of the Sultan of Sokoto*, 3.

68. Arewa House Archive, 1/37/291, *Confidential Report on the Visit of the Sultan of Sokoto*, 3.

69. Arewa House Archive, 1/37/291, *Confidential Report on the Visit of the Sultan of Sokoto*, 3.

70. "African Rulers Tour: Visit to Portsmouth Dockyard," *Western Morning News and Daily Gazette*, June 27, 1934, 7.

71. Arewa House Archive, 1/37/291, *Report on the Visit of the Sultan of Sokoto*, 4.
72. Arewa House Archive, 1/37/291, *Confidential Report on the Visit of the Sultan of Sokoto*, 4.
73. Photo caption in *Illustrated London News*, July 14, 1934, 52.
74. Photo caption in *Illustrated London News*, July 14, 1934, 52.
75. "Puzzling Scene for African Potentates," *Illutsrated London News*, June 30, 1934, 1052
76. "African Chiefs at the Colonial Office: Ministers Charmed by Their Dusky Visitors," *Western Daily Press*, July 6, 1934, 8.
77. Arewa House Archive, 1/37/291, *Confidential Report on the Visit of the Sultan of Sokoto*, 3.
78. Arewa House Archive, 1/37/291, *Confidential Report on the Visit of the Sultan of Sokoto*, 3.
79. "King's Visitors," *Dundee Evening Telegraph*, Monday, July 2, 1934, 1.
80. Arewa House Archive, 1/37/291, *Confidential Report on the Visit of the Sultan of Sokoto*, 3.
81. Ousmane Kane, *Muslim Modernity in Postcolonial Nigeria: A Study of the Society for the Removal of Innovation and Reinstatement of Tradition* (Leiden: Brill, 2003), 70–71.
82. Arewa House Archive, 1/37/291, *Confidential Report on the Visit of the Sultan of Sokoto*, 7.
83. Arewa House Archive, 1/37/291, *Confidential Report on the Visit of the Sultan of Sokoto*, 7.
84. Arewa House Archive, 1/37/291, *Confidential Report on the Visit of the Sultan of Sokoto*, 8.
85. Arewa House Archive, 1/37/291, *Confidential Report on the Visit of the Sultan of Sokoto*, 8.
86. Arewa House Archive, 1/37/291, *Confidential Report on the Visit of the Sultan of Sokoto*, 13.
87. Arewa House Archive, 1/37/291, *Confidential Report on the Visit of the Sultan of Sokoto*, 13.
88. "Princes See Margarine Made," *Taunton Courier: Bristol and Exeter Journal and Western Advertiser*, July 11, 1934, 1.
89. "Princes See Margarine Made."
90. "Princes See Margarine Made."
91. "Princes See Margarine Made."
92. "African Chiefs' Birds Eye View of London," *The Nottingham Journal*, June 28, 1934, 11.
93. Ibid.
94. "Emir's Visit to York," *The Yorkshire Post*, June 29, 1934, 4.
95. Ibid.
96. "Princes See Margarine Made."
97. Arewa House Archive, 1/37/291, *Confidential Report on the Visit of the Sultan of Sokoto*, 10.
98. See Lugard, *The Dual Mandate*.
99. Arewa House Archive, 1/37/291, *Confidential Report on the Visit of the Sultan of Sokoto*, 13.
100. Arewa House Archive, 1/37/291, *Confidential Report on the Visit of the Sultan of Sokoto*, 11.
101. Arewa House Archive, 1/37/291, *Confidential Report on the Visit of the Sultan of Sokoto*, 8.
102. Arewa House Archive, 1/37/291, *Confidential Report on the Visit of the Sultan of Sokoto*, 11.
103. "West African Chiefs: Picturesque Rulers at Plymouth," *Western Morning News*, June 25, 1934, 6.
104. "West African Chiefs," 5.
105. "Our Nigerian Visitors: What Manner of Men Are They?" *The Sphere*, July 7, 1934, 8.
106. "West African Chiefs," 5.
107. "West African Chiefs," 5.
108. See Charles Temple, *Native Races and Their Rulers: Sketches and Studies of Official Life and Administrative Problems in Nigeria* (Cape Town: Argus, 1918).
109. Arewa House Archive 1/37/291, *Confidential Report on the Visit of the Sultan of Sokoto*, 5.
110. Arewa House Archive 1/37/291, *Confidential Report on the Visit of the Sultan of Sokoto*, 6.
111. British National Archives, FO 141/699/5, From H. E. the Governor of the Sudan, dispatch # 69 (18-3-1933), Pilgrimage of the Emir of Katsina (of Nigeria) via Sudan. The author

of the report of Emir Dikko's visit to England in 1921, Mr. G. W. Webster, based his report on "a diary of the Emir of Katsina's visit to England and Mecca."

112. "Foreign Potentates Visit to Portsmouth: Quaint Letters of Thanks to Sir Harold Pink," *Portsmouth Evening News*, December 24, 1934, 3.
113. "Foreign Potentates Visit to Portsmouth," 3.
114. "Foreign Potentates Visit to Portsmouth," 3.
115. "Foreign Potentates Visit to Portsmouth," 3.
116. "Gaskiya Ta Tabbata Ga Allah."
117. "Gaskiya Ta Tabbata Ga Allah."
118. "Gaskiya Ta Tabbata Ga Allah."
119. "Gaskiya Ta Tabbata Ga Allah."
120. "Gaskiya Ta Tabbata Ga Allah."
121. "Gaskiya Ta Tabbata Ga Allah."
122. "Gaskiya Ta Tabbata Ga Allah."
123. "Gaskiya Ta Tabbata Ga Allah."

4

THE DIKKO-NAGOGO BRITISH CONNECTION

> I do not feel free in London. I feel overshadowed. Life here is not simple.
> Your amazing inventions have lengthened your powers
> but shortened your chances of happiness.
> —Muhammadu Dikko

IN THE 1930S, THE DIKKO CLAN MADE THREE trips to Britain, one of which was paired with the pilgrimage to Mecca. Taken together, these midcolonial trips and the metropolitan explorations, resources, and appropriations that marked them helped transform the cultural identity of Katsina, consolidating the emirate's reputation within and outside Nigeria as a hub of colonial modernization. This chapter inscribes the traveling and modernizing agency of the father-son duo of Dikko and Nagogo in this story of travel, metropolitan cultural immersion, and an attempted re-creation of metropolitan-inspired institutions, objects, and symbols. The chapter begins with Dikko's trip to Britain in 1933.

Emir Dikko's third visit to Britain in 1933 was perhaps his most elaborate in terms of itinerary and resonance. Like that of 1921, the visit was paired with the Muslim pilgrimage to Mecca, which made detailed logistical planning and prior epistolary exchanges necessary. It was Dikko's idea to make a detour to Britain for a three-week sightseeing and shopping vacation on his way home from the pilgrimage. However, colonial protocol demanded that he obtain permission from several superintending colonial authorities, beginning with the district officer, continuing with the resident of Katsina Province, and ending with the governor.

Dikko had originally proposed visiting Britain in 1931, but archival evidence suggests that colonial authorities "abandoned" the proposal "for reasons of economy" since the Great Depression had eroded revenue and the state's ability to finance the logistics of metropolitan travel for its aristocratic partners.[1] In 1932, the emir requested that the proposal be reconsidered. This request triggered formal discussion on the matter. Correspondence on the proposed visit began in earnest in the same year with a set of proposals for the itinerary, number of visitors, outlines of logistical necessities, and a sightseeing list for the emir and accompanying officials. Safe passages and diplomatic protection had to be requested for Dikko and his group, who would be traveling through French colonial territory, other British colonial domains, and the Kingdom of Saudi Arabia. In Britain, chauffeur-driven cars had to be arranged for the metropolitan transportation of the emir and his entourage, and tours had to be booked in advance. Other logistical instruments had to be arranged through formal and informal channels.

In January 1933, discussions intensified about details and arrangements. G. S. Browne, a former district officer of Katsina Division and the lieutenant governor of Northern Nigeria, outlined the proposals in a letter to his liaison in London, H. S. Goldsmith. The emir was to depart for the pilgrimage with "a party of 26," traveling overland through French and British colonial territories. Thereafter, Dikko would proceed to Britain with seven people in his entourage for a stay of "2 or 3 weeks."[2] Browne would not be able to guide the tourists in England because he had to travel to Barbados to be with his sick mother. As a result, he requested that Goldsmith, who had served in the colonial bureaucracy in Northern Nigeria, "take charge of the party or get some old Nigerian in England to do it or to help you."[3] Browne suggested that since the party "will eat nothing provided by the hotel," presumably for fear of ingesting pork-based foods, it would be best if they took "rooms in a small hotel" and for Goldsmith and other metropolitan logistical officials to "arrange facilities for them to cook their own food."[4]

The logistical instructions and forethought were as detailed as they were intimate, including the types of beds to secure for married and unmarried members of the entourage, who spoke little English and would need a full-time slate of translators, how items would be paid for, and other such details. Browne stated that Dikko "will want to do a lot of shopping," which required making arrangements with the Bank of British West Africa to provide checks to pay for goods. Dikko also wanted to meet the king. Since the secretary of state for the colonies had been informed of Dikko's visit, Browne surmised that he would arrange "an audience with the King."[5]

Late in January 1933, the outlines of a final logistical plan emerged, articulated in correspondence between the district officer of Katsina Division and the resident of Zaria Province. A memo from the former to the latter stated that Dikko would travel to Britain with £2,000, the equivalent of £126,400 in today's money.[6] This money would be supported by a letter of credit. Furthermore, the Bank of British West Africa would be instructed to enable the emir to "draw from his current account through [the bank] should the Letter of Credit become exhausted."[7] The memo stated further that those traveling from the pilgrimage to England had been provided regular passports while the pilgrimage party had been issued special pilgrims' passports. Other arrangements outlined in the memo include fuel dumps along the overland route in Maiduguri, Djamena, and El-Obeid in Nigeria, Chad, and Sudan respectively.[8] Letters of introduction had been issued to Dikko to enable him to access the diplomatic and logistical support of British and French colonial authorities along the way.

Governor Donald Cameron approved Dikko's visit shortly thereafter, permitting the emir to travel with three of his wives; six relatives, including his brothers, his two sons, the wives of his sons; and fifteen servants—twenty-seven people in all. In a memo communicating the approval to Sir Philip Cunliff-Lister, the secretary of state for the colonies, Governor Cameron requested Cunliff-Lister to "inform the authorities at Khartoum, Jeddah, and Port Said of the Emir's proposed journey in order that if he should be in difficulties at any of these places he could be given such help as would be possible."[9] What Cameron was requesting was that the logistical, military, and diplomatic assets of the British imperial system be put at the disposal of Dikko and his entourage. The lieutenant governor of Northern Nigeria subsequently sent a letter to his counterpart in the French colonial district of Fort Lamy (Djamena), asking him to "facilitate the passage of . . . the Emir and his party."[10] In a later correspondence, the Foreign Office would urge the British ambassador to France to "bring the matter to the notice of the French Government"—in other words, to formally request diplomatic passage for Dikko and his group through French colonial territory.[11]

Another imperial logistical business concerned formal requests from the Colonial Office and the Foreign Office to colonial authorities and officials in the Anglo-Egyptian Sudan axis, through which the party would travel, lodge, and transition from land to sea. On February 8, the Foreign

Office formally wrote to the British colonial authorities in Sudan and Egypt to request support and protection for Dikko and his group: "I request that you will invite the Government of the Anglo-Egyptian Sudan to extend, if they see no objection, such assistance as may be possible to the Emir and his party during their journey through Sudanese territory, and that you will endeavor to arrange for the provision of appropriate facilities for the party on their return journey through Egypt."[12] The Foreign Office also sent a similar letter to "His Majesty's Minister at Jedda," requesting a similarly high level of diplomatic support for Dikko and his entourage during their pilgrimage in the Hejaz.

Correspondence from the British governor of Egypt and Sudan at the Cairo Residency directed officials of the British Legation in Jeddah to facilitate Dikko's passage to Suez in Egypt, where the emir's entourage would land and be quarantined on their return journey before some of them would depart for England through Port Said and others for Nigeria. Specifically, the missive directed the Legation to "arrange for the passport section and instruct the Egyptian consulate at Jeddah that visas . . . may be granted to the Emir and his party on application."[13] The Legation was further requested to ask the "Resident of the quarantine branch" to "do what is possible . . . to facilitate the Emir's progress."[14] Earlier correspondence from the Colonial Office had requested "His Majesty's Minister at Jeddah . . . to do all in his power to assist the Emir and to secure a favorable reception from the Saudi,"[15] and that the governor of Egypt and Sudan would "accord such assistance to the Emir as may be possible, especially in matters of customs and quarantine formalities."[16] British colonial diplomatic clout and the transnational administrative and bureaucratic networks that embodied it preceded and facilitated the transnational mobility of Dikko and his group.

Trip Planning as Colonial Regimen

Colonial arrangements for Dikko's visit underscore the British colonial obsession with regimen, control, and detail and point to the workings of a bureaucratic machine focused on micromanaging every aspect of the subaltern's entry into metropolitan society. In the months before Dikko's trip, a flurry of correspondence among officials located in British colonial nodes in London, Nigeria, Sudan, and Cairo touched on a wide array of preparations for the trip.

Officials asked G. S. Browne, who had chaperoned Dikko's trip in 1924, to apprise current planners of the emir's feelings regarding the hotel in which he previously stayed. They also wanted to know what sights he had seen on his previous visits so they would "avoid showing him sights that he has already seen."[17] Other preparatory protocols included determining who would guide the party through the excursions in Britain. On that question, officials defaulted to Browne. A British colonial officer in Nigeria, Browne was transiting through London to Barbados for his annual holiday. He and his wife would "take charge of the Emir."[18]

When the correspondence shifted to additional guides, especially for the emir's wives, Browne volunteered the services of his wife and stepdaughter, stating that the two had helped guide Dikko's wives during the emir's visit to the Wembley British Empire Exhibition in 1924.[19] In this correspondence, Browne positioned himself as an expert on Dikko's tastes and preferences, the equivalent of today's country expert who, through direct field interaction with Dikko in Nigeria, could advise on the latter's interests. He told Goldsmith, who was coordinating the logistics of Dikko's visit, that the emir would want to meet the king at Buckingham Palace. The emir, Browne further stated, would want to attend "race meetings, polo matches, [and see] a hospital, the Houses of Parliament and the Colonial Office."[20] Dikko's senior wife, Browne told Goldsmith, was interested in seeing "a girl's school."

In addition to regular updates from Browne, trip planners fielded requests from a certain Colonel Blythe, who wanted the emir to visit his school; a suggestion from one Captain Rattray that Dikko make "phonographic records in Hausa" for the BBC; and a request from Windsor Castle for an updated "note about the Emir and his state" to be used by the king as a reference and conversational prompts during their proposed meeting in Buckingham Palace.[21]

Other preparations included issuing "half-fare first class train tickets" to Dikko and his entourage on the Sudan Railways for their overland journey to Port Said, from where they would sail on the SS *Talodi* to Jeddah.[22] Even before other arrangements had been concluded, the lieutenant governor of Northern Nigeria wrote to Goldsmith to request that since Dikko and his party were not traveling from Nigeria with a British guide, Goldsmith should arrange a welcoming party composed of "retired [colonial] officers" or officers "on leave" to "meet [the party] on arrival and look after them during their stay."[23]

The logistical and epistolary processes that preceded Dikko's 1933 trip underscore the important role that imperial networks and diplomatic resources played in organizing and shaping aristocratic visits to Britain. In this and other trips, Dikko and his party moved within the empire and beyond it on the good diplomatic graces of the British imperial system. Imperial resources, even in faraway Jedda and Mecca, proved useful and were a reminder of the empire's reach, ubiquity, and power. The diplomatic efforts of various British colonial institutions facilitated the mobility and reception of Dikko and his team of pilgrims in the Hejaz/Saudi Arabia. For their part, the emir and his entourage explored the Muslim Holy Land extensively, traveling from Jeddah to Medina and then to Mecca to perform the hajj.

The British government's representatives in Saudi Arabia were instrumental to the logistics of the travels there. Fulfilling one of Dikko's requests, British officials in Saudi Arabia arranged for the emir to visit the governor of Medina and King Abdul Naiz Ibn Fa'ad. Beyond the satisfaction of fulfilling a personal aspiration, Dikko was reportedly delighted that the Saudi king "received him personally and placed him on his right hand."[24] The political import of British imperial might reaching all the way to Saudi Arabia and smoothing his path through the Hejaz would not have been lost on Dikko and would have reinforced existing imperial affinities and loyalties. It also probably dissolved any residual antipathy the emir might have harbored against the British on account of his Muslim faith since culturally Christian British officials were enjoying much goodwill and consequential influence in the holiest place of Islam.

The logistical lengths to which metropolitan and Nigeria-based colonial authorities went to arrange imperial protection for Dikko and his party suggest that these efforts were not just about protecting a valued imperial ally but also about demonstrating to that ally that the British imperial system could do almost anything, and on any scale, and that what it could not do by itself, it could use its global diplomatic clout to make others do. It was a powerful message to send to an emir visiting Britain; it signaled British claims to imperial greatness and stood in for the alleged power and reach of British colonial might.

Dikko Returns to England

Upon the completion of the pilgrimage, Dikko and his party left Mecca on April 8, 1933 (see map 4.1). Parting with other members of his pilgrimage

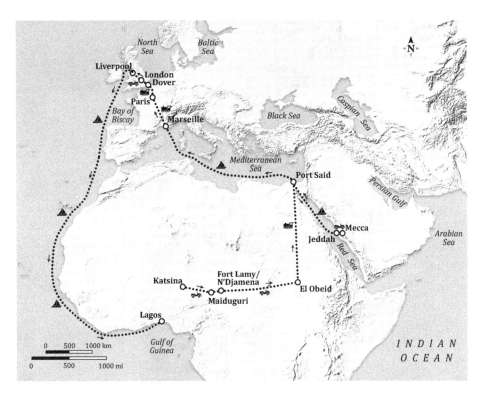

Map 4.1. Itinerary of the journey of Emir of Katsina, Muhammadu Dikko, and his entourage to the Hejaz and Britain in 1933.

group, Dikko took his two sons, his brother, two grandsons, and his wife Ummulhairi on the journey to Britain. The smaller group sailed from Jeddah to Port Said to Marseilles, where they took a train to Paris and then another to Dover, where Lieutenant Governor Browne met them and took them to London. In London, they lodged at the Hyde Park Hotel for two weeks. Like Dikko's previous visits to Britain, this one was packed full of sightseeing and other adventures (see figs. 4.1 and 4.2), and it included a meeting with both the king and the Prince of Wales. He was the first Northern Nigerian emir to meet the two royal figures during one visit.

British newspapers reported extensively on Dikko's visit, sensationalizing his otherness as usual, and making sloppy errors about his title and domain. Because of his extensive metropolitan itinerary, Dikko provided the British press ample opportunities to satisfy their readers' curiosities about exotica, Africa, Islam, and empire. Journalists followed Dikko to

Figure 4.1. Photographic news coverage of Emir Dikko's 1933 visit in the *Illustrated London News*.

Figure 4.2. Dikko and his entourage admiring a traffic light in London.

every engagement, shouting out questions, taking pictures from multiple angles, and sometimes getting in the way as he and his party entered or exited buildings. The overarching editorial slant of the British press regarding Dikko and his entourage turned on a single theme: the emir and his entourage were primitive colonial subjects discovering and fawning over the wonders of civilization. This trope was merely rearticulated to accommodate evolving itineraries. Commenting on the visit, the *Montrose Standard* explained to its readers that Dikko and his grandsons "left their somewhat primitive country to see the wonders of modern Western civilization" and that they had already "received many surprises" and had "been amazed at the sights they have seen."[25] Underscoring a pattern of press "mobbing" discussed in previous chapters, Browne stated that the emir's visit "has been a trying time . . . with journalists and photographers and people who want to sell [the emir] something."[26] He added without elaborating that "women journalists are the worst."[27]

This last comment could be an indication that the female journalists were questioning Dikko about the whereabouts of his wives, a holdover from the press speculations (discussed in chap. 2) about the women allegedly being left at the hotel while the male members of the entourage toured sites. The speculation about the Muslim emir barring his wives from appearing in public was shown to be unfounded during the 1921 visit when the women, guided by Maud Gowers, visited theater shows and the zoo and subsequently joined Dikko and his entourage to tour several sites. In 1933, any lingering speculation about the wives' exclusion should have dissipated. Mrs. G. S. Browne, "who is acting as guide, adviser, and friend during the visit," responded to the request of Dikko's fourth and youngest wife, Maidaki [Salamatu] "to be shown those institutions which cater to the needs of children," by "arrang[ing] sightseeing trips . . . which include visits to a Montessori Kindergarten, a Children's Hospital, and Roedean School."[28]

Maidaki and Dikko's senior wife were guided around London by Mrs. Browne and were photographed alongside their guide at some London touristic sites, with their reluctance to be photographed on full visual display (see fig. 4.3). Browne's statement regarding female journalists could also reflect his and Dikko's unfamiliarity and discomfort with professional interactions involving women. Browne complained in another report that, although "the press . . . were delighted with the chance of getting hold of some unusual 'copy,'" he was not sure "they did not rather over do it."[29]

On this visit, Dikko's grandsons were a hit with the British media and seem to have upstaged their grandfather as the principal visual attraction of the entourage. On May 5, the day the king received Dikko at Buckingham Palace, the *Scotsman* published a photo of the grandsons dressed in traditional royal regalia.[30] The *Illustrated London News* then published two iconic photos of Dikko's grandsons, one showing them playing with a tadpole jar during a visit to an elementary school in London (see fig. 4.4)[31] and another showing them posing by the wheel of an Imperial Airways aircraft at the Croydon Aerodrome and at a traffic light (see figs. 4.1 and 4.2).[32] The grandsons' visit to the London Zoological Gardens was visually documented in a picture of them walking excitedly with a penguin, which was published in the German magazine *Berliner Illustrirte Zeitung* (see fig. 4.6). The mutual fascination between Dikko's grandsons and London continued and survives in multiple photographs. At the West Acton Film Studios in London, Dikko's two grandsons would once again be the center of attention as they fiddled with the studio equipment and then marveled while watching a newsreel clip of themselves and listening to the commentary on their headphones (see fig. 4.5).

Figure 4.3. Dikko's wives on a guided tour of London.

Figure 4.4. Dikko's grandsons admiring a tadpole jar at a London elementary school.

Figure 4.5. Dikko's son and grandsons at the Acton Studio in London.

Figure 4.6. Dikko's grandsons walking with a penguin at the London Zoological Gardens.

The previous day, May 4, several newspapers had published stories on the entourage's visit to two airfields. The emir and his group traveled to the North Weald Aerodrome, where "the Royal Air Force staged a miniature pageant" in his honor. RAF fighter jets dazzled the visitors with "a takeoff in formation of a fighter squadron and a quick getaway attack."[33] As the jets thundered above, Dikko reportedly exclaimed, "I never want war to

Figure 4.7. Dikko and his sons and grandsons at the Croydon Aerodrome.

come to my country when such fighting aircraft exist,"[34] a profound statement indicating that the emir's awe was tempered with anxiety about the military technologies the British imperial system had at its disposal. The RAF fighters also demonstrated how they dropped supplies in remote war zones. Dikko and his retinue then flew to Croydon, where the emir toured the aircraft fleet and watched an Imperial Airways airliner take off for Paris (fig. 4.7).[35] Dikko and his group inspected different kinds of aircraft on display as an instructor guided them and made pilots demonstrate the workings of each aircraft. The visitors later flew in one of the planes.[36]

The visits to North Weald and Croydon were part of an elaborate scheme of awing the visiting aristocrats with graphic evidence of British imperial military might. In addition to the aerodromes, Dikko toured the naval dockyard at Portsmouth, where he and his retinue were taken aboard two warships, the HMS *Hood* and the HMS *Victory*, and thereafter toured the submarine *Thames*. While in the warships, Dikko was shown different components of their operations as well as their combat capabilities. The commander of the fleet, Admiral W. M. James, conducted them "through the engine rooms, the galley, the lower and upper decks, and on to the bridge,"[37] communicating the operations of the battleships to the emir through Browne, who interpreted.

As usual, Dikko's meeting with the king was the highlight of the visit. The meeting at Buckingham Palace followed the emir's audience with the Prince of Wales, with whom he "had a long conversation."[38] Accompanied to the palace by his two sons, his brother, and Browne, Dikko's return visit to Buckingham was as grand as his first in 1921. The king received him at the grand entrance, and both men spent "some time" together while the emir's sons remained "in the Palace quadrangle, watching the Changing of the Guard ceremony."[39]

As was Dikko's tradition, he took his entourage to the London Zoological Gardens, where the *Yorkshire Post and Lead Intelligencer* reported that his two grandsons, Wakili and Yusufu, "walked about in wide-eyed wonder looking at the various animals, birds, and reptiles."[40] It was further reported that they "rode on the camels, fed the penguins and macaws, and went for a ride on an elephant."[41] Later in the tour, Wakili and Yusufu were reported to have been terrified when, as they were feeding one giraffe, another in the next pen stretched its neck and "made a grab at the food."[42] Such stories of the party's metropolitan adventures made them something of a novelty act in British public spaces.

Britain as Recreational Escape

If British journalists and other interlocutors saw Dikko and his entourage as a curious, entertaining presence, Emir Dikko saw the metropole as a playground—a recreational escape from the drudgery of quotidian colonial and emirate work in Katsina. For him, going to Britain was an opportunity to be introduced to new forms of leisure and to reinforce the aristocratic hobbies he had cultivated and nurtured in the framework of empire. Two sights satisfied this curiosity: the circus and animal racing. After their tour of the battleships in Portsmouth, the emir and his entourage visited the Bertram Mills Circus. There, Dikko, an avid horseman, took a particular interest in the horses in the circus's stable, "asking numerous questions" that Bertram Mills answered through Browne.[43] Dikko then rode one of the liberty horses that had been specially fitted with a harness for him. He was so impressed with the harness's "gay trappings and plumes" that he declared he would buy some for his horses in Nigeria.

As Dikko engaged the circus personnel in small talk about horses and the rest of the entourage alternately encountered "an affectionate" reception from the elephants and "a growling" from one of the tigers,[44] his sons asked questions about the origins of the circus ponies and made notes on the answers.[45] Dikko requested that a photograph be taken of him and a tiger trainer and handler named Togare, who also signed his autograph for the emir's sons in their notebooks. Dikko wanted to know how the circus traveled with all the animals and expressed awe when he was told that the circus ensemble traveled weekly and that railway coaches transported the animals from town to town for their weekly shows.

In Britain, where animal racing of different kinds was a popular pastime supported by a large betting operation, Dikko satiated his interest in the equestrian arts enthusiastically, giddy at his immersion in a wide variety of equestrian sports and entertainment forms. During this trip, he also took his retinue, including his wife, to see the White City greyhound race. The emir and his group were the guests of honor at the event and "received a great ovation when they preceded the procession of dogs on to the track."[46] As he had done during previous visits, Dikko bet on several races, picking the winning dog in three out of five races and picking two others who came in second and third.

In a moment of irony, one of his picks won while he was saying his prayer outside the venue. This convergence of betting and prayer is instructive because it once again reinforces the argument that Dikko, like other Northern Nigerian aristocrats who were enamored with the metropole and its modernist displays, saw no contradiction between their metropolitan social indulgences and their Muslim devotion and identity. The emir was ecstatic at winning and reportedly remarked, "I have never seen dogs run so fast . . . we hunt with dogs in my country, but I have not seen them run like this before."[47] When asked about the secret of his successful picks, Dikko said simply, "I look for the strongest-looking dog, particularly the dog with strong [hind]quarters."[48] During the race, organizers named one of the events the Nigerian Stakes in Dikko's honor. The emir then presented the silver trophy to the winner of that event.[49]

The aforementioned visit to the White City greyhound race was the offshoot of an elaborate rendezvous with Dikko's old friend and former British resident in Katsina, E.H.B Laing. The metropolitan reunion with Laing, who was now the senior resident for the northern provinces, was a detour from the official itinerary, and it allowed Dikko and his entourage the freedom to explore Britain with a private itinerary arranged by the Laings around a lunch invitation to their residence at Wanborough. As reported by the *Surrey Advertiser*, the party was accompanied by the Brownes, and they traveled to the Laings' home in two groups.[50] After lunch, the party was photographed as a group and individually in the garden of the Laings' home. The Laings then accompanied Dikko and his team on their road trip to Reading to tour the Huntley and Palmer's biscuit factory. Thereafter, the Laings arranged for the tourists to "watch the greyhound racing at the White City."[51]

Dikko and his entourage also visited the Kempton Park races in Surrey on May 7. The emir, whom a local newspaper described as "a clever judge of horseflesh,"[52] and his "picturesque party" attended the event as guests of Sir Frederick Eley, the owner of one of the competing horses in the Kempton Park Jubilee race. The emir's attendance at Kempton Park is immortalized in a photograph published in the *Illustrated London News* that shows Dikko and his entourage interestedly inspecting the "totalisation" board at Kempton Park Racecourse (fig. 4.1).[53]

As shown in chapters 2 and 3, ritualized tours of industrial settings where metropolitan goods were made were common features of these itineraries. This visit was no exception. Dikko visited Unilever establishments twice during his 1933 tour. On his first visit, he toured the company's boardroom. Col. E. H. Beddington, the chairman of the United Africa Company (UAC), made a traditional offering of kola nuts on a silver platter and delivered a welcome address that was then translated for the emir and his relatives.[54]

Ever the master of imperial protocol, Dikko laughed when Beddington's remark about higher groundnut prices was translated to him.[55] The laughter was a polite disagreement. The groundnut export was a touchy subject in 1933 because the price had collapsed at the onset of the Great Depression that was still raging in Northern Nigeria, where groundnuts were the primary agricultural export. Beddington had obviously advanced that remark to preempt Dikko, who might have asked about the dwindling price of groundnuts had Beddington not brought it up. Not wanting to be a rude imperial guest, the emir simply laughed at the comment to communicate his disagreement without directly criticizing the low prices or blaming Unilever and other British colonial raw material buyers for the price slump, a narrative staple of the Northern Nigerian colonial grapevine.

As one of the concluding activities of their visit to Britain, Dikko and his entourage toured the Lever Brothers soap factory at Port Sunlight on May 17. Lord Leverhulme, who had invited them, was on hand to receive them at the factory in Liverpool at the beginning of a three-day program of final sightseeing in the Merseyside region of England. At Port Sunlight, Lord Leverhulme presented Dikko and his party with a bowl of kola nuts as "a symbol of friendship" and then welcomed them in the Hausa language.[56] During his tour of the factory complex, Dikko told Lord Leverhulme that he would like to see the fire brigade in action. Lord Leverhulme obliged, sending out a false fire alarm.[57] The fire brigade appeared within minutes of the alarm. Dikko's son Nagogo then put on a fireman's helmet and asked to be photographed in it. Dikko's grandsons climbed atop a fire engine and were "given a thrilling ride at top speed" in a simulated fire response as they were allowed to blow whistles and ring the fire bell in imitation of a real fire emergency.[58] Later, Dikko was driven through the newly constructed Mersey tunnel, an experience he described as going to hell and coming back.[59]

At the end of his tour of Port Sunlight, Dikko reportedly told Lord Leverhulme and his other hosts that he felt that as a person of "small importance" he had been treated better than a white person.[60] Over the next three days, Dikko and his group toured the model village on the factory grounds, and "the women and children of the party were shown round the village institution, the schools, the hospital, and Lady Lever Art Gallery."[61] The lord mayor of Liverpool hosted Dikko and his entourage at a reception at the city hall. Dikko's final tours complete, he and his entourage left Liverpool for Lagos and arrived in the Nigerian colonial capital on June 6, 1933.

Before leaving Britain, Dikko and his entourage repaid the labor of H. B. Goldsmith, who had worked hard on the logistical planning of their trip and helped guide the tourists to sites around Britain. Dikko and his party paid Goldsmith, Dikko's "old friend" and former lieutenant governor of Northern Nigeria, what the *Hampshire Telegraph* called a "surprise visit" at his Barncroft home near Eastergate and Bognor.[62] The two colonial friends had the customary tea and conversed about Britain and Nigeria.

Dazzling the Guest

Metropolitan tour guides and planners took extraordinary steps to ingrain visiting African guests with impressions they hoped would stay with them. Investments in material and audiovisual instruments intended to dazzle important visitors were a priority. New audio and visual technologies proved particularly useful in this effort to awe visitors from the colonized world. As Dikko and his entourage approached the end of their visit, two encounters arranged by his metropolitan minders expressed this audiovisual razzmatazz. Dikko's grandsons were presented with model toy cars. Officials arranged for a photographer to take photos of them and "their famous grandfather."[63] The emir was then presented copies of the photographs, but there was a perplexing twist to the story. Dikko received photographs in which, "instead of looking coloured," he and his grandsons "have white complexions," or, as the *Montrose Standard* explained, "they are just like an old British gentleman and his two little boys in white robes."[64]

Was this the result of a photographic or laboratory mishap or a bizarrely lighthearted attempt at a photographic racial makeover? There is no definitive clarity in either direction, but the evidence points to a flaw in the photographic process, which had not been designed to be faithful to the pigmentational singularities of nonwhite photographic subjects. As Olaf Bloch, the head chemist of Ilford Photograph Company, explained, "The pigment in a dark skin is able to reflect a certain amount of infra-red light. Therefore when infra-red plates are used it gives a dark picture in the negative and a white picture in the print."[65]

Clearly, metropolitan photographic technology was struggling to catch up with the desire to provide visiting Africans with race-neutral photographic souvenirs. The technology had apparently not reckoned with the possibility of photographing high-melanin colonial subjects from Nigeria. Technology lagged behind the colonial desire to dazzle visiting colonial aristocrats. This technological deficit, it should be noted, also meshed with the casual journalistic racism of metropolitan newspapers that covered and wrote about Dikko's adventures in Britain.

The second aspect of the audiovisual propaganda was the newsreel. As analyzed elsewhere in this book, the newsreel medium was deployed for visiting emirs as an improvised cinematic gateway into events in other corners of the British Empire and to showcase the staged glories of an imagined imperial community, to paraphrase Benedict Anderson.[66] Toward the end of the 1933 visit, Dikko and his entourage were subjected to a different newsreel experience. As the *Merthyr Express* reported, the emir "for the first time in his life . . . saw himself on the screen and heard his voice reproduced by microphone when he visited the editorial department of the British Paramount News."[67] The sound newsreel company had made a film feature about Dikko's visit to the Croydon Aerodrome. Once again, metropolitan technology wrestled with the subtleties of color and pigmentation in audiovisual representation. The *Merthyr Express* reported that Dikko was "greatly amused by the fact that while his dusky features assumed a decidedly milk-white tint, those of the surrounding Europeans temporarily took on a tropical tan"—a result, the report explained, of editors shooting news films in negative "to save time."[68] Fidelity to accurate representation of the filmed and photographed colonial subject was subordinated to the expediencies of a metropolitan journalistic and audiovisual enterprise that had no experience with representing racial colonial Others in film and photograph.

Dikko's Evaluation of Britain

Dikko's journal entries are sprinkled with opinions and commentary on several spheres of British society he observed, but the entries are more descriptive than evaluative in tone and texture. Part of the limitation is that journaling in a touristic situation is essentially an exercise in experiential chronicling. Additionally, the fact that the experiences Dikko documented in his journal occurred largely in official touring itineraries skewed the narrative in the direction of the descriptive. It is in less scripted sources, mostly in media interviews and informal chats, that Dikko's complex evaluations of British society are revealed.

After Dikko and his entourage departed for Nigeria, the *Tatler*, a companion magazine of the *Illustrated London News*, published an interview it had conducted with the emir. Dikko's responses to questions, published along with pictures of him and his grandsons, give us a glimpse into his thoughts on British society, his position within the British imperial realm, his anxieties and hopes about his immersion in British modernity, and his discomfort with aspects of British metropolitan life. Dikko proceeds in the interview from fawning approval to biting critique. On his meeting with the king and Britain's regal and martial customs, Dikko had this to say: "His Majesty the King is wonderful. He spoke of all my hobbies when he saw me the other day, and recalled that he himself had invested me with his medal for the African chiefs. May Allah aid him! Who could help being loyal to a remembering king? . . . Then came the soldiers at Aldershot, who move about as though they were part of a machine. Your machines are human, your men are machines."[69] Dikko then returned to a theme he had broached after seeing a display by fighter jets of the Royal Air Force, which was analyzed earlier in this chapter: his disdain for and the unintelligibility of what he regarded as a British obsession with war making, war preparation, and military industrialization. "Why do you prepare for war, when everywhere I hear that the world is at peace?" Dikko asked rhetorically. Dikko proceeded to extend this incipient critique of what one might call the British military industrial complex and its imperial war mongering: "In Katsina when the English settled the province, they disbanded the troops saying: 'that is our way of peace'"[70] Dikko was highlighting the contradiction of purportedly pursuing peace through imperial war making and perpetual arms buildup. Here Dikko was not only decrying the intense militarization of British imperial power and the ubiquity of martial symbols in metropolitan life; he was also pointing to the British hypocrisy of disarming colonized peoples while turning metropolitan industrial spaces into vast armament production zones and maintaining a growing military arsenal in peacetime.

Since the British conquest of Katsina at the turn of the twentieth century and Dikko's role in enabling the occupiers to consolidate their administrative control, the emir had been dogged by local gossip that he was too enamored with British culture and was losing his Islamic piety in the process of ingratiating himself with British colonizers.[71] This was clearly a source of anxiety for the emir, whose disposition toward British ways of life was more complicated than a simple desire to adopt and emulate. Dikko told his interviewers that while "my people think I am so pro-English" and that "I have come to England to buy a house and settle here," he would never leave Katsina, where he was "cock of the walk."[72] His adamant unwillingness to swap Katsina for England was not just because he was the emirate's number one citizen and would be a commoner in Britain but also because "in Katsina we laugh" while "the English have so much to think about." He continued, "Your amazing inventions have lengthened your powers but shortened your chances of happiness."[73] This was a profound critique of the mechanization of British life by the progress of technology, which, in Dikko's view, undermined the humanity, spontaneity, and happiness of the British people. Dikko's contention was that the very things that made Britain strong as an imperial power also made Britons unhappy, encumbered, stiff, and incapable of simple, spontaneous human pleasures. Technology and modernization, he contended, were both a blessing and a burden and so needed to be humanized and mitigated by an embrace of simple, rustic living, which he surmised was not possible in Britain.

Like other Northern Nigerian visitors to Britain analyzed in this book,[74] Dikko regarded Britons as a people enslaved by their obsessions with technological advancement, power, industrialization, and a punishing and dehumanizing work regimen. The regimentation of socioeconomic life was marked, Dikko argued, by the ironic absence of freedom in a society that proclaimed itself a democracy and professed progress. He declared, "I do not feel free in London. I feel overshadowed. Life here is not simple."[75] As Dikko saw it, life in Britain was suffocating and stifling, as humans were drowned out by machines, automobiles, and the competing presence of inanimate embodiments of British modernity. These were bold, frontal critiques articulated by an aristocratic subaltern understood by both his subjects and British interlocutors to be enamored with Britain and its culture and unquestioningly loyal to British power. This was a totalizing critique of British modernity, British imperial obsessions with and claims to power, and technological superiority.

And yet, for all his strident, unsparing critique of British political, martial, and cultural attributes, Dikko was invested in British ideas of progress, modernity, and cultural advancement, declaring that his grandsons "will be educated in England," which would represent "progress," help position them to surpass their grandfather, and prepare them for the challenges of a new era.[76] His critique of the excesses and pitfalls of British modernity was tempered by a deeply held pragmatism about the utilitarian value of colonial education, which required at least a partial acceptance of British claims about progress and civilization.

What Dikko's commentaries on Britain reveal is a nuanced perceptual scheme in which adulation for the practical and symbolic benefits of British metropolitan culture is entwined with discomfort regarding certain aspects of British society. Dikko offered a complex experiential and ethnographic commentary that defies simplistic notions of colonial engagements and subaltern collaboration posited in dichotomous historiographies of imperial loyalism and African colonial history.

Reenacting Britain in Nigeria

As indicated in the earlier chapters of this book, the journey to Britain and the subsequent tours in the metropole were only one aspect of an elaborate process of metropolitan resonance in Northern Nigerian aristocratic and colonial circles. If going to Britain to behold the majesty of the empire and swoon over the material and symbolic markers of imperial modernity was the primary investment, returning to Northern Nigeria to immortalize and narrate what the traveler had seen and done in Britain was the return on that investment. Because of this underlying cultural economy that entailed the mining of metropolitan signs for domestic prestige, what travelers like Dikko did upon their return from Britain is as instructive as what they did or saw in the imperial metropole.

Because Dikko's 1933 trip was the most elaborate of his tours in terms of planning, sightseeing adventures, and personal investment, it is not surprising that he did more to recall and inscribe its memories in his politics of self-representation in Nigeria. Upon his return, Dikko wrote a remarkable number of letters of gratitude to his numerous metropolitan hosts and the firms that had lent him their logistical expertise. He wrote Sir William Morris, the owner of the Morris motor company, whose factory in Cowley he had toured, thanking him for the "kindness" he had "showed us when we visited your place in England"—a visit that, according to Dikko, "thrilled and delighted" his entourage.[77] Dikko accompanied the missive with a gift of a leopard skin—a token, Dikko wrote, of his recognition of Sir Morris's "excellent hospitality and patience."[78] Another letter went to the managing director of Elder Dempster Line, which had transported Dikko and his entourage from Liverpool to Nigeria. This letter was also accompanied by a gift of a leopard skin.[79] Dikko wrote similar letters of gratitude, accompanied with leopard skins, to the lord mayor of London, Lord Leverhulme, and the general manager of the Hyde Park Hotel where Dikko and his group had stayed in London.[80] Dikko penned a letter to the chief secretary of the Nigerian colonial government in Lagos "for all the kindness and for the honour you did me when I disembarked at Lagos, in giving me a car, and for all the kind help that you rendered to me."[81]

Dikko's most significant letter went to the king of England. It deserves to be fully reproduced because it departs in style and substance from the perfunctory formula of the other letters.

> From the Emir of Katsina to the Illustrious the Representative of our great and glorious King-Emperor of England, may God grant him victory, Amen. I address the Great One Sir Donald Cameron [governor of Nigeria], may God grant him victory and give success to his deliberations and prolong his life, Amen. Greetings and friendship and good wishes and honour to you again and again. It gives me great pleasure to write this letter to you in order to thank you and to render you honour for all that you did for my journey to Mecca when you helped me by so kindly giving me letters. I did not forget your kindness from the time I left home and reached French country and the Sudan. At every place till we reached Mecca when they saw the letter that you

gave me, they overwhelm[ed] me with honour. I did not fail to receive much honour and deference at sight of your letter in my hand. I am full of gratitude and praise for the wonderful kindness that you rendered me by your letter. I pray God to lengthen your days, to increase your happiness, and to help you and all your staff—Amen. May peace be on you.[82]

Dikko was clearly cognizant of the role played by the diplomatic clout of Britain in facilitating his journey from Nigeria to Mecca and Britain. His obsessive reference to the introductory letters and their requests for diplomatic passage and assistance was a testament to this acknowledgment of imperial protection in far-flung lands. It was a gesture, on Dikko's part, to British imperial might, which he believed caused his interlocutors in Saudi Arabia to "overwhelm me with honor." It was also a rhetorical strategy since Dikko was seizing an opportune event to reassure British overlords that he remained awed by and appreciative of the might of the empire.

Except for the one sent to the king of England, all the letters were generic, repetitious, and predictably bureaucratic protocols of gratitude. Dikko wrote to perform the gratitude that was expected of him, which was crucial for maintaining himself in the good graces of British colonial patrons. However, the letters of gratitude also reveal Dikko to be an astute participant in and master of imperial protocols of power, clientage, and patronage. Dikko was a master of diplomatic niceties; he knew how to work the colonial system by being a model ally. He was the emir of Katsina and a favored aristocratic subaltern of the metropolitan colonial officialdom by the grace of his British friends and the British colonial institutions and networks to which he belonged. When presented with an opportunity to acknowledge and return the patronage of colonial interlocutors, Dikko seized it robustly.

Dikko's Narrative of Metropolitan Modernity

Apart from writing personal travel memoirs, publishing serialized travelogues in *Gaskiya*, and giving public lectures on Britain, some aristocratic travelers took to the pages of the Northern Nigerian colonial official newssheet, which was published monthly and circulated to all agencies and departments of the colonial bureaucracy, to peddle their travel accounts. The readers of the newssheet included hundreds, perhaps thousands, of African colonial staff for whom travel to the imperial metropole was an enterprise signaling colonial favor and privilege. We do not know whether colonial authorities required returning travelers to pen summaries of their trip for publication in the newssheet or whether the travelers themselves volunteered to share their stories of Britain with the multiracial colonial bureaucratic community in Northern Nigeria, but a few of the travelers, including Dikko, published abbreviated versions of their travel narratives in the official newspaper.

After his return from Britain in 1933, Dikko began "preparing the account of the wonderful things that I saw in England." As his narrative developed, however, he decided to immediately share some of his most striking experiences because, as he put it, "there are three things which impressed me as being so marvelous that I have not the patience to finish my account before telling about them."[83] For Dikko, the "three wonders" were things that would "always equal all other wonders."[84] The first were the traffic lights on London's roads. Dikko described a traffic light for his readers as "a lamp which works like a 'dan doka' [policeman or law enforcer] on the motor roads."[85] Dikko then detailed, either from memory or from notes in his diary, the workings of the traffic light and motorists' interaction with it:

> This lamp has different coloured lights, each colour showing what is intended. If some motors meet at a cross-roads one light shows which motor is meant to stop and when the driver sees this light he stops. Another light shows which of them is to go on and signals him to proceed. All the rest of the motors have a light turned towards them so that they may either stop or go on. Thus the light works until no more danger remains. There are so many motors running about that it is beyond a man's powers to control their continuous passing if they come to a cross-roads and so the scheme of the lamps has come about.[86]

Dikko's detailed account would be fawningly unsettling were it to be told today, but in 1930s Northern Nigeria, this was nothing short of the white man's magic. The idea that lights and not people controlled traffic on the streets of London and that these lights worked independently of manual human control and with the rhythm and flow of traffic reinforced the mystique of London and Britain. What Dikko was highlighting, whether wittingly or unwittingly, was the distant, exotic modernity of the imperial metropole, which trickled to the colony but not in the awe-inspiring forms it allegedly manifested in Britain. Dikko made sure to ascribe the technological agency of the traffic light to colonial "wisdom." At first he thought "this wisdom comes from the motor drivers," but he later realized "it came from the lamps."[87] The traffic lights of London were metaphors,

Dikko suggested, for manifestations of the white man's inscrutable technological "wisdom."

The second wonder in Dikko's trifecta was what he called "the talking pictures," a reference to cinema newsreels: "To us Hausas a photograph itself is a very wonderful thing. So it was until we saw many photographs moving as though they had life. And now surpassing this here are photographs of a man speaking so that everyone can hear his words as well as if they came from his mouth."[88] Perhaps intuiting that his audience would find this iteration of the white man's magic implausible, Dikko added, "this is no idle gossip"[89] and proceeded to tell his readers the story of how he ended up in a newsreel as one of the moving and talking pictures on the screen: "I went in an aeroplane which could take 14 people. When I alighted the white men asked me what I thought about the aeroplanes and I said, 'Truly these things are very wonderful. If they are brought to Hausaland I shall be the first to buy one.' I heard myself saying these very words in the Cinema. And what, you readers, could be more wonderful than that? Nothing."[90]

Dikko's moment as a newsmaker—as a newsworthy guest of colonial metropolitan authorities—coincided with his discovery of the cinema newsreel as a technological genre of communication and information dissemination. Dikko's subjectivity had become an integral part of the message. He was a character in the story of metropolitan modernity he was relaying. Herein lie the ways these travelogues performed the dual functions of underscoring imperial metropolitan modernity while inscribing the traveler-narrators in that modernity.

Dikko's third British wonder was something that again involved him as a participant observer and, like the previous two, involved an object of British technological wonder: "a trip in a war vessel [submarine] which dives under the sea and comes to the surface at will,"[91] a reference to his experience in the submarine *Thames* at Portsmouth. According to Dikko, the "boat" had a periscope through which one could view the surrounding waters below the submarine and "on the surface of the water," all while remaining "closely shut up."[92]

Memorabilia of Metropolitan Travel

On May 30, 1933, one F. S. Dapp, acting for the United Africa Company, a subsidiary of Unilever, authored a memo to the manager of the company's Northern Nigerian branch headquartered in Kaduna. The letter asserted, "It

Figure 4.8. Commemorative tray, produced to mark Dikko's trip to Britain in 1933, depicting the polo and equestrian feats of the Dikko clan.

has been suggested that we should manufacture for sale a souvenir article such as a plate or enamel tray" as a commemorative souvenir "in connection with the visit of the Emir of Katsina to England."[93] The memo reveals that there had been considerable internal deliberation within the UAC hierarchy and that the decision was that photographs or prints could be placed on the plate and tray but not "statues and representations in relief" since that would offend the Islamic prohibition of lifelike images and statues (see fig.4.8).

The memo proposed that the souvenir items be printed with "a photograph of the Emir and His Majesty King George side by side, or those of the

Emir and his two grandsons."[94] The UAC manager in Kaduna was directed to contact the secretary of the Northern Nigerian colonial government to seek Dikko's permission "for the use of his photograph" on the souvenirs.[95] What followed was a flurry of triangular epistolary exchanges involving the UAC, various levels of the colonial bureaucracy, and Emir Dikko. Finally, on August 9, the District Office of Katsina Division conveyed Dikko's approval and permission to the resident of Zaria Province. Dikko, according to the district officer's memo, had "readily agreed to the idea of a souvenir in some form of a plate."[96] However, the emir would chose "flat representations of Nagogo, the two grandsons and himself so that the unique journey of the three generations together [could] be commemorated."[97] It is not clear from the archival records who first suggested the commemoration of Dikko's visit to Britain with usable souvenirs, but the emir clearly mediated and shaped the visual representations in the proposed commemorative items. With the emir's permission obtained, the UAC proceeded to manufacture the plates and trays, with metal replacing porcelain.

The colonial record is silent on how many of the souvenirs were manufactured or whether they were commercially distributed or simply given out as collectors' items. The souvenir room of the Katsina Emirate, where trophies won in polo games sit side by side with medals and awards received in Britain (see fig. 4.9), does not contain the commemorative tray and plate, but many descendants of Dikko remember seeing and using the souvenir items.[98] My efforts to track down any existing copies of these souvenirs led me to Dikko's granddaughter Hajiya Binta, in the village of Jibia, who still possesses two of the commemorative trays manufactured by the UAC to mark Dikko's visit to Britain in 1933.[99] The prints on one of these surviving trays—the one depicting Dikko, Nagogo, and Dikko's two grandsons—are now almost completely faded, probably worn from being used to serve food or from decades of exposure to the elements. The other commemorative tray showing a regally attired Dikko, his two sons, and British colonial officials all on horseback playing the game of polo is well preserved, with the printed images approaching relief quality (see fig. 4.8). Hajiya Binta stated that specially printed balloons were produced and released in Katsina as part of the commemoration, but there is no archival corroboration for this.[100]

Dikko was an avid consumer of metropolitan goods and images and a self-conscious cultivator of an identity anchored on claims of superior familiarity with such objects and technologies. The souvenirs were one

Figure 4.9. The Katsina Emirate trophy, memorabilia, and souvenir room housing the Dikko clan's polo trophies, medals, plaques, and commemorative items at the palace in Katsina.

facet of an elaborate personal investment in the instruments of metropolitan modernity. Another was the consumption of metropolitan technologies unfamiliar to local eyes and tastes. While visiting the Morris motor factory in Britain, Dikko ordered five lorries and paid for them to be shipped to Nigeria through the Morris dealership and agent in Lagos. In September, the lorries arrived in Lagos and set off a rash of correspondence between officials who could not believe that Dikko, an individual, would order multiple lorries for personal use and therefore assumed that the emir had ordered the trucks on behalf of the Katsina Native Authority. A memo from the resident of Zaria Province to the secretary of the northern provinces clarified that Dikko had indeed purchased the trucks for his own personal use and that there was thus no need for Morris Motors Limited to communicate with the Native Authority about the delivery of the trucks.[101] Clearly, Dikko parlayed his metropolitan connections into his vision of pioneering the adoption of the material, technological, and symbolic accoutrements of British imperial modernity in Northern Nigeria.

Colonial Medical Tourism

Dikko made his fourth trip to Britain in 1937, arriving in Plymouth on July 31 (map 4.2). The main purpose of this trip was cataract surgery, but the emir used the opportunity to shop, sightsee, and rekindle his metropolitan aristocratic relationships. Dikko's party included his wife Maidaki, his brother, his brother's wife, and his son Nagogo.[102] G. S Browne, the former chief commissioner of Northern Nigeria, was designated to take charge of Dikko and his party in Britain. He would coordinate and supervise the activities of other colonial guides and volunteers, including K. Dewar and D. C. Fletcher, who were district officers in the Nigerian Colonial Service.[103] According to an itinerary prepared by the office of the governor of Nigeria and sent to the secretary of state for the colonies, Dikko and his party would stay at the Hotel Great Central, Marylebone, London. Dikko would undergo an eye operation with an oculist, Dr. R. Foster Moore, and then spend about two weeks at a nursing home located at Mandeville Place, London.[104] Thereafter, Dikko and his party would do some sightseeing and shopping.

Like Dikko's previous visits to Britain, this one was preceded by a rash of epistolary exchanges on the logistical aspects of the trip. From June 6, 1937, when the deputy governor of Northern Nigeria gave his permission for Dikko's trip, a network of colonial officials, private individuals in Britain, and prospective guides exchanged letters and telegrams on various aspects of the trip. The archive of these exchanges is an enduring testament to the elaborate bureaucratic practices and processes around such visits.

Several of the letters were from individuals and organizations in Britain who, upon learning of Dikko's forthcoming visit, requested a meeting with the emir or a visit to their organization. On July 7, one Miss E. S. Fegan wrote to the trip organizers to state that she "would like to meet the Emir of Katsina and his wife while they are in England."[105] On the same day, a certain Mr. Rankin, a resident of southwestern London and a longtime friend of the Dikkos, wrote to one of the organizers of the trip, Sir George Tomlinson, saying he would love to see the emir in London and to "visit him in hospital if he is left there for some time."[106] Furthermore, Rankin stated that he would love to see Maidaki, Dikko's wife, whom he described as "a real friend." He would "do anything to help in entertaining her or taking her about."[107]

On July 27, an official of the Carlton Club of Pall Mall, Harry B. Hermon Hodge, wrote to Tomlinson to confirm that "my old friend, the Emir

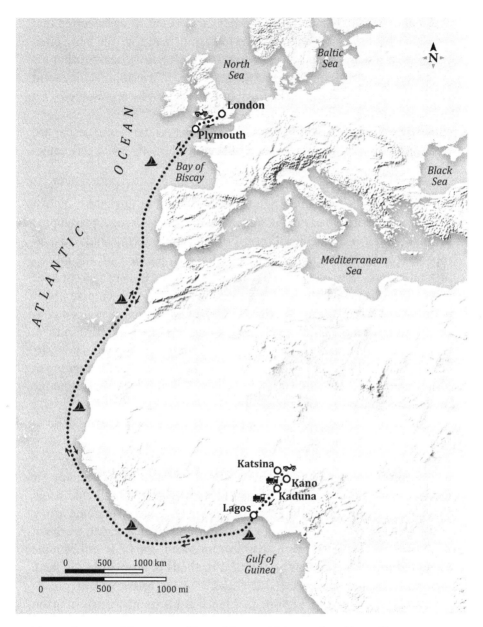

Map 4.2. Itinerary of the journey of Emir of Katsina, Muhammadu Dikko, and his entourage to Britain in 1937.

of Katsina," was arriving England on July 31. Hermon Hodge asserted that he knew that "the emir wants to see me again" and that the emir often wrote to him from Nigeria.[108] Hermon Hodge further disclosed that his "late father" and Dikko were "mutual admirers."[109] Hermon Hodge went on to outline the request of the Carlton Club, which he represented: "I'd be glad—and so would the Club be—if [Dikko] would bring his son for a game of Polo at Kirtlington Park (of which I am Secretary) on Tuesday 3rd August. Failing that, Thursday 5th might be possible—if I could get enough players."[110]

The polo prowess of Nagogo, who had won many tournaments in Nigeria and had the emirate's best handicap, had spread to England.[111] Dikko himself was a fairly good polo player who, along with Nagogo, played polo at metropolitan venues. Official correspondence introducing Dikko to metropolitan audiences routinely referenced his polo profile with the following statements: "Some years ago [Dikko] made an excellent polo ground just outside the town halls [and] his son, Nagogo, . . . is a keen polo player with the highest handicap in Nigeria."[112] This reputation developed connections between the Dikko clan and polo institutions in Britain. In turn, this shared recreational interest caused people in the metropolitan polo circuit to invite Dikko and Nagogo to play on their ground upon learning of his visit to Britain. On this occasion, it is not clear if there were competing invitations from other polo clubs.

Ahead of his visit, other metropolitan actors wrote to invite Dikko to social events they planned to host in his honor. Sir William Nevill M. Geary wrote to the undersecretary of state to invite "the Emir of Katsena [*sic*]" to a luncheon he wanted to organize in honor of Dikko and his entourage. Sir Geary, a renowned British aristocrat, was well aware that both Dikko and the colonial organizers of his trip favored sights of industrial manufacturing in the postsurgery itinerary. This fact had been amplified by the itineraries of previous visits, as well as by missives that indicated "the Emir will be more interested to see such things as practical methods of farming in England, rather than to do a round of social activities."[113] Nonetheless, Sir Geary made his case for the luncheon, arguing that lunch at his country estate at Oxon Hoath, Tonbridge, would open other vistas to the visiting emir. Sir Geary opined that "it may be as interesting and instructive for an African Ruler to see an English country house well furnished, than a manufacturing."[114]

Dikko spent a total of six weeks in Britain, two of them in a London hospital. His first social business in London was a visit to Buckingham Palace to receive the King George VI Coronation Medal from the king. Dikko had been awarded the King's Medal for African Chiefs in 1921, was knighted as Commander of the British Empire (CBE) in 1930, and would receive the King's Jubilee Medal in 1935. This was another royal honor. Waiting for Dikko at Buckingham were the lieutenant governor of Northern Nigeria, G. S. Browne, who had helped arrange the trip, and Frederick Lugard, whom Dikko referred to as "my old friend Governor Lugard" in his journal.[115]

Upon his discharge from the hospital, and after being told to return to treat the other eye in two years, Dikko hit London to explore, shop, sightsee, and socialize with his British friends and acquaintances, declaring in his journal that "whenever you visit London you will surely find new things to amaze you."[116] As had become a ritual of these visits, Dikko visited his "old friend" Lugard for tea at his Abinger home, where they had a profound and intimate exchange that is instructive about both the level of comfort the two aristocrats had with each other and the lingering, unspoken tensions that remained as colonizer and colonized courted each other within the growing rubric of aristocratic kinship. The exchange is worth quoting in full:

> We were sitting together with Governor Lugard having tea when he asked me, "What did Katsina intend to do when you heard that the British were coming?" I told him that we intended to make peace with them even though we were so frightened of them. Governor Lugard erupted in laughter, saying, "If you had fought us and killed me we would not be sitting here having tea together." And I said to him, "If you had killed me I would not be here having tea with you in your house." We both laughed. I told him that I am delighted to be having tea with the first British official I set my eyes on in 1903. We continued our conversation and reminisced about the old days.[117]

This exchange is profoundly insightful in several ways, but for context, it is important to stress that Dikko had been a critical player in the moment when sovereignty transferred from Katsina's precolonial rulers to British colonizers. He was a member of the royal delegation that surrendered to Lugard's troops in Katsina in 1903. He was also one of the royal advisers who had swayed the emir of Katsina at the time to surrender to the British and save lives rather than embark on a futile resistance. Thereafter, in the postconquest political order in Katsina, Dikko had served as the logistical liaison for the occupying colonial army, attending to their quotidian needs and building a strong rapport with them. This relationship put him in the good graces of the British and ultimately helped him become emir in 1906.[118]

More than thirty years later, Lugard and Dikko could reminisce about that foundational encounter over tea as though that moment had been more transactional than tragic. The reduction of the traumatic event of colonial conquest to a casual teatime conversational topic is indicative of how far the aristocratic fraternity binding Dikko and Lugard had come. Revisiting their first encounter points to a mature friendship in which no conversational topic, no matter how tragic or tense, was considered too sensitive. The exchange also portrays the ways the event—and, in particular, the crucial decisions made by the Katsina aristocracy—remained a backdrop for current relationships and fraternal interactions thirty-four years after that foundational moment of colonial occupation. Finally, Dikko demonstrated in this exchange that he could match his metropolitan interlocutors wit for wit. He emerges in the exchange as an empowered and self-assured colonial interlocutor.

Dikko's Final Metropolitan Adventure

On July 4, 1939, Emir Dikko arrived in Britain on what would be his final trip to the imperial metropole, flying into Croydon Aerodrome via Marseille, France (map 4.3). This was his first flight to Britain. The trip was a follow-up to his 1937 visit to treat his eye and, like that previous trip, quickly devolved into a sightseeing adventure. For this trip, Dikko had expressed to colonial planners his desire to once again meet the king at Buckingham Palace and "to see a submarine."[119]

Accompanied by his two sons, the seventy-four-year-old monarch packed his itinerary full of his favorite activities, both social and official. At the invitation of King George VI, he visited Buckingham Palace on July 14, holding audience with the king. Dikko visited and received an award from the Royal Society for the Prevention of Cruelty to Animals. During the visit, Dikko's son, Nagogo, played polo with British polo acquaintances (fig. 4.10). The emir was interviewed at the British Broadcasting Corporation (BBC) (fig. 4.11).[120] There, Dikko broadcast a goodwill message in Hausa to his kinsmen in Northern Nigeria, which was relayed to Nigeria through the radio diffusion service of the colonial information bureau and translated into Arabic by his son Nagogo for broadcast to other parts of the world.[121]

This trip saw a robust display of the familiar imperial politics of affect and hospitality, with several serving and retired colonial officials and Dikko's

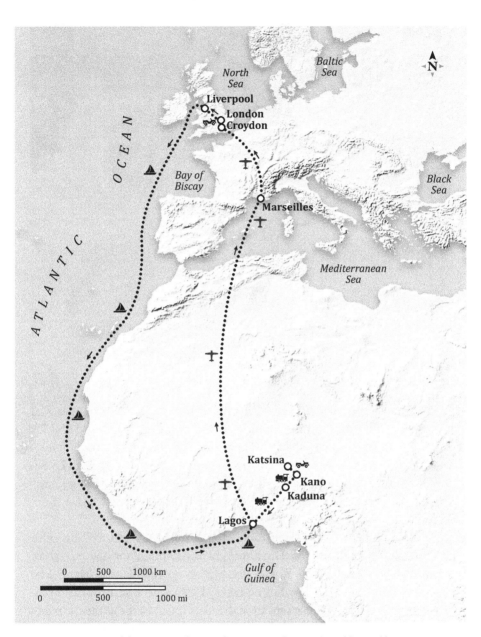

Map 4.3. Itinerary of the journey of Emir of Katsina, Muhammadu Dikko, and his entourage to Britain in 1939.

Figure 4.10. Usman Nagogo playing polo at Kirtlington Park polo ground while being observed by H. B Hermon Hodge in 1939. Credit: Kagara, *Sarkin Katsina*, 36.

many friends and acquaintances writing to his metropolitan guides and handlers to inquire about his health after the operation on his eye and his recuperative stay in the hospital. Notably, Secretary of State for the Colonies Malcom MacDonald sent flowers to Dikko's hospital bed.[122] Although Dikko and his family managed to include a sizable itinerary of metropolitan touring after his recovery, interactions with British interlocutors were at times indexed in his health crisis and the focus on recovery.

Dikko and his sons visited the Colonial Office on July 17. The colonial secretary, Malcom MacDonald, held a reception for the party, an event widely covered in the British press.[123] As during his 1933 trip, Dikko attended the White City greyhound races, a visit whose sartorial and religious visuals the local press sensationalized as much as it did the drama of the emir's participation in the betting frenzy. Here is how the *Lancashire Daily Post* reported Dikko's visit:

> In the middle of dinner in the restaurant at the White City last night three dusky Mohammedans in white robes prostrated themselves on the ground and performed devotions towards the sunset. They then returned to their table

Figure 4.11. Dikko, his son Usman Nagogo, and the district head of Musawa, Usman Liman Yero, at the British Broadcasting Corporation in London. Credit: Kagara, *Sarkin Katsina*, 66.

and continued with the task of picking winning greyhounds. They were the Septuagenarian Emir of Katsina, his son, and the keeper of his Privy Purse, who came to see the inauguration of a new dog race entitled in his honor, the Katsina Stakes. Pundits of the O.R.A. surrounded the Emir and gave him the benefit of their knowledge of form. But their tips proved consistently wrong, and the disconsolate Emir was losing money from the Privy Purse at the rate of two shillings per race. Finally, on the quiet, he took the initiative, rose to his feet, and after an inspection of the dogs, picked his own winner. It won, and the Emir broke into delighted laughter, rocking to and fro. The Emir bases his judgment of greyhound on an expert knowledge of the points of horses. He has won 75 horse-racing cups in Northern Nigeria, and to his delight, has now ousted a local wealthy Syrian from the position of leading owner. His son is one of the best polo players in Africa, with a handicap of six. He was coached in polo by Mr. G. S. Browne, till recently Chief commissioner of Northern Nigeria, who interpreted for the emir at the White City on Thursday.[124]

Unpacking this reportage requires a prefatory caveat about its condescendingly avuncular undertone. Remarks about Dikko's appearance, the substitution of his religion for his entire identity, and the snide comment about "devotions to the sunset" all represent facets of this racist and Orientalist reportorial frame. With this disclaimer out of the way, it is important to point out that Dikko and his sons engaged in familiar metropolitan pastimes and basked in the social latitudes and contrived hospitalities afforded them by the metropole. One of these social liberties was that of betting on races, which, like all forms of gambling, is outlawed in Islam and was unavailable to them in Katsina. However, it should be noted that it is clear that Dikko approached and partook in the betting not as gambling but rather as part of the recreational ritual of the racing pastime and in order to be a good, participatory guest.

The morality of betting aside, Dikko, as on previous visits to Britain, demonstrated his superior knowledge of animal capabilities—dogs and horses in particular. The emir's ability to recalibrate his knowledge of racehorses as a breeder into a knowledge of the racing capabilities of dogs awed his metropolitan interlocutors, who had assumed the emir's ignorance simply on account of his origin and circulating idioms of African backwardness. In his own polite way, Dikko confounded stereotypes of African ignorance of competitive race betting. Dikko's success compelled reluctant acknowledgment from his metropolitan hosts. It became a footnote, perhaps an appendix, in the reportage, which acknowledged Dikko's expertise and superior knowledge of racing animals. Dikko and his entourage also visited the Hurst Park horse races, where the emir again demonstrated his knowledge by picking the first winner.[125]

Before leaving Britain, Dikko and his sons visited the Whipsnade Zoo and safari park in Bedfordshire. The party rested and then returned to Nigeria. Although this was Dikko's last trip to Britain, his son Usman Nagogo, who accompanied him on all the trips and was himself a keen student of imperial aristocratic protocol, would succeed him and extend Katsina's reputation as an emirate in the orbit of British metropolitan modernist influences.

In a condensed travelogue published in *Gaskiya*, Usman Nagogo recalled the highlight of the trip. He discussed flying in an airplane for the first time, which he described to his readers as a "fascinating object": "We were so relaxed on the plane that it felt like being in our car."[126] He described being met upon arrival in Britain by "Mr. Browne, Mr. Laing, former Resident whom we called *Karangiya*, and Captain Masterton Smith."[127] He told his readers how Captain Masterton had guided them to the palace of the king of England when they visited the monarch and how they attended the commissioning of a warship christened *Nigeria* and met Governor Cameron, Commander Carrow, Mr. Whiteley, and other Nigeria colonial officials at the ceremony.[128]

In addition to Nagogo's narrative, the editors of *Gaskiya* published a series of travelogues focusing on the activities of Dikko and his sons in Britain, a trove of information they would have obtained from the emir himself through his journal. From the August 8 installment, we learn that Dikko and his entourage had added a new item to their itinerary. Their arrival in England coincided with the annual Royal Agricultural Show, which the king was hosting at Windsor Castle. Dikko, a lover of animals and a farmer, was intrigued and decided to visit the show.[129] There, he met and chatted with the king, who "brought 32 animals and other agricultural products from his own farms to showcase."[130] Relying on the accounts of Dikko and his sons, *Gaskiya*'s editors proceeded to educate the newspaper's readers on the purpose of the show: "The show is held to enable people from all over the world come and see animals and other agricultural products of England. If people saw a big cow that when cross-bred with their own cow could produce a superior breed, they would buy the seed and ask questions about how to grow it on their own farms. This is why this kind of exhibition is very helpful to people around the world."[131]

As noted in previous chapters, *Gaskiya* was an important instrument for aristocratic travelers to the metropole to transmit their observations and recollections about metropolitan objects, cultures, and practices. Even an emir as savvy and as intent on narrating his own metropolitan story as Dikko had to rely on the reach of *Gaskiya* among Northern Nigeria's Roman-literate Hausa people to disseminate his personal stories of metropolitan adventure.

In His Father's Path

Usman Nagogo was born in 1905, a year before his father, Muhammadu Dikko, became emir of Katsina. According to his biography, Dikko "knew that Nagogo would be his successor" and treated him as one.[132] Nagogo's biographers tell a story of an affection-filled upbringing in which his father could not bear to be away from him, which was the reason his father interrupted his education to include him on the trip to Mecca and England in 1921 at the age of sixteen and shortly after he enrolled in Katsina Provincial School. Nagogo accompanied Dikko on his four subsequent trips and, in the process, acquired his own predilection for the metropolitan trappings of colonial modernity. Nagogo ingratiated himself with the British colonial authorities and attracted metropolitan favor and recognition, including a knighthood of his own.

Dikko set the stage for Nagogo's rise in the Katsina Emirate political hierarchy when he appointed him head of the Native Authority Police in 1929. As head of law enforcement, or wakilin doka, Nagogo understudied his father's administrative reforms and activities. He also began to construct his own identity as a cultivator of colonial governmental modernity. He reformed the Katsina Native Authority Police by increasing recruitment and expanding the operational office.[133] He also purchased vans and other policing gear in a conscious replication of the metropolitan policing techniques he had seen in Britain. Nagogo's elaborate reenactment of metropolitan police culture in Katsina had other dimensions. He trained some of the policemen to form a band and a ceremonial unit,[134] a decisive departure from the Native Authority traditional emirate police model and a self-conscious adaptation of British metropolitan police culture. He did this even though the Native Authority Police was under the control of the emirate and was thus not expected or required to adopt colonial policing templates.

Upon his return from Britain in 1933, Nagogo sent some of his men to Scotland to learn how to play ceremonial Scottish bagpipes, a remarkable investment in the appropriation and adaptation of metropolitan police culture. The Katsina Native Authority Police bagpipes players later became a major feature and attraction in Katsina's ceremonial processions and entertained dignitaries on important occasions. It was probably the only bagpipes-playing police regiment in Northern Nigeria at that time. To complete the neocolonial ensemble, Nagogo later established a mounted police regiment.

From an early age, Nagogo engaged in aggressive repurposing and creative domestication of imperial policing and martial traditions. He proved himself an independent and impatient modernizing agent. Nagogo's appropriation of metropolitan symbols of power and authority was a classic instance of invented tradition—one that fused emirate notions of law and order with British policing culture.[135] When Nagogo transitioned to the higher office of magajin garin Katsina (mayor of Katsina town), he continued to champion modernization projects that complemented his father's modernist profile.

Polo and Modernization in the Age of Nagogo

Nagogo learned to play polo, a close cousin of the emirate equestrian sport of horse racing, under the tutelage of European officials. Nagogo was one of several African players of aristocratic background who struggled to learn to play the game and adopt its sartorial traditions. Nagogo's biographers wrote that he and other local players "looked comical, dressed in big flowing gowns with turbans around their heads... [on horses] adorned lavishly as if they were in a ceremonial function."[136] Difficult adjustment or not, Nagogo stuck to polo and improved to become one of the best players in Nigeria for about forty years. During his active playing days Nagogo won several tournaments, had an admirable handicap of seven, and would later become the president of the Nigerian Polo Association.[137]

Nagogo's playing circuit extended from the colony to the metropole. When he accompanied his father to Britain in 1939, Nagogo slipped away on his own to Kirtlington Park, home of the famous Kirtlington Polo Club outside Oxford, to play with his European polo-playing friends under the guidance of one H. B. Hermon.[138] In later years, as emir, Nagogo made several visits to Britain, each time organizing his itinerary around his polo-playing adventures and making logistical arrangements to play in Britain's iconic polo parks. For instance, in 1952, when Nagogo was preparing to visit the United Kingdom, the Nigeria Office, the official liaison for the trip, informed R.L.B. Maiden, the resident of Katsina Province who organized the logistics of the trip, that because of the emir's well-known penchant for metropolitan polo-playing adventures, especially his desire for "playing polo at Cowdray Park, or at other Grounds in another district," it would be preferable to reserve a hotel "in the neighborhood of the Ground."[139] For Nagogo, polo was a central aspect of an immersive experiential connection to British colonial modernity and an important aspect of a broader modernist self-fashioning that was forged in the cultural context of metropolitan travel.

Nagogo the Modernizer

Emir Dikko passed away in 1944 and was succeeded by Nagogo, a predictable succession that Dikko had planned and arranged before his death. Nagogo immediately stepped into Dikko's position as the preeminent modernizing emir in Northern Nigeria and the emir with the most intimate familiarity with British metropolitan culture. Colonial authorities noted Nagogo's socialization into an imperial system, his many royal and aristocratic acquaintances in Britain that were facilitated and lubricated by his travel there in the company of his father, and his own conscious continuation of his predecessor's modernist projects. It was not long before this visibility produced colonial recognition and prestige. In October 1944, only a few months after he became emir, British colonial and metropolitan authorities selected Nagogo to visit and boost the morale of Nigerian and other Anglophone West African troops fighting for Britain in the Indian theater of World War II.[140] This was a rare honor that bypassed at least five senior emirs in the Northern Nigerian caliphal hierarchy.

Nagogo's carefully choreographed itinerary was complex. He flew from Kano to Cairo and then to New Delhi, where he was received by the staff officers of the West African regiment as well as General Sir George Giffard, commander of Britain's Eleventh Army.[141] The emir and his private secretary, Mallam Isa Kaita, were then hosted at a lavish reception as guests of the viceroy and vicereine, Field Marshal and Lady Wavell. Nagogo was later hosted at a dinner by the commander in chief, General Sir Claude Auchinleck, at his residence. Prior to his departure for the front lines, Nagogo toured the Mughal ruins and a temple complex, a South Asian extension of his practiced excursions to sites of imperial grandeur and awe.[142]

Accompanied by officers, Nagogo toured the living quarters of West African troops on the front lines in Burma and later addressed the soldiers. The emir told the troops that he had come to the front lines "with the approval of the Government, the Military authorities, the Sultan of Sokoto and his brother Emirs" to "personally greet them and to see for himself the good work they were doing to help their cause and that of all freedom loving people of the world."[143] Nagogo stated that he and other Africans were proud of the troops, telling them, "You are the descendants of fighting men" and that the troops' contribution to the war effort would "win for our countries an honoured position and a worthy place in the Commonwealth of Nations, so that one day it can be said that we played our part worthily in the downfall and defeat of those enemies of mankind, the Germans and the Japanese."[144]

From the colonizers' perspective, Nagogo's speech clearly justified his selection. Like Dikko, he was a loyal imperial aristocratic ally, but this loyalty was on his own terms. He consciously enjoyed and nurtured his position as the colonialists' favorite Northern Nigerian emir. Like his father, Nagogo was also a master of the imperial politics of mutual patronage and knew what imperial recognition required from a subaltern ally. In other words, Nagogo understood the unspoken, unwritten rules of colonial relationships. The last paragraph of his speech is a perfect illustration of this sensibility: "The links between our countries and the Mother country are everlasting and strong. We are proud to belong to the British

Commonwealth of Nations. When the world was at peace the Mother country made all efforts to further the social progress and advancement of our countries so that our sons may prosper."[145]

Here, Nagogo may seem to be pandering to his British colonial benefactors, but he was also doing exactly what was expected of him. This should not erase his own agency as a traditional ruler who was consciously desirous of the imperial visibility represented by the tour of India. Nagogo was comfortable upholding and promoting the banner of imperial solidarity. The emir, it should be stressed, had a stake in the imperial system whose center, Britain, now stood threatened by Germany. Nagogo's investment in the empire and its organizational successor, the Commonwealth of Nations, was not only predicated on the premise that his domain, Katsina, remained in the universe of metropolitan influences, but he also had personal, symbolic, and material connections to Britain that were worth preserving. Furthermore, Nagogo understood the reciprocal economy of patronage that had brought him so far in his aristocratic ascendancy, and it would have been self-sabotaging for him to relinquish it. Like his father, Nagogo unabashedly craved the validation and recognition of British political institutions, and this recognition followed him as he made his way through the British imperial system. In 1948, Nagogo, a young and relatively new emir, was one of a few West African chiefs invited to a conference with King George VI in England. At the conference, Nagogo was placed in a prominent position and stood to the right of the king in the newsreel and official public photo of the event as recorded by the British Pathe News Agency.[146]

The Afterlives of Katsina's Metropolitan Outreach

The Dikko ruling dynasty brought Katsina enormous metropolitan visibility. It inscribed the emirate firmly in multiple spheres of imperial modernity. Whatever other emotions characterized the relationship between the people of Katsina and their successive father and son emirs and between Katsina and the British, the people of the emirate seemed to have appreciated the modernization projects—schools, hospitals, motorcars, a modern police force, polo, and others—that transformed their sleepy town into a hub of colonial cultural business in Northern Nigeria. Central to these projects of modernization was the travel of members of the Dikko dynasty to Britain and the imperial relationships these trips established or helped consummate.

There was an acknowledgment on the part of Katsina's people that much of the inspiration for the modernization of Katsina in the colonial period came from the many visits of Dikko and Nagogo to the imperial metropole. One evidence of this appreciation is the fact that the people of the emirate lavishly welcomed Dikko and Nagogo back from their trips to Britain. They even composed special songs for their welcome parties that are illustrative of this appreciation. One particular song composed to welcome Dikko back is inscribed in Katsina lore. The song is simple but evocative:

> You are the first to go to Mecca.
> Dikko, you are the first to go to England.
> Hero, son of Isa, on whom poison could be tested,
> Let others learn from you.[147]

Implicit in the lyrics is a robust acknowledgment of the role of Dikko's metropolitan connections in making him an emir and of his British adventures in increasing his and Katsina's prestige. The song also suggests that other emirs could "learn from" Dikko's expansive access to metropolitan resources and aristocratic symbols that became central to Katsina's self-image.

Dikko's and Nagogo's metropolitan travels brought other imperial cultural benefits to the people of Katsina, especially the large, extended Dikko clan. Some influences were direct and tangible, such as the fact that Dikko's multiple tours of Buckingham Palace left him desiring the grandeur of its regal appearance and caused him to order a major remodeling of the front facade of his palace in Katsina. On Dikko's instruction, the old palace's mud facade built by Ibrahim Soro (reigned 1405–8) in the traditional emirate royal architectural style common in Northern Nigeria (see fig. 4.13) was demolished to make way for a concrete facade that Dikko visualized as a replica of the front facade of Buckingham Palace (see fig. 4.12).[148] In 1952, Emir Nagogo commissioned a prominent Katsina aristocrat, Mamman Nasir, to oversee a remodeling of the front facade to its present form—a renovation that preserved the Buckingham Palace-inspired frame cherished by Dikko.[149] The ceremonial attire of Katsina's princes were also products of Dikko's metropolitan sartorial adaptations.[150] Several members of the Dikko clan remember that Dikko's and Nagogo's metropolitan agricultural sightseeing inspired them to introduce improved fruit, vegetable, and grain seed varieties to Katsina's farmers.[151]

Katsina royal oral traditions credit the metropolitan trips of the two successive emirs, especially the modernist technological devices and signifiers they brought to Katsina, with inspiring an emirate-wide awareness about

Figure 4.12. The Katsina palace front facade.

Figure 4.13. The old Katsina palace mud front facade. Credit: M. T. Safana Archive.

and love affair with transistor radios, gramophones, electric fans, and other gadgets. In their metropolitan travels, the two emirs brought back these items and introduced them to the people of Katsina.[152] Several members of the Dikko clan remember Dikko and Nagogo returning from Britain with technological and decorative items as presents for family members. Dikko's granddaughter Hajiya Rakiya remembers her mother proudly displaying a gold chain and a gramophone she said her father, Dikko, had purchased for her in Britain, and Nagogo's daughter Hajiya Hassatu remembers receiving a wristlet from Dikko as a present from England.[153]

The metropolitan engagements of Dikko and Nagogo and the modernist inclinations that these engagements inspired and incubated in Katsina have become part of the emirate's royal traditions, and stories of Dikko's and Nagogo's relationship with white colonial officials and their adventures in Britain are fondly retold and passed down from generation to generation.[154] Apart from these recollections, several members of the Katsina ruling family credit the metropolitan travels of the two emirs with making a way for several family members to study, work, and vacation in Britain.[155]

Across Northern Nigeria, the legend of Dikko as a pioneer modernizing emir whose metropolitan connections and travels opened his domain to a disproportionate European cultural influence lives on and is encapsulated in the popular factoid that Dikko was the first emir from Northern Nigeria to visit the colonial metropole as well as the first emir from the region to make the hajj in the colonial era. In my years of hearing interlocutors and informants in Northern Nigeria repeat this factual, widely known narrative, I never sensed that they were doing anything other than acknowledging and praising Dikko's pioneering and repeated exploration of the metropolitan cultural and sociological landscape—his modernist firstness, as it were. Nor does the popular retelling of Dikko's beneficial friendship with colonial institutions in Nigeria and Britain betray any contradiction between the image of Dikko as a devout, upright Muslim and his image as an influential colonial ally and cultural broker.

Conclusion

The full repertoire of Muhammadu Dikko's travels to Britain can only be captured by analyzing the ways he mined the cultural resources and commodities of the metropole toward his ambition of increasing the prestige of his court in Katsina. This chapter documented this conscious cultural appropriation, consumption, and repurposing on the part of Dikko and his son Nagogo. In particular, I highlight the duo's modernization of Katsina Emirate, which they did by drawing consciously on the symbolic and spatial examples of Britain. This landscape of inspiration and modernist example defined much of the cultural and physical changes Katsina underwent during the reigns of Dikko and Nagogo.

Furthermore, being an avid polo player opened up additional metropolitan spaces to Nagogo. This participation in metropolitan polo circuits added another layer to the Dikko dynasty's British connection. On the polo fields of Britain, as during the guided tours of metropolitan sites, the hierarchies of colonialism became subordinated to the imperatives of imperial hospitality. This caused British colonial guides and officials to observe a ritualized deference to their valued guests from Nigeria, which empowered Dikko and his entourage to claim social liberties absent in their interactions with colonial officialdom in Katsina and participate in new pastimes.

This chapter explored the afterlives of Dikko's extensive mobility within the vast metropolitan world of Britain. In the aftermath of his travels to Britain, Dikko, more than any other Northern Nigerian traveler to the metropole, sought to replicate the architectural, sartorial, and symbolic accoutrements of British aristocratic and bureaucratic culture. His son Nagogo continued in that mold, implementing a set of modernist reforms inspired by metropolitan institutions and governmental practices.

From the 1940s, aristocratic travel to Britain was routinized as an annual ritual of colonial mediation. Simultaneously, the institution of metropolitan travel pioneered by Dikko and carried forward by his son and successor expanded both within and outside the scripted official touristic circuits. A similar expansion was also occurring in the discursive techniques and technologies Nigerians were deploying to make sense of British society and translate it to curious colonial subjects in Northern Nigeria. As local curiosities increased for metropolitan phenomena, so did the appetite of aristocratic travelers for the replicable or adaptable artifacts of British modernity. The symbolic and practical utility of metropolitan travel in local cultural transactions and politics became even more apparent in this period, as will be demonstrated in the next chapter.

Notes

1. NAK/Katprof 110/Vol. I, Number 14827/5, November 21, 1932, From the acting secretary of the Northern Provinces to the Chief Secretary, Lagos.

2. NAK/Katprof 110/Vol. I, Correspondence Number 14827/30, Browne to Goldsmith.
3. NAK/Katprof 110/Vol. I, Correspondence Number 14827/30, Browne to Goldsmith.
4. NAK/Katprof 110/Vol. I, Correspondence Number 14827/30, Browne to Goldsmith.
5. NAK/Katprof 110/Vol. I, Correspondence Number 14827/30, Browne to Goldsmith.
6. NAK/Katprof 110/Vol. I, Number 68, January 20, 1933, From district officer I/C Katsina Division to the Resident, Zaria Province.
7. NAK/Katprof 110/Vol. I, Number 68, From district officer I/C Katsina.
8. NAK/Katprof 110/Vol. I, Number 68, From district officer I/C Katsina.
9. NAK/Katprof 110/Vol. I, Number 68, From district officer I/C Katsina.
10. NAK/Katprof 110/Vol. I, Number 14827/50, January 27, 1933, Lieutenant governor of Northern Nigeria to the lieutenant-gouverneur, Colonie Du Tchad, for Lamy.
11. NAK/Katprof 110/Vol. I, Number 235 (L667/667/405), The secretary of state to the Right Honorable Lord Tyrrell, Paris.
12. NAK/Katprof 110/Vol. I, Number 235 (L667/667/405), The secretary of state to Sir Percy Loraine, British high commissioner to Egypt, Cairo.
13. British National Archives, FO 141/699/5, Katsina (Emir of).
14. FO 141/699/5, Katsina (Emir of).
15. FO 141/699/5, Katsina (Emir of).
16. FO 141/699/5, Katsina (Emir of).
17. British National Archives, CO 383/187/11, Emir of Katsina, Proposed Pilgrimage to Mecca and Visit to England.
18. CO 383/187/11, Emir of Katsina, Proposed Pilgrimage to Mecca and Visit to England.
19. CO 383/187/11, Emir of Katsina, Proposed Pilgrimage to Mecca and Visit to England, Mr. Browne to Mr. Goldsmith.
20. CO 383/187/11, Emir of Katsina, Proposed Pilgrimage to Mecca and Visit to England, Mr. Browne to Mr. Goldsmith.
21. CO 383/187/11, Emir of Katsina, Proposed Pilgrimage to Mecca and Visit to England, Mr. Browne to Mr. Goldsmith.
22. CO 383/187/11, Emir of Katsina, Proposed Pilgrimage to Mecca and Visit to England, From the British Resident in Khartoum to the Acting High Commissioner for Egypt and the Sudan, the Residency, Cairo.
23. CO 383/187/11, Emir of Katsina, Proposed Pilgrimage to Mecca and Visit to England, From Lieutenant Governor, Northern Provinces to Mr. B. S. Goldsmith.
24. CO 383/187/11, Emir of Katsina, Proposed Pilgrimage to Mecca and Visit to England, From British Legation to Sir John Simon, April 15, 1933.
25. "Shock for Emir of Katsina," *Montrose Standard*, May 26, 1933, 7.
26. CO 383/187/11, Emir of Katsina, Proposed Pilgrimage to Mecca and Visit to England, Browne to Lieutenant Governor.
27. CO 383/187/11, Emir of Katsina, Proposed Pilgrimage to Mecca and Visit to England, Browne to Lieutenant Governor.
28. "Maidaki Unveils: Interview with Emir's Wife Who Is Coming to Liverpool," *Liverpool Echo*, May 10, 1933 [page number not legible].
29. CO 383/187/11, Emir of Katsina, Proposed Pilgrimage to Mecca and Visit to England, Browne to Lieutenant Governor.
30. "Nigerian Reactions," *Scotsman*, May 5, 1933.
31. "Home Events in Pictures," *Illustrated London News*, May 20, 1933, 725.
32. "The Emir of Katsina's Visit," *Illustrated London News*, May 13, 1933, 688.

33. "Flying Emir," *Sunderland Echo and Shipping Gazette*, May 5, 1933, 13.
34. "No War for Me: What the Emir Said After Seeing R.A.F. Maneuvers," *Western Daily Press*, May 5, 1933.
35. "No War for Me."
36. Kagara, *Sarkin Katsina*, 70.
37. "The Emir of Katsina," *Portsmouth Evening News*, May 8, 1933, 7.
38. "Mainly Personal," *Western Daily Press*, May 6, 1933, 8.
39. "Emir of Katsina: Received by the King at Buckingham Palace," *Portsmouth Evening News*, May 10, 1933, 9.
40. "Emir at the Zoo: Grandsons' Fright in Giraffe Pen," *Yorkshire Post and Leeds Intelligencer*, May 8, 1933, 8.
41. "Emir at the Zoo."
42. "Emir at the Zoo."
43. "Emir of Katsina at the Circus," *Portsmouth Evening News*, May 9, 1933, 3.
44. "Emir of Katsina at the Circus."
45. "Emir of Katsina at the Circus."
46. "The Emir at the Dogs," *Portsmouth Evening News*, May 10, 1933, 2.
47. "Emir's Success at 'the Dogs'—One Wins While He Is at Prayer," *Courier and Advertiser*, May 10, 1933, 7.
48. "Emir's Success at 'the Dogs.'"
49. "The Emir at the Dogs," *Portsmouth Evening News*, May 10, 1933, 2.
50. "Emir of Katsina at Wanborough to Visit Mr. and Mrs. E.H.B Laing," *Surrey Advertiser*, May 13, 1933, 4.
51. "Emir of Katsina at Wanborough."
52. "Emir at the Zoo."
53. "The Emir of Katsina's Visit," *Illustrated London News*, May 13, 1933, 688.
54. "Received by the King: The Emir of Katsina at Palace in Native Robes," *Lincolnshire Echo*, May 10, 1933, 3.
55. "Received by the King."
56. "Emir Greeted in How Own Language—Lord Leverhulme's Guests at Port Sunlight," *Western Daily Press*, May 17, 1933, 11.
57. "Emir Will Never Forget," *Bristol Mirror*, May 18, 1933, 12.
58. "Emir Will Never Forget."
59. "Emir Will Never Forget."
60. "Emir Will Never Forget."
61. "Emir Will Never Forget."
62. "Eastergate: An Emir's Visit," *Hampshire Telegraph*, May 12, 1933, 10.
63. "Shock for the Emir," *Montrose Standard*, May 26, 1933, 7.
64. "Shock for the Emir."
65. "Shock for the Emir."
66. Anderson, *Imagined Communities*.
67. "Emir Sees His Picture," *Merthyr Express*, May 27, 1933, 23.
68. "Emir Sees His Picture."
69. "The Wise-Cracking Emir and His Grandsons," *Tatler*, no. 1665, May 24, 1933, 327.
70. "The Wise-Cracking Emir."
71. For a full account of the early gossips about Dikko's dalliance with British colonizers and its alleged impact on his Muslim devotions, see Kagara, *Sarkin Katsina*.

72. "The Wise-Cracking Emir."
73. "The Wise-Cracking Emir."
74. See, for instance, my analysis of *Etsu Nupe*, Muhammadu Ndayako's metropolitan travel memoir, in chapter 5.
75. "The Wise-Cracking Emir."
76. "The Wise-Cracking Emir."
77. NAK/Katprof 110/Vol. II, Number 177, From emir of Katsina via divisional officer in charge of Katsina to Sir William Morris, Bart.
78. NAK/Katprof 110/Vol. II, Number 177, From emir of Katsina via divisional officer in charge of Katsina to Sir William Morris, Bart.
79. NAK/Katprof 110/Vol. II, Number 180, From emir of Katsina via divisional officer in charge of Katsina to the managing director, Elder Dempster & Coy Ltd.
80. These letters are contained in file number NAK/Katprof 110/Vol. II.
81. NAK/Katprof 110/Vol. I, 130, From the emir of Katsina via district officer in charge, Katsina Division to the chief secretary, Lagos.
82. NAK/Katprof 110/Vol. I, From emir of Katsina via divisional officer in charge of Katsina to the king.
83. NAK/Katprof 110/Vol. II, Number 151, Manuscript of Emir's Account of Travel to England in Newssheet.
84. NAK/Katprof 110/Vol. II, Number 151, Manuscript of Emir's Account.
85. NAK/Katprof 110/Vol. II, Number 151, Manuscript of Emir's Account.
86. NAK/Katprof 110/Vol. II, Number 151, Manuscript of Emir's Account.
87. NAK/Katprof 110/Vol. II, Number 151, Manuscript of Emir's Account.
88. NAK/Katprof 110/Vol. II, Number 151, Manuscript of Emir's Account.
89. NAK/Katprof 110/Vol. II, Number 151, Manuscript of Emir's Account.
90. NAK/Katprof 110/Vol. II, Number 151, Manuscript of Emir's Account.
91. NAK/Katprof 110/Vol. II, Number 151, Manuscript of Emir's Account.
92. NAK/Katprof 110/Vol. II, Number 151, Manuscript of Emir's Account.
93. NAK/Katprof 110/Vol. I, Memo Ref FED/M. No. 4, From the United Africa Company, Unilever House, London to the manager, The United Africa Co. Ltd. Kaduna.
94. NAK/Katprof 110/Vol. I, Memo Ref FED/M. No. 4, From the United Africa Company.
95. NAK/Katprof 110/Vol. I, Memo Ref FED/M. No. 4, From the United Africa Company.
96. NAK/Katprof 110/Vol. I, Number 171, From the district officer in charge, Katsina Division to the Resident, Zaria Province.
97. NAK/Katprof 110/Vol. I, Number 171, From the district officer in charge, Katsina Division.
98. Some members of the Dikko family confirmed in interviews that the commemorative souvenirs circulated when they were growing up.
99. Interview with Hajiya Binta, Jibia, November 6, 2015.
100. Interview with Hajiya Binta.
101. NAK/Katprof 110/Vol. I, Memo Number 74/146, From acting resident of Zaria Province to the secretary, Northern Provinces, September 14, 1933.
102. British National Archives, CO 583/223/1, Visit of the Emir of Katsina 1937.
103. CO 583/223/1, Visit of the Emir of Katsina 1937.
104. CO 583/223/1, Visit of the Emir of Katsina 1937, Governor of Nigeria to W.G.A. Ormsby Gore, Secretary of State for the Colonies, June 18, 1937.
105. CO 583/223/1, Visit of the Emir of Katsina 1937.

106. CO 583/223/1, Visit of the Emir of Katsina 1937, Rankin to Tomlinson.
107. CO 583/223/1, Visit of the Emir of Katsina 1937, Rankin to Tomlinson.
108. CO 583/223/1, Visit of the Emir of Katsina 1937, Hermon Hodge to Tomlinson.
109. CO 583/223/1, Visit of the Emir of Katsina 1937, Hermon Hodge to Tomlinson.
110. CO 583/223/1, Visit of the Emir of Katsina 1937, Hermon Hodge to Tomlinson.
111. The October 9, 1948, edition of the *Illustrated London News* published a story accompanied by two side-by-side polo photos on page 10, one of Nagogo and other polo players in Katsina and the other of metropolitan polo players. The story proclaims Nagogo as a "first class polo player."
112. CO 583/223/1, Visit of the Emir of Katsina 1937, "The Emir of Katsina."
113. CO 583/223/1, Visit of the Emir of Katsina 1937, "The Emir of Katsina."
114. CO 583/223/1, Visit of the Emir of Katsina 1937, "The Emir of Katsina," Sir William Geary to the Under Secretary of State.
115. The journal entries on this trip were reproduced verbatim in Kagara's *Sarkin Katsina*, 80.
116. Kagara, *Sarkin Katsina*, 80.
117. Kagara, *Sarkin Katsina*, 80.
118. Moses Ochonu, "Colonial Itineraries: Muhammadu Dikko's Metropolitan Adventures," *Journal of African History* 61, no. 2 (2020), 179–200.
119. British National Archives, CO 583/243/21, Visits of Native Chiefs.
120. Kagara, *Sarkin Katsina*, 84.
121. Some interviewed family members remembered his famous BBC address to his people, which has now become part of Dikko family lore. Interview with Hajiya Mairo Yarkawu, wife of late Sarkin Maska Shehu II and granddaughter of Dikko, eighty-four years, at Kaduna, April 8, 2015.
122. CO 583/243/21, Visits of Native Chiefs, E. S. Laing to Malcom MacDonald, May 23, 1939.
123. "Emir at the Colonial Office," *Birmingham Mail*, July 18, 1939, 7.
124. "The Emir Goes Racing," *Lancashire Daily Post*, August 19, 1939, 4.
125. "The Emir of Katsina Goes Racing," *Daily Record and Mail*, August 21, 1939, 26.
126. Magajin Gari Alhaji Usuman Nagogo, "Tafiyan Sarkin Katsina London a Jirgin Sama," *Gaskiya ta fi Kwabo*, October 16, 1939, 8.
127. Nagogo, "Tafiyan Sarkin Katsina London," 8.
128. Nagogo, "Tafiyan Sarkin Katsina London," 8.
129. "Sarkin Katsina Dal na London," *Gaskiya ta fi Kwabo*, August 8, 1939, 2.
130. "Sarkin Katsina Dal na London," 2.
131. "Sarkin Katsina Dal na London," 2.
132. Imam and Coomasie, *Usman Nagogo*, 24.
133. Imam and Coomasie, *Usman Nagogo*, 26.
134. Imam and Coomasie, *Usman Nagogo*, 27.
135. See Ranger, "The Invention of Tradition in Colonial Africa."
136. Ranger, "The Invention of Tradition in Colonial Africa," 30.
137. Ranger, "The Invention of Tradition in Colonial Africa," 30.
138. See Kagara, *Sarkin Katsina*, 36. This page of his biography includes a photograph of Nagogo on his polo horse at Kirtlington Park.
139. NAK/Katprof 3381/14/178-5, From E. K. Featherstone, Nigeria Office, London to R.L.B. Maiden, Resident, Katsina Province.
140. NAK/Katprof 3381, Emir of Katsina's visit to India.
141. Ibid.

142. Ibid.

143. Ibid. Press release on the emir's visit to India and Burma.

144. Ibid.

145. Ibid.

146. See British Pathe News Agency, "The King with African Delegates to Conference (1948)," April 13, 2014, YouTube video, 1:23, https://www.youtube.com/watch?v=WeCMcxSCpjA.

147. S. J. Hogben and A.H.M. Kirk-Greene, *The Emirates of Northern Nigeria* (Oxford: Oxford University Press, 1966), 177, quoted in Umar, *Islam and Colonialism*, 149.

148. Interview with Dan Madamin Katsina, Alhaji Usman Sabo, district head of Daddara, grandson of Dikko, fifty-five years, December 27, 2015; interview with Alhaji Idris, grandson of Nagogo, fifty-four years, at Filin Sami Quarters, Katsina, December 29, 2015.

149. Personal communication with Dr. Musa Jibril, May 11, 2020. Mamman Nasir later rose to become justice of the Supreme Court of Nigeria.

150. Interview with Dan Madamin Katsina, Alhaji Usman Sabo. Also interview with Hassan Kabir Usman, great-grandson of Emir Dikko, forty-four years, at Kofar Soro, Emir's Palace, Katsina, April 18, 2015.

151. Interview with Hassan Kabir Usman. Also interview with Hajiya Hassatu An Turai, Nagogo's daughter, April 16, 2015.

152. Interview with Hajiya Binta Titi, Dikko's granddaughter, ninety-one years, April 16, 2015; interview with Hajiya Rakiya, Dikko's granddaughter, seventy-two years, April 17, 2015.

153. Interview with Hajiya Hassatu 'yan Turai, Nagogo's daughter, at Katsina, April 17, 2015.

154. Several members of the Dikko family interviewed for this book testified to having heard some of the details of Dikko's metropolitan travels from their parents, with the refrain "My parents told me" prefacing several of their comments and answers to questions.

155. Interview with Hassan Kabir Usman; interview with Dan Madamin Katsina, Alhaji Usman Sabo; interview with Hajiya Binta Titi.

5

METROPOLITAN TRAVEL AND UTILITARIAN LITERACY

> The things Europeans put so much emphasis on seem rather insignificant to the African mind.
> —Bashir Tukur

MANY TOPICAL EXPLORATIONS FEATURED IN THE WRITINGS THAT circulated in the Northern Nigerian colonial intellectual public sphere, but travel narratives had a particularly resonant appeal among readers. Unlike fiction, nontravel biography, poetry, folktales, and oral performative literature rendered in text, narratives of travel to the imperial metropole intersected poignantly with a widespread desire to know the colonizer. In a colonial setting, discerning the ways of the colonizer had a utilitarian value that, when combined with the imperative of aesthetic satisfaction, produced a travel-animated literary form that was capable of enthralling a broad range of literate subalterns.

Those who claimed to know the metropole through their travel there commanded enormous intellectual and cultural capital. Travel narratives had immediate and practical utility as educational guides to the strange, socially distant ways of the colonizer. From the perspective of subalterns, there was indeed something distant and mysterious about colonial officials who worked in the colonies. Their "strange" predilections were seemingly discrete and inscrutable epistemological enigmas. Colonial enigmas fed into curiosity about why colonial officials acted the way they did, what informed their "strange" habits, and why they had unfamiliar expectations of colonized Africans. Northern Nigerians wondered why particular colonial officials preferred this or that method of executing a task or enjoyed particular pastimes while being indifferent to others. Travel by Northern Nigerian aristocrats to the metropole to observe the sociological drama of the metropolitan everyday was seen as a way of unlocking these mysteries, a way to satiate the curiosities and questions Northern Nigerians harbored about colonizers and their natal society.

This chapter analyzes the culture and economy of literary production and consumption that emerged from and catered to the intellectual and epistemic hunger for metropolitan stories among Northern Nigeria's growing community of readers and writers. Northern Nigerians literate in the Roman script desired to both epistemologically unlock the metropole and derive aesthetic fulfillment from reading new texts written in the Romanized script. These desires were sated by expanding literacy and literary spaces that increasingly privileged the experiential writings of Northern Nigerian been-tos, mostly aristocratic travelers to the United Kingdom, who, upon their return, found themselves drawn into a deepening Northern Nigerian vernacular public arena in which readers prodded writers to provide narratives of wonder, adventure, and the white man's way of life.

Students of Britain

The textual tradition established by Abubakar Imam and other early Northern Nigerian writers on Britain continued long after the literary effect created by *Tafiya* had peaked. The enduring cachet of stories purporting to translate and vernacularize the metropole created a diffuse genre wherein narrations of metropolitan sights and practices constituted a treasured literary and intellectual performance in Northern Nigeria's expanding public sphere. In telling these stories, narrators performed their identities as been-tos, as people involved in the stories they relayed.

The travel narratives were semi-biographical texts in the sense that the writings said as much about the writers' explorations and activities in Britain as about British peoples and cultures. Readers simultaneously encountered narratives that humanized and lionized their authors and revealed the underbelly of the white man's world. Throughout the colonial period and until Nigerian independence in October 1960, the testimonial narratives of travelers to Britain captivated diverse groups of subalterns, particularly students and those involved in Northern Nigeria's colonial secular school system. Seeing Britain and returning home to testify about its material and quotidian realities became a particularly resonant mode of self-definition for aristocratic students. The small number of students who won the lottery of overseas cultural excursions returned to pen their travelogues in school magazines supported by colonial educational officials, who regarded these writing endeavors as laboratories for cultivating responsible intellectual and literary expression.

Demonstrating the staying power of this literary imaginary, as late as the eve of independence in 1960, the cultural seduction of these overseas tales continued to captivate students at Northern Nigeria's few elite colonial schools. For instance, in June of that year, as the timetable of independence was winding down, two essays appeared in *Barewa*, the student magazine of Barewa College in Zaria, the relocated and renamed elite Katsina College.[1] The essays purported to reveal the ways of the British—an audacious authorial claim to metropolitan sociological expertise. The first of these travel essays, written by Bashir Tukur, was titled "Britain as I Saw It."[2] Tukur had been selected as a student representative of Northern Nigeria at the Centenary Celebrations of the Combined Cadet Forces in London. Tukur's narrative is a familiar reflection on the inquisitive bent of the English, "the interest they place in all things—natural, artificial or otherwise," and their "great affinity for learning."[3] In this text, Tukur remains faithful to the binary narrative of enunciating metropolitan cultures that are allegedly at odds with and therefore unintelligible to African cultural sensibilities. "The things Europeans put so much emphasis on," declared Tukur, "seem rather insignificant to the African mind"—interests such as "paintings and souvenirs from foreign countries," sports, and recreation. During his time in Britain, Tukur's British interlocutors asked him repeatedly what he thought of sports and the Olympic Games, and he was unable to answer with any substance. Now, in his postvisit reflection, he wondered if "anybody in this college is interested in this particular example [the Olympic games]."[4] Even more than Abubakar Imam before him, Tukur's narrative is heavily inflected by the idiom of contrast and metropolitan alterity. So different were the British from Northern Nigerians that even the books that "English boys of the same age [as us]" read were different from those read by students in Barewa College, Tukur wrote.

In Tukur's narrative, British culture is rendered radically distant from Northern Nigerian Muslim culture. Although he does not always engage in direct comparison and does not consistently invoke the foil of Northern Nigerian difference, the colonial region and its culture are the silent referents in his narrative. They foreground descriptions of effete British indulgences, such as the recreational and conservationist habituation of wildlife to green urban spaces and the social utility of parks as arenas of intellectual sociability: "Even in the city of London, there are places, called parks, in which wild life is allowed to exist so that even metropolitan people can know about that wild life which is abundant here in the North. This is not the only use of these parks: they are a sort of *'filin fadi souka'* in which you could come along, collect an audience for yourself and put forward ideas to them unmolested."[5] Tukur had apparently witnessed speaking engagements at London's famed Speakers' Corner and was relaying his experience there to his readers.

Without declaring or suggesting that such intentionality underpinned Tukur's narrative, the travelogue would have been received by his fellow students and other readers as both a confirmation of the assumed mysterious ways of metropolitan people and a demystification of some of the more esoteric, seemingly inscrutable aspects of metropolitan life. Tukur's narrative provided both a context and an interpretive logic for his student readers to make sense of the ways of the British, including why they invested in the instruments of recreation and intellectual nourishment. Like other self-accredited local narrators of metropolitan society, Tukur was supplying a scheme for reading the visual, symbolic, and material texts emanating from the metropole and circulating in Northern Nigeria.

Tukur capped his narrative by effusively discussing his meeting with Queen Elizabeth II. "The opportunity to meet and speak with Her Majesty, the Queen and his Royal Highness, the Duke of Edinburg" was the high point of the trip, Tukur told his fellow students.[6] For many literate Northern Nigerians, both fantastical and factual stories about the metropole would have been a staple of a shared, communal reading culture. Like many others, Tukur thought he knew much about the metropole, but visiting Britain caused him to recognize the gaps in his knowledge: "There were certain aspects of the British I had not known until [I took the trip]."[7] Like Imam before him, Tukur posits the metropole as both familiar and unknown; it was only by constructing this ambivalence that the value of travel, discovery, exploration, and the narratives that flowed from them could be inscribed in text and appreciated by Northern Nigeria's reading audience. Tukur was urging his readers to set aside what partial familiarity they had with the metropole through their prior readings and take his words as a more authentic and fuller perspective on the cultures of Britain. Tukur meandered his way to a fairly simple point: the eyewitness testimonial of a Northern Nigerian traveler was more authoritative than news reports on the metropole, which reached Northern Nigeria through colonial filters and controls.

School culture was a beehive of intellectualism in Northern Nigeria and mirrored the intellectual tastes of Northern Nigeria's growing community of Romanized readers. By the late colonial period, writing and reading about the metropole was an established feature of this public sphere. The school space, with its aspirational elevation of Britain as a model of modernity, became a zone of intellectual exchange about all things metropolitan. Several other students who had visited Britain felt obliged to write their own narratives and pontificate authoritatively on what they presented as metropolitan mannerisms and cultures.

In the same June 1960 edition of *Barewa* magazine, Magaji Inuwa, who signaled his authorial authenticity by declaring that he was among "those who have been to their country," formulated his own theories on British life and invited his readers to learn about the "very strange" ways of the British. Inuwa's essay, titled "Some Ways of Foreigners Which Seem Strange to Me," was half travelogue and half travel advice.[8] Inuwa compared the undignified "shirt and a pair of shorts" attire of the British with the dignified "flowing gowns and voluminous trousers" of Hausa "gentlemen."[9] Inuwa went on to dramatize the contrast between Hausa youthful subordination to gerontocracy and seniority and the culture he claimed to have observed in England, where "whatever the difference between their ages might be, each [English person in a conversation] has his eyes glued to the other's face."[10] "Even their women," Inuwa explained to his readers, "are not shy enough to avoid the fixed look of a man talking to them."[11] Inuwa then contrasted the Hausa culture of aristocratic monetary patronage of the poor or service-providing lower-class people with what he described as the "Englishman [who] does not like offering gifts occasionally, even to somebody of lower status than himself."[12]

The literary economy of contrast that characterizes other descriptive and morally pedagogical narratives of metropolitan travel dominates Inuwa's observations. The Englishman emerges in Inuwa's text as a bland, rigid, overly formal, and individuated agent and, alternately, as an inordinately informal, liberal figure of unregulated freedom. On the one hand, "the Englishman is never free" and is imprisoned "by the clock" of regimen and schedule, a stark contrast to Hausa culture, in which "we do things as we wish."[13] On the other hand, in Inuwa's eyes the Englishman is so liberal that he "is not ashamed of having his child monopolize his attention in a gathering of friends."[14] An Englishman, Inuwa informs his readers, finds "nothing more delightful ... than answering very silly questions from his child," while "we Hausas ignore the foolishness of a child and send him out when a visitor calls so that he might not do or say something offensive."[15] Contrast, distance, and difference were frequently used devices in the literary tool kits of these been-to writers.

These semi-didactic pontifications were profound statements of self-fashioning among Inuwa's generation of writers, travelers, readers, and students. Travel to the metropole gave Inuwa and other Northern Nigerian literary mediators of metropolitan culture a cache of social instruments that enabled them to stand in the cultural gap between colony and metropole as self-installed interpreters. The fact that these two narratives were written and published just a few months before Nigeria's independence indicates the longevity of the metropolitan travel genre under discussion. To understand this longevity and the literary-cultural space into which Tukur and Inuwa wrote their treatises, we must step back and map the earlier intellectual ferment that produced a vibrant Northern Nigerian discursive public sphere.

From a Community of Readers to a Community of Writers

The processes that culminated in the popularity of these narratives crystallized into two catalytic factors: the intellectual restlessness of Western-educated youth and the emergence of a colonially mediated public sphere of discussion and debate. Rupert East and his team of educators had set out to build what they called a "nation of readers," but between the 1930s and 1940s, a scribal revolution enveloped Northern Nigeria and deepened and complemented the emerging culture of reading.

Northern Nigeria's school culture engendered the fertilization of ideas of various provenances. In the 1930s, the region's overlapping first and second generations of Western-educated teachers and colonial civil servants voraciously read books, journals, and newspapers. As noted in chapter 1, these intellectual resources were largely Southern Nigerian in origin, causing concerns about importing subversive ideas into conservative Northern Nigeria. Colonial anxiety and a concomitant desire to channel the intellectual cravings of Northern Nigerian youth into controllable and allegedly constructive outlets of political discussion intersected with a fledgling informal intellectual congregation through a book club in the city of Bauchi. There, the most radical elements of Northern Nigeria's intellectual class of readers and writers, such as Mallam Aminu Kano, Yahaya Gusau, and the poet Sa'adu Zungur, mingled intellectually with more conservative organic intellectuals such as Abubakar Tafawa Balewa.[16]

Anxious colonial officials in Bauchi wanted these discussions brought into the open so they could be better managed. British officials subsequently formed the first official organ of public intellection, discussion, and debate in Northern Nigeria, convening the Taron Tattauna Al'Amuran Bauchi (Bauchi Discussion Circle, or BDC) in 1943.[17] The circle met in the local middle school every Friday evening to discuss a wide range of topical political, social, and cultural issues. These discussions demonstrated the vibrancy of the Northern Nigerian intellectual space. Some of the members of this public forum were creative writers, poets, and regular newspaper op-ed and letter writers.

The BDC proved a transferable template whose infectious impact was felt directly or indirectly in other Northern Nigerian urban centers where Western-educated youth similarly shared ideas, books, and critical reflection on colonial policies. As both Trevor Clark and A. M. Yakubu have shown, the public intellectual space the BDC offered acquired its own uncontainable intellectual momentum and proved too expansive for anxious colonial officials wary of unfettered intellectual ferment in the region.[18] After barely a year, British officials disbanded the BDC's formal structure and dispersed the participating intellectuals through administrative postings to different parts of Northern Nigeria.[19] Nonetheless, the template of intellectual activism embodied by the BDC had taken hold. The making of the Northern Nigerian public intellectual sphere of actively engaged readers and writers predated the BDC, but it was the reverberation and contagion of that inaugural, formal public forum that gave this intelligentsia its form. It was the BDC and its replicas elsewhere in Northern Nigeria that glamorized the vernacular colonial culture of writing, reading, and debate.

This diffusion of writing, reading, and discussion was aided by the increased proliferation of organs of colonial sociability such as African social clubs, which began to serve as forums for intellectual and literary transactions. Clubs such as the Kaduna Club, Gusau Club, Zaria Club, Yola Club, Kano Club, and others were designated as arenas for the emergent African colonial civil service intelligentsia to socialize outside the workplace since the colonial color bar forbade their membership in exclusive

European social clubs.[20] These African clubs were sites of vibrant literary and intellectual discussions. In these clubs, the BDC model was replicated in various informal forms outside the intrusive gaze of British colonial officials. No history of the intellectual ferment and the emergence of Romanized reading and writing cultures in the region would be complete without recognizing the instrumental influence of the BDC and its seductive demonstration of the social utility of reading, writing, and discussion. A vibrant public sphere, no matter how fragmented, was complementary to the burgeoning realm of literary production and consumption, a crucial aspect of which was the genre of metropolitan travel writing.

Newspaper Travel Narratives and Ways of Knowing the Metropole

The desire to know the metropole produced a community of both readers and writers, but, more crucially, it engendered the emergence of a distinct newspaper culture in Northern Nigeria in which periodicals became a village square—a public forum for telling, embellishing, marinating, and consuming stories of travel to the metropole. This was a dialogic culture in which readers interacted with travelers and authors of travelogues, with the ensuing exchange facilitated by the active editorial oversight and mediation of newspaper editors and publishers.

Dialogue between writers and readers persisted on the pages of *Gaskiya* because the writers and editors at the newspaper engaged readers with a variety of techniques. Writers adopted a conversational storytelling style in which readers could imagine themselves as participatory actors in the textual descriptions and experiential reenactments. Another popular technique was to parcel out stories in small installments, the narrative served in bits with the narrators stopping and announcing the pauses as one would in a verbal narration, with words such as, "Let's pause here and await the next edition of *Gaskiya*."[21] Another technique that deepened this dialogic travel journalism and sustained this economy of knowledge production was the use of what looked like a modified Socratic method of posing or repeating audience questions and then answering them. In this way, the editors made these stories seem driven by the curiosities and palates of their readers rather than any preconceived editorial agenda. By starting with the premise of audience inquiries, the editors justified some of their densely descriptive, esoterically foreign narrations.

Over time, the publishers and editors themselves developed infrastructures and procedures for soliciting and acquiring narratives from returned travelers. Although informal at the beginning, this complex intellectual loop of translating and mediating the sights and cultures of the metropole morphed into a process in which metropolitan travel and the public narration of these trips became entwined as frames of elite self-fashioning. This self-making enterprise benefited from the authorial and experiential capital conferred by the privilege of colonial travel. The culture of constituting elite subaltern subjectivities through travel was facilitated by the increased travel of Northern Nigeria's aristocrats and Western-educated men to Britain from the 1940s to the early 1960s. The increased pace of travel was sustained by establishing formal colonial bureaucracies and processes for cultivating the goodwill of Northern Nigeria's mainly Muslim elites and rewarding aristocrats for their instrumental partnership with British colonial administrators.

Gaskiya ta fi Kwabo was the primary organ for constructing and disseminating metropolitan travel stories in midcolonial Northern Nigeria, and this continued to be the case in the 1940s. The newspaper's popularity rested, in part, on its editors' deft exploitation of a widespread appetite for stories of travel to the United Kingdom by the region's elites. This desire was expressed in the form of letters to the editor, inquiries, and requests for new travel stories, clarifications on previously published ones, or continuations of truncated ones. Readers of Northern Nigeria's vernacular newspaper were an engaged audience, and they pressured editors to publish more details about metropolitan life.

Abubakar Imam, *Gaskiya*'s pioneer editor, felt this pressure. Upon his return from his tour of the United Kingdom in 1943, the newspaper's readers inundated him with questions about various aspects of British life. "How are the English at home?" Imam was repeatedly asked. "Do they have poor people like us?" was another question put to Imam by several readers in the newspaper's feedback pages.[22] The volume of inquiries and requests for particulars of metropolitan life led the newspaper's editors to devote a substantial amount of space to responding with detailed accounts and narratives evidently mined from the travel diaries and notes of returned travelers, supplementing these sources with other informational materials.

Most of the newspaper's stories on the people, politics, and cultures of Britain were published in response to readers' inquiries and requests, lending the stories a certain dialogic and pedagogic purpose. Upon receiving a preponderance of inquiries about a particular metropolitan topic, the editors consulted *Gaskiya*'s growing library of travel narratives and supplementary materials and responded with descriptive stories on the topic. In 1947, when the newspaper's readers began requesting more information on the duties of the colonial secretary and what informed Britain's relationship with its protectorates, the editors turned the inquiries into a platform to explain and describe the ways the colonial secretary functioned within and in relation to the British Parliament. The main supplementary material for this story was a wireless metropolitan broadcast transcribed by the newspaper's editorial staff.[23]

Inquiries sent in by the newspaper's readers ranged from the mundane to the political. Sometimes the inquiries embraced both realms, seeking to understand a British political phenomenon through its commonplace material culture. In July 1947, several readers wanted to know more about the English Crown Jewels, their interest having been piqued by previously published narratives about the English monarchy and the material symbols of its majesty. In response, the editors published the recurring questions, providing a glimpse into how and from what socioeconomic perspectives readers approached this subject. The editors' preface to the story recapped its origins: "Many people have been asking, 'Why is the King of England hoarding such precious jewels when many of his subjects are living in abject poverty and hunger? Why not sell them and provide succor to the needy?'"[24] The editors then proceeded to provide a detailed answer, establishing the newspaper's metropolitan travel section as a referential asset for readers seeking knowledge about metropolitan affairs.

Sometimes readers' inquiries touched on questions whose deterministic tentacles reached or led to the metropole. In November 1947, *Gaskiya*'s editors reported "receiving letters with questions" about why commodities remained scarce despite the end of World War II and despite, in the readers' estimation, Britain's complete economic recovery from the war. The editors seized on these inquiries to educate the readers on "the damage done to England" by the war, noting that "it is true that the war is over but England is still nursing the wounds inflicted on her."[25] Drawing on their sources— returned travelers, other eyewitness accounts, and *Gaskiya*'s library of materials on the metropole—the newspaper's editors were able to clarify, describe, and translate metropolitan cultures and affairs for their readers.

Metropolitan travel accounts published in *Gaskiya* were not only animated by the dialogic interaction between the newspaper and its readers. The newspaper's editors developed elaborate techniques for accessing returning travelers' stories and experiences. The newspaper routinely sent reporters to cover welcoming ceremonies for these travelers, and stories of their return would then be published as teasers for the stories to come about their experiences in Britain. The newspaper's editors "would let [the travelers] rest first before getting their stories,"[26] which would then be published in small, serialized bits that left the readers yearning for more.

Another way to obtain stories was to secure travelers' travel notes and diaries, rewrite and refine the entries and observations into coherent narratives and topical categories, and then publish individual or serialized stories. In one special instance, Ahmadu Bello, the sardauna of Sokoto and future premier of Northern Nigeria, sent *Gaskiya* editors a report on his travel to the United Kingdom in 1948, which the editors published under the title "Our Visit to England."[27] It is not clear how much editorial intervention was brought to bear on the report or whether the editors rewrote the travel report to give it a journalistic quality, but the published account was clearly informed by excerpts from Bello's travel notes and retained the sequential itineraries of the trip. Furthermore, the story was told in the first-person voice of Bello, indicating that the editors allowed the traveler to relate his experiences in and observations about England directly to the newspaper's readers. This decision made sense given Bello's status as the most influential political and aristocratic figure in Northern Nigeria in the postwar period and his embodiment of a growing political and social affinity between Northern Nigeria's aristocrats and British colonial officialdom.

Many travelers, aware of the newspaper's reputation as an epistemic gateway into the metropole for many Roman-literate Northern Nigerians, sought to spread their own experiences through the newspaper's reach and connection to an audience of Hausa-language readers. By the mid-1940s, several Northern Nigerian students on colonial or Northern Nigerian student scholarships had found their way to Britain to study. These students routinely sent stories to *Gaskiya* about events, sights, and experiences in Britain, as well as commentaries purportedly describing and explaining aspects of British life, mannerisms, and ethical systems. In some cases, returning students or students visiting Nigeria during school holidays reached out to *Gaskiya* to pitch their narratives to the newspaper's editors. In other cases, the returnees orally narrated their experiences to *Gaskiya*'s editorial staff, who put their own slant and narrative imprimatur on the stories before publishing them. This pattern of editorial mediation of unsolicited metropolitan stories is illustrated by the copious deployment of a reportorial tone as well as the second- or third-person narrative pronouns of *he* and *they*.[28] Publishing excerpts or entire travel diaries of returned aristocratic travelers was consistent with the pattern established earlier by Abubakar Imam. As discussed in chapter 1, Imam's serialized stories of his metropolitan experiences published over many editions of *Gaskiya* captivated his Hausa-speaking audience with a vivid narrative portrayal of the sights and spaces he had observed in Britain, affording them a vicarious immersive participation in the trip.

Northern Nigerian aristocrats who were trying to fashion themselves as modern been-tos cultivated ties to *Gaskiya* as both readers and writers. Imam's *Tafiya Mabudin Ilimi* set a standard for those entering this literary and political endeavor of colonial cultural translation. In the late 1940s, *Tafiya* continued to inspire and structure how travelers to the metropole narrated their experiences. *Tafiya*'s influence is discernible in several stories about Britain published in *Gaskiya*. Some stories, especially those designed to inform and educate and those with a descriptive bent, outright repeated details that were part of Imam's narration.

These stories upheld the tradition of narrating mundane metropolitan topics to a captive audience attracted to the quotidian footnotes of British life. Other stories in *Gaskiya* acknowledged the inspirational influence of and paid homage to *Tafiya*. Given *Tafiya*'s topical versatility, some authors felt compelled not only to declare their intellectual and literary gratitude to the text but to also acknowledge that their own stories merely built on Imam's iconic portrayal of Britain. When he returned from Britain by air in June 1948, Mallam Garba Kafin Madaki, a titleholder in Zazzau Emirate, referenced *Tafiya*, remarking on the entry protocol in Britain that "the inspections were not as thorough as that described by M. A. Imam in his travelogue, *Tafiya Mabudin Ilimi*."[29]

One travel writer in *Gaskiya*, Mallam Bayaro, took a slightly different tack in acknowledging the foundational influence of *Tafiya*. For him, England was a land overflowing with so many stories—a land possessing so much narrative material—that *Tafiya*, for all its breadth, only offered an abridged narrative of what England was about. His own story, he seemed to be suggesting, complemented previous ones, filled gaps, and extended the infinite narrative trajectories that England projected to a visitor. By his own account, he sought to explore topics left out by *Tafiya*'s necessarily limited narrative focus. He prefaced his narrative thus: "I am Bayaro, the former chief of Wusasa [a town outside Zaria]. I have spent exactly 10 months and five days studying in England. There are so many things to tell about England. Even M. Abubakar Imam who wrote *Tafiya Mabudin Ilimi* only summarized it."[30] It is clear that the travelogue writers read each other's narratives and that aristocratic explorers of the metropole read the narratives of previous travelers to Britain before their own trips.

The Other Colonial Other

Scholars of empire argue that the quest to know and understand is a colonial instrumental imperative. However, they often assume that only those seeking to use information to dominate, rule, and control had an appetite for information about the Other in the reductive colonial dyad of conqueror and conquered, colonizer and colonized. In this frame, colonizers are posited as possessing bureaucratic, political, and cultural curiosity animated by a desire to accomplish the task of domination. It is easy to slip from this valid but incomplete articulation of colonial informational curiosity into an even more problematic conceptual realm in which only colonizers are seen to invest in efforts to understand, classify, document, and quantify the colonial Other.

Colonialism is rarely unidirectional. As a complement to the colonizers' need to understand the peoples they were ruling, colonized peoples possessed an arguably greater impulse to know who their colonizers were, what motivated them, what kind of societies they lived in, what kinds of values and cultures were normative, and in what ways the colonizers were different from or similar to them. Northern Nigerian travel writers and readers did not have the cultural leverage or representational power of their British counterparts, given the existing colonial hierarchies, but their curiosities were no less generative of informational resources about the societies of their British colonial interlocutors.

In a colonial situation, whether operating from a position of strength or weakness, the desire to know the Other was a logical emotion of unequal relations. Regardless of where one stood in the equation of colonial power and race, knowing one's interlocutor was a useful asset. While the colonizer needed to know the origins and ramifications of "native" character, colonized peoples needed to know the origins of colonial violence, colonial oppression, colonial modernity, and the strange predilections and quirky mannerisms of colonial officials. For the people of Northern Nigeria, the answers to this curiosity lay in a vigorous probing of the colonizing country—its peoples, cultures, politics, flora and fauna, technologies, values, family structures, religious life, and social relations. Northern Nigerians craved knowledge about the metropole for reasons instrumentally similar to those of colonial ethnologists, who sought to pry open the underbellies and cultures of colonized peoples in order to more effectively dominate and rule them. For Northern Nigerians, every bit of information about the metropole was helpful in completing the composite cognitive profile of the colonizer. More important, information about the metropole was a guide that could help colonial subjects navigate colonial politics and the maze of colonial bureaucracy or ingratiate subalterns with colonial authorities.

Northern Nigerians' quest to know the oppressor explains the vigorous newspaper engagements with the subject of the metropole; it also conferred credibility on the narrative craft of travelers who claimed to know the metropole through travel. This social imaginary of curiosity further clarifies the popularity of *Gaskiya*'s stories about Britain and the experiences of Northern Nigerians who traveled there. The following analysis of the substantive discussions regarding the metropole on the pages of *Gaskiya* is set against an intense appetite for information on Britain among Northern Nigeria's Roman-literate people.

Ethnographic Minutia and the Subaltern Gaze

Because a similar utilitarian ethos underpinned both the colonizer's quest to know the native and his environment and the subaltern's appetite for information about his oppressor, the metropolitan narratives of Northern Nigeria's travelers mirrored the same homogenizing discourses, cultural generalizations, forced comparisons, and boring minutia found in colonial ethnographic texts on African societies. Why was a lengthy story on "summertime in England" published in the June 18, 1947, edition of *Gaskiya*?[31] An obvious answer would be that many among the newspaper's aristocratic readers aspired to visit England and would find the meteorological contrast with the tropics useful. In the prescriptive tone and substance of the story, they would also find a manual on how to thrive in the English summer. Details about how "the sun doesn't set ... until 9 pm" and how "light persists until 11 pm" were usable informational resources for would-be travelers.

Many other details in the story fall within the realm of the mundane, esoteric, boring, and distant. I argue, however, that the distance of readers from that which is being described transforms the trivial into something fascinating since distance exoticizes and vivifies the mundane. In this case, the distance between Northern Nigeria and Britain, dramatized in the rarity and logistical difficulty of travel and in the curiosities that distance creates, rehabilitated the mundane metropolitan sphere into an object of infinite fascination among Northern Nigerians. Discussions of "the branding of swans on the Thames," the "traditional summer rites performed by the English before the emergence of Christianity,"[32] and other minutia that would be tediously uninteresting to British people filled out the story. To Northern Nigerian readers, the distant novelty and exotic character of these details gave them a new valence.

In piecing together such a densely detailed narrative about summertime in England, the editors of *Gaskiya* were catering to a curiosity that made sense in the colonial situation. Colonial ethnographic texts are often dominated by irrelevancies, detailed asides, and esoterically boring discussions of seemingly idle "native" activities and objects. This same logic was at work in *Gaskiya*. Published colonial ethnographies and travel narratives often became bestsellers in Europe. They were often little more than compilations of the fantasies and curiosities of European colonial travelers, but such seemingly useless details pandered to Europeans' desire to know the African "native." These representations found a ready, enthusiastic audience even though they were little more than what we might justifiably consider the exoticizing frivolities of European colonial ethnographers and travelers. Thus, in both African and European travelogues, the rehabilitative effect of distance was at work, transforming minutia into treasured information in the minds of curious readers.

Like Europeans in the colonial period, Northern Nigerians had a vigorous thirst for the minutia of metropolitan life. This informational quest could only be sated by authoritative and esoterically unfamiliar details about the colonizer's home society. In this universe of epistemological production and consumption, the more exotic and unfamiliar the text the better its reception; hence, detailed descriptions of metropolitan conditions and material culture, bland and boring to today's discriminating and short-spanned informational palates, were common empirical elements in travelers' narratives. For instance, the narrative jumble of the summertime story was not rendered in English or for those with some familiarity with England; rather, the signified meteorological phenomena were translated through the filter of vernacular Hausa storytelling, further intensifying their exotic character. Set against circulating myths and mystiques of a seemingly inscrutable British metropole, boring details in this context of linguistic and cultural translation became desirable answers to long-held curiosities about colonizers and their society.

Other metropolitan stories in *Gaskiya* in the 1940s privilege densely descriptive, almost pedagogical descents into minute details. A story titled "Forestry in England," published in the July 9, 1947,[33] edition, illustrates this abiding trope. The article begins with the following: "The nature of fields in England is fast changing nowadays. In the past, you would see fallow fields but they have now been replaced by forests. Forests have now dominated the lowlands of Wales and Scotland as well as the fields of Hampshire and Dorset. You will now see blue fields filled with pine, spruce and larch trees. These are soft wood trees. You know that there are two varieties of wood; hard and soft. Soft wood is used in making kerosene and soft boxes. Hard wood is used in buildings."[34] The article delves into great detail about forestry in England, setting the scene by first outlining the history of afforestation in Britain, the evolution of government policies on forest management, the creation of large forest reserves, the large-scale planting of trees, and even the wartime harvesting of forest wood to support the war effort.[35]

Clearly, the editors of *Gaskiya* sourced the story from multiple informational venues, including materials brought back by travelers interested in Britain's forests. Why did *Gaskiya*'s editors deem such a story worth publishing, and what economy of reader interests drove its publication? To the extent that stories pandered to readers' interests, and controlling for the story's potential entwinement in colonial policy on afforestation, it is important to understand how such a dull subject would have found reception among *Gaskiya*'s readers, who may have imagined Britain as a space developed beyond the rusticity of thick flora. To answer this question, one must understand the depth of the readers' quest for an all-encompassing dossier of knowledge on the colonizing society. The allure of the foreign and the unfamiliar was strong, but the end point was to know the colonial Other by juxtaposing his world with the moral, material, and semiotic worlds of the writers and readers of metropolitan travel narratives. Contrast, difference, and details shaped this informational transactional economy.

Another explanation for the narrative minutiae in these travel texts can be found in one of the overarching arguments of this book: the mutuality of ethnography and observation in the colonial ideational space. As composites of colonized peoples, Northern Nigerian metropolitan travelers engaged actively in the ritualized art of ethnographic fascination and the observational obsessions that scholars have long associated with European colonial ethnography and travel writing. Northern Nigerian narrators who staked out space in *Gaskiya* to write about British metropolitan ways did not merely do so to satisfy the curiosities of their readers; they themselves were participating in the same colonial economy of curiosity that animated their readers. The writers were ethnographically gazing at the white man's society and leveraging their firsthand observations to curate the world of the colonizer for both aesthetic and utilitarian purposes in Northern Nigeria. The parallels between this narrative genre and the writings of colonial travelers and observers of Nigerian societies is apparent even when we account for power differentials and the diverging subtleties of vernacularization. The abiding idiom in both iterations of colonial gazing is the work of minutiae as ways of accessing the cultural and material world of the colonial Other.

An aesthetic of the mundane framed *Gaskiya*'s accounts of the metropole, and minutiae legitimized a technique of colonial ethnography discernible in and perfected by *Gaskiya*'s metropolitan travel writing. An article titled "Linen Manufacture in England" painstakingly traced the history of English textile manufacturing to the era of wool, its functional response to the bitterly cold weather—a weather so cold that one could not "compare it to Nigeria's"—and the eventual advent of cotton fabric, the raw material for which came from British India.[36] The article then addressed the basics of linen manufacture: "Linen is made from a shrub called flax, [and] flax is grown in England and the Island of Ireland to the West of England, so linen making is big business in Ireland."[37] The authors even offer a primer on the difficulties of making linen from flax compared to ginning and weaving cotton, concluding, "In short it takes about a year from harvesting flax to manufacturing the linen."[38] The authors included three pictures with the caption: "Here are three pictures taken in Northern Ireland showing the process of turning flax into linen."[39]

Subsequent editions of *Gaskiya* carried similarly esoteric descriptions of processes, industries, and material objects in Britain. The October 8, 1947, edition offered an extremely detailed description of granite mining in England. This story included photos of an actual granite mine in Britain showing "the breaking [of] granite into building stones."[40] A whole series of stories on various industrial and quasi-industrial processes ran throughout 1947 with titles ending with the phrase "in England." Because these stories actually focused on the entire British Isles, by October 1947,

Gaskiya's editors realized they had to define their metropolitan geography more precisely for their readers. In the story on granite mining, the bulk of which focused on the granite and building-stones industry of Aberdeen, Scotland, the editors included the following prefatory note: "Whenever we say England we refer to the whole of Britain."[41]

One long story titled "European Ships" was a maritime treatise on merchant and military ships in the British fleet, their mercantile connections to trade in Nigeria, and a detailed description of the *Queen Elizabeth* and the *Queen Mary*, "the biggest, most beautiful, most comfortable, and fastest ships ever built."[42] This story also included illustrative photos meant to enhance the readers' sense of awe and connect them visually to the object of the story. A story titled "The Port of Liverpool" contained painstaking descriptions of Liverpool's centrality to British marine mercantile engagements. As was typical of such stories, the authors made unexpected digressions into mundane descriptions of Liverpool's origin as a mercantile city, the entertainment culture of the people of Liverpool, the university, the "beautiful church on a hill," the Mersey River, and the difficulties of "maneuvering ships to harbor . . . during the winter."[43] The authors seemed to be exploiting the pedagogical efficacy of contrast, detail, the visual, suspense, and meandering digressions to satisfy the curiosities of *Gaskiya*'s readers. Readers desired stories on the more remote, unfamiliar sectors and objects of British society, prompting *Gaskiya*'s editors to publish ever more esoteric details of British life.

When a metropolitan object was generically familiar to the audience, the authors of treatises stoked interest by invoking contrast and rendering the object sufficiently British to attract and sustain the interest of readers. A story titled "Sheep in England" had a subtitle that sought to make it more exotic and less familiar to Northern Nigeria's readers, who were well acquainted with sheep and sheepherding. "Their sheep are different from Nigerian sheep," the rider declared. The article, a lengthy, multifaceted discussion that ran for two consecutive editions of the newspaper, outlined the distinguishing feature of British sheepherding culture: "In this country, we keep sheep for their meat and skin; in England, sheep are not only kept for meat and skin but also for their wool."[44] The story zigzags across various aspects of Britain's sheepherding culture, commenting on the economics of sheepherding; the belief that "the best mutton is Scottish"; the evolution of heavy fleece on British sheep to protect them in the long, harsh winter; the use of herding dogs to control and corral large herds of sheep; the grazing fields of Britain; and how the "cold and rain wreak havoc" on the sheep population.[45]

Stories included one on "Merchant Marine Training in England,"[46] another was a turgid description of the role of the Bank of England in the British economy,[47] and yet another story dwelled extensively on boat racing in England and veered off into a detailed discussion of what the author called "the English love of sport."[48] This story, a meandering multisport commentary, invokes the register of sports in Zaria and Kano and the emotions at play to help guide the reader in understanding British sports and recreational culture; the pride, passion, and money at stake in British sporting contests; and the annual spectacle of the London Boat Race.[49] Another story in that series focused on the Port of London; its "role in developing the British Empire"; its emergence, along with the city of London, as "the commercial center of the world"; and its function in the postwar period as "the heart of England's economy."[50]

These textual and visual details about the material culture and industrial projects of Britain had obvious appeal to readers familiar with imported British goods, including textiles, and how raw materials were transformed through industrial processes into finished goods. However, in publishing stories on topics and subjects so far removed from the experiential repertoires of Northern Nigerians, the editors counted on their readers' fascination with British phenomena, appealing to their xenophilic colonial imagination. The permutation appeared to be that readers would read about anything if the setting was England, hence the recurrence of the phrase "in England" in most of the metropolitan stories published in *Gaskiya*.

The writers' ethnographic and observational practice thrived on a symbiotic partnership between existing curiosities and the narratives produced on various aspects of British metropolitan life. As with European colonial travel and ethnographic texts that could not exist independently of the extant racist curiosities about African peoples and societies, *Gaskiya*'s metropolitan travel writers could not practice their craft outside the fascination with metropolitan society. Metropolitan and Nigerian readers desired details about their respective colonial Others. This desire, in turn, catalyzed the ethnographic production of minutiae and esoterically detailed narratives.

Some returned travelers who published their metropolitan accounts in *Gaskiya* took a decisively prescriptive tack. Mallam Bayaro Nuhu Zariya's piece titled "Winter in England" was, in addition to being a description of

Britain's wintry conditions, a how-to manual for travelers to Britain during the winter season. The following excerpt presents Zariya's prescriptions for surviving winter in England.

> Winter starts in November and lasts till March. In those months, the sun sets by 4:30pm and doesn't rise until 8:00am. Shirts must of necessity be tucked in. Before wearing anything, one has to wear a tight woolen pair of trousers with long sleeved woolen singlet. One would then put on about two to three long socks before putting on a suit and long overcoat. One would then put on gloves. Sometimes even two or three. After wearing this much clothes one would still feel the cold. In the night, you would have to wear the thermal underwear and pajamas. Then sleep under four or five heavy blankets. Even so you will still feel the cold until you hug a warm water bottle before going to sleep.[51]

Here Zariya implicitly proclaims his experiential authorial authority on the subject, his detailed prescriptions being the mark of that authority. By underscoring the cold temperatures of winter in Britain—"whoever visits England in the summer will not realize how it really is"—Zariya hoped that prescribing winter survival gear to would-be travelers to Britain would serve as an indirect description of the harshness of winter. He thus combines the descriptive with the prescriptive, much like what other stories had subtly done.

Forging Imperial Community

The travel writers were staking out an authorial ground from which they felt their pontifications and observations about British society could not be challenged. This assumption may also say something about the dependent relationship between writers and readers, especially readers without metropolitan travel experience who would not have possessed the informational resources to challenge the authors' pronouncements. The inability of readers to judge what they were reading about Britain against their own knowledge or experience meshed with an intense curiosity about the metropole to confer credibility and the appearance of facticity on the claims of traveler-writers, no matter how embellished or outlandish.

The consistent focus on British society, culture, and quotidian objects in *Gaskiya* contributed to and was nourished by the existence of what one might call an imperial communal imagination—a feeling of imperial solidarity that enabled many Roman-literate Northern Nigerian colonial subjects to identify with Britain and invest emotion, interest, and passion in its affairs. This mode of imperial identification found expression in the tone of some of the travel narratives, as well as in the elaborate domestic rituals that preceded and followed trips to the metropole. In several published stories, the writers were not content to simply describe and explain the topic or subject at hand; they pontificated on what was wrong with British life and prescribed what should be done. In the aforementioned story on forestry in England, the anonymous writer transitions fluently between description and prescriptive punditry. Amid the writer's detailed treatise, he noted that "even though forestry development is vital to the survival of England, farming is also very important; therefore forestry managers have to be careful not to take over all the arable land in the country. Also this might affect sheep owners as they are not allowed to rear their animals in the forests."[52] Here, the detached aesthetic of the travel-writing genre meshes with what reads like colonial agricultural instruction. The boundary between the descriptive and prescriptive is again blurred.

The fluid, authoritative, and passionate pivot to opinionating on a matter of strictly metropolitan importance is indicative of the imperial communitarian identification that drove *Gaskiya*'s editorial staff to focus so inordinately on metropolitan matters and Roman-literate Hausa readers to consume these writings. Both groups were forging and participating in an imperial cultural economy that enabled colonized elites to see themselves, at least at an aspirational level, as part of a metropolitan culture of modernity and as invested in its making and remaking. Modernity was defined as emanating from and residing permanently in Britain, and elite subalterns—consumers of colonial modernist goods and aspirants to the paradigmatic markers of metropolitan high culture—understood themselves as being imbricated in metropolitan matters, goods, and ways of living. This explains the intense passion with which they consumed metropolitan information and their eagerness to register their opinions and prescriptions on British matters.

Gaskiya was a fulcrum and clearinghouse of the informational and discursive universe created around metropolitan realities, but, as indicated earlier, the newspaper depended on a variety of informational streams. Like the newspaper's readers, its editors regularly listened to British wireless broadcasts. The British Broadcasting Corporation began worldwide broadcasts in 1934 with the establishment of its World Service focusing on global and empire issues. The BBC's Hausa-language wireless broadcasts in Northern Nigeria played a central role in a multipronged propaganda effort against the Germans during World War II. In the 1940s, many Western-educated Northern Nigerians continued to tune in to these broadcasts, which took on a more professional form after the end of the war. In at least one instance, the editors revealed that they had gleaned some of the information included in their stories on Britain from the wireless broadcasts.[53]

This universe of intersecting informational sources constructed a metropolitan consciousness among Northern Nigeria's Western-educated elites. A sociopolitical space already saturated with imperial and metropolitan information caused imperial solidarity to evolve and identification with metropolitan affairs to emerge. Given this preexisting condition, not only was *Gaskiya*'s consistent coverage of metropolitan realities intelligible to its readers, but many of the readers who traveled to Britain became part of the newspaper's network of interconnected and overlapping readers, wireless listeners, and travelers who were fairly well acquainted with metropolitan affairs and cultures. Returnees from Britain who worked with *Gaskiya* perpetuated the belief that travel to Britain was critical to attaining epistemic intimacy with the metropole and becoming an imperial citizen-subject.

While recapping the experiences of a contingent of Northern Nigerian teachers who visited Britain in May 1947—a group that included Mallam Aminu Kano of the famed Bauchi Middle School referenced earlier—a story in *Gaskiya* extensively discussed the visitors' intense program of touring. Much of the tour focused on introducing the visitors to Britain's agricultural technology and "farming techniques which they hope to transplant to Nigeria."[54] We are told that the visitors' immersion in British agricultural practices and other aspects of British life was so thorough that "they went to Wales as strangers and left as locals."[55] The idea that travel to the metropole could transform the subaltern into an honorary Briton by virtue of the immersive experience of observing and participating in British life was actively cultivated by *Gaskiya* and its network of travel writers.

In the late 1940s, the network of travelers to Britain expanded, giving *Gaskiya* more narratives to publish and more visibility as a gateway to information about the metropole. Moreover, most of Northern Nigeria's prominent aristocrats actively patronized the pages of *Gaskiya* to peddle their metropolitan stories. Stories about visits to Britain by prominent or emergent figures in the postwar colonial political scene began to proliferate in *Gaskiya*. *Gaskiya*'s editors sometimes anticipated these firsthand accounts with their own stories on the visit, interviewing the travelers and soliciting their diaries or summaries of the trips' highlights.

On June 23, 1948, an eleven-man contingent returned from Britain. The group, composed of some of Northern Nigeria's most important political figures and aristocrats, was led by Ahmadu Bello, the sardauna of Sokoto and future premier of Northern Nigeria. *Gaskiya* reported that a large delegation of Native Authority officials—aristocratic auxiliaries in the colonial bureaucracy—welcomed the delegation at Kano's airport. While the editors stated that they would allow the returnees to settle in before obtaining their stories, the story declared that members of the delegation had relayed "the highlight of the visit" to the newspaper's correspondent on the sidelines of the welcome ceremony. This, the newspaper stated, "was the luck they had on Thursday 17th of June of seeing His Majesty the King together with the Queen and their children at the Royal Ascot races."[56] As stated in previous chapters, more than anything else, Northern Nigeria's aristocratic visitors to Britain craved a chance to behold the king. In this case, the visitors, according to *Gaskiya*'s reportage, caught a glimpse of the king by chance: "As they were seating, His majesty the King of England, Her majesty the Queen, Princess Elizabeth and her husband arrived in a carriage. Luckily for our representatives, the royal entourage disembarked close to them and they were able to see them free of charge."[57] The serendipitous sighting of the king was cited as the climax of the visit, but the visitors also "learned how the English rule themselves . . . [as well as] modern farming techniques."[58]

Following the publication of *Gaskiya*'s report on the delegation's visit, two prominent Northern Nigerian political figures, Mallam Garba Kafin Madaki and Ahmadu Bello, published their own accounts. The former's report focused on the logistics of the travel rather than on the group's experiences in Britain, while Bello narrated his observations and memories from the trip. Bello remarked about the early sunrise and late sunset as well as "the days of cold and rain" that had them "shivering."[59] Bello stated that "the major lesson" he and his fellow visitors learned in Richmond and Yorkshire, where they spent much of their time, "was about the domestic social setting of the British." This educational socialization was facilitated by the distribution of the visitors among local host families. The overarching impression Bello and his fellow visitors conveyed about their experience congealed into one recurring point: "The English are kind at home."[60]

Bello and his entourage observed the political life of small-town Britain: "We studied how this small town conducts its own affairs; we witnessed local elections of the mayor and the councilors."[61] Bello fondly remembered their visits to farms, forest reserves, local industries, and museums. His account was clearly excerpted from his diary, which underwent little to no editing.[62] The unrefined authenticity of these narratives, sometimes mixing first-person narrative with reportorial third-person language, gave the recollections a unique appeal for *Gaskiya*'s readers.

Like Bello, other returnees commented in their published narratives on the hospitality of the English. Mallam Bayaro Nuhu's narrative, published in August 1948, contrasts the kindness of British people to visitors in their homes with the public aloofness of Britons to strangers: "They are very helpful at home. As soon as they see a stranger, they will rush to him offering assistance. The only peculiar thing that a stranger would notice especially in London is their silence in public transport vehicles. You would reach your destination without hearing anyone saying hello to another person."[63] For Nuhu, the public social indifference of the British people was such a departure from their domestic hospitality that it had to be explained outside the stereotypical British attitudinal fabric. He hypothesized that public "silence is to avoid saying anything that might discomfit you as the government shows its fury to anyone that exhibits the slightest form of racism."[64] There is, of course, no evidence to substantiate Nuhu's theory since it was based on conjecture, but this confident punditry on metropolitan affairs, this plugging of informational gaps with personal conjecture, is precisely what established the authorial authority of the traveler-writers. It is important to note, first, Nuhu's bold willingness to proffer an explanation for an aspect of British life he considered anomalous and, second, the ways his proclamations represent a broader eagerness on the part of these traveler-writers to plug empirical and logical holes they identified while constructing their own theories and explanations for observed metropolitan incongruities.

Nuhu was one of the boldest claimants to metropolitan explanatory expertise, weighing in on an eclectic body of topics and phenomena. He was declarative in several of his pronouncements, with a tone of finality that would have come across to his readers as the confident eyewitness account of a writer reeducated by travel. His section titled "Leaders serve their people" states that "England practices true democracy" because "political leaders in England serve their people rather than the people serving their leaders."[65] British leaders, Nuhu proclaimed, "hate anything that would harm their people."[66] This was, of course, a romanticized perspective on British politics, but to his impressionably Anglophilic readers, the contrast would have been reasonable because it affirmed what they had already gleaned from colonial propaganda: that British political organization was more egalitarian than that of Northern Nigeria.

Nuhu's streak of authoritative claims about British society extended to his pronouncement that "there are no lazy people in England." He elaborates by resorting to the recurring technique of contrast, comparison, and invocation of Northern Nigerian opposites: "Here, in our country you can see unemployed people feeding on the efforts of others. It is not so in England. Every person—male or female—is busy. In fact, the women work almost more than the men."[67] Women, Nuhu explained to his readers, "take care of their homes, husbands, and children and [still] go out to work side by side with the husbands. . . . Women serve as parliamentarians in England . . . and take part in the discussions like men"; he concluded that "there is nothing that women do not do in England."[68]

Nuhu's meandering, multitopic travelogue touched on the subject of education in England, observing that education was "free and compulsory to all citizens." For Nuhu, "the most helpful group of people in England are the police."[69] He made a point of explaining to his readers the multiple functions of the police as guardians of public safety, noting with a tinge of embellishment that "English police do not even carry batons" and that "they would politely ask you to move back and thank you for complying with their request." Nuhu reminded his readers of "stories about [the British police] that had appeared in earlier editions of *Gaskiya*" and concluded, "It is in England that the police is indeed everybody's friend."[70]

Was Nuhu opaquely contrasting the high-handed, law-and-order policing in colonial Northern Nigeria with the polite, nonviolent policing he described as being the norm in Britain? Was he, like previous writers on the metropolitan police in *Gaskiya*, romanticizing and humanizing the British metropolitan police as a way of drawing attention to the contradictory reputation among subalterns of colonial police units as people to be feared rather than respected? A counterpart, unasked question implicit in Nuhu's narrative is why British colonizers policed differently and more aggressively in Northern Nigeria than in Britain. We may never definitively answer these questions, but one thing appears fairly clear: Nuhu's reference to earlier stories in *Gaskiya* about the British police indicates a fixation of traveler-writers on the sharp contrast between policing in the colony and policing in the metropole. Like contrasts in other sectors of life, this divergence was portrayed to sensationalize both the assumed nonviolent policing of the metropole and the violent, forceful policing of the colony.

The quotidian conduct of British people held a particular fascination for Northern Nigeria's writers and consumers of these travel narratives. The question of whether British behavior at home was truly the key to understanding British behavior in the colony seemed to have been displaced by an explanatory fetish centering on a monolithic British character that could be found frozen in time and space in Britain—the kind of sociobehavioral homeostasis that early colonial anthropology is accused of having promoted about African peoples. For writer-travelers like Nuhu, British attitudes needed to be understood outside the colonial context to grapple with both deviations from and conformity to those attitudes in the colony. In other words, British behavior, accessible through travel and metropolitan experience, was the paradigm against which the conduct of British colonial officials in Northern Nigeria could be judged. Nuhu makes this point poignantly in a section of his travelogue titled "Behavior of the British."

Although analysis of behavioral transmission and influence often assumes that the more powerful colonizer always influenced the weaker colonized peoples,[71] in this section, Nuhu develops a strangely intriguing theory about what he saw as a dissonance between "the bad behavior exhibited by some Europeans in this country [Nigeria] such as haughtiness and verbal abuse" and what he observed in Britain as a general attitude of ecumenical respect, decorum, and kindness.[72] Nuhu opined that abusive behavior by British colonial officials was "learned from our people." The officials, he claimed, had had their attitudes altered by the antagonizing disposition of some colonial subjects in Northern Nigeria. The colonizers' behavior in Northern Nigeria, Nuhu argued, was a departure from metropolitan behavioral norms. However, it was "neither our hot weather nor excessive work that makes them boorish," Nuhu opined. Rather, since "they don't work as much as their fellow Europeans in Britain" and since hot weather "is their preferred weather in Britain" and causes them to "become happier and friendlier,"[73] the bad behavior of colonial officials was attributable, Nuhu claimed, to the contagion of similar behaviors they encountered in Nigeria. The idea that colonized Northern Nigerians corrupted the character of their British colonizers and taught their colonizers to behave badly is a bizarre explanation for the erratic and domineering behavior of colonial officials. Yet Nuhu's diagnosis inverts the colonial order of impact and, however perversely, imbues Northern Nigerians with impactful agency, capacity, and influence on colonial relations that are not often emphasized in colonial historiography.

Two months after excerpts from Ahmadu Bello's British travel diary were published in *Gaskiya*, Northern Nigeria's foremost aristocrat and political figure continued to reflect on his experiences in Britain. In September, he published another story in *Gaskiya* recalling and distilling his observations on Britain. Like other traveler-writers before him, Bello was intrigued by the pace of British life and by a disciplined work culture whose unmentioned antipode was the less rigid, less consuming work culture of Northern Nigeria. He titled his story "There Are no Idlers in England, Everybody Is Busy."[74]

> Life in England is not idle. By 7:30am, the lady of the house would provide tea for the family. By 8:00am, the whole family would gather for breakfast. From there, the father would set off to work while the children go to school. The lady of the house will continue her domestic chores. Neither the father nor the children goes back home for lunch. In every village and town, there are restaurants that sell food to customers. Male or female, young or old, customers are all served in the restaurant. Additionally, big corporations provide canteens for their staff, while schools provide food for their pupils for a fee. Therefore nobody goes back home for lunch as the distance between your house and your office may be as much as two to ten miles.[75]

Bello sought to capture the assembly-line, impersonal efficiency of British work culture and its intrusion into routines that Northern Nigerian readers may have assumed were universal, such as leaving the farm to return home for lunch. The established tradition of explaining the quotidian rhythms of observed British life to Northern Nigerians informed Bello's subsequent commentary on what he saw as a mastery of the domestic sphere by the British "lady of the house." "The wife," Bello informed his readers, "takes care of all domestic chores." He continued, "After the husband and children have left for work and school respectively, she cleans the rooms, makes the beds, washes the bathrooms and wipes windows and mirrors. She then inspects used clothes and sews those in need of sewing. If there is a garden in the house, she moves there and takes care of it. Afterward she indulges in some form of handcraft before it is time for shopping."[76] Such quotidian details of the familial sphere of British life would have been refracted through the personal gender politics of the aristocratic paternal figure of Bello, and this is evidenced by the fact that Nuhu's commentary on the role and status of British women contrasts radically with Bello's. Since Bello would have read Nuhu's earlier commentary that claimed British women worked alongside men in the British public sphere, it is possible that Bello was responding to the claims of his fellow traveler-writer. For our purpose, however, there is a more productive question to pose, which is why such fine details of British family life and domestic gender relations captivated *Gaskiya*'s writers and readers. There existed an undeclared Northern Nigerian comparative foil for these discussions. When the discussion moved to children, this comparative frame became apparent.

Bello discussed children's after-school play and the British culture of ensuring that children got "enough sleep, which would improve their health and physical development."[77] The comparative foregrounding for the discussion is a subtle critique of children's routines in Northern Nigeria, a point substantiated by the writer's claim that "a two year old girl in England is as big as a twelve year old in Nigeria," the difference in growth patterns being a function, according to Bello, of "good food, enough sleep, and exercise."[78] In other words, Bello was making the contrastive argument that British children had more balance in their lives and thus developed faster than Nigerian children. Bello then extended this contrastive discussion to parenting techniques in Britain: "Children are raised through persuasion, not through threats; they are shown their mistakes and persuaded to do the right thing." Here, again, the unsaid is as instructive as the said since the unspoken referent appears to be the Northern Nigerian parenting tradition of instilling discipline in children through threatened or actual corporal punishment. The real genius of Bello's narrative is his ability to draw these contrasts without appearing to endorse the British referent or condemn the contrasting Northern Nigerian phenomenon.

Bello concluded his treatise on British society by distinguishing between the attitudes of rural and urban Britons: "Just like urban dwellers behave differently than rural dwellers here, that is what obtains in England," he stated. "If you become familiar with English villagers you will find them to be very friendly," but in Bello's English cities, "there are gentlemen and of course there are rascals."[79] Bello's celebration of English rustic attitudes and his concomitant devaluation of British urbanity echoes the British colonial devaluation of urbanized African populations purportedly dislodged from the stabilizing, humanizing, and disciplining influences of rural African life. It is not clear if Bello's perspective drew on or was subconsciously influenced by this dominant colonial rhetoric venerating rural Africa and criticizing urban Africa as polluting, detribalizing, and thus de-Africanizing. The interplay between colonial ethnological registers and methods of valuation, on the one hand, and the contrastive impulse of traveler-writers seeking to find and explain difference, on the other, made for a complex travel script of the metropole.

The Etsu Nupe Testament

Northern Nigerian aristocratic testimonials to metropolitan life were compelling because the aristocrats telling the stories rendered metropolitan signs as memories—as memorable etchings on the consciousness of those giving the testimonies. These retrospective, recollected experiences were powerful because Northern Nigerian readers saw them as important precisely because they were worth remembering and were therefore instructive and fascinating tidbits of metropolitan life. Like all remembered and textually disciplined narratives, the testimonials were mediated by the intrusions of time, distance, the idiosyncratic biases of the colonial space, colonial relations, and the privileged subaltern position of the narrators.

In 1952, the Etsu Nupe Alhaji Muhammadu Ndayako penned a travel memoir about his six-week tour of the United Kingdom along with Abdulkadir Shuaybu, the emir of Ilorin (Map 5.1). This memoir, although heavily mediated, became one of the most widely read travelogues in the Northern Nigerian metropolitan travel canon. Written from mental notes and the paramount ruler's diary, the text contains the full range of expressive gestures that had come to characterize this genre. Ndayako and the emir of Ilorin toured several sites in Britain between the first week of June and July 17, 1952. Ndayako's book on the trip, *Tafiyan Etsu Nupe Ingila* (Etsu Nupe's travel to England), was published by Gaskiya Corporation in 1954.[80] It is a remarkably detailed narration of the metropole through the lens of travel, mobility, and touristic adventure. It is also a heavily mediated narrative, tempered by Ndayako's eagerness to accentuate the import of his account. So involved was he that he invariably became a part of his own story of metropolitan awe. As the following analysis reveals, the traditional ruler of Northern Nigeria's predominantly Muslim Nupe people was awed by his invitation to the metropole and sought, it seems, to both repay the gesture and maximize the importance of the invitation by constructing an exaggerated tale of metropolitan glory, albeit tinged with subtle but stinging critique.

Upon their arrival in London, Ndayako and Shuaybu walked the streets of the city guided by colonial officials arranged by the organizers of the visit, the British Council. The reader learns from Ndayako's narrative that over the next six weeks, the duo and their aides traversed the breadth of

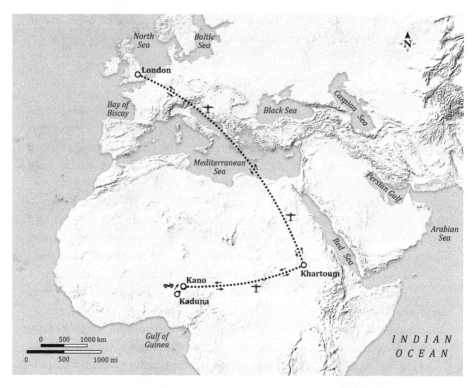

Map 5.1. Itinerary of the journey of Etsu Nupe, Muhammadu Ndayako, and Emir of Ilorin, Abdulkadir dan Shuaybu Bawa, to Britain in 1952.

Britain, seeing, hearing, and touching multiple objects of British imperial significance. The book includes a retelling of the elaborate preparations and meandering itinerary of travel within Nigeria that ultimately saw Ndayako and other members of his tour group fly out of Kano to London via Khartoum. By the time we get to Ndayako's narrative of his metropolitan adventures, we see not just his vivid recollections of sights and sounds but also, more instructively, scattered personal commentary on what he saw and did in Britain.

Ndayako and his fellow tourists visited an unnamed minting and printing facility, presumably the Royal Mint, and saw the process of minting coinage and printing paper money: "We were so excited to see how metal was miraculously transformed into money within the short time [and] we were also shown how paper money was produced."[81] Ndayako then tells the story of their visit to a circus: "We were taken to a big hall. I had never seen a room as big as this one. We saw many people playing different games there. We saw three people riding motorcycles, displaying their riding skills and scaling through rings of fire. We were fascinated by the skills displayed by the riders. In that big room we saw trained dogs jumping over items one after the other. Really, we had never seen such displays."[82] Ndayako next describes what one might call metropolitan order and discipline, remarking that he and his fellow tourists were impressed by "the display of maturity by the spectators while leaving the big hall." Circus attendees, Ndayako notes, "conducted [themselves] in an orderly manner [and there was] no rushing, not to talk of stampeding."[83] Ndayako frequently returns to this theme of metropolitan orderliness in his narrative. While commenting on an open-door gathering at Windsor Castle, Ndayako remarks that "even though the people present there were so many, none stepped on anybody's feet," and that "the British are so tolerant of and patient with one another."[84]

During a tour of a school, Ndayako narrates how their presence stirred much curiosity in the students: "The pupils kept staring at us as if we were aliens from another universe." When told to return to their classes, however, "they all left, not minding our presence again." Ndayako recalls being fascinated by "this act of obedience displayed by the pupils."[85] His focus on appearances of order, social discipline, and what he deemed obedient, responsible conduct by metropolitan interlocutors should be read partly as reflecting his own orientation in a monarchical tradition in which such social gestures were treasured. In other words, Ndayako was reading the metropole through his own experiences and aristocratic values, much like European colonial ethnographic commentators on African societies had done and continued to do.

When Ndayako and his fellow aristocrats attended a military parade in honor of the queen's birthday at Windsor Castle, his narration of the event reveals two instructive discursive strategies. One expresses disappointment that the metropole failed to live up to what he had expected, and the other deploys creative hyperbole to capture and translate the grandeur of metropolitan aristocratic sights. Ndayako notes with surprise that despite the fact that "many people attended" the queen's birthday parade, "a great number of people did not attend the event, minding their businesses at different places."[86] How could subjects of the great English queen and head of the empire skip her birthday? Here, his imagining of and assumptions about the queen's monarchical clout and positioning in British society clearly failed to align with the apparent indifference of many Britons to her birthday celebration. Perhaps the British monarch—despite her unmistakable visual prestige, the tales of her power that circulated in the colony, and the artifacts and ceremonial rituals of empire in Northern Nigeria—was not so powerful at home after all.

The second strategy Ndayako utilizes is the deliberate deployment of hyperbole to convey his sense of awe at the sartorial and regal excess around the British monarch and at the dizzying mobility of London's urban life. Ndayako writes of the streets of London being filled with cars, stating that "no fewer than 1000 cars were present in each street of London," a "large number of cars" that does not seem to keep people from walking the streets: "You will still find many people walking on foot. . . . God is wonderful!"[87] The "1000 cars" reference was an almost direct appropriation of Hausa folkloric invocation of aesthetic hyperbole. *Dubu* (thousand) is a figure of Hausa literary speech. In many Hausa traditional tales, reference to *dubu* is a recurring narrative device meant to convey unquantifiable, awe-inspiring numerical largeness. Elsewhere in Ndayako's engrossing narrative, he recalls seeing a warplane in Portsmouth that was "said to be over 400 years old."[88] Given that the aircraft did not exist even two hundred years ago, this was an obvious, calculated hyperbole designed to underscore the longevity of Britain's aeronautic prowess as well as the antiquity of its military supremacy, which Ndayako would have encountered in Nigeria through popular tales of British military might.

Ndayako and his group visited a public housing project where the occupants paid no rent and lived there "on the mercy of the King of England." Ndayako also describes a newspaper firm where a picture of the two emirs was taken and printed "in less than 30 minutes," as well as visits to Middlesex Hospital in London and the British Parliament, where the visitors "met people like Mr. [Winston] Churchill, Mr. Attlee, and Mr. Henry Hopkinson."[89] At the London Museum, a tour guide showed the group an exhibit on West African peoples that included a photo of the Etsu Nupe himself, which caused everyone to laugh when Ndayako recognized himself and the guide told him jokingly that he had known him long before they met in person. Not only did Ndayako view himself on exhibition, an amusingly awkward exercise of anthropological self-observation, he also recognized several materials from Northern Nigeria in the exhibit. He recalls, "He also showed us historical materials from West Africa, such as mats and other items from our region. From there we were shown other traditional items from other countries and in the process I saw a hand woven textile from Northern Nigeria and I asked the head if he would accept a very nice hand-woven cloth that I brought to London to protect me from the cold weather."[90] The museum's head accepted and appreciated the impromptu gift giving, and Ndayako later sent the cloth to the museum.

The group toured the Royal Air Force Museum in Southampton, where they inspected decommissioned planes, simulated a flight, and viewed photos of pilots. A tour of Windsor Castle, where they noticed that "the queen was not at home" and found the grounds swarmed by foreign tourists, was followed by a visit to Eton College, the bastion of English aristocratic education and socialization with its stone walls and "beautifully constructed" classrooms. The group visited the Oxford police headquarters, where, upon being conducted around the station, Ndayako asked the head to "give us the guideline for recruiting police officers so that I can apply the strategies in recruiting our own police officers."[91]

In London, the visiting emirs and their aides attended a formal reception in their honor, where Ndayako and old British friends rekindled their friendships, reminisced about their interactions in Northern Nigeria, and discussed common acquaintances. The visitors and their old British friends seemed eager to reenact and renew the old relationships in the relaxed hierarchies, hospitality, and less regimented colonial spaces of the metropole. As Ndayako conveyed, "There was this day when an event was organized to formally welcome us to London and I saw faces that I recognized, such as that of Mr. Featherstone and the Resident of Sokoto, Carrow, and Mr. Tegetmier. We had a long discussion with Mr. Tegetmier, and he asked me about some legislator that he knew when he was staying in my country. Unfortunately most of the people he asked about were dead. We had a very long, interesting discussion with him as it had been long that we had seen each other."[92] Ndayako and his group toured a cattle market and an agricultural engineering school, "where we saw different kinds of agricultural implements and the farmers." The group then proceeded to a racecourse, where they bet on horse racing, losing their bets while their guide, Mr. Greatbatch, won twice.[93] The group witnessed the commencement ceremony of Oxford University, visited a fire station where the firemen put on a fire drill for them, and toured a blanket factory where sheep's wool was processed by "hundreds of workers" and machines into thick blankets.[94]

While having lunch at the Richmond Hill Hotel, the aristocrats witnessed ballroom dancing, which Ndayako describes thus: "A nice music was being played and the Britons there danced to it in twos, male and female hugging each other, they are really experts in this kind of dance."[95] The group visited electricity-generating plants as well as organic waste-treatment facilities. They then traveled to the town of Taunton to visit with Usman Nagogo, the son of the emir of Katsina, who was studying there at a boarding school. The emirs also visited other aristocratic children studying in schools in the town of Leicester, which caused Ndayako to remark in his travel memoir that "our children ... [had] changed completely into Britons as they were not wearing our traditional clothes."[96]

Henry Hopkinson, a Conservative MP representing Taunton who was now serving in the government of Prime Minister Winston Churchill as minister of state for the colonies, invited the tourists to his Taunton home for dinner. Ndayako's memoirs describe the event:

> We went to Mr. Henry Hopkinson's house and he showed us a lot of things. We ate good food and we were really honored in his house. He showed us around his garden, his horses, and gave us nice fragrant flowers from the garden. I put mine on the traditional turban I was wearing and they all burst out laughing. The Emir of Ilorin put his in his breast pocket. Mr. Hopkinson also gave me and the Emir of Ilorin each a gift of nicely decorated walking sticks. We left the house very happy with the reception we got from him.[97]

Following the dinner at Hopkinson's house, the mayor of Taunton invited the tourists for tea in her office, where the aristocrats took several pictures with their hosts. Receptions, teas, and dinners were choreographed to leave visiting Northern Nigerian aristocrats feeling honored, treasured, and important in the culture of empire. Such ritualistic and elaborate gestures of imperial hospitality were grounded in the ethos of imperial kinship that either informed or haunted the many metropolitan encounters analyzed in this book.

Ndayako and his fellow emir visited a car factory in Birmingham, a soap-making factory, a tannery, and a textile factory in Liverpool, where, according to Ndayako's account, the group was impressed by the processes of converting familiar Northern Nigerian raw materials, such as hides and groundnuts, into finished consumer products. These industrial visits highlight the instrumental intentions of the British Council, which clearly wanted the aristocrats to get a taste of British industrial processes as well as the commodity and consumption cultures the industrial processes supported. British factories displayed the British imperial capacity to make and remake things and transform raw objects into impressive quotidian items of high value. The emirs also spoke with the head of Britain's Colonial

Development Corporation, an imperial bureaucracy established during the Great Depression to create jobs for British citizens by funding public works and social projects in the colonies.[98]

The highlight of the tours was an invitation to Buckingham Palace for tea with the queen. Here is Ndayako's account:

> We were wearing our traditional regalia and we were all holding our staff of office; our appearance made us stand out from the rest of the people there. I saw a huge crowd at the venue and when I later asked I was told that about 7,000 people were invited to have tea with the queen. With some difficulty, Mr. Greatbatch managed to get us two seats. Most of the invited guests kept watching us due to our mode of dress. We wanted to see the queen but due to the crowd we could not and Mr. Greatbatch suggested that we maintain our position and that we may be lucky to have a glimpse of the queen.[99]

Readers of Ndayako's travel account would have imagined the queen as regal and the occasion as momentous for the emirs, important monarchs in their own right. Ndayako was setting up for his readers the privileged access he and his group secured to see the queen. In the next paragraph, Ndayako followed this tease by narrating their eventual, climactic one-on-one encounter with the queen.

> We were there when the queen's presence was announced. We saw her from afar, and she was led from a beautifully decorated pavilion where she sat for at least 15 minutes before she was led through the gathering while security officials made a way for her. Before she came to where we were standing we were told that she doesn't speak to anyone and that no one speaks to her. But when she came to where we were standing she stopped and stared at us for a while. We stared back at her. She then smiled at us; we did not say a word to her, mindful of what we had been told about the queen not speaking to anyone. The queen later spoke to us. She asked us about the number of days we had spent in London and we replied that we had spent 38 days.[100]

Ndayako supplies further details of their short conversation: "She asked if we had finished visiting places to which we replied yes." According to Ndayako, the emirs then asked the queen for permission to depart Britain for Nigeria the following day, and "the queen bid us farewell."[101] The tourists, Ndayako noted, "were so elated by the gesture the queen made to us." For him, the queen's brief conversation demonstrated the "trust" that existed between them and the queen, a trust "we prayed we wouldn't breach."[102]

Ndayako's travelogue evolved from a play-by-play narration of the visitors' itinerary to a more evaluative commentary on metropolitan Britain. He was "impressed with the British system of agriculture," particularly the productive integration of "animal rearing" and "crop cultivation." British buildings, Ndayako stated, "have good structures" and were lined up in rows, with their interior beauty eclipsing their impressive outer appearance. Ndayako's commentary was not all positive, however. One flaw in British architecture, Ndayako noted, was that British houses had a bland uniformity to them: "If you went out you could forget the house you wanted to go into because the houses usually have similar looks."[103] Here Ndayako critiqued the metropolitan obsession with order, pattern, and the predictable architectural logic and uniformity of the planned, built urban space.

Ndayako lauded Britons for their "trustworthy, kind, and accommodating" character. However, while he admired "the way [Britons] arrange their food," he found it "difficult to adapt to their kind of food," stating, "I did not like their food throughout my stay in London."[104] Ndayako's subtly critical comments on the monotonic predictability of British architecture and the strangeness of British cuisine to an untrained African palate round out a narrative dripping with general reverence for the aristocratic trappings of Britain, the technological repositories of British modernity, and the quaint ways of the British aristocracy.

Conclusion

Northern Nigerian aristocratic travelers positioned themselves to demystify the colonizers by translating the metropole and giving their readers a metropolitan cultural referent against which to understand and evaluate the conduct of on-ground colonizers. The veracity of their portrayal, its fidelity to metropolitan life, and its completeness as a reflection of British culture are robustly debatable. Nonetheless, these narratives functioned in the mutually unintelligible world of colonial cultural relations as primers for Northern Nigerians seeking a deeper understanding of the colonial oppressor. The foregoing analyses have focused on four varieties of metropolitan travelogues: those published in *Gaskiya ta fi Kwabo* by the travelers themselves, those written and published by the newspaper's editors using notes and diaries supplied by the travelers and supplemented by widely available print and broadcast resources on the metropole, those published by students in school publications, and metropolitan travel memoirs written and published by travelers.

When travel writers discussed their trips to Britain, they were standing in the gap, so to speak, and decoding the ways of the white man. They supplied a usable manual, wrapped in captivating metropolitan experiential narratives, of how to engage the white man and how to gain access to the white man's character, a strategically homogenizing characterization of metropolitan culture that aligned with the undifferentiated registers through which Northern Nigerian subalterns saw their British colonial interlocutors. In this frame, understanding the white man preceded and underpinned productive, profitable engagement with him in the colony, and the metropole was the perfect cultural laboratory to behold and study the colonizer in his natural habitat.

Travel writing made the quirks and individual eccentricities of colonial officials more legible because it enabled literate Hausa readers to discern which mannerisms and predilections were rooted in metropolitan conventions and which were attributable to the individual characters of colonial officials. The travel writers were broaching the ubiquitous debate about the causal relationship between structure and agency and helping their readers unravel the metropolitan cultural scripts and norms from which British colonial officials in Nigeria acted or deviated. Separating the cultural from the idiosyncratic was a valuable epistemic asset for subalterns, and it was critical to the process of engaging strategically with the colonizer. At a systemic level, travel had a utilitarian value and hence was uniquely popular among the many literary genres that circulated in the Northern Nigerian colonial public sphere. Travel was a practical ethnography whose findings could be deployed in the quotidian interactions of colonialism. Metropolitan travel literature provided a lens through which readers could understand Anglo-imperial culture and its relational expectations and etiquette. In turn, this understanding helped readers better engage with colonial policies and better negotiate their position in relation to colonial obligations.

The appeal of written narratives animated by metropolitan travel rested, in part, on their expressive latitude, stylistic freedom, relatability, and flexible idiomatic properties. The metropolitan travelogues of the Northern Nigerian elite moved freely between the casual and the densely instructive. They combined the serious with the lighthearted, the informative and philosophical with the aesthetic, and the historical with the contemporary. These texts bore the weight of Nigerians' curiosities about Britain. As a result, they peddled minutiae and were steeped in seemingly boring details about metropolitan objects, practices, processes, and phenomena. They also expressed the ethnographic and sociological fantasies of Nigerians whose inability to visit the colonial metropole made them hungry for the stories and experiences narrated and curated by aristocratic returnees from the white man's land.

Notes

1. Katsina College was moved from Katsina in 1938 and briefly operated in Kaduna before being permanently relocated to Zaria.
2. Rhodes House, MSS. Afr. s. 1933, Bashir Tukur, "Britain as I Saw It," *Barewa* (June 1960): 9–11.
3. Rhodes House, MSS. Afr. s. 1933, Bashir Tukur, "Britain as I Saw It," 10.
4. Rhodes House, MSS. Afr. s. 1933, Bashir Tukur, "Britain as I Saw It," 10.
5. Rhodes House, MSS. Afr. s. 1933, Bashir Tukur, "Britain as I Saw It," 11.
6. Rhodes House, MSS. Afr. s. 1933, Bashir Tukur, "Britain as I Saw It," 11.
7. Rhodes House, MSS. Afr. s. 1933, Bashir Tukur, "Britain as I Saw It," 12.
8. Rhodes House, MSS. Afr. s. 1933, Magaji Inuwa, "Some Ways of Foreigners Which Seem Strange to Me," *Barewa* (June 1960): 12–14.
9. Rhodes House, MSS. Afr. s. 1933, Magaji Inuwa, "Some Ways of Foreigners Which Seem Strange to Me."
10. Rhodes House, MSS. Afr. s. 1933, Magaji Inuwa, "Some Ways of Foreigners Which Seem Strange to Me."
11. Rhodes House, MSS. Afr. s. 1933, Magaji Inuwa, "Some Ways of Foreigners Which Seem Strange to Me."
12. Rhodes House, MSS. Afr. s. 1933, Magaji Inuwa, "Some Ways of Foreigners Which Seem Strange to Me."
13. Rhodes House, MSS. Afr. s. 1933, Magaji Inuwa, "Some Ways of Foreigners Which Seem Strange to Me."
14. Rhodes House, MSS. Afr. s. 1933, Magaji Inuwa, "Some Ways of Foreigners Which Seem Strange to Me."
15. Rhodes House, MSS. Afr. s. 1933, Magaji Inuwa, "Some Ways of Foreigners Which Seem Strange to Me."
16. Clark, *A Right Honourable Gentleman*, 51–52.
17. Clark, *A Right Honourable Gentleman*, 52.
18. Clark, *A Right Honourable Gentleman*, 52. See also A. M. Yakubu, *Sa'adu Zungur: An Anthology of the Social and Political Writings of a Nigerian Nationalist* (Kaduna: Nigerian Defense Academy, 1999).
19. Yakubu, *Sa'adu Zungur*.
20. KSHCB R.532 (Government Service: Promotion of Africans, Northernisation, Etc.). This file briefly discusses the activities of the Kano Select Party, a sociopolitical club in Kano promoting socialization and intellectual exchange among the Nigerian staff of the colonial bureaucracy.
21. "London University," *Gaskiya*, May 21, 1947, 8.
22. "How the English Live at Home," *Gaskiya*, August 30, 1944, 6.
23. "Our Ministry in England," *Gaskiya*, April 30, 1947, 11.
24. "The English Crown Jewels," *Gaskiya*, July 23, 1947, 4.
25. "The Damage Done to England," *Gaskiya*, November 5, 1947, 8.

26. "The Guests of England Have Arrived, They Saw the King at Ascot," *Gaskiya*, June 30, 1948, 13.
27. "Our Visit to England: The English Are Kind at Home," *Gaskiya*, July 7, 1948, 5.
28. An example is the story "Northern Students in England," which was published in the May 28, 1947, edition of *Gaskiya*.
29. M. Garba Kafin Madaki, "Kano to England by Air," *Gaskiya*, June 16, 1948, 3.
30. "There Are No Jobless People or Beggars in England, Leaders Serve Their People (Says M. Bayaro Nuhu, Who Recently Returned from England)," *Gaskiya*, August 18, 1948, 6.
31. "Summertime in England," *Gaskiya*, June 18, 1947, 7.
32. "Summertime in England."
33. "Forestry in England," *Gaskiya*, July 9, 1947, 14.
34. "Forestry in England."
35. "Forestry in England."
36. "Linen Manufacture in England," *Gaskiya*, September 10, 1947, 9.
37. "Linen Manufacture in England."
38. "Linen Manufacture in England."
39. "Linen Manufacture in England."
40. "Building Stones in England," *Gaskiya*, October 8, 1947, 3.
41. "Building Stones in England."
42. "European Ships," *Gaskiya*, October 15, 1947, 6.
43. "European Ships."
44. "Sheep in England (1)," *Gaskiya*, February 4, 1948, 4.
45. "Sheep in England (1)." Also "Sheep in England (2)," *Gaskiya*, February 11, 1948, 6.
46. "Merchant Marine Training in England," *Gaskiya*, July 30, 1947, 12.
47. "Bank of England Today—Established More than 250 Years Ago," *Gaskiya*, December 10, 1947, 9.
48. "Boat Race in England," *Gaskiya*, March 31, 1948, 8.
49. "Boat Race in England."
50. "London Port, One of the Busiest in the World," *Gaskiya*, June 9, 1948, 10.
51. Mallam Bayaro Nuhu Zariya, "Winter in England," *Gaskiya*, February 11, 1948.
52. "Forestry in England."
53. "Our Ministry in England."
54. "Northern Students in England."
55. "Northern Students in England."
56. "The Guests of England Have Returned; They Saw the King at Ascot."
57. "The Guests of England Have Returned; They Saw the King at Ascot."
58. "The Guests of England Have Returned; They Saw the King at Ascot."
59. "Our Visit to England: The English Are Kind at Home."
60. "Our Visit to England: The English Are Kind at Home."
61. "Our Visit to England: The English Are Kind at Home."
62. An indication of this absence of editorial meddling is the clause "we will leave London on the 22nd and arrive Kano on the 23rd."
63. "There Are No Jobless People or Beggars in England," *Gaskiya*, August 18, 1948, 9.
64. "There Are No Jobless People or Beggars in England."
65. "There Are No Jobless People or Beggars in England."
66. "There Are No Jobless People or Beggars in England."
67. "There Are No Jobless People or Beggars in England."

68. "There Are No Jobless People or Beggars in England."
69. "There Are No Jobless People or Beggars in England."
70. "There Are No Jobless People or Beggars in England."
71. An exception to this historiographical tendency is Catherine Hall's *Civilizing Subjects:Metropole and Colony in the English Imagination 1860-1867* (Chicago: University of Chicago Press, 2002).
72. "There Are No Jobless People or Beggars in England."
73. "There Are No Jobless People or Beggars in England."
74. "There Are No Idlers in England, Everybody Is Busy (Says Sardauna of Sokoto)," *Gaskiya*, September 22, 1948.
75. "There Are No Idlers in England, Everybody Is Busy."
76. "There Are No Idlers in England, Everybody Is Busy."
77. "There Are No Idlers in England, Everybody Is Busy."
78. "There Are No Idlers in England, Everybody Is Busy."
79. "There Are No Idlers in England, Everybody Is Busy."
80. Muhammadu Ndayako, *Tafiyan Etsu Nupe Ingila* (Zaria, Nigeria: Gaskiya Corporation, 1954). Portions translated for this book by Abdulrahman Abdullahi, with my modifications.
81. Ndayako, *Tafiyan Etsu Nupe Ingila*, 65.
82. Ndayako, *Tafiyan Etsu Nupe Ingila*, 65.
83. Ndayako, *Tafiyan Etsu Nupe Ingila*, 65.
84. Ndayako, *Tafiyan Etsu Nupe Ingila*, 66.
85. Ndayako, *Tafiyan Etsu Nupe Ingila*, 66.
86. Ndayako, *Tafiyan Etsu Nupe Ingila*, 66.
87. Ndayako, *Tafiyan Etsu Nupe Ingila*, 66.
88. Ndayako, *Tafiyan Etsu Nupe Ingila*, 67.
89. Ndayako, *Tafiyan Etsu Nupe Ingila*, 66.
90. Ndayako, *Tafiyan Etsu Nupe Ingila*, 66.
91. Ndayako, *Tafiyan Etsu Nupe Ingila*, 67.
92. Ndayako, *Tafiyan Etsu Nupe Ingila*, 67.
93. Ndayako, *Tafiyan Etsu Nupe Ingila*, 67.
94. Ndayako, *Tafiyan Etsu Nupe Ingila*, 68.
95. Ndayako, *Tafiyan Etsu Nupe Ingila*, 68.
96. Ndayako, *Tafiyan Etsu Nupe Ingila*, 70.
97. Ndayako, *Tafiyan Etsu Nupe Ingila*, 68.
98. For a history and assessment of the Colonial Development Corporation, see Mike Cowen, "Early Years of the Colonial Development Corporation: British State Enterprise Overseas during Late Colonialism," *African Affairs* 83, no. 330 (1984): 63–75; see also E. R. Wicker, "The Colonial Development Corporation," *Review of Economic Studies* 23, no. 3 (1955–56): 213–28.
99. Ndayako, *Tafiyan Etsu Nupe Ingila*, 69.
100. Ndayako, *Tafiyan Etsu Nupe Ingila*, 69.
101. Ndayako, *Tafiyan Etsu Nupe Ingila*, 69.
102. Ndayako, *Tafiyan Etsu Nupe Ingila*, 69.
103. Ndayako, *Tafiyan Etsu Nupe Ingila*, 70.
104. Ndayako, *Tafiyan Etsu Nupe Ingila*, 70.

6

DEEPENING IMPERIAL EXPLORATION, IMAGINING THE POSTCOLONY

> During my short stay of two months [in Britain] I traveled thousands and thousands of miles by air, trains, and cars to see for myself... the industrial centers where agricultural machineries are manufactured. I attended various social gatherings and tea parties at which I gathered valuable impressions.
> —Mallam Garba Kafin Madaki

BETWEEN THE 1940S AND THE EARLY 1960S, NORTHERN Nigeria's aristocracy and emergent Western-educated elite viewed travel to the United Kingdom as a political and social rite of passage. During this period, British colonizers made colonial organizational resources that supported metropolitan tours more widely available. This standardized and now annual trip became something of a routine—an undeclared induction into a colonial fraternity. The British also accommodated the adventures of important notables who could not participate in the annual tours. Furthermore, colonial authorities opened the trips to non-Muslim chiefs from the Middle Belt, as well as to a few carefully selected women. The trips became an expected ritual for those craving recognition, visibility, and further patronage through a touristic pilgrimage to Britain. Travelers, in turn, helped institutionalize the culture of metropolitan travel and, more crucially, the practice of returning to publish travel memoirs and deliver lectures on observations and experiences in Britain.

This chapter maps the evolution of overseas colonial touring from the postwar period to the first decade of independence in the 1960s and analyzes and distills the epistemological insights of this revamped travel culture. In particular, it considers the impact of this routine of metropolitan travel on the changing cultural ecology of Northern Nigeria, the self-fashioning of Northern Nigerian elites in the late colonial period, and the reverse courtship that saw Northern Nigerian aristocrats and bureaucrats actively seek out British travel, British technocratic expertise, and British cultural goods in the period of transition to independence.

Institutionalizing Metropolitan Travel

By the 1940s, members of the Northern Nigerian aristocracy viewed travel to the metropole as an endeavor that enhanced their prestige at home. These elites also recognized that the informational resources collated from such travel had to be rendered accessible and available to the Roman-literate masses of the region. To do this, the elites delivered public lectures on their experiences abroad. These public lectures were highly scripted affairs designed to talk up the allure of the metropole and the benefits of exposure to British markers of modernity. The lectures served as platforms for travelers to socially leverage their travel experiences, thus boosting their domestic intellectual and political stature.

When Garba Kafin Madaki, the chief scribe of Zazzau Emirate and holder of the emirate's traditional title of sarkin ruwa, returned with the Ahmadu Bello–led Northern Nigerian "study" and sightseeing delegation to Britain in 1948, he scheduled two public lectures on his experiences. On July 5, Madaki delivered an English-language lecture on his observations about Britain at Zaria Middle School. The next day, he delivered a Hausa-language lecture at the Zaria City Reading Room on the same theme.[1] Similarly, when Ihas Daura, the wakilin gonan Daura (supervisor of agriculture in Daura Emirate), returned from a visit to Britain in 1952, he toured the emirate to give lectures "in terms of what I have seen and experienced [in the United Kingdom]."[2] Daura summarized his adventures in a written primer circulated for his lectures: "During my short stay of two months I traveled thousands and thousands of miles by air, trains, and cars to see for myself the main centres that deal with Nigerian exported raw materials, English system of Agriculture, to listen to the lectures on rural Education and craft, English system of Local Government, and to see the industrial centers where Agricultural machineries are manufactured. I attended various social gatherings and tea parties at which I gathered valuable impressions."[3] Priming his audience with a summarized itinerary of his adventure was a way to underscore his immersion in British metropolitan life, which was the basis of his claimed expertise and the crux of his lectures. In his lecture, Daura spoke on three broad themes: impressions, public service, and British agriculture. He stated that his first impression of English people was "the way they tackle their duties." "An English worker," Daura told his listeners, "does not has [sic] to be supervised or pushed to execute his duties," adding that "once he knows it is his duty he is prepared to do it to the best of his abilities and honesty."[4] Among other attributes Daura observed in English people was their consistent willingness to answer questions posed to them, an indication of "goodwill and co-operation" and the existence of "confidence between senior and junior people."[5] With general pronouncements on the character of English people out of the way, Daura's lecture then devolved into atomistic details about observed governmental and agricultural practices and institutions in Britain, a level of esoteric detail that worked, once again, to reinforce the lecturer's claimed experiential and observational expertise on metropolitan society.

In addition to published travelogues and treatises on British society in *Gaskiya* and public lectures by visitors to Britain, inscribing the cachet of metropolitan travel in the consciousness of Roman-literate Northern Nigerians required its institutionalization. This, in turn, necessitated an elaborate bureaucratic infrastructure. Institutionalization required the standardization and bureaucratization of aristocratic travel to the metropole as well as the expansion of travel sponsorships beyond the demographic of aristocratic Hausaphone Muslim males. The following analysis explores the process of bureaucratization, the colonial politics that underpinned it, and the logistical complications and innovations that emerged to render it a normative aspect of the cultural interaction between the colony and the metropole.

The Colonial Bureaucracy and the Mechanics of Travel

The groundwork for the formal bureaucratization of metropolitan travel as part of imperial relational rituals in Northern Nigeria was laid in the early 1940s, although the process began as early as the mid-1930s. As stated in chapters 2 and 3, the early travels in the 1920s and 1930s saw superintending colonial authorities experimenting and improvising with different itineraries and programs and then soliciting feedback from traveling emirs on how the trips could be improved for future travelers. One of the contentious issues was funding. The treasuries of different Native Authorities and, by extension, taxpaying Northern Nigerian colonial subjects under the jurisdiction of those Native Authorities bore the financial burdens of the early trips, which emirs supplemented with their own personal funds for personal purchases or private detours.

As early as 1935, officials began discussing ways to codify and bureaucratize these trips as part of a permanent colonial gesture of cultivating harmonious social relations with Northern Nigeria's elites. The discussions culminated in several important decisions in November 1935. Regarding "visits of chiefs to the United Kingdom," the chief commissioner of Northern Nigeria decided that the government would take over the funding of these trips from the Native Authorities. The government also decided that British colonial officials who served as guides and performed other logistical tasks associated with the visits would have all their out-of-pocket expenses refunded and their travel costs covered.[6]

The sponsorship decision was significant in two respects. First, Native Authorities often had little surplus revenue to devote to these trips. Making them pay for what appeared to be self-indulgent vanity strained the treasuries and potentially opened the door to scandal if commoners made this an issue in their repertoire of anticolonial and antiaristocratic critique. Second, unlike the Native Authority treasuries, the regional colonial government had a variety of revenue streams outside the taxes and levies collected directly from subjects, and it could accommodate sponsorship in its maze of budgetary jargon to avoid such criticism. From this perspective, it made sense for the regional colonial government, a more distant and opaque entity, to take over the funding, and thus officials signaled their willingness to do that for future metropolitan tours. Once the important matter of financial sponsorship seemed tentatively resolved, the visits became routinized as essential elements in satisfying two entwined impulses: the thirst of Northern Nigerian elites for immersive metropolitan experiences and the desire of colonial authorities to reward and consolidate the loyalties of Nigerian aristocratic partners in the colonial enterprise.

The next phase of the bureaucratization process was the formalization of the logistical and organizational role of the Colonial Office and the British Council. In the late 1930s, the Colonial Office solicited volunteer hosts for visitors from Northern Nigeria. These volunteers began contacting the Colonial Office from 1938 and offered to host any visiting "northern emirs."[7] The standardization process continued through the early 1940s, but since there were few aristocratic visits to Britain during World War II, much of the implementation of the new, formalized arrangements only took shape in the postwar period.

When regular tours recommenced in 1947, the postwar financial crisis in the colonies seems to have compelled the colonial government to renege on its earlier promise to finance the trips. In an August 1947 memo to residents of all provinces in Northern Nigeria, the chief commissioner made several proposals regarding restarting the aristocratic visits. One prominent proposal was for Native Authorities to bear the entire travel costs for visitors from their domains, estimated at £240 per head.[8] This was a reversal of the decision reached in 1938, but it was nestled in a broader package of guidelines for the revamped tours and so escaped scrutiny.

The chief commissioner's other proposals included suggestions that the trips be undertaken by groups of between eight and ten people and that they should be open only to those "who have already attained positions of responsibility and have a record of service to the community and who would thereby benefit themselves and their communities."[9] Another aspect of the plan was to have a regular schedule of these tours every summer, with each "study tour" lasting two months and each month devoted to a more disciplined program of lectures on topics such as "public administration in a rural district" and "local government in a small country town."[10] Here the chief commissioner was reconceptualizing the visits as colonial pedagogical projects designed to instruct and reeducate the visitors in particular British bureaucratic imaginaries and political orientations. A final, important aspect of the emerging arrangement was that the British Council would assume logistical and bureaucratic control over the visits, treating them as part of Britain's cultural outreach for cultivating the goodwill of overseas peoples.

At the time the chief commissioner issued this memo, some provinces had already submitted names of potential visitors. He thus proposed that the visits under the new guidelines should commence in 1948 and requested an additional four names be submitted. The 1948 visit of the eleven-man delegation led by Ahmadu Bello was the first trip undertaken under the new bureaucratized arrangements. The 1948 "study tour" of Britain was pivotal in several ways, not least because it tested the viability and sustainability of regular visits under the new guidelines. The trip brought to the fore several unforeseen problems. When the party arrived in Britain, several of the visitors complained that their salaries had been docked to provide them with pocket money "and that they had no money of their own" as a result.[11] The British Council, the organizers of the trip, had seven members of the group sign statements declaring how much they had been docked, after which the council reimbursed the declared amounts. Upon the party's return to Nigeria, the amounts were collected from each traveler's respective Native Authority and remitted to the government, which then repaid the British Council.[12]

The visitors' complaints and the financial complications they generated prompted colonial authorities to further clarify the financial rules governing the visits. In October 1948, a new circular went out from the chief commissioner stating that in order to bring a "measure of uniformity" to the financial aspect of the trip, future travelers would be paid five pounds per week as pocket money; he directed that an advance should then be recovered from the traveler's salary, using "discretion with regard to the amount to be recovered" after due consideration was given to "each person's salary and legitimate commitments."[13] Each future visitor, the commissioner's memo further stated, would receive twenty pounds as an "outfit allowance," and this expense would be financed from "Native Treasury funds."[14] The taxpayers of Northern Nigeria would finance the metropolitan expenses of the tourists, with the British Council funding the transportation and logistical aspects of the trip.

The continued financial misunderstanding that necessitated the multiple clarifications outlined prior was a window into a broader dissonance between the priorities of the visitors and those of the organizers. Some of the aristocrats who participated in the tours understood the trips to be entirely colonial affairs, part of the state's obligations to them as colonial partners. As a result, they did not expect to incur any personal expenses and instead expected the government to pay for both the trip and whatever personal spending they conducted in Britain. Philosophically, they thought of the trip as a dividend accrued to them for the goodwill, support, and loyalty they had offered the Colonial Office.

Colonial officials, on the other hand, saw the visits as a ritual of mutual understanding and benefit, the cost of which should thus be borne by the Native Authorities, the travelers, and the British Council. Officials sought to redistribute the financial burden of the exercise and disabuse potential travelers of the notion that the visits were deserved or earned largesse. The proposal emanating from this understanding would place only some of the financial burden on the British government and its appendages in Nigeria. The commissioner made the government's position clear in a forceful commentary bookending his directive: "These visits should not be regarded as being entirely at the expense of Native Authorities. Any person who proceeds to the United Kingdom on a visit has the opportunity of gaining considerable personal benefit and experience and it is thought only reasonable that he should not expect to be absolved from all expenses incurred . . . travelers should take all their money with them during those short visits. . . . The British Council should not be expected to make any payments to visitors or to receive remittances on their behalf while they are in the United Kingdom."[15] The clarifications and directives were also a response to feedback obtained from some members of the 1948 tour, notably Mallam Garba Kafin Madaki. Upon his return from Britain, Madaki suggested through the resident of Zaria Province that minor changes be made to the tour program. Madaki advised that the British homes chosen to host the visitors "should be as close as possible to the transport rendezvous" and that "if possible all meals should be taken in the [hosts'] houses." In addition, Madaki suggested that pocket money of four pounds per week be paid to each visitor. His final two suggestions were that religious services should be removed from the itinerary and that "the party should stay in as many counties as possible in order to obtain a balanced view of the country as a whole."[16] Despite official efforts at standardization, the architecture of the tours remained provisional since new issues emerged with each traveling group.

Accordingly, the official posttour report of the 1948 trip recommended that the itinerary be reworked to respond to the feedback and predilections of recent tourists. The elusive objective in the assessment exercises was to construct an accurate, composite profile of the Northern Nigerian aristocratic traveler to Britain and his interests. Despite the tour's acknowledged shortcomings, the report sought to justify the practice of metropolitan travel as an exercise that gave the visitors a glimpse into British society: "From comments made by those who went to the United Kingdom this year, it is apparent that a considerable broadening of outlook resulted from their being able to see what the English are like at home and from their being given an opportunity to experience European conditions at first hand; there is little doubt that visits made by suitably selected persons fully justify the expenditure of Native Authority funds."[17] The report, which contained an assessment of the 1948 trip as well as proposals for the planned 1949 trip, proceeded to offer a full breakdown of the visitors' itinerary. For the first three weeks of the six-week tour, the visitors engaged in a program of lectures on a variety of topics, attended meetings with various local organizations, and participated in "visits to places and institutions of interest."[18] In the second three weeks, the visitors "were occupied with a programme of sightseeing which covered Cambridge and Redford and the neighboring country" and then "rounded off with ten days in London."[19]

For the summer 1949 trip, organizers increased the duration from six weeks to two months, as proposed by the chief commissioner. They also increased the cost to £368 per person. Furthermore, the tour was significantly revised to make it more educational and give it the pedagogical character the chief commissioner envisioned. Officials wanted the "study tours" to reflect the implied idea of touring as a form of study and pedagogy. The tours would thenceforth encompass quasi-academic content. Organizers packaged three modules of study: "Local Government in Transition," "Britain and the British People," and "Britain—its Life and People."[20] The modules included a program of lectures, especially on "the historical background of British life," as well as visits to factories, schools, public utilities, and "places of local historical interest."[21]

Officials continued to tweak the itinerary in subsequent years. In the 1950s, organizers increased the number of participants in each batch to thirty, citing demands from emirs and aristocrats across the northern provinces.[22] The modules were revamped and expanded to four, with each visitor required to enroll in at least two. The new courses were "Life in an English City," "Local Government," "The British Commonwealth of Nations," and "English Language."[23]

Even with these changes, the organizers still struggled with the possibility that the trips could be viewed by nonaristocratic Northern Nigerians as vain, expensive colonial patronage with little or no educational or practical value to justify the use of Northern Nigerian taxpayers' money. Pedagogy, or elaborate pretensions to it, was conceived as a solution to this concern. The organizers' anxiety was partly predicated on the fact that, despite efforts to change local perceptions of the metropolitan visits, the travelers continued to view the trips to Britain as little more than prestige-enhancing adventures that provided opportunities to purchase metropolitan goods and memorabilia and amass usable memories that could be deployed for the purpose of distinguishing themselves back home. It was against this backdrop that organizers expanded and deepened the educational content of the program to lend it the appearance of educational depth. Even so, a scrutiny of the courses' contents reveals they were dignified touring itineraries punctuated by "lectures" that were more propagandistic fluff than educative, rigorous discussions of British life.

Complicated Imperial Explorations in Late Colonialism

Organizers of the visits had reason to worry about how the expensive annual tours would be perceived. By the late 1940s, Northern Nigeria's Roman-literate elite had bifurcated into two distinct ideological trajectories. On one side, the conservative wing, which had congregated politically in the Northern People's Congress (NPC), aligned with the traditional aristocratic establishment; on the other side, the smaller, radical anticolonial wing gradually demonstrated its antiestablishment bona fides in the form of strident critiques of colonial policies and practices. Abubakar Imam and Ahmadu Bello were the most recognized members of the conservative wing, while Sa'adu Zungur and Mallam Aminu Kano were the faces of the radical wing until the death of Sa'adu Zungur in 1958, when Aminu Kano became the sole, symbolic figurehead of the northern political Left.

By 1950, the radical wing had coalesced rather coherently into a political party called the Northern Elements Progressive Union (NEPU). NEPU's radical politics placed it in an antagonistic relationship with colonial authorities and with the conservative wing of the Northern Nigerian elite. For many of the radicals, the metropolitan trips were the capstone of an exploitative colonial partnership between British colonizers and Northern Nigerian aristocrats. When the colonial secretary issued a release in August 1950 declaring that he would not meet with a delegation from Nigeria seeking talks on a road map to self-rule, NEPU saw an opening to criticize the annual ritual of the metropolitan visits and pounced. NEPU published a scathing critique in the August 21 edition of the *Daily Comet* newspaper, with the following poignant excerpt: "Such a delegation would cost Northern taxpayers thousands of pounds, which could be used beneficially in other pressing problems. Now, the Colonial Secretary through his recent release has vindicated his stand, which clearly shows that he would not welcome any delegation from Nigeria that aims at separation. This is a good gesture from the Colonial Secretary in that in the name of democracy and economy he does not allow the chiefs' delegates to leave Nigeria before he makes his stand clear. This shows that not even a farthing will be spent again on an unwelcomed delegation."[24] Since the tour only involved Northern

Nigerian aristocrats, NEPU regarded the trip as a perpetuation of a sectional parochial agenda antithetical to the colonial secretary's pronouncements against such visits. Understandably, NEPU's criticism caused much anxiety to the organizers of the tours, who suggested that an official press statement should explain that the colonial secretary's statement referred to a proposed pan-Nigerian delegation seeking talks on the future of the colony and not to touristic delegations of chiefs and aristocrats from Northern Nigeria.[25]

Despite the opposition from NEPU and its supporters, the annual tours forged on and even expanded in the 1950s. The 1952 delegation included the emirs of Gombe and Ilorin and the lamido of Adamawa. In addition to the usual itinerary of touring, sightseeing, and lectures, the chiefs spent ten days in Oxford and fourteen days on a structured sightseeing tour of London and saw "the Royal Tournament, The Richmond Royal House Show, and the Trooping of the Colour on the birthday of His Majesty the King."[26] In a new tweak to the itinerary, the emirs spent a week in the British home of an unnamed officer in the Northern Nigeria colonial service who was on leave in Britain at the time of their visit.[27]

After 1950, the tours became an extension, at least programmatically, of a more elaborate gesture of aggressive colonial acculturation in Northern Nigeria. The focal point of this renewed cultural enterprise was the British Council. By this time the council had a functioning library in Kano that catered to Northern Nigerians' appetite for British culture through its outposts and traveling film shows. The council ran a comprehensive slate of cultural activities and programs. The highlights included a robust book-rental service; a membership drive; radio broadcasts on topics such as "Agriculture in Britain" and "Trooping the Colour"; and film shows that included segments on British news, English continuation classes, and exhibitions of photographs on strategically complementary topics such as English costumes and British architecture.[28] In addition, the council facilitated multiple film-show tours across Northern Nigeria and arranged public lectures by British "experts" on various subjects in major Northern Nigerian cities such as Kaduna, Kano, Zaria, and Jos.[29] These programs helped establish a climate of awareness on British affairs, society, and ways of life within the Northern Nigeria elite, priming future metropolitan tourists for their overseas adventures. For would-be visitors to Britain, the council's activities and the textual and visual materials on offer at its library provided an invaluable navigational guide for such visits.

"A Weekend in Paris"

The large size of Northern Nigeria's aristocratic community meant that at any given time, there was a stream of emirs and chiefs making their way through metropolitan towns and cities, beholding the sights of Britain and making mental and written notes they would translate for local audiences upon their return. Sometimes the tours took the aristocrats beyond the traditional imperial metropole of Britain into other parts of Europe, detours the British colonial officialdom and their superiors were all too happy to enable. Such was the case in June 1951, when two emirs and one important titleholder on a six-week tour of England requested a detour to Paris. The British Council, the Colonial Office, and Britain's diplomatic institutions mobilized at a moment's notice to organize a guided tour of Paris for the visiting aristocrats.

On June 1, 1951, the Lamido of Adamawa, Mallam Ahmadu; the emir of Gombe, Abubakar Muhammadu Ribadu; the native treasurer of Adamawa Native Authority, Mallam Jauro, a member of the House of Representatives; P. A. Greer, their designated colonial guide and an assistant district officer in the Nigerian colonial service; and Greer's wife flew from London to Paris on the BEA *Viking* to spend a weekend shopping and sightseeing.[30] Mallam Ahmadu and Abubakar not only desired to add Paris to their touristic repertoire but also wanted to shop for Parisian perfumes, whose "fame had spread to Yola and Gombe."[31] Paris was agog with ongoing celebrations of the city's bimillenary. The city was teeming with tourists, complicating the British Council's efforts to secure accommodations and logistical support for the party on such short notice. The British Council had to arrange for traveler's checks, tickets, hotel reservations, passports, and visas, a frantic and logistically complex undertaking.

With preparations concluded, the group managed to avoid "a press photographer who had trailed [the tourists] to London Airport"[32] and flew into a boisterous Paris animated by overlapping, rolling parties. In Paris, British embassy officials produced diplomatic plate numbers for the party's vehicular convoy, easing their way through the raucous summer traffic. With diplomatic cover granted, they traveled through Paris as a "privileged class,"[33] skirting the gridlock on highways and city roads. Their drive from the airport to the opulent Hotel St. Petersbourg on the Rue Caumartin was smoothed by French authorities, who, at the urging of the British embassy, "waived all formalities so that we were able to drive away in some style while less favoured travelers were still searching for their keys."[34] Parisians, high and low, accorded the group the attention due treasured guests, with Greer, whose French was passable, acting as interpreter.

Their first evening in Paris presented a few challenges. Greer brushed up on both his French and Hausa, using a mélange of languages to facilitate the tourists' communication and translation needs. Another early problem arose regarding the direction of Mecca, which the tourists needed to face during their prayers. A concierge at the hotel solved the problem after Greer explained the confusion to him. The group had dinner and then drove to the Paris Casino, where the performance theater was hosting a circus with jugglers and acrobats. The emirs were unimpressed, remarking that "the London Casino was more interesting and that we might as well go home early to prepare for an orgy of shopping next day."[35]

The emirs were tired at the theater and were seated so far back that they barely saw the action. To compound their frustration, their seats received little or no cooling in the summer heat, causing them discomfort. As with other Northern Nigerian aristocratic tourists, it was clear that the scripted itinerary had little appeal and that, for them, shopping was the essence of such a high-profile touristic adventure. There were no colonial officials to meet and no colonial institutions to visit, and whatever Paris had to offer by way of entertainment, London could also provide. Paris's appeal for the aristocrats was its shops, which offered something distinctly French, and French products conferred a prestige that could not be replicated by British metropolitan goods. With their interest in the performance sapped by these considerations, the tourists left before the show ended and headed back to their hotel to prepare for a hectic Saturday of shopping.

The next morning, the tourists, all desirous of the perfumes of Paris, descended on the Galeries Lafayette, an upmarket department store in central Paris. Here, under the enthusiastic guidance of Mrs. Greer, the aristocrats obtained samples of assorted designer brands—Lanyin, Coty, Guerlain, and Molyneux; they were dabbed with fragrance after fragrance and then chose the "very strongest."[36] The tourists then moved to the jewelry section of the store, where, assisted by a coterie of shop assistants, they spent their collection of traveler's checks purchasing multiple sets of jewelry. The shopping spree lasted until lunchtime.

Later that afternoon, British embassy cars arrived at the hotel to pick up the tourists for a tour of Paris. The group toured the Place de la Concorde, drove along the Champs-Élysées, and made a stop at the Arc de Triomphe before proceeding to the Eiffel Tower, which the emir of Gombe climbed with the rest of the group. The Lamido of Adamawa "preferred to await our return on solid ground." Braving the touristic scramble in the lift as visitors crammed in, the group made its way to the summit, getting a memorable "view from the 300 meters high top platform" that they described as "well worth the turmoil."[37]

In the evening, the group made its way to the British embassy, where they dined with the ambassador, his wife, and several dignitaries. Paris was not on the regular itinerary of Northern Nigerian emirs, so the ambassador considered the emirs' visit a rare opportunity to learn about their emirates and societies. Dinner was followed by a tour of the embassy grounds. The visiting aristocrats were shown around the sprawling estate, a network of impressive Victorian buildings purchased by the Duke of Wellington from Napoleon's sister, Pauline Borghese, in 1814. Since the purchase, the compound had been the official residence of the British ambassador and had, by virtue of its history and ornate magnificence, become a touristic site in its own right. The emirs toured Pauline's preserved bedroom with "its original long mirrors." The ambassador led "his eminent and stately guests in their silk robes gently down" a long staircase that opened into a large hall on the lower floor.[38] The emirs were particularly taken by the throne room, with all its preserved accoutrement of royal splendor—symbols that resonated with their own monarchical and aristocratic sensibilities.

With the tour concluded, the tourists signed the visitors' book and drove away past a crowd of tourists and sightseers gathered outside. On Sunday, the tourists window-shopped the closed but elegantly decorated shop fronts of Paris. They drove to the Palace of Versailles and joined thousands of other tourists to view the palace's many rooms and gardens. The tourists then drove to Saint-Germain-en-Laye, casually walking through its quiet, ornate gardens.[39] On their way back to Paris, the emirs spontaneously decided to stop at a fair in Neuilly, getting on a switchback ride, "which hurtled round and round at a terrifying speed" and caused Mallam Jauro to momentarily betray a noticeably terrified demeanor.

Evolving Metropolitan Itineraries

Aside from the annual summer tour, the central feature of the program of metropolitan tours was that the chief commissioner of Northern Nigeria routinely used his discretion to request that the British Council arrange solo visits for some emirs and chiefs. In these instances, the aristocrats could travel to Britain with their chosen aides rather than with unfamiliar aristocratic peers from other parts of Northern Nigeria. Such was the case in 1952, when the emirs of Ilorin and Bida traveled to Britain accompanied by favored officials of their respective emirates. On this occasion, a certain Mr. Greatbatch of the Northern Nigerian colonial service was the guide for the two emirs and their two aides.[40] The program for this trip was not as structured as that of the big annual summer tour—partly because, given its size and smaller budget, organizers felt no compulsion to justify the visit as an educational enterprise and partly because the emirs regarded the trip as something of a personal sightseeing tour and thus contributed to the process of formulating an itinerary. These trips lacked a regimented program of lectures; instead, they were packed with sightseeing adventures, tours of institutions, and meetings with important political and cultural actors from the upper crust of British society. Between June 2 and July 17, 1952, the two emirs toured an eclectic array of sights and institutions in a bid to, as the official report of the visit put it, conduct a "survey of life in contemporary Britain."[41]

In London, the two emirs visited the Colonial Office, the Imperial Institute, the Islamic Cultural Center and London Mosque, the Royal Mint, the Zoological Gardens, several schools, the House of Commons, Middlesex Hospital, London County Council Housing Estate, Windsor Castle, Eton College, and the Richmond Royal Horse Show. Between June 16 and 27, the duo visited the cities of Portsmouth, Southampton, Guildford, and Oxford, where they toured several sights, including town halls, Oxford University, a dock, the Royal Counties Agricultural Show in Guildford, and a cattle market.[42] Between June 28 and July 17, the emirs visited Witney, Bath, Bristol, Birmingham, and Liverpool, among other cities. Their program of sightseeing included tours of several town councils, the Roman Baths at the Museum of Bath, water reservoirs, the Austin Motor Company at Longbridge, the Northern Tanning Company at Bootle, and the Lever Brothers factory at Port Sunlight.[43] The list of sites the emirs toured indicates an effort on the part of the organizers to develop a mix of attractions that satisfied the interests of the emirs and the colonial tour planners. These sites aligned with the eclectic interests and tastes of the Northern Nigerian aristocracy. Colonial preferences were represented by locations clearly designed to give the emirs a glimpse into what could crudely be described as metropolitan governmental and cultural modernity.

The British Council hosted the group at tea receptions in London, Oxford, and Liverpool. The minister of state for colonial affairs hosted the visitors at the House of Commons and at his private home in Devon. The emirs witnessed the Trooping the Colour ceremony and were special guests at a musical show on ice, "Ranch in the Rockies." The highlight of the visit was the emirs' attendance at the Royal Garden Party at Buckingham Palace on July 10 and their subsequent presentation to the queen and the Duke of Edinburgh.[44]

In October 1952, the emir of Bedde, Umar dan Sulayman, visited the United Kingdom. Among other activities, he visited the International Commercial Show at Earls Court. The emir, "his long baggy green brocade trousers and long, flowing white robes" providing a "picturesque" appearance,[45] was reported to have taken a ride on a motor bus at the show. His guides and officials at Guy Buses, one of the automotive exhibitors at the show, arranged for Sulayman to "try the controls" on one bus and ride in another.[46] Thrilled by the ride, the emir described his experience as "magnificent" and told his guides that he would tell his friends in Nigeria about it.

Seeing that Sulayman was taken by "a big Red Indian mascot on the front of one of the new Guy buses,"[47] Sidney Guy, the managing director of the company, proceeded, unprompted, to tell Emir Sulayman of an incident he claimed happened during his son Robin's visit to "Central, East, and West Africa."[48] Upon arrival at "a native rest house," his son found himself being introduced by his driver to a chief as the "Bwana Guy, who makes the big trucks and buses."[49] The reference to "Bwana Guy" discloses the setting of the story as the Swahili-speaking regions of East and Central Africa. The chief remarked that Robin was too young to make buses and trucks but that he had seen a picture of his father, the elder Mr. Guy, "the big Chief" who was the real automaker.[50] The chief then went into his hut and brought out a picture of "the Red Indian mascot," remarking that this was the real bus maker and that he was wearing a chief's headdress.

Guy's point in telling the story was first to underscore the popularity of the Red Indian mascot, the brand image of his automotive company, and, second, to display his and his son's familiarity with Africa. It is this secondary layer of meaning that is of interest to this study. Perhaps Guy hoped that invoking this register of geographical familiarity would make him more relatable to Emir Sulayman. In telling the story of another African chief's connection to the Red Indian mascot, Guy probably sought to reassure Sulayman that he was not the only African who was drawn to the company's chiefly, regal motif.

The story simultaneously and perhaps unintentionally reveals an instructive facet of the discursive encounters between visiting Northern Nigerian aristocrats and their metropolitan hosts. It is a powerful reminder of the British colonial discursive homogenizing of Africa and Africans that Guy thought a story about an African chief in East or Central Africa and his son's visit there was appropriate for breaking the proverbial ice with an emir from Nigeria. Metropolitan interlocutors regaled Northern Nigerian emirs and chiefs with tales of their or their acquaintances' travels in different parts of Africa, expecting the visitors to be familiar with or at least relate to any part of Africa they chose to talk about.

The colonial trope of an undifferentiated Africa peopled by a homogenized humanity often influenced how metropolitan hosts engaged with visitors from colonized African territories. The aristocratic visitors may have been from Northern Nigeria, but in the imperial metropolitan space of Britain, they were Africans, accountable for all of Africa. Like other visitors from the empire, Emir Sulayman was a stand-in for other subalterns of the British Empire—a representative of the exotic humanity in far-flung imperial peripheries.

The Women's Tour

The year 1952 witnessed the beginning of a new phenomenon in the metropolitan touring culture: the introduction of sponsored women's tours of Britain. Planning for the summer 1952 trip began in late 1951, when Northern Nigerian authorities began to compile the names of potential female visitors. They declared that the trip, like its counterpart for males, would be financed by Native Authorities, and they set the cost at £300 per person.[51] The women would stay with host families and "share in the life and work of the house," but arrangements would also be made for them to "see interesting things in the neighborhood."[52] The trip would be characterized by strategically selected "educational visits and sight-seeing tours."[53]

The women's tour would last between six and eight weeks and would entail trips to see "schools of various types, village institutes, District Nursing Organizations, School Clinics, all types of women's voluntary work as well as women's work in factories and elsewhere."[54] The itinerary and choice of sites to be visited reflected the professional orientation of the selected visitors. Six of the eight female visitors were teachers or health-care workers. One was a Native Authority secretarial staff, and one was a stay-at-home wife of a Native Authority official from Adamawa Emirate.[55] The itinerary also reflected the Victorian gender understandings and expectations of British colonizers, a view of gender relations that meshed conveniently with the dominant gender norms in Northern Nigeria at the time.

Officials insisted on the group being housed "in the country, or in a country town," and declared that the visitors would live at least "for a time in an English home."[56] Once the logistics and pedagogical content of the visit were finalized, the Northern Nigerian colonial authorities solicited volunteer Hausa-speaking British hosts "who know the North." In all, three volunteers emerged—two retired colonial officials who had served in Northern Nigeria and one, Robert Wright, who was serving in Bauchi Province and had offered to host some of the visitors in his home in Warwickshire.

The records do not indicate the outcome of the tour, and I have not located a formal report of the visit. What can be gleaned from the available record is that the organizers selected the visitors more carefully than they did male visitors. They tapped professional women but also women married to treasured Native Authority officials, hoping to both cultivate what one official called "educational propaganda" and reward male aristocratic allies in the Native Authority system by selecting their wives. Furthermore, officials insisted on giving the women an experience dominated by immersion in the dynamics of rural British life as well as in the humanitarian and familial arts, which broadly defined a skewed itinerary consistent with British colonizers' efforts to inscribe Nigerian women more securely in a Victorian gender trope of domesticity.

Metropolitan Touring as Colonial Validation

In 1953, the program of tours became an even more significant routine in the human, material, and ideational traffic between colony and metropole. With the British Council assuming a superintending and organizational role over logistics, the annual tours expanded further. The council organized three formal "study tours" in 1953 in addition to the special tours like those arranged for the emirs of Ilorin and Bida.[57] So elaborate and regular had the tours become that the British Council's Kano office, established in 1943, began to organize "short introductory courses on what to do and what to expect on first arrival in the United Kingdom" for aspiring visitors.[58]

Despite efforts to steer potential visitors to preferred informational and cultural precincts, the evidence indicates that many visitors viewed the acquisition of knowledge about British life as only half their mission. They viewed the trips as forms of social self-fortification, opportunities to shop for rare metropolitan goods, and avenues to deepen long-standing imperial aristocratic connections. The visitors' occasional insistence on alternative agendas and their predilections caused frustration for British Council officials, who complained that only a small minority of Northern Nigerians attended and appreciated the council's public presentation of the "British Way of Life" show.[59] The other issue was that even those few whom the council credited with appreciating the presentation would have considered going to Britain and actually observing the British way of life superior to an artistic audiovisual presentation on the topic.

The trips grew in popularity, and high demand among high-ranking Native Authority staff for slots forced the expansion of each delegation to thirty-four persons, with another candidate placed on a waiting list. Not only was the raw number increasing, but the ethnic and religious demographics of selected visitors were also changing. The 1954 delegation included an ethnic Yoruba Native Authority official from Ilorin Emirate; an Igala from Lokoja Province; Michael Audu Buba, a Christian from Shendam in Plateau Province; and Ortsenenger Dekke, a Tiv from Benue Province.[60]

The shift to a more inclusive touring regime that reflected the aristocratic diversity, spread, and geography of Northern Nigeria enabled the Och'Idoma, Ogiri Oko, to spend two months in the United Kingdom in 1955. Although there had been discussions about pairing him with another chief or emir or including him in the annual summer tour, the British Council eventually arranged a special two-month tour for him in conjunction with the secretariat of Northern Nigeria in Kaduna. The circumstances that led to his selection for the trip are instructive.

In February 1955, the district officer of Idoma Division, over which Oko presided as chief and head of the Native Authority, wrote to the Northern Nigerian colonial authorities through the resident of Benue Province to recommend the chief for a special tour of Britain. His rationale was that the chief needed a vacation, the trip would have an educational impact on Oko, and the visit would reward him for his service to British colonialism: "I consider that the chief could do with this break in his work—he has never taken a holiday since his installation in 1947—and it would be, as well, in the nature of a reward for his unrelenting efforts to further progress in his division. I think he would gain considerable benefit from the visit."[61] In March 1955, a program of tours was packaged for the Och'Idoma, with organizers proposing a tour in which "the emphasis should largely be on a visual programme."[62] The chief's two-month visit would take "the form of a road tour round England visiting places and events . . . and seeing as much of the country as possible." The plan was to "hire a car for the period of the visit outside London" and have a colonial guide drive the chief around the country.[63]

The declared emphasis on the visual rather than other sensory mediums was a clear gesture in the direction of trying to awe the chief by exposing him to the spectacular material culture and technological processes of Britain. That organizers wanted to dazzle the chief with the sights of the imperial metropole rather than organize a study tour replete with a deliberate educational agenda perhaps reflected a shift back to the emphasis on visual impressions of the 1920s and 1930s. It may also illustrate the difference between the structured, capstone summer tours and the special ones arranged on a case-by-case basis for individual chiefs or pairs of chiefs.

The Och'Idoma, Ogiri Oko, left Nigeria for Britain on June 14, 1955, accompanied by Ogah Oko, a mission-educated Christian who served as the chief's secretary and interpreter. His party included a group of "study tourists" embarking on an "introduction tour" of Britain, but a separate arrangement had been made for a special guide dedicated to Oko alone. The visit coincided with the annual leave of A.C.E. Long, the district officer who had worked with the chief in Idoma Division for the previous four years and had volunteered to "give up a large part of his leave to be the conducting officer." Long would "conduct" the chief and "take care of all disbursements in the U.K.," according to his brief from the British Council.[64] Funds from the Idoma Native Authority were used to finance the trip, with its estimated cost already included in the budget estimates for the year.

Upon arriving in the United Kingdom, Long hired a car and retained a driver for the countrywide tour.[65] The chief and his interpreter were accommodated at the Regent Palace Hotel in London, from where they set out for their daily tours. Ogiri Oko visited several agricultural shows. During his stay, he had tea with the mayor of Manchester and met with members of the Manchester Chamber of Commerce. Over several weeks, the chief, accompanied by Long, visited football matches, a textile factory, a ballet performance, a farm, both Houses of Parliament, a coal mine, a circus, a motorcar factory, a car race, and a horse-racing school. He also walked along the Thames, and visited the London docks, schools, the *Queen Mary* battleship, the Zoological Gardens, and a few London shops.[66]

Oko was a savvy and calculating aristocratic tourist who sought to put his own imprimatur on the tour itinerary, and he aimed to extract maximum symbolic utility from it. For instance, he planned to build an archive of visual materials from the trip and leverage these materials in his domain to communicate his ties to colonial power and modernity. Given his intentions, visual representations of the metropole preserved in photographs and material culture had a special appeal to him. Oko "made it clear that the publicity side of the visit was important . . . in his own area [Idoma Division]."[67] If the British were trying to awe him, he would, in turn, use the acquired visual and material objects from the trip to awe his subjects, especially his aristocratic rivals in Idomaland. Oko directed Long to take "many photographs . . . of him in the [English] South-west, of which he has had copies."[68] Ogiri Oko was continuing a popular tradition that began much earlier: African kings who visited Britain memorialized their visit by having their pictures taken close to important sights and institutions and commissioning the "Durrant Press Cuttings agency in London to clip the newspapers for references to themselves."[69] Furthermore, when Oko met the colonial secretary at the Colonial Office, he arranged for the latter to sign his photographs—a valuable mark of validation that the Och'Idoma saw as integral to the "publicity side" of the trip.[70]

Ogiri Oko visited Aberdeen in Scotland, where he toured a vacuum-dried fish factory as well as the local fish market. There, a local newspaper described him as being dressed in "flowing robes" that drew "quite a lot of attention" and as saying that the dried fish "industry was one of the most interesting things he had seen on his tour of Britain."[71] In Taunton, Ogiri Oko visited the press of the local newspaper, the *County Gazette*. Oko toured the newspaper's printing facilities, conducted by its two managing directors. He reportedly asked many questions regarding the newspaper's operations. The newspaper described him as appearing for the tour in "his handsome cloak and turban, and wearing the King's Medal, awarded to African chiefs who have given outstanding services to the Crown."[72]

Although he was not a Muslim, Ogiri Oko liked the sartorial appearance of emirs and dressed in the colorful robe and turban worn by emirs and Muslim aristocrats. While members of the emergent, Western-educated Idoma elite in Otukpo and other urban centers derisively described the chief as embracing a foreign regal sartorial ensemble unrepresentative of Idoma culture and, for good measure, connected his sartorial accoutrements to his alleged conservative political inclinations and his loyalty to the NPC, Oko's emirate-style robes and regal headgear drew fascination and curiosity in the United Kingdom. He was accorded the same treatment as was extended to Northern Nigeria's visiting emirs, despite the newness of the Idoma central chieftaincy.[73] Given the attention it drew, Oko would have considered his sartorial appropriation a success. In a colonially infused metropolitan space where exotic Muslim attire and those who wore it reinforced Britons' established Orientalist fascinations, Oko probably felt flattered by the attention his royal attire received, given his personal politics of regal self-representation, reckoning that the attire and attention put him in the same league as his Muslim emirate peers who presided over older, more established chieftaincies.

Oko took back a sizable collection of regal artifacts that would enhance his prestige in the eyes of his subjects in Idomaland, such as a throne stool purchased for nine pounds and shipped to Nigeria for another ten pounds.[74] These investments in the afterlives of the tours were as important as the tours themselves as Northern Nigeria's aristocrats sought to extend the symbolic lives of their experiences in Britain. For Oko, the purchase of a throne and his insistence on photographically curating his own travels through the white man's country were particularly poignant. They point to the importance of these trips for the domestic politics of chieftaincy and for consolidating precarious positions in a competitive aristocratic environment. When Oko traveled to Britain, he was facing the residual effects of a long-running opposition to his rule from a group of Western-educated Idoma men who considered him too conservative and insufficiently committed to a progressive agenda.[75] In this crisis of legitimacy, and given the colonial cachet of metropolitan validation, Oko had reason to acquire and flaunt the visual evidence of his visit to the center of British colonial power and to invest in exotic royal objects that would remind opposing and supporting Idoma subjects alike of his British-bestowed prestige and the majesty of his realm. Oko's elaborate leveraging of his trip to Britain bespoke a calculated aristocratic project of self-fashioning.

The Late-Colonial Allure of the Metropole

The year 1955 was one of the busiest for metropolitan touring; the summer was packed full of simultaneous and overlapping tours. While the British Council was completing arrangements for Chief Oko's visit, it was also organizing a tour of Britain for the emir of Dikwa. The emir departed for the United Kingdom on July 20, 1955, with J. A. Reynolds—a colonial official who was on leave in Britain and serving his colonial tour of duty in the Dikwa Native Authority—designated as the official guide to the traditional ruler.[76] We do not have the full itinerary of the emir's visit, but correspondence sent to Reynolds indicates the trip entailed visits to the usual assortment of metropolitan sites.[77]

The touring regime had evolved in many ways, and the new practice of creating an ethnically and religiously diverse group of tourists seems to have endured and become the norm. The 1956 summer tour included Mallam Gwamna Awan, the Christian chief of Kagoro, who had been disqualified from participating in 1950 purportedly because of his insufficient facility with the English language.[78] The 1956 group also included V.M.C. Tay, the president of the Mixed Court in Kano; Peter Akpeto Tion, the administrative councilor of Tiv Native Authority; Mallam Ahmadu Tijani, the scribe of the Igbirra Native Authority; and Mallam Ibrahim, the supervisor of Community Development in the Sokoto Native Authority and holder of the traditional title of sarkin malamai (head of Islamic scholars). Others were Mallam Bello, the emir of Agaie; Mallam Ahmadu Bawa, holder of the title of madawakin Kontagora and a senior councillor in the Kontagora Native Authority; Mallam Abdullahi Zuru, the native treasurer (ma'aji) of Zuru Emirate; and Mallam Abdullahi Dan Buran, for whom no official affiliation was given.[79] There were also representatives of the Katsina, Bornu, Bauchi, Ilorin, and Kano Provincial Native Authorities. These new, ecumenical demographics of the tour inadvertently helped to forge a Northern Nigerian sociopolitical solidarity that Ahmadu Bello would nurture into a "one North" political ideology.[80]

The pedagogical itinerary of the 1956 tour included the familiar assortment of lectures on a variety of topics. Some of the topics covered included "Public Cleansing," "Present Day Britain and Its System of Local Government," "Sanitary Administration and Control," "Education and Schools," "The British People Today," "Women in Britain," "Municipal Transport Service," "The English Social Behavior," "The English Concept of Democracy," and "British Agriculture."[81] Tours of cultural sites, farms, factories, the docks, and colleges, as well as luncheons and teas with members of British high society, occupied the visitors. The group was also treated to multiple film shows, including instrumental propaganda films on road safety and those with didactic titles such as *Local Government* and *The New Councilor*. On June 16, the group saw the film *The Overlanders*, and on June 23, they saw two films, *The Heart of England* and *West Country Journey*.[82] All three movies were propaganda movies that respectively portrayed heroic wartime innovations and improvisations in the British imperial realm and the alluring expanse of Britain.

From the Personal to the Official

By 1956, Northern Nigeria had entered a phase of colonization in which its colonial status was gradually giving way under the weight of intense negotiations on independence for Nigeria as a whole. Under the terms established by the quasi-self-rule constitutions of 1947 and 1954, a regional legislature and a council of chiefs were established in Northern Nigeria, both peopled by representative elites and aristocrats. In 1954, Ahmadu Bello became the premier of Northern Nigeria. In theory, Northern Nigeria was thus inside the overarching overlay of British imperial power and a functioning albeit circumscribed self-rule government with its own budgets and programs. It had a cabinet of officials with portfolios and representatives in a few countries. One of the most powerful of these representatives was Northern Nigeria's commissioner in Britain, a quasi-ambassadorial position established in 1955. The holder of the position was assigned the task of coordinating the northern region government's metropolitan affairs. The commissioner lived in London but was expected to oversee the interests of Northern Nigeria in all of Britain. Beginning in 1956, the Northern Nigerian commissioner in Britain, Alhaji Abdulmalik, embarked on regular and elaborate tours around one or more of the countries of the United Kingdom.

Between October 15 and 20, 1956, Commissioner Abdulmalik toured various sites in Belfast, Northern Ireland. The tour was packaged and logistically underwritten by the British Council. The program of the tour included visits to the abattoir, the House of Parliament, the Faculty of Agriculture at Queens University, and shipyards.[83] The commissioner met with Nigerian students studying in Belfast; the event was held in the British Council Center and thenceforth became a routine event in the itinerary of this quasi-diplomatic tour. Abdulmalik then met with a smaller group of students from Northern Nigeria in his hotel. The commissioner attended several plays, had tea with local dignitaries, and went to a dinner party with several prominent officials and aristocratic citizens of Belfast. The lord mayor of Belfast, Alderman R.J.R. Harcourt, conducted the commissioner and his aides around Belfast City Hall.[84] Abdulmalik subsequently visited a tannery, a "visit of practical interest" where it was reported that he saw "piles of goatskins from Kano, Zaria, and Maiduguri" and took a keen interest in the industrial process of "turning these skins into leather."[85]

The commissioner's report on the five-day tour gives us a glimpse into the evolution of the culture of metropolitan tours, which gradually mutated into a diplomatic touristic adventure that combined the sightseeing of old with new imperatives for cultivating official bureaucratic and technocratic ties between a semi-autonomous Northern Nigerian government and British cities, agencies, and institutions. In this new configuration, tourists such as Abdulmalik not only craved the symbolic and material signs of British modernity but also the technological capacities that made that modernity possible. They sought technical assistance, hoping to leverage it to replicate desired aspects of British modernity in Northern Nigeria as part of a broader developmental aspiration.

In this late-colonial vision, modernization and development were entwined in symbiosis, and tours of metropolitan institutions were expected to supply usable ideas for catalyzing re-creations of these institutions and their practices in Northern Nigeria. As the commissioner's report stated, he toured several factories and tanneries because he wanted to learn how they were run "should similar institutions be established in Northern Nigeria."[86] The tour was conceived in a deliberately instrumental way and on the initiative of the Northern Nigerian government rather than that of colonial authorities. Aside from his secretary, the commissioner was accompanied by the director of veterinary services of Northern Nigeria, buttressing the *Belfast Telegraph*'s claim that the commissioner was in Belfast to study "our agricultural methods."[87]

A noteworthy footnote to this itinerary is the persistence of the trope of imperial transatlantic kinship highlighted in chapter 3. As the analysis of several subsequent tours and trips has made clear, organizing officials and the travelers themselves often rekindled ties and friendships with retired or holidaying colonial officials in Britain, and these British colonial actors were happy to shepherd the tourists through the cultural maze of Britain. This element endured with the advent of semi-diplomatic tours. Commissioner Abdulmalik relied on his acquaintance with retired colonial officials to navigate Belfast, notably depending on a certain Mr. Denton, a retired colonial district officer who had served for many years in Northern Nigeria, to implement a packed itinerary of touring.[88]

Another important shift had to do with the amount of input from would-be tourists regarding planning. When emirs, chiefs, and other aristocrats had traveled to the metropole, they generally had limited say in framing the program of sightseeing and determining the quotidian contours of the tours, although they could do so informally once in Britain and could express their preferences prior to the trip. Their other formal avenue for expressing their views on the tours was the posttour feedback ritual, an expressive space constrained by the expectations of melodramatic subaltern gratitude. In the quasi-diplomatic tours of this period, the would-be tourists were consulted more often and more substantively in the planning stages, enabling them to make concrete input into the structure and finer logistical details of the tour. Because of these more robust preparatory conversations, which read more like diplomatic communications than colonial exchanges, Abdulmalik was able to request spatial and temporal provisions for Islamic prayer ahead of his visit, unlike others who made such requests during their trips. He was also able to ask his hosts to "impress on the hotel not to have any alcohol in the sauces, and not to serve any ham, bacon, or similar pork products with the chicken."[89]

As these official tours continued, they became more structured quasi-diplomatic exercises that were more removed from the tours analyzed earlier. In April 1959, the new commissioner of Northern Nigeria in Britain, Mallam Abba Gana, toured Belfast. He visited the city's mayor, was treated to a film show and a reception, met with Northern Nigerian students, and went on a "drive around" arranged by the British Council in which a guide lectured him about sites as he was driven around the city.[90] Mallam Gana also visited the House of Parliament, where he met with the prime minister, Lord Brookeborough. The April 29 edition of the *Northern Whig and Belfast Post* newspaper carried a front-page picture of Mallam Abba Gana, the lord mayor of Belfast, and Alderman W. Cevil M'Kee at Belfast City Hall.[91]

Like his predecessor, Mallam Gana aggressively courted the technocratic and technological assistance of institutions in Belfast. He arrived in the city with a wish list of requests, which he unfurled at each high-profile meeting. Northern Nigeria was readying itself for independence and since 1956 had been implementing a deliberate and controversial policy of regional development, institution building, and bureaucratic preparedness called northernization.[92] Northernization stemmed from the realization that Northern Nigeria was chronically short of trained personnel in multiple technocratic fields critical to running the bureaucracy of an autonomous government.

Due to discrepancies in colonial investment in Western education between Northern Nigeria and Southern Nigeria, as well as historical antipathy toward Western education in the predominantly Muslim region of colonial Nigeria, most of the civil service and institutional positions in Northern Nigeria were occupied by expatriate British personnel and Southern Nigerians. This asymmetrical distribution of expertise was a source of anxiety for Northern Nigeria's political leaders and elites, who feared what they regarded as southern domination, an anxiety dramatized by the North's reliance on Southern Nigerian bureaucratic labor. With independence in view, officials sought to replace the Southern Nigerian personnel by the dawn of complete self-rule. This anxiety intensified in the late 1950s and caused Northern Nigeria's government to pressure representatives like Abba Gana to initiate and consummate technical assistance agreements in different parts of Britain. With this imperative in mind, the official tours of the commissioners assumed new importance. By 1959, with independence only a year away, the prevailing pressures and uncertainties of imminent independence led to a frenzied, aggressive effort on Gana's part to attract skilled British personnel to the region.

Political Independence in the Shadow of Metropolitan Courtship

Political independence in 1960 did little to alter the symbolic cachet or practical utility of metropolitan connections. These relationships only assumed new forms, dictated not by the imperatives of rewarding African colonial allies but by a new, deliberate Northern Nigerian policy of tapping into existing metropolitan networks and connections to both modernize the region and accomplish the goals of northernization.

In 1962, Mallam Baba Gana, now the agent-general of Northern Nigeria in Britain, embarked on a tour of several cities in England and Wales. The central goal of his tour, which he expressed in different forms to various official interlocutors, was to obtain special admission considerations for Northern Nigerian students "who may not fulfill the admission requirements" of metropolitan institutions but whose higher training was desperately needed in Northern Nigeria.[93] The imperative of northernization framed the agent-general's postindependence tours of British cities and institutions. Gana's request resonated with and was authorized by the renewed urgency of northernization.

As he and his entourage traversed Britain, Baba Gana requested that universities and training institutes empathize with the dire problem of Northern Nigeria's educationally handicapped postindependence modernization project. He pleaded with them to set aside procedures and precedents for admitting applicants from the region. At British medical colleges, the agent-general appealed to officials to extend admissions to "locally trained medical officers" and to "sympathetically consider the applications of Northern Nigeria as it lags educationally behind other parts of the Federation of Nigeria."[94]

The agent-general made a similar appeal at the University of Liverpool, where he urged the dean of the university's medical college to consider exempting medical personnel from Northern Nigeria from the regular preparatory qualifications and accepting their Northern Nigerian training as a basis for further medical training and certification in Britain.[95] Emotional appeals of this type were powerful indicators of how the anxieties of self-governance activated a new touristic tradition rooted in the search for technocratic expertise in British institutions.[96] These appeals yielded mixed results, but Northern Nigerian officials were unfazed in their pursuit of metropolitan expertise, certification, and validation as they sought to modernize their territory and close a glaring educational and personnel gap.

In the wake of independence, Northern Nigerian authorities pursued a two-pronged engagement with Britain. One was official and diplomatic and echoed the tours of the late 1950s—a plea for technical assistance for a variety of modernizing projects. The other was a cultural path of exchanges that recalled and continued the touristic cultural explorations of the previous decades.

One plank of this cultural exchange had the imprimatur of Ahmadu Bello, the prime minister of the Northern Region. Bello was an avid fives player and fan.[97] He had learned to play the metropolitan sport through his British aristocratic networks, much like other Northern Nigerian aristocrats had learned to play polo. Specifically, Bello learned to play fives from S. J. Hogben, an education officer and teacher at Katsina College, who had introduced the game at the college and in Sokoto in the 1920s.[98] Bello's keen interest in fives further endeared him to Hogben, fives pioneer in Northern Nigeria.

In 1961, on the initiative of the prime minister's office, a Northern Nigerian Eton fives team—composed mostly of Northern Nigerian bureaucrats, including at least one official who was taking a six-month course in Britain—toured the cities of Oxford, Cambridge, and Birmingham.[99] We know from a story in the *Eton College Chronicle* that the team's visit was part of a cultural and sports exchange that had been discussed between visiting leaders of Northern Nigeria and the authorities of Eton College in the summer of 1960, just a few months before Nigeria's independence. John Holt and Company, a Liverpool-based trading firm and one of the major British companies operating in Nigeria, funded the team's trip, indicating the ways colonial and neocolonial institutions continued to sustain and subsidize postindependence metropolitan travels and adventures. After the team returned to Nigeria, a British expatriate official of the Northern Nigerian Ministry of Land and Survey, W. T. Gordon-Marshall, sent the prime minister the *Eton College Chronicle* article detailing the visit:[100] "One day last summer a procession of a dark bearded figures [sic], with richly embroidered flowing robes, was seen making its dignified way through the Cloisters. It was the Premier of Northern Nigeria, the Hon. Alhaji Sir Ahmadu Bello, the Sardauna of Sokoto, and suite, coming to lunch with the Head Master to discuss an exchange visit of Etonian fives players with schools in N. Nigeria. The suggestion had been made originally by the Head Master: the formal invitation to Nigeria came at this luncheon party from the Sardauna himself."[101]

Following this outreach by Bello and his entourage, Eton College's fives team visited Northern Nigeria in January 1961. The team toured Kano, Zaria, Katsina, and Kaduna, where they met with the prime minister. When he received the team, Bello referred to the "delicious dishes" he and his team had enjoyed during their exploratory visit to Eton in the summer of 1960 and presented each team member with "a Muslim hat and gown, all gaily coloured, and a 'luru' (a blanket of locally woven cloth)."[102] In the afterglow of independence, Northern Nigeria's problems with building the human competencies required for a modern governmental bureaucracy necessitated a cultural outreach designed to lubricate and transition into more concrete technocratic relationships between former colony and metropole. These efforts relied on a remembered history of prior social, experiential engagements with the metropole and in some ways paralleled prior British metropolitan travel programs.

Although their courtship of British metropolitan expertise and culture was aggressive, it would be inadequate to simply understand Bello and other

Northern Nigerian aristocrats who consumed, courted, and domesticated imperial culture as Anglophiles. Bello and his cohort found a skillful way to weave imperial cultures and other modernist inventions into Northern Nigeria's burgeoning elite cultural codes, producing a distinct marker of identity that was simultaneously anchored in caliphal and British aristocratic practices and objects. The centrality of Eton College to this project of self-making is understandable. Eton was and still is the bastion of English aristocratic socialization, education, and fraternity, much like Katsina College and its successor, Barewa College, in colonial Nigeria. Eton and the sport of fives provided a model for Bello's own vision of a conservative aristocratic political dynasty that embodied a gradualist politics suffused with tradition, religion, and a set of modernist symbols and mannerisms. This vision mirrored the overlapping sensibilities of the British aristocracy and British political formations. Bello and many Northern Nigerians who imitated his personal and political example embodied a similar intertwinement of aristocratic tradition, secular political dominance, and cultural modernity.

Postcolonial Anxieties and Metropolitan Outreach

In the first few years after independence, Northern Nigerian officials frantically courted metropolitan institutions, cities, and influential individuals to cultivate concrete ties of cooperation and assistance that harkened to prior connections facilitated by elite travel and tours. In the new period, official and semi-official delegations from Northern Nigeria traveled to Britain to build more concretely beneficial relationships.

The defining imperative of this early postcolonial outreach was that of enlisting British institutions in the effort to overcome what Isa Kaita, the minister of education, called "the magnitude of our staffing problems."[103] Independence sharpened the dissonance between the region's avowed policy of northernization on the one hand and the paucity of trained Northern Nigerian personnel and the resultant continued dependence on contracted British expats on the other. Solicited and incentivized by the Northern Nigerian government, many British expats remained in the country, and several others took up appointments in the region after independence. Still, the problem of staffing and inadequate instructional personnel in educational and training institutions persisted.

In the early independence period, the task of correcting this imbalance, which began with the aggressive courtship of British educational institutions in the late 1950s, became a high government priority. It was no longer a task to be left to the representative of the Northern Nigerian government in Britain but one to be pursued by Northern Nigerian government officials overseeing the educational affairs of the region. Accordingly, in December 1963, Minister of Education Isa Kaita and an entourage of officials from his ministry visited Britain and held a series of meetings with London County Council officials about "problems facing [the Northern Nigerian] Government in connection with the recruitment of teachers from Britain."[104] Kaita and his team requested the formation of an educational relationship between the Northern Nigerian government and the London County Council "with a view to maintaining and improving the supply of expatriate teachers and other educationists from the United Kingdom to Northern Nigeria."[105] The team also invited the council's assistant education officer, L.G.A. Saunders, to visit Northern Nigeria to tour schools and educational facilities and hold further discussions.

Upon his return from Britain, Kaita penned a memo formally proposing a linkage to the executive council of the Northern Nigerian government. The memo laid out a comprehensive assessment of the North's educational crisis. According to the memo, there were 230 unfilled job vacancies in Northern Nigerian schools, including 13 open school principal positions.[106] At a time when the North was expanding educational access as part of its determined effort to northernize its workforce, the shortages threatened to derail any effort to achieve both substantive bureaucratic autonomy and the modernization that northern leaders understood to depend on a sound, educated bureaucracy. The shortages, the memo noted, stemmed from two sources: British experts returning to Britain and difficulty in attracting new expat recruits from Britain: "[Expat] teachers feels [sic] that when they have completed their professional contracts with the Northern Nigerian Government they will not obtain posts in their country of origin commensurate with their age and experience."[107] The minister recommended that the Northern Nigerian government forge links and relationships with British "institutions and organizations that employed teachers." These institutions would then "encourage teachers . . . to come to Northern Nigeria, or recruit in conjunction with our recruitment Agency teachers especially to come out here."[108] Kaita argued that more teachers should be recruited from Britain to help "raise the morale of overseas teachers in the employment of this Government, who are becoming increasingly worried by the cessation of recruitment from overseas, and the consequent shortage of staff in Government post primary Educational Institutions."[109]

The council approved both requests, and Saunders visited several schools in different districts of Northern Nigeria. The London County Council thereafter approved a formal educational linkage, assuring the Northern Nigerian government that "the Council will do everything possible to encourage London teachers to apply for posts in Nigeria provided that the conditions of service are satisfactory."[110] The terms of the proposed link included "liaison between the educational services of London and Northern Nigeria and between individual schools and colleges in London with corresponding establishments in Northern Nigeria," with the council acting as a recruitment promoter for the Northern Nigerian government and sending some of its experienced teaching staff to work for specific periods as school inspectors.[111] On April 11, 1964, Kaita wrote to Marjorie McIntosh, the chairman of the Educational Committee of the London County Council, to accept the terms of the partnership, promising to extend Northern Nigeria's "jealously-guarded tradition of hospitality" and "traditional respect for teachers and men of learning" to recruited British teachers.[112]

Meanwhile, the efforts of Agent-General Mallam Baba Gana to court British technocratic patronage continued. Between November 22 and December 1, 1963, the agent-general and his aides toured several major cities in Scotland and Northern Ireland as well as Newcastle, England. The agent-general held multiple, extensive discussions with administrative officers at Queens University in Belfast. He and his team also visited Aberdeen, Glasgow, Dundee, and Edinburgh, meeting with officials of several higher educational institutions to request teachers and spots for prospective Northern Nigerian students. Everywhere he went, the refrain and request were the same: "the recruitment of graduates to teach in Northern Nigeria" and the recruitment of experienced "Scottish teachers for Northern Nigeria Civil Service."[113]

The agent-general distributed the Northern Nigerian government's employment brochure at all the institutions he visited, aggressively making the case that Northern Nigeria provided an attractive work environment and that recruited expat teachers would be treated well. He also suggested to his hosts that a mechanism be created to address the professional anxieties of potential recruits as a way to ensure that British teachers who took up appointments in Northern Nigeria "would be assured of their rightful position when they returned to their country."[114] At factories and firms, the agent-general requested training slots for Northern Nigerian engineers, and at the College of Pharmacy of the University of Edinburgh, he discussed "the possibility of attracting pharmaceutical lecturers to teach in Northern Nigeria's School of Pharmacy."[115] These efforts to access metropolitan expertise and technocratic resources grew stronger, and Northern Nigerian postcolonial leaders repurposed the old networks of colonial metropolitan touring developed by colonial tourists in the previous decades.

Colonial Adventures and Postcolonial Metropolitan Tourism

As the independence decade of the 1960s progressed, the touristic networks established in colonial times endured, maintained by new governmental connections and rekindled aristocratic kinships. The colonial metropolitan circuits traversed by members of the Northern Nigerian aristocracy in earlier decades remained busy as more emirs and their associates continued to visit Britain for touristic adventures, reviving old itineraries and pathways. In Britain, they played or watched polo on their favorite polo grounds while interacting with old British colonial acquaintances who had retired to Britain.

In 1968, one group of emirs toured familiar touristic sites in Britain. Robert Longmore, who had served for more than a decade in the Northern Nigerian colonial service, was on hand to welcome and entertain the visitors and recalls the visit in his colonial service memoir thus:

> During evening polo as practised in Goodwood Week I had gone after work with my spaniel, Twinkle, to watch an evening match. I was talking to Colonel Kennedy, retired Indian Cavalry and the Chief Umpire, when I sensed a swish of skirts behind me and suddenly heard in Hausa: "Ga wanda ya ke a nan!" = "Look who's here." Looking round I found advancing on me Mamman Kabir, the son of the Emir of Katsina, followed by Alhaji Usman Nagogo the Emir of Katsina himself, together with another Emir whom I did not know but who from the way in which his turban was tied, with two rabbits ears, I realised was a new, to me, Emir of Kano.[116]

The entourage was in Britain for a conference but traveled to the Cowdray polo ground to watch the tournament being played there that week. Conversations in Hausa were a ritual of reacquaintance in these circumstances. Shared pastimes such as polo helped facilitate postcolonial interactions. During this visit, the polo-playing adventures of the emir of Katsina,

Usman Nagogo—who had accompanied his father, Muhammadu Dikko, on multiple visits—helped ease the current encounter. As Longmore recalled, "the Emir of Katsina, who had when a young man in England before the war played [polo] a little at Cowdray," was already deeply familiar with the protocols of the Cowdray Polo Ground.[117] Nagogo asked to see and greet Lord Cowdray, the owner of the ground, so Longmore took Nagogo and his entourage to an "enclosure" to meet him. Lord Cowdray welcomed, entertained, and conversed with his guests. Longmore recalled chatting with Mamman Kabir and the Madakin Kano, "enquiring about old friends" and rekindling old memories. The reminiscences continued later that day over drinks as Longmore "took [Madakin Kano] off to get a drink at the bar (nonalcoholic of course!)" and "then sat with him to watch the polo and ask for news of all my friends in Kano."[118]

These affective continuities from colonial times were part ritualistic in nature and marked by the formalities and strictures of aristocratic sociability. They were steeped in the theatrical hospitalities of the metropolitan touristic encounters analyzed in previous chapters. Nonetheless, their longevity is a testament to the depth of unlikely colonial relationships, which imperial travel, curiosity, adventure, and touristic observation helped sustain. This mobility in the orbit of empire and the tangible and intangible cultural exchanges they spawned were central to the circulation and remaking of modernity in Northern Nigeria and elsewhere. They complicate conventional understandings of colonialism as a unidirectional flow of ideas, cultures, tastes, consumption, curiosity, adventure, and touristic ethnography.

Conclusion

The persistence of Britain, its technologies of problem solving, its modernist material culture, and its assumed expertise in the science of development in the Northern Nigerian postcolonial touristic and diplomatic imagination provide another lens on the multiple, evolving lives of colonial relationships and networks. This perspective troubles the adversarial conception of a colonizer/colonized dyad. Postcolonial human traffic between the former colony of Northern Nigeria and the metropole of Britain turned on the practical needs of a newly independent bureaucratic entity. However, the networks and pipelines that underpinned and facilitated this traffic dated back to the touristic explorations of the metropole by Northern Nigerian aristocrats in the preceding decades and through the well-worn networks of empire.

This chapter analyzed a momentous time in metropolitan touring by Northern Nigeria's aristocrats—the late 1940s to the 1960s. This period witnessed the expansion of the metropolitan tours, the diversification of the participating demographics, and the evolution of a late-colonial and postcolonial touring regime informed by the novel anxieties, initiatives, and desires of a self-ruled and later independent Northern Nigeria. The particular anxieties and politics of self-making in the late-colonial period of post–World War II Northern Nigeria lent additional popularity to the touring culture of the region's elites. The result was an intense quest for more metropolitan validation and resources.

In this period, modernization was understood to come from a plethora of British material goods and metropolitan associations, including diplomatic and technocratic partnerships. The most significant shift in this period was that Northern Nigerians drove and initiated tours and, in so doing, consciously fulfilled needs outside the strict frame of colonialism. These needs intersected with local political aspirations, developmental and modernizing ambitions, and regional identity formation in the competitive reconfigurations of Nigeria's postindependence nationhood.

Notes

1. NAK/ZariaProf 4427/S, 1: British Council Visits to UK (2), Study Course (3) Summer School, 1947–57. Lectures by Sarkin Ruwa, Circular Number 4427/19.
2. NAK/Katprof, Lecture by Wakilin Gona, Daura, September 5, 1952.
3. NAK/Katprof, Lecture by Wakilin Gona.
4. NAK/Katprof, Lecture by Wakilin Gona.
5. NAK/Katprof, Lecture by Wakilin Gona.
6. NAK/ZariaProf 4427/S, 1: British Council Visits to UK (2), Study Course (3) Summer School 1947–57; Memo Number NAK/Zariaprof 25323/3, Kaduna, November 20, 1935, Memorandum From Secretary, Northern Provinces to The Residents All Provinces.
7. NAK/ZariaProf 4427/S, 1: British Council Visits to UK (2), Study Course (3) Summer School 1947–57. See, for instance, the volunteer offer letter from one Sir William N. M. Geary to the undersecretary of state in the Colonial Office touting his experience hosting the Alake of Egbaland and a detachment of the Royal West African Frontier Force the previous summer.
8. NAK/ZariaProf 4427/S, 1: British Council Visits to UK (2),Study Course (3) Summer School 1947–57; NAK/DDN/CDN/6/15/KADMIN/ Circular 38796/s.3/5, Kaduna, August 19, 1947, British Council Short Visits to United Kingdom, 1948.

9. NAK/ZariaProf 4427/S, 1: British Council Visits to UK (2), Study Course (3) Summer School 1947–57.
10. Ibid.
11. Ibid.
12. NAK/ZariaProf 4427/S, 1: British Council Visits to UK (2), Study Course (3) Summer School 1947–57. Memo Number 38796/s.3/156, Kaduna, July 7, 1948, From the acting secretary, Northern Provinces to the Resident, Zaria Province, "British Council Short Visits."
13. NAK/ZariaProf 4427/S, 1: British Council Visits to UK (2), Study Course (3) Summer School 1947–57. Circular Number 266/1949; 38796/s.5, Kaduna, October 21, 1948, From the acting secretary, Northern Provinces to the Resident, Zaria Province, "British Council Short Visits."
14. Ibid.
15. Ibid.
16. NAK/ZariaProf 4427/S, 1: British Council Visits to UK (2), Study Course (3) Summer School 1947–57. Correspondent Number 4427/29, From acting Resident, Zaria Province to the Secretary, Northern Provinces, "Visits to England Arranged by the British Council."
17. NAK/ZariaProf 4427/S, 1: British Council Visits to UK (2), Study Course (3) Summer School 1947–57, Circular Number 38796/s.3/213. From secretary, Northern Provinces to the Resident, Zaria Province, "Short Visits to the United Kingdom 1949, Sponsored by the British Council."
18. Ibid.
19. Ibid.
20. NAK/ZariaProf 4427/S, 1: British Council Visits to UK (2), Study Course (3) Summer School 1947–57, Circular Number 38796/s.3/228, February 3,1949, From secretary, Northern Provinces to the Resident, Zaria Province, "Short Visits to the United Kingdom 1949, Sponsored by the British Council."
21. Ibid.
22. NAK/ZariaProf 4427/S, 1: British Council Visits to UK (2), Study Course (3) Summer School 1947–57. Circular Number 38796/S.9/12, Kaduna, February 1, 1950, "Short Visits to the United Kingdom 1949, Sponsored by the British Council."
23. Ibid.
24. *Daily Comet*, August 21, 1950, 6.
25. NAK/Zaria 4427/S, 1: British Council Visits to UK (2), Study Course (3) Summer School 1947–57. Circular Number 7084/24, Kano Provincial Office, Acting Resident, Kano Province to the secretary, Northern Provinces, Kaduna.
26. NAK/ZariaProf/4427/S, 1: Nigerian Visitors to UK (2), Nigerian Office in London (1950–55)—Emir of Ilorin to London, File 5158, "Visit to the UK by the Emir of Ilorin" (Circular Number 46103/51, October 2, 1951), from the secretary, Northern Provinces to the Residents of multiple provinces.
27. Ibid.
28. NAK/Kanoprof/BCC/5, The British Council, Kano, Northern Provinces Monthly Reports. Specifically, see the report for September 1952.
29. NAK/Kanoprof/BCC/5, The British Council, Kano, Northern Provinces Monthly Reports. The available monthly reports at the National Archive in Kaduna range from 1952 to 1954 and show a vibrant organ of British colonial public relations at work.
30. Rhodes House MSS. Afr. S. 1403, Fol. 1, A Weekend in Paris, 1951.

31. Rhodes House MSS. Afr. S. 1403, Fol. 1, A Weekend in Paris.
32. Rhodes House MSS. Afr. S. 1403, Fol. 1, A Weekend in Paris.
33. Rhodes House MSS. Afr. S. 1403, Fol. 1, A Weekend in Paris.
34. Rhodes House MSS. Afr. S. 1403, Fol. 1, A Weekend in Paris.
35. Rhodes House MSS. Afr. S. 1403, Fol. 1, A Weekend in Paris.
36. Rhodes House MSS. Afr. S. 1403, Fol. 1, A Weekend in Paris.
37. Rhodes House MSS. Afr. S. 1403, Fol. 1, A Weekend in Paris.
38. Rhodes House MSS. Afr. S. 1403, Fol. 1, A Weekend in Paris.
39. Rhodes House MSS. Afr. S. 1403, Fol. 1, A Weekend in Paris.
40. NAK/ZariaProf 4427/S, 1: British Council Visits to UK (2), Study Course (3) Summer School 1947–57. The British Council Report on the Visit of Muhamadu Ndayako, C.B.E., emir of Bida and Abdul Kadiri, C.B.E., emir of Ilorin, Northern Nigeria.
41. The British Council Report on the Visit of Muhamadu Ndayako, C.B.E., emir of Bida and Abdul Kadiri, C.B.E., emir of Ilorin, Northern Nigeria.
42. The British Council Report on the Visit of Muhamadu Ndayako, C.B.E., emir of Bida and Abdul Kadiri, C.B.E., emir of Ilorin, Northern Nigeria.
43. The British Council Report on the Visit of Muhamadu Ndayako, C.B.E., emir of Bida and Abdul Kadiri, C.B.E., emir of Ilorin, Northern Nigeria.
44. The British Council Report on the Visit of Muhamadu Ndayako, C.B.E., emir of Bida and Abdul Kadiri, C.B.E., emir of Ilorin, Northern Nigeria.
45. "Emir of Bedde Enjoys Bus Ride at Earls Court Grand Display," *West African Pilot*, October 21, 1952, 3.
46. "Emir of Bedde Enjoys Bus Ride."
47. "Emir of Bedde Enjoys Bus Ride."
48. "Emir of Bedde Enjoys Bus Ride."
49. "Emir of Bedde Enjoys Bus Ride."
50. "Emir of Bedde Enjoys Bus Ride."
51. NAK/DDN/CDN/6/15/KADMIN/Ministry of Education, Visit of Hausa Women to UK (1952).
52. NAK/DDN/CDN/6/15/KADMIN/Ministry of Education, Visit of Hausa Women.
53. NAK/DDN/CDN/6/15/KADMIN/Ministry of Education, Visit of Hausa Women.
54. NAK/DDN/CDN/6/15/KADMIN/Ministry of Education, Visit of Hausa Women.
55. NAK/DDN/CDN/6/15/KADMIN/Ministry of Education, Visit of Hausa Women, Confidential Circular Number 51057/7/1952, From the civil secretary, Northern Region to The Resident Provinces, "Proposed Visit of Hausa Women to the United Kingdom in 1952."
56. Ibid.
57. NAK/ZariaProf 4427/S, 1: British Council Visits to UK (2), Study Course (3) Summer School 1947–57; NAK/DDN/CDN/6/15/KADMIN, Correspondence Number 38796/S.7/74, Ministry of Education and Social Welfare, Northern Region, to the financial secretary, Nigerian Secretariat, Lagos, Kaduna, September 20, 1954.
58. NAK/DDN/CDN/6/15/KADMIN, Correspondence Number 38796/S.7/74, Ministry of Education and Social Welfare, Northern Region, to the financial secretary, Nigerian Secretariat, Lagos, Kaduna, September 20, 1954.
59. Ibid.
60. NAK/Zaria 4427/S, 1: British Council Visits to UK (2), Study Course (3) Summer School 1947–57, Circular Number 38796/S.17/40, Ministry of Education and Social Welfare, Northern Region, Kaduna, May 10, 1954,. "British Study Tours, 1954."

61. NAK/Zaria 4427/S, 1: British Council Visits to UK (2), Study Course (3) Summer School 1947–57, Correspondence Number 266/S.1/10, From the Resident, Benue Province to the civil secretary, Northern Region, Kaduna, "Visit of Chief of Idoma to United Kingdom."
62. Correspondence Number 266/S.1/10, "Visit of Idoma Chief to United Kingdom."
63. Correspondence Number 266/S.1/10, "Visit of Idoma Chief to United Kingdom."
64. Correspondence Number 266/S.1/10, "Visit of Idoma Chief to United Kingdom."
65. NAK/Zaria 4427/S, 1: British Council Visits to UK (2), Study Course (3) Summer School 1947–57. British Council Report Number NIG/331/58, November, 1955, "Visit of Mr. Ogiri Oko, Paramount Chief of Idoma and Mr. Ogo Oko, his Secretary."
66. NAK/Zaria 4427/S, 1: British Council Visits to UK (2), Study Course (3) Summer School 1947–57. Correspondence Number 266/S.1/117A, March 22, 1955, From the Resident, Benue Province to the civil secretary, Northern Region, Kaduna, "Visit of Chief of Idoma to United Kingdom."
67. NAK/Zaria 4427/S, 1: British Council Visits to UK (2), Study Course (3) Summer School 1947–57, British Council Report Number NIG/331/58, "Visit of Mr. Ogiri Oko."
68. Ibid.
69. Parsons, *King Khama*, 4.
70. NAK/Zaria 4427/S, 1: British Council Visits to UK (2), Study Course (3) Summer School 1947–57, British Council Report Number NIG/331/58, "Visit of Mr. Ogiri Oko."
71. "Mr Ogiri Oko, Paramount Chief of the Idoma Tribe, Northern Nigeria," *Aberdeen Evening Express*, August 8, 1955, 5.
72. "Nostalgia: Special Visitor to the Gazette Offices," *Taunton Gazette*, September 15, 2016, 8.
73. Chief Ogiri Oko was the first to fill the position of Och'Idoma, which was created in 1944.
74. NAK/Zaria 4427/S, 1: British Council Visits to UK (2), Study Course (3) Summer School 1947–57. British Council Report Number NIG/331/58, "Visit of Mr. Ogiri Oko."
75. See Alvin Magid, *Men in the Middle: Leadership and Role Conflict in a Nigerian Society* (Teaneck, NJ: Holmes and Meier, 1976), 242–45; see also Moses Ochonu, "The Idoma Hope Rising Union and the Politics of Patriarchy and Ethnic Honor," *International Journal of African Historical Studies* 46, no. 2 (2013): 229–54, 237–38.
76. NAK/Zaria 4427/S, 1: British Council Visits to UK (2), Study Course (3) Summer School 1947–57. Correspondence Number 5337/74, The Provincial Office, Maiduguri to the civil secretary, Northern Region, Kaduna, June 1, 1955, "Visit of Emir of Dikwa to the United Kingdom."
77. NAK/Zaria 4427/S, 1: British Council Visits to UK (2), Study Course (3) Summer School 1947–57. Correspondence Number R. 658/247, From the civil secretary, Northern Provinces, to J. A. Reynolds Esq., c/o Division Office, Dikwa Division, Bama, June 1, 1955, "Visit of Emir of Dikwa to the United Kingdom."
78. NAK/Zaria 4427/S, 1: British Council Visits to UK (2), Study Course (3) Summer School 1947–57. Correspondence Number 4427/68, Zaria, October 5, 1950, Daga Babban Bature D. O Zaria zuwa ga Sarkin Kagoro "Tafiya Ingila."
79. NAK/Zaria 4427/S, 1: British Council Visits to UK (2), Study Course (3) Summer School 1947–57, The British Council in Association with Burton Manor College and the Corporation of Birkenhead, Study Tour of Northern Nigerian Native Authority Officials.
80. See George Amale Kwanashie, *The Making of the North in Nigeria, 1900–1960* (Kaduna, Nigeria: Arewa House, Ahmadu Bello University, 2002).

81. Kwanashie, *The Making of the North in Nigeria*.
82. Kwanashie, *The Making of the North in Nigeria*.
83. NAK/AGNN 1005/Vol. I, Agent-General Official Tours of the UK 1956–1963, British Council Report on Tour.
84. NAK/AGNN 1005/Vol. I, Agent-General Official Tours of the UK 1956–1963, British Council Report on Tour.
85. NAK/AGNN 1005/Vol. I, Agent-General Official Tours of the UK 1956–1963, British Council Report on Tour.
86. NAK/AGNN 1005/Vol. I, Ministry of Internal Affairs, Agent-General Official Tours of the UK 1956–1963, From commissioner of Northern Nigeria in London to the secretary to the governor, Governor's Office, Northern Region, Kaduna, "Visit to Belfast, Northern Ireland, October 15–20, 1956."
87. "Nigerian's Visit Tops A Full Diary," *Belfast Telegraph*, October 29, 1956, 16.
88. NAK/AGNN 1005/Vol. I, Ministry of Internal Affairs, Agent-General Official Tours of the UK 1956–1963, From commissioner of Northern Nigeria in London to the secretary to the governor, Governor's Office, Northern Region, Kaduna, "Visit to Belfast, Northern Ireland, October 15–20, 1956."
89. NAK/AGNN 1005/Vol. I, Ministry of Internal Affairs, Agent-General Official Tours of the UK 1956–1963, Correspondence from secretary to commissioner to Miss Logan, British Council Area Officer in Belfast, September 19, 1956, and October 9, 1956.
90. NAK/AS TO/British Council Tours 1959–1964, Programme of Visit to Belfast by The Commissioner for the Northern Region of Nigeria, Mallam Abbah Gana, April 27–30, 1959.
91. "Nigerian Visitor at the City Hall," *Northern Whig and Belfast Post*, April 29, 1959, 1.
92. For a discussion of northernization, see Isah Odidi and Baba Adam, "Sir Alhaji Ahmadu Bello, the Sardauna of Sokoto: The Seasons of a Man's Life," *Gamji*, accessed July 16, 2018, http://www.gamji.com/article5000/NEWS5668.htm. The article describes the policy thus: "The development strategy of the government under Ahmadu Bello may be summarized as trying to achieve regional parity through affirmative-action politics. This 'northernization policy' was the basic agenda for development, and reflected a profound belief on the part of Ahmadu Bello that northerners had the capability for rapid development, if given the opportunity." See also J.D.Y. Peel, "Two Northerners Contrasted in their Visions of Nigerian Unity," *Canadian Journal of African Studies* 22, no. 1 (1988): 144–48. Northernization authorized massive investments in several critical sectors with the express aim of catching up with Southern Nigeria socioeconomically but more immediately replacing southerners with northerners in the region's governmental, economic, and educational sectors.
93. NAK/AGNN 1005/Vol. I, Ministry of Internal Affairs; agent-general's Official Tours, 1956–1962.
94. NAK/AGNN 1005/Vol. I, Ministry of Internal Affairs; agent-general's Official Tours, 1956–1962.
95. NAK/AGNN 1005/Vol. I, Ministry of Internal Affairs; agent-general's Official Tours, 1956–1962.
96. NAK/AGNN 1005/Vol. I, Ministry of Internal Affairs; agent-general's Official Tours, 1956–1962.
97. See John Paden, *Ahmadu Bello, Sardauna of Sokoto: Values and Leadership in Nigeria* (London: Hodder and Stoughton, 1986), 97; Ahmadu Bello, *My Life* (Cambridge: Cambridge

University Press, 1962); and Kwasi Kwarteng, *Ghosts of Empire: Britain's Legacies in the Modern World* (New York: Public Affairs, 2011). The *Eton College Chronicle*'s story on the visit of the Northern Nigerian team to Eton states, "Fives in Northern Nigeria owes a considerable amount of its popularity, in the few towns where it can be played, to the Premier himself, who is still a keen player."

98. "Visit of Eton Fives Team to Northern Nigeria," *Eton College Chronicle*, February 3, 1961, 3251.

99. NAK/Prem. ASI/387/Vol. II, Visit of Northern Nigerian Eton Fives Team to England (1961), Correspondence from permanent secretary, Ministry of Education to the secretary to the premier, Premier's Office, Kaduna, and two others, "Visit of Northern Nigerian Eton Fives Team to England."

100. NAK/Prem. ASI/387/Vol. II, Visit of Northern Nigerian Eton Fives Team to England (1961), Correspondence from W. T. Gordon-Marshall to Sir Ahmadu Bello, premier of Northern Nigeria.

101. "Visit of Eton Fives Team to Northern Nigeria," 4760.

102. "Visit of Eton Fives Team to Northern Nigeria," 3251.

103. NAK/AGNN 1005/Vol. II, Ministry of Internal Affairs, Agent-General Official Tours to UK 1963–64, CDN. B.G., Proposed Link with London City Council, 1963–1964.

104. NAK/AGNN 1005/Vol. II, Ministry of Internal Affairs, Agent-General Official Tours to UK 1963–64, Correspondence from London City Council to Alhaji Isa Kaita, minister of education, Northern Nigerian Government, Kaduna, April 7, 1964.

105. NAK/AGNN 1005/Vol. II, Ministry of Internal Affairs, Agent-General Official Tours to UK 1963–64, Correspondence from London City Council to Alhaji Isa Kaita.

106. NAK/AGNN 1005/Vol. II, Ministry of Internal Affairs, Agent-General Official Tours to UK 1963–64, Memorandum by the minister of education, Proposed Educational Link with London City Council.

107. NAK/AGNN 1005/Vol. II, Ministry of Internal Affairs, Agent-General Official Tours to UK 1963–64, Memorandum by the minister of education, Proposed Educational Link with London City Council.

108. NAK/AGNN 1005/Vol. II, Ministry of Internal Affairs, Agent-General Official Tours to UK 1963–64, Memorandum by the minister of education, Proposed Educational Link with London City Council.

109. NAK/AGNN 1005/Vol. II, Ministry of Internal Affairs, Agent-General Official Tours to UK 1963–64, Memorandum by the minister of education, Proposed Educational Link with London City Council.

110. NAK/AGNN 1005/Vol. II, Ministry of Internal Affairs, Agent-General Official Tours to UK 1963–64, Correspondence from London City Council to Alhaji Isa Kaita.

111. NAK/AGNN 1005/Vol. II, Ministry of Internal Affairs, Agent-General Official Tours to UK 1963–64, Correspondence from London City Council to Alhaji Isa Kaita.

112. NAK/AGNN 1005/Vol. II, Ministry of Internal Affairs, Agent-General Official Tours to UK 1963–64, Correspondence from Alhaji Isa Kaita to Mrs. Marjorie McIntosh.

113. NAK/AGNN 1005/Vol. II, Ministry of Internal Affairs, Agent-General Official Tours to UK 1963–64, The British Council Report, Touring Note—Northern Ireland and Scotland.

114. NAK/AGNN 1005/Vol. II, Ministry of Internal Affairs, Agent-General Official Tours to UK 1963–64, The British Council Report, Touring Note—Northern Ireland and Scotland.

115. NAK/AGNN 1005/Vol. II, Ministry of Internal Affairs, Agent-General Official Tours to UK 1963–64, The British Council Report, Touring Note—Northern Ireland and Scotland.
116. Robert Longmore, *Notes on My Time in Northern Nigeria*, http://www.britishempire.co.uk/article/notesonmytimeinnorthernnigeria.htm (accessed June 8, 2020).
117. Longmore, *Notes on My Time in Northern Nigeria*.
118. Longmore, *Notes on My Time in Northern Nigeria*.

EPILOGUE

The Persistent, Evolving Fraternities of Empire

> Contact with [British] friends enriched my experience.
> —Dadasare Abdullahi

ON APRIL 15, 2017, JA'AFAR JA'AFAR, A NIGERIAN journalist and editor of the online newspaper *Daily Nigerian*, published a story in the paper criticizing various aspects of the stewardship of the then emir of Kano, Muhammadu Sanusi II.[1] The story was half op-ed and half investigative journalism. Its theme was financial recklessness. The respected emir was accused of mismanaging the funds of his emirate, including billions of naira he allegedly inherited from his predecessor when he became emir three years earlier. Because the emir had publicly criticized some policies of Kano state governor Dr. Umar Ganduje, many Nigerians viewed the series of exposés on the emir's financial management as payback sponsored by Ganduje's administration. In subsequent online commentaries, Ja'afar rejected accusations that he was being used to silence the vocal emir, who had publicly berated Northern Nigeria's elites for failing to educate the populace, marginalizing women, and creating a religious environment that he claimed was hostile to development, Western education, and other progressive trends in a globalizing world.

As the debate over the emir's conduct and his criticism of the governor raged and Ja'afar found himself in the middle of the controversy, it was clear that financial matters alone were not the crux of the accusation against the emir. Ja'afar's article framed Sanusi's alleged lack of financial discipline as part of a broader allegation that the emir had assaulted the established traditions of the emirate and the revered artifacts of the palace, which were integral to the emirate's identity and prestige. The op-ed accused the emir of abandoning centuries-old palace traditions and changing an emirate culture nurtured and cultivated over the reign of several emirs, including that of his grandfather, Emir Muhammadu Sanusi I (reigned 1954–63).

One of the emir's most egregious violations, Ja'afar alleged, was that he had sought to destroy the architectural symbol of the Kano Emirate's proud connections to the British imperial realm and the British Crown. Specifically, Ja'afar claimed that the emir had "demolished the century-old Soron Ingila, built by Emir Abbas and used by British colonialists as a base of administrative operations shortly after the colonial occupation of Kano in 1903."[2] Soron Ingila (England Chamber) was a wing of the palace preserved as a permanent spatial reminder of and monument to the emirate's connection to the history of British imperialism in Northern Nigeria. That wing of the palace had been showcased to visitors since colonial times.

Soron Ingila was originally the room in which Frederick Lugard worked after the military conquest of Kano in 1903 (see fig. Epi.1). It functioned as Lugard's office and military command center. The building symbolizes Kano's status as the first major British base in the Sokoto Caliphate, other than Zaria, which British troops and officials had used as a lynchpin for capturing Kano and other emirates farther north. In 1956, when Queen Elizabeth visited Kano along with the Duke of Edinburgh, she and her entourage were received in Soron Ingila, further ossifying the imperial imprimatur of that section of the Kano palace. Emir Sanusi I had the hall remodeled and spruced up for the occasion and proudly showed his guests around a palatial space dedicated to the memorialization of an imperial relationship forged in conflict and lubricated in transracial aristocratic solidarity. It was during the visit of the queen that the name of the chamber was officially changed from Soron Aljannar Duniya (chamber of earthly paradise), so named because it was decorated with exotic rugs, furniture, and accessories imported from Turkey, to Soron Ingila.

The existence of a wing in the Kano palace that memorializes the connections between Kano and the British imperial establishment in Northern Nigeria amplifies a major contention of this book. Northern Nigerian elites preserved and venerated the artifacts of their connections to imperial Britain during and after the end of formal colonization. Northern Nigerian aristocratic institutions and personalities, constructed in colonial historiography as suffering a terminal blow from the British conquest, continued to make seemingly contradictory but strategic symbolic and curatorial investments to announce, celebrate, and perpetuate their imperial connections as a way of boosting their prestige and enriching their traditions.

Arguments about a colonial assault on African cultural authenticity and traditions run counter to any suggestions that African subalterns drew on the symbols and institutions of the colonizer to enhance their traditions.

Figure Epi.1. Frederick Lugard working in England Hall inside the Kano emir's palace in 1903.

Such perspectives also ignore the permeability of tradition and the capacity of African aristocratic cultures to absorb foreign influences and adapt to new sociopolitical orders.[3] The conscious preservation of and appeals to colonial modernity and aristocratic connections embodied by Soron Ingila represent a certain vision of political legitimacy and authenticity. Tradition is conventionally defined in terms of what predated colonization, but in this context, tradition derives from colonial interactions, and modernity is accessed through a sophisticated interweaving of colonial and precolonial histories of the Kano Emirate.

For visual effect, Ja'afar added to his story a Royal Geographic Society photo showing Frederick Lugard at work in his office in Soron Ingila in 1903 (fig. Epi.1). It is difficult to determine why Ja'afar published the allegation of demolishing an important symbol of the emirate's prestige in a story about alleged financial recklessness. However, it is not far-fetched to conjecture that he included this seemingly tangential allegation to cast the emir as having a flippant attitude to the traditions of the emirate. This choice is instructive. It points to the continued resonance of British imperial references and symbols in the emirate's self-imagining and in the self-fashioning of its aristocrats. Knowing that the people of Kano regarded the palace and the histories of its various sections and wings as repositories of the emirate's history and prestige, Ja'afar's reportorial strategy may have aimed at presenting the emir as someone who was undermining rather than enhancing the prestige of the court.

Why did Ja'afar conflate the alleged demolition of Soron Ingila, a space in which the trauma of colonial conquest is physically etched, with a desecration of the palace? Why did he believe that an allegation that the emir had destroyed a key architectural relic of British colonization, an act that would, in a different context, be praised as a courageous gesture of decolonization, would resonate with his readers in Kano instead of making the emir a decolonial hero? The emir, through his spokesperson, predictably denied the allegation that he had demolished Soron Ingila, stating that he had only renovated it and made it better. The veracity of the allegation is up in the air, but that is not the pertinent issue. Rather, the issue is the existence of an elite consensus in Kano, which understands Soron Ingila as a sacred component of Kano royal identity, making outrage at the allegation of its destruction plausible and expected. That the allegation resonated in the first place and necessitated a public denial from Sanusi is revealing. That the emir felt a need to defend himself against an allegation that he destroyed a colonial relic in his palace speaks to the ways in which colonial material and nonmaterial signs and symbols have become imbricated in the "traditional" instruments and identities of Northern Nigerian emirates.

The Kano palace, in colonial times the richest and most populous Native Authority in Northern Nigeria, is steeped in a history of imperial connections and mutual courtship. The rulers of Kano consciously forged far-reaching symbolic ties to Britain and its institutions. For instance, in 1938, the emir of Kano, Abdullahi Bayero, and his council proposed spending some of the emirate's revenue to honor King Edward V, who had died three years earlier.[4] Under the proposal, the emirate would pay a British engraving firm, Bromsgrove Guild Limited, to engrave a bronze tablet with a portrait and text. The plaque was to be fixed on a tower built in Kano in 1936 as a memorial to the late king. As conceptualized by the rulers of Kano, the tablet would be engraved with the following text in English, Hausa, and Arabic: "This tower erected in 1936 is dedicated to the memory of His Majesty King George V during whose reign the Kano Emirate has prospered and progressed; thanks be to God."[5] Such effusive declarations of loyalty to and admiration for the regal institutions of Britain were fairly common in colonial times.

The Crown Agents for the Colonies approved Kano's King George V memorial proposal in August 1938. Eight months later, two contiguous Native Authorities, Gumel and Hadejia, wrote through the acting British resident of Kano Province to have similar memorials for the late English monarch approved.[6] The Gumel and Hadejia memorials would carry text similar to that on Kano's memorial tower, but in these two cases, the memorials were buildings, not towers, and they were built in 1937 and 1938 respectively.[7] Such gestures from Northern Nigeria's aristocratic institutions helped solidify their connections to their metropolitan counterparts. Material and symbolic memorializations of the relationship were preserved and expanded through spatiohistorical projects and rituals recalling a shared, if fraught, colonial history.

Kano's aristocracy, for whom the palace embodies the collective identity of a privileged elite, has mastered a colonial and postcolonial modernization template in which tradition can be conscripted to enrich modernity and vice versa. The resulting "invention of tradition" incorporates colonial histories, symbols, and relationships.[8] Even a spatial symbol connected to the tragic moment of colonial conquest was appropriated and reconfigured to serve the political end of fortifying the palace's postcolonial identity. So deep is this constructed imaginary of honor and aristocratic prestige that it rejects analysis and categories that cast colonial conquest and colonial domination as little more than a prolonged tragedy of humiliation and subordination. Postcolonial aristocracies' continued memorialization and lionization of imperial transactions point to the depth of imperial relationships that were cultivated and consummated through the touristic adventures of subaltern imperial allies, as well as Northern Nigerian aristocrats' conscious appropriation of the residues and signs of British adventures in Northern Nigeria. It is telling that the aristocrats of Kano and other emirates consider the material debris of colonization worth preserving.

Across Northern Nigeria, the desire of aristocratic institutions and actors to reaffirm their membership in the empire and identify with its symbols produced self-conscious projects of imperial solidarity that complicate the assumptions of nationalist historiography and simplistic notions of imperial loyalism. At the same time that emirates in Kano Province were installing memorials to King George V, Emir Muhammadu Dikko of Katsina was building his own monument to honor his friend Frederick Lugard. On November 28, 1938, during the Eid al-Fitr Muslim celebrations in Katsina, Dikko unveiled an inscribed bronze tablet commemorating

Lugard and his colonial troops entering Katsina in March 1903.⁹ Installed at Kofar Yandaka (Yandaka Gate), through which Lugard and his troops invaded the walled city, the tablet's inscription in Arabic and English reads: "Brigadier General Sir F. D Lugard, K.C.M. G, C.B, D. S. O., entered Katsina by this gate on the 28th March, 1903."¹⁰ Unveiling the tablet during a Muslim festival underscores Dikko's reconciliation of his Muslim devotions with his imperial connections. The most compelling testament to Dikko's dexterity in moving fluently between the registers of Islam and colonialism is his speech at the unveiling ceremony:

> We are here today to unveil this tablet in commemoration of the great European whose name is known to you, Governor Lugard, who entered Katsina town through this gate, the Kofar Yandaka, on Saturday, the 28th March, 1903. The gentleman in whose memory we are gathered here today is still living. I see him whenever I visit England, and we still talk about this country. He has been honored by the King of England with a peerage and is now called Lord Lugard. This tablet, which I am going to unveil, will strengthen the ties of friendship and loyalty between this country and England. My earnest prayers are that God gives him and us long life and good health, as it was that gentleman who made it possible for us to enter the British Empire, which has given us peace and prosperity. We pray that the Empire and His Majesty the King will long endure, Amen.¹¹

Dikko's speech connected the secular themes of empire to the religious idiom of offering Islamic prayers for the sustenance of that empire. The connection was then extended to Lugard, who brought the empire to Katsina—or, as Dikko put it, took Katsina into the empire. It is also noteworthy that Dikko deemed it necessary to tell his audience that he visited Lugard during his trips to Britain. This rhetorical maneuver posited the trips as a continuum, a never-ending colonial ritual that Dikko and other travelers continued to draw on for their political self-fashioning in their domains in Nigeria. Lugard was an iconic colonial figure in Northern Nigeria, and Dikko's confident assertion of their continuing friendship and visits on his trips to Britain was meant to underscore his intimate relationship with Lugard and, by extension, the citadel of colonial power in Britain. This reading is bolstered by the line about Lugard being knighted by the king. The homage to empire was completed by the effusive expression of gratitude to Lugard for initiating Katsina into Britain's imperial family—an imperial membership that Dikko claims had brought the emirate "peace and prosperity."

Lugard, who could not attend the ceremony in person, sent a message to Dikko through Secretary of State for Dominion Affairs Malcom MacDonald.

In the message, Lugard told Dikko that he was delighted that "by this tablet you desire to express your loyalty to His Majesty the King, and your gratitude for having been included in the British Empire."[12] Lugard praised Dikko as an astute leader who had "cooperated with" British colonial officers to bring "peace and prosperity" to Katsina. Dikko, Lugard wrote, had "led the way in every path of progress, and loyalty."[13]

Metropolitan travels and connections remained central to the commemorative colonial projects of Northern Nigerian aristocrats. When they were not traveling to Britain to reinforce their imperial symbolic capital, the aristocrats were invoking the signifiers of imperial power and prestige to underscore their membership in imperial political networks and enhance their prestige at home. Because such networks were transnational, travel and mobility between colony and metropole indexed gestures, invocations, and commemorations of imperial symbols. Furthermore, commemorative rituals sought to domesticate and appropriate colonial actors deemed capable of bestowing prestige by association and invocation.

Metropolitan Travel and the Colonial Sublime

British officials envisioned the travel of Northern Nigerian emirs, chiefs, and aristocrats to Britain as a pedagogical experience. The colonial architects of these trips expected the travelers to return and become evangelists for a certain idealized image of the empire as a redemptive, glorious entity worthy of support and sacrifice. The careful selection of metropolitan sites for inclusion in the travelers' itineraries, the management of their mobility within the metropolitan physical and sociopolitical space, and the focus group–like requests for feedback all contributed to a desire to obtain maximum awe from the subaltern visitors.

In the first chapter of his book *Signal and Noise*, anthropologist Brian Larkin executes an insightful cultural analysis of colonial infrastructures, seeing them as both instruments of state power and forms of cultural reorientation.[14] Both identities of colonial infrastructure, he argues, were interlinked, united by colonialists' desires to impress and hypnotize Nigerian colonial subjects into a reverence for colonial modernity and cultural forms expressed through dazzling technocultural objects. British colonizers constructed a causal connection between subaltern awe and subaltern loyalty, assuming that an overawed colonial subject was likely to remain in the orbit of the imperial system rather than seek exit from it. This colonial sublime, as Larkin calls it, provides a conceptual and theoretical crutch for what I have argued in this book regarding the motive behind the elaborate logistical infrastructure that British colonizers established or mobilized to support and encourage Northern Nigerian aristocrats' travel to the metropole.

Clearly, the purpose of this travel aligns with Larkin's insightful construct of the colonial sublime, a capacious idiom for capturing the ways colonizers sought to leverage the power and cultural resonance of technical objects and infrastructures to dazzle and manage the minds of their subjects. Mind management was an important structuring device for shaping the contours of colonial metropolitan travel, but it was not the only factor at work. The travel adventures of Northern Nigerian aristocrats were marked by other subtle gestures. Most notably, during these travels the colonial hierarchy was reversed since British officials, who would normally lord it over emirs, chiefs, and aristocrats, became guides to the visitors, performing obsequious tasks of hospitality and lavishly exhibiting the ethos of humility that one would consider appropriate for treasured guests.

Nigeria's traveling aristocrats were, of course, not passive or naive participants in this arena of performed hospitality. It is difficult to tell if they were seduced by the subliminal gestures of the guides and peoples they encountered in Britain. However, the aristocrats consciously seized the opportunity presented by these metropolitan rituals. They asserted themselves with dignity, unfazed by the unfamiliar grandeur and choreographed spectacle of metropolitan Britain. The travelers clearly imagined themselves in this temporal and spatial context as the equals if not superiors of their British guides, as some of the images in this volume attest. This is borne out by the bold demands the aristocrats made of their metropolitan interlocutors for additional logistical arrangements and the accommodation of personal predilections, religious faith, and curiosities.

The performance of imperial hospitality was matched if not surpassed by an elaborate and equally contrived performance of gratitude on the part of the visiting aristocrats. It is not that the two parties were oblivious to the performative character of the gestures on display. The performance was precisely the point; the colonial interactive space was one of mutual mimicry, emotional exchanges, and learned, reenacted protocols. Moreover, there was an ethos of masculine honor that underpinned these interactions. The mutual understanding in this relationship was that it was expected to be performed, in addition to being declared. Intended or not, these performances added depth, texture, and detail to the texts the travelers produced about their trips.

Dadasare Abdullahi, Colonial Victimhood, and Colonial Kinship

The chapters of this book examine the affective economy of colonial relationships through the lens of subaltern travel to imperial Britain. As argued throughout the book, these relationships flourished across the colonial racial divide, masking but also rupturing the familiar tensions of colonialism. These kinships—transactional and aristocratic—confound the traditional logic of empire as a consistently adversarial interaction. Unlikely emotional connections saturated the space of empire. These unusual emotional and affective itineraries point to the pragmatic ethos of transracial connection that is often neglected in colonial studies.

In many instances, Northern Nigerians who interacted with British actors in colonization had little leverage in choosing the terms of the interaction or rejecting engagement altogether. Yet in several cases, when the moment of colonial coercion had receded and Northern Nigerian colonial subjects had the opportunity to extricate themselves from the stranglehold of colonial oppressors, they not only balked but extended the relationship, embracing the oppressor with a passion that defies the familiar binaries of colonial rule. The pertinent question is thus not whether pathos and affection are emotional possibilities in the context of domination but, rather, what kind of affect is possible under such circumstances. I argue in this book that strategic, transactional affective connections were not only possible but indeed marked several facets of the relationship between colonizers and African aristocratic subalterns. Sometimes this situational relationship rested on the Africans' dexterity in taking strategic advantage of colonizers' self-appointed role as avuncular benefactors to Africans. At other times, Africans proactively cultivated European colonial interlocutors as allies in the quest to access privileges or enter exclusive networks.

It is possible to extend this argument further while bracketing it in attenuating and clarifying caveats. If colonization was a brutal political regime designed to inflict violence on the body of the colonized, which it often was, it is difficult to imagine predatory violence coexisting with or preceding rapprochement or social connection between the victim and the perpetrator. However, in rare situations—their extreme atypicality illustrating the possibilities of transracial relationships—colonial violence was coterminous with or triggered interracial intimacies that make plausible and understandable the argument about unusual affective relations in nonviolent and violent colonial encounters. It is precisely because this strange, rare colonial logic of affect and utilitarian fraternity challenges conventional understandings of colonization as a consistently adversarial encounter that the contradiction is worthy of exploration.

No story illustrates this paradoxical intimacy more than that of Hajiya Maimunatu Dadasare Abdullahi. Dadasare's biography disrupts several analytical bromides of colonial studies. Born in 1918 into a fairly privileged Fulani family in Gola District in Northeastern Adamawa Province, Dadasare and her immediate family moved to the town of Jambutu when she was a toddler. During a 1929 trip with a relative to Gola, the headquarters of Gola District, Dadasare was abducted on the orders of a European colonial official who desired the companionship of a young Fulani girl. Dadasare was eleven years old at the time. The colonial official, whom Dadasare described in her memoir as a man "who was feared by the people," had ordered a parade of three kidnapped pubescent Fulani girls. He then picked Dadasare from the lineup.

The abduction itself had been an elaborate conspiracy involving some of Dadasare's own relatives, including the older male cousin with whom she had traveled to Gola. Her unnamed British colonial abductor, a much older man, had an English wife and children in Britain. Dadasare effectively became a kidnapped child victim of her British colonial abductor, a traumatic experience compounded by the knowledge that members of her own family had participated in the kidnap plot and that her parents and other relatives were powerless to challenge her powerful colonial abductor and retrieve her.

Separated from her family, Dadasare was put under the watch of a member of her abductor's colonial staff named Sidiki, who "accompanied me everywhere to ensure that I did not run away."[15] Upon learning of Dadasare's kidnapping and forced appropriation by a European official, her family in Jambutu erupted in outrage, armed themselves, and threatened to invade Gola to rescue her. Some of her clan members persuaded the armed men to back down, preferring instead to instigate an inquiry. The colonial authorities at the provincial headquarters in Yola launched the inquiry, gathering information from multiple sources and then—as a final, anticlimactic end to the inquest—asked Dadasare herself if she wanted to return to her parents or stay with her abductor. Dadasare recounts in her memoir that each time she was asked, she stated her "earnest wish to return to my mother."[16] The inquiry was a sham; much to her horror, the investigating colonial authorities ordered Dadasare to remain with her abductor.

When it dawned on Dadasare that neither colonial judicial instruments nor her own family's determination to rescue her would secure her release, she took matters into her own hands, executing a daring escape in the middle of the day when her abductor and his African servants and policemen were napping. When her escape was discovered hours later, a search party on horseback was dispatched to recapture her. She spent the night in the cold, damp Adamawa bush as she made her way in the direction of her hometown of Jambutu. Meanwhile, her abductor's wrath ensured that no one was willing to take her in or aid her journey to freedom. Exhausted, hungry, and knowing she would endanger others if she sought help or would come to harm if she identified herself, she hid in the bushes between Gola and Jambutu until the colonial policemen in the search party found her and returned her to her abductor. She wrote in her memoir that her abductor "was furious and slapped me hard" and that she "got no second chance at running away."[17] Suspecting that her family had abetted Dadasare's attempted escape, her abductor relieved her uncle, the district head of Gola, of his chieftaincy. Her kinsmen and kinswomen, fearing more reprisals and "afraid that [their] daughters might suffer a fate similar to mine,"[18] fled the district. Dadasare's encounter with the capricious sexual predation of a colonial official had devastated her life and the lives of her family.

Shortly thereafter, her abductor was transferred to Ibbi in Benue Province, and she had to leave with him, increasing her geographical separation from her family and her natal roots. At Ibbi, she appears to have reluctantly accepted her fate and resolved to make the best of her situation. There, she interacted with a coterie of colonial officials and their wives, just as she had in Gola. She made peace with her role as her abductor's informal Nigerian "wife." She was being socialized, however problematically, into a new social community of colonizers. At Ibbi, Dadasare also met a colonial official with whom she would, in her own words, fall in love—she considered him "very attractive" and taught him Fulfulde, her mother tongue. Her new British colonial acquaintance "aroused" in her a "strong interest in Western music" that remained with her for the rest of her life.[19] But that chapter of the story was in the future.

Meanwhile, Dadasare's abductor impregnated her. She gave birth to a son, but shortly thereafter, her abductor's term of service was over, and he was asked to retire and return to England. He told Dadasare he was going to England on leave and would be back, asking her to go with her child to her mother until he returned. During the difficult boat journey on the Benue River back to Adamawa Province, she lost her son to malaria. She described the tragedy thus: "I spent the night at a small place called Bajabure. Mosquitoes swarmed everywhere. My baby was badly bitten all through the night. He quickly got malaria, and as he was not very strong and I could not get to a doctor, he died in my arms at Song on the way to Gola. I shall not dwell on this event. Only a mother can know how I felt."[20] Returning alone to Gola, Dadasare was traumatized and confused. Her kinsmen resolved to marry her to a local man, forbidding her to return to her abductor. This was designed to salvage the clan's honor, which had been violated by her abduction.

It is in this moment that we get a glimpse of Dadasare's transformation and the ironic connection she had forged with the colonial social network of her abductor. The tragic circumstances of her induction into the small, exclusive world of colonial officials and their wives notwithstanding, Dadasare had become part of that world and wanted to continue in it. When her kinsmen proposed that she marry a local man instead of returning to her abductor upon his return, she wrote in her memoir that "the prospect filled me with gloom."[21] Dadasare further wrote that she was no longer the "child who had been unscrupulously carried off" and that "something . . . had fundamentally changed and my horizon had widened."[22]

Why does Dadasare write about a fundamental shift in her aspirations and a widening of her horizons in the context of a traumatic abduction and sexual abuse by a British colonial figure? Why did she appear to treasure her exposure to new colonial worlds and her acquisition of new tastes and aspirations in the context of colonial trauma? Why does she ascribe this broadening of her horizons to the influence of her abductor and his friends? Was this, to use a modern psychological jargon, Stockholm syndrome? I suggest that the emotional economy at play and the anxieties and experiences unleashed by this moment of colonial trauma defy a one-dimensional moral commentary. I also argue that a strange logic of affect rooted in the utilitarian attractions of colonial association was in operation in Dadasare's thought processes as she navigated the colonial violence of abduction and rape and her new colonial social connections. For most people in a noncolonial situation, this would not present an emotional conflict, but as Frantz Fanon theorizes so compellingly, colonial situations present colonized subjectivities with a dual impulse of both aspirational attraction to and disdain for the colonial Other.[23] Colonialism, Fanon argues, was a fundamentally adversarial relational encounter suffused with mutual hatreds and resentments. However, it was not always this originary animosity, he argues, that dictated how colonial actors on different sides acted toward one another. At times, perhaps most times, it was the realization by both colonizers and the colonized that they could never measure up to their constructed notions of the Other, rather than an implacable hatred of the Other, that motivated acts of oppressive and liberatory violence.

In Fanon's psychoanalytic analysis, for white colonizers it was the realization that they could never compete against or measure up to their constructed ideal of virile, sexually unlimited black manhood, rather than innate hatred, that caused much violence on their part. Insecurity, masculine anxiety, and a sense of failed aspiration were the catalysts for violence. For Africans, revolutionary and vengeful violence were logical and legitimate, but Fanon argues that some of that violence, too, was a product not of an irreconcilable hatred for the white man and his vaunted modernity but of a failure to attain the white man's constructed and policed "civilizational" status and thus a failure to access the exclusive racial privileges of white colonizers. If failed colonial aspirations provoked resentment, the same aspirations also produced the opposite emotion: affect. In this context, aspirations to the imagined abilities and privileges of the Other activated mutual curiosities, and those curiosities, in turn, sometimes motivated unlikely relationships, explorations, and cross-racial connections.

For the colonized, in particular, the aspirational quest to attain the paradigmatic standards of the white colonizer was often complicated by resentment of those same standards, those same conditions of modernity. Even more traumatizing for colonial subjects was the realization that they could never fully attain the standards prescribed for them by colonial oppressors and that even if they did, they could never be fully accepted as equal humans but would instead be subjected to the colonizer's wrath, which was rooted in envy and the fragility of colonial whiteness. Yet the violence of the colonizer on the body of the colonized did not always trigger a total rejection of the colonial abuser. At times, it instead activated, on the part of colonized people, a more aggressive pursuit of acceptance in the world of the colonizer, seeing such acceptance as the ultimate protection against further abuse and perhaps as an opportunity for upward socioeconomic mobility. The elusive but visible privileges of colonial whiteness were an ever-present aspirational attraction for colonized people, even those who had been victims of egregious colonial violence.

In the case of Dadasare, the fact that the allure of colonial privilege and access competed with the desire to reject her abuser and return to her family speaks to this persistent dilemma of colonial victimhood: trauma competed with aspirational connection, with the latter concealing and perhaps mitigating the former. The story of Dadasare is a tragic illustration of gendered colonial violence. Instructively, it is also a story of how colonial violence and its lingering traumas could coexist with an aspirational relationship that brought colonial subjects ever deeper into the intimate networks of the colonized. Such connections were, as Florence Bernault argues, often transactional and situational, verging on strategic.[24] Whatever form they took, such colonial kinships forged in the crucible of violent and oppressive colonial encounters provide a window into the strange trajectories of imperial relationships analyzed in this book.

Colonial Stimulus and Unlikely Affections

In the face of this unspeakable manifestation of colonial evil, Dadasare found an emotional space to appreciate the social cachet conferred by her association with her abductor and his colonial friends. At stake was a strange colonial privilege Dadasare now enjoyed and wished to extend. Extending this social experience required the rejection of her kinsmen's effort to rescue her from her captor through marriage to a local Gola man, effectively rejecting an opportunity to regain the freedom she had longed for and had sought to claim during her failed escape. She was also spurning the chance to reintegrate with her family and natal community.

Around 1933, four years after her abduction, Dadasare found herself paradoxically wanting to rejoin her British colonial social group. Her wish was fulfilled when Rupert East, whom she had met and admired in her abductor's social circle, asked her to move in with him at his new station in Zaria. He was serving as an education officer and the inaugural director of the Translation Bureau in Zaria, which soon morphed into the Literature Bureau, the mass literacy and literary publishing division of the Northern Nigerian colonial bureaucracy discussed in chapter 1. Dadasare eagerly accepted the invitation, securing a chaperone, an escort, and a horse from the district head of Gola for the journey to Zaria, five hundred miles away. On her way to Zaria, the district head of Gola made one last attempt to persuade her to abort the journey and return to Gola to marry and settle down in her hometown by sending a message to her to return home. Instead, Dadasare sent home her chaperone and horseman, "engaged a new horseboy," and proceeded to Zaria to join Rupert East.[25]

Dadasare was well aware of the strangeness of her choice to rejoin the colonial network into which she had been violently inserted against her will. She explained her choice to move in with East, whom she affectionately called Jaumu-sare (Master of the House), in these philosophical words: "This time I did not have to be kidnapped. I had decided of my own free will to go to a man I felt I could love and who, I was sure, had real feeling for me. I do not propose, now or later, to expatiate on the personal relationship that grew up between Jaumu-sare and myself. Those who have deeply loved will not need to be told, and those who have not, could never understand."[26] In this passage, Dadasare wrestles with the strange and seemingly unlikely but not too uncommon attractions that colonized people, including those who personally experienced the brutality and injustice of the colonial system, felt toward colonial objects, processes, and personnel. It was not a forbidden emotion, but it was not a normative one, either. Yet many colonial subjects somehow found a way to compartmentalize the horrors of colonization and the allure and privileges of colonial kinship. Like many Northern Nigerian elite men and women who discovered that associating with the material cultures, symbols, and networks of the colonizer conferred privileges and prestige, Dadasare seemed to have found a way to deactivate the memories of her abduction in order to appreciate her privileged position as the informal wife of Rupert East—a position of instant visibility and prestige in the exclusively European circles of colonial urban society in Northern Nigeria.

Having resolved the seeming contradiction of embracing her abductor's colonial circle and their social predilections, Dadasare soon settled into a new life with her British partner. She writes in her memoirs that her years with East in Zaria were "happy days."[27] East found her a teacher who taught her how to read and write in the Roman alphabet. She also began to learn Hausa in the Roman script. Within a short time, Dadasare was reading Hausa books faster than her partner could secure them. She reports in her memoir that despite being a Muslim, her newfound love of reading led her to the Hausa version of the Bible, which she read three times.[28] East also hired an English teacher to help Dadasare improve her spoken and written English. She was soon reading English fiction. She became particularly fond of Jane Austen and developed what she called a passion for detective stories.

She also learned English social etiquette and mannerisms from interactions between East and his English colonial friends when they visited their home.

From the unpublished memoirs of H. P. Elliot, a friend of East's and a member of his colonial social circle who was a frequent guest at the home of the interracial couple, we learn that East, to the unease of his British colonial colleagues and friends, insisted on Dadasare being accepted and treated as his wife and like any other colonial spouse.[29] On her part, Dadasare enjoyed enormous prestige, power, and attention as the companion of a powerful colonial official—at least among the African workers who surrounded her lover at his job and among the African domestic staff. She hosted parties and dinners and played the role of a colonial wife while reveling in its privileges.

Subaltern Privilege and Colonial Connections

Dadasare kept a diary in which she recorded the mundane routines of her life in Zaria. Put in charge of the domestic realm, Dadasare relished the supervisory authority she had over servants, stating that she had learned "how to handle servants" from her parents.[30] She indicated that being in an intimate relationship with East was a fulfilling and rewarding period in her life, that living with East in Zaria enabled her to learn and do many things, and that she was "happy." This happiness, she wrote, ripened her as the sun "ripens the corn and sweetens the mango."[31] Furthermore, her relationship with East opened the door to other relationships and to an expansive network of social and professional associations in the British colonial metropole in the United Kingdom. Dadasare wrote that "contact with [East's] friends enriched my experience" and birthed friendships that "survived the upsets of later years."[32]

As discussed in chapter 1, Dadasare soon became a fixture in the Zaria literary and journalistic arena, inhabiting an emerging scene of intellectual activity in Northern Nigeria that had been dominated by men. In the 1940s, she launched her own literacy campaign in Zaria that targeted women in purdah, or Islamic seclusion. She then began volunteering for the Church Missionary Society (CMS) Mission Hospital in Wusasa, Zaria, where she started training to become a nurse. At the Wusasa Hospital, she helped in a medical outreach to Hausa Muslim women in purdah and mediated in dicey medical situations touching on taboos and honor in a Muslim society.

In 1949, Dadasare traveled to Oxford, England, on a yearlong course to train as a certified nurse. Her commentary on her time in England betrays an effusively favorable disposition toward the colonial metropole. She praised the British Council, which had sponsored her study trip. She writes in her memoir of making friends in Britain, meeting host families who became lifelong friends, and returning to England on holidays in the years after her study to stay with her new friends, whom she remembered with "deep affection."[33]

In 1951, Rupert East returned home to England, married the former Gaskiya Corporation worker and Belgian artist Jacqueline de Naeyer, and retired. Dadasare apparently sustained her relationship with East and his new family, writing in her memoir that she had a "wonderful relationship" with East's two children until their father passed away in 1975.[34] She visited the couple and their children at their home in Wiltshire, England, several times while on holiday in Britain. Furthermore, Dadasare remembers East in her memoir as a person she continued to cherish, someone who left a piece of himself in her and made her who she was—a high level of praise signifying the intimate sense of connection Dadasare felt for East and the colonial network he inducted her into. She credits her immersion in that British colonial world with constituting her own sense of personhood.

The Limits and Possibilities of Colonial Kinship

In August 1986, Dadasare passed away in circumstances many people in Zaria believe to have been suicide.[35] We may not know for certain how she died, but it is clear she had been under considerable psychological strain and had been nursing a broken heart due to Rupert East, whom she regarded as the love of her life, returning to Britain to marry someone else. Hence, this is not a story of a successful navigation of the colonial divide and colonial trauma, complete with a happy ending. In forging ties to East's British family, Dadasare tried to recreate a relationship that was probably no longer there, a colonial intimacy that was already in remission. A subaltern woman accustomed to colonial patronage had perhaps been reminded that she belonged with her African kinfolk in Zaria and not with East, his colonial friends, and his British metropolitan associates. Her life of happy colonial hybridity had been reset to conform to the familiar hierarchies and fault lines of colonialism.

Yet Dadasare's life is instructive for pointing to the possibilities of transracial connections in the vortex of colonial racial oppression. Dadasare had not been pushed to commit suicide by the trauma of her capture and enslavement, as tragic as that experience was, but ironically by a scorned desire to extend her association with Rupert East, who shared a direct filial, political, and ideological relationship with her abductor. Dadasare's biography is particularly illustrative of the possibility of transracial imperial affective association because of the tragic circumstances in which she encountered oppressive colonial power as well as the directness of her victimhood.

If Dadasare could momentarily transcend this originary moment of colonial trauma to cultivate and treasure the colonial networks around Rupert East, it becomes plausible to imagine that the Northern Nigerian colonial arena was a site of strange but understandable connections and interactive relationships between British officials and African subalterns. I do not, of course, discount the persistent presence of colonial violence and trauma and the overarching psychic encumbrance of colonial racism and hierarchies of power in subaltern lives that, on the surface, appear enamored and entwined with the personnel and accoutrements of colonialism. The life of Dadasare illustrates, with tragic intensity, these tropes of stricture and victimhood.[36] Simultaneously, however, her unusual biography suggests the possibility of pragmatic affective relationships in the interstices of colonization. Such relationships were lubricated and consolidated by the mobilities enabled by the logistics and technologies of empire.[37]

Dadasare's story dovetails, albeit imperfectly, with that of Emir Dikko, a key subject of this book. The foundational circumstances in which Emir Muhammadu Dikko of Katsina encountered Frederick Lugard are fairly similar to those in which Dadasare was introduced to her abductor. Both Africans had no choice and were forced or intimidated into a subordinate status in an imposed colonial relationship. However, like Dadasare, Dikko found ample room to maneuver once he had ingratiated himself with metropolitan and local colonial authorities and personnel. He secured enough leverage to cultivate productive and personally rewarding ties to British colonial officials. These types of relationships were enhanced by the location and locution of subalterns, their ability and willingness to travel to the metropole (thereby changing their location), and their skill in writing and speaking strategically about empire, the metropole, and their relationships with British imperial actors.

Metropolitan Explorations in the Late Colonial and Postcolonial Periods

In the late 1950s and 1960s, Britain continued to attract Northern Nigerian officials who sought to accelerate the pace of the region's development through education, training, and expatriate assistance (chap. 6). Courting British institutional patronage and assistance required travel to Britain. The culture of metropolitan travel so crucial to the self-making and modernist claims of the Northern Nigerian aristocracy became redefined as a diplomatic undertaking designed to attract British technological and technocratic assistance to the government of Northern Nigeria.

Private postcolonial metropolitan adventures continued beyond independence in 1960. Aristocrats, long socialized into a British modernist universe, continued to travel to the metropole for health reasons, business, vacations, and leisure. These postcolonial tourists designed their own itineraries and scripted their travel themselves. However, the fact that the postcolonial elite of Northern Nigeria were largely nurtured on government patronage and were, in fact, directly or indirectly a part of the governmental infrastructure meant that such visits often had a quasi-official texture. Visitors combined official and personal itineraries and explored familiar metropolitan leisure spaces while on official diplomatic or institutional tours.

Postcolonial African explorations of Britain may not connect directly to the elaborately planned tours of colonial times, but they, too, entailed the kind of interactions and connections characteristic of colonial tours. In the 1960s and 1970s, many of the affinities and friendships developed in colonial times endured. At that time, many British colonial officials had retired to various British towns, but they maintained correspondence with their aristocratic colonial interlocutors in Northern Nigeria. Many of the postcolonial tourists from Northern Nigeria had been auxiliary officials, emirs, and chiefs in the colonial administration and had interacted with the retired British colonial officials. The persistence of these colonial-era relationships into the postcolonial period is perhaps a subject worthy of a separate study. For our purposes here, it is sufficient to note that the postcolonial challenges of nation building and the imperative of catching up with a much more socioeconomically developed Southern Nigeria increased rather than reduced transatlantic interactions and mutual patronage between the new political elites of Northern Nigeria and the neoimperial government of the United Kingdom. At this time, Britain had assembled its former colonies into the Commonwealth of Nations to preserve ties between the former colonizer and the formerly colonized.

Furthermore, the mobile materialism that marked subaltern touristic adventures in colonial times, which saw travelers purchasing, amassing, and then bringing back imperial goods of various levels of technological sophistication, continued to characterize the Northern Nigerians who traveled to Britain after independence. Shopping was just as big an item in the itineraries of postcolonial metropolitan tourists as it had been for colonial-era tourists. The operative denominator remained: the allure of a technomodernity forged in the asymmetries of empire and the normative, paradigmatic centrality of British goods and infrastructures to ideas of development, progress, self-improvement, and aristocratic prestige.

Even today, Britain continues to exert its quasi-imperial seduction on the so-called children of empire. The old, unspoken connections and affinities that connected Nigerians emotionally and psychically to Britain in colonial times and underwrote the metropolitan travels and explorations of Nigerian elites still persist. The discernible difference is that the category of "metropole" became less territorial and less identifiable with a particular assemblage of peoples and cultures. At present, it is probably more accurate to designate a Euro-American metropolitan zone of cultural and technological modernity and contact than to insist on a geographically narrow British one.

An Ambivalent Gaze

In recent postcolonial times, scholars and observers have posited a growing ideological divide between Northern Nigeria and the interests and foreign policy priorities of the United States and the West in general. Contemporary Northern Nigeria is narrated as a hotbed of Islamist awakening and grassroots anti-Western political ferment and as a part of Nigeria where public opinion has soured on the Western ideals of liberalism and modernity. Some scholars have cautioned against self-fulfilling exaggerations of this ideological disconnect, but even these more restrained voices acknowledge that today's Northern Nigeria harbors a seemingly irreconcilable ideological resentment against Western values more broadly and American ideals in particular. They urge more constructive American sociopolitical and economic engagements with the region's leaders and peoples as a solution.[38]

It is true that public opinion at the Northern Nigerian grassroots level has grown suspicious and even hostile to professed Anglo-American ideals and that some members of today's Northern Nigerian political elite regard America and her British allies with suspicion and cynicism. In today's Northern Nigeria, Western products and interventions, no matter how neutral or humanitarian in conception, are sometimes regarded as part of a larger global war on Islam and Muslims and as part of a conspiracy to harm Muslims or tame their critique of the West. Perhaps the most eloquent testament to this anti-Western attitude is the recent response of the *talakawa* (rural and urban poor) to immunization in the region.[39] This attitude also manifests in a growing apathy to Western education. In addition, a portion of Northern Nigeria's Muslim population has become vulnerable to the influence of a few charismatic anti-American Islamists, leading to radicalization and a deepening resentment of the West. The number of extremist elements remains small in proportion to the population, but they are vocal and uncompromising, prompting some observers to erroneously claim the existence of a generic, historical anti-Western antipathy in the region.

Given the current disposition of these radicals to the West, their dominance of the public religious and ideological sphere, and their ability to sporadically set the rhetorical agenda for Muslim conversations about modernity and its material culture, it is tempting to assume that this discernible divide between Northern Nigeria and the West has always been present or that it is occasioned by a "clash of civilizations" confrontation.[40] Such a position is problematic. Northern Nigerian political elites have not always constructed their internal or external politics against perceived British—and, by extension, Western—values, but have instead embraced and adopted some Western influences as part of their sociopolitical repertoires as argued in this book. The ideological divergence visible today is thus fairly recent and needs to be put into its proper historical perspective in light of the intimate connections forged between Northern Nigerian aristocrats and British colonizers in past decades, as analyzed in the chapters of this book.

The travel-aided cultural appropriations that connected colony to metropole, Muslim Northern Nigerians to Christian Britons, and Africans to Europeans weaken claims of an endemic anti-Western angst in Northern Nigeria. In the 1950s and 1960s, traditional Northern Nigerian politicians had much more in common with Britain and America than the current strain in mutual perceptions may indicate. Today, Britain is rarely seen as the embodiment of Western modernity. That honor, dubious and problematic as it is, belongs to America. In the 1950s and 1960s, Northern Nigeria's Muslim political figures openly and proudly flaunted their American associations. They parlayed their travels to Britain and their appropriation of British modernity into new socioeconomic flirtations with America and its Western values.

Who were these political actors? In the late colonial and early postindependence period, there was little distinction between the traditional Islamic elite and the political elite. The two, as several scholars indicate, were one and the same.[41] Most of the Muslim politicians in the Northern People's Congress (NPC) were, in fact, traditional rulers, emirs, and title-holding aristocrats with immense legitimacy and sway over large numbers of Muslim subjects and followers at the grassroots level. Understandably, then, these elites were not drawn to radical anticolonial or decolonial political shifts. Instead, they cultivated a more sympathetic view of the political and colonial status quo and a more suspicious disposition to rapid change than was the case among the elites of Southern Nigeria.

In embracing America and her Western values, and in openly expressing admiration for America, the inheritor and embodiment of Britain's colonial and Anglo-Saxon modernist ideals, Northern Nigerian politicians and elites cultivated a large audience of *talakawa* Muslims (commoners) for America's declared cultural and political values. One could thus argue, albeit with copious qualifications, that in the 1950s and 1960s, there was a large field of socioeconomic, cultural, and political convergence between the United States and the West on one hand and Muslim Northern Nigeria on the other, a convergence that belies today's mutual antagonisms.

American Courtship and the Balewa Visit

Like Britain in colonial times, America courted Northern Nigerian aristocrats and emergent political elites. Cold War calculations undoubtedly dictated much of this outreach, but some of the courtship is attributable to the existing affinity of Northern Nigerian aristocrats to Western modernist values. It made them receptive targets of American Cold War cultural and political evangelism. Northern Nigerian aristocrats were themselves active seekers of Euro-American modernity and all the political and cultural values associated with it. They wanted to visit America, in their eyes the new metropole of modernity, to extend their repertoires. There was, in this

Figure Epi.2. US president John F. Kennedy welcomes Nigerian prime minister Tafawa Balewa to the White House, 1961.

sense, a convergence between the American desire to befriend Northern Nigerian Muslim leaders and the latter's desire to access Euro-American modernity through travel to the United States. It was in this spirit of mutual courtship that between July 25 and 28, 1961, Nigeria's first postindependence prime minister, Sir Abubakar Tafawa Balewa, toured the United States at the invitation of US president John F. Kennedy (fig. Epi.2). In addition to the usual official niceties of high-level diplomatic visits to Washington, the visit took Balewa to two of America's largest cities, New York and Chicago, and to the southern agricultural backwater of Knoxville, Tennessee.[42]

Upon his arrival in Washington, DC, Balewa, ever the confident orator, acknowledged the welcoming remarks of Vice President Lyndon Johnson, balanced his agbada, and expressed gratitude for his warm reception. Even as he basked in the attention of one of the world's superpowers, Balewa could not have anticipated the lavish courtship Washington would extend to him and his large entourage. Over the next three days, Balewa waved to crowds, signed autographs, hosted and attended presidential banquets, viewed the sights of high and low cultures, accepted an honorary doctorate from New York University, and shook many hands.

Balewa was less than a year in office and had considerably less nationalist and pan-African influence than Ghana's Kwame Nkrumah, who was in his fourth year as independent Ghana's leader. While conservative, Balewa's politics were not necessarily less anticolonial than Nkrumah's; this was, after all, a period of nationalist ferment in Africa in which elites were separated not by whether they were pro- or anticolonial but by their method of anticolonial nationalism. Yet Washington pulled out all the stops to give Balewa and his entourage a memorable reception. The reason was fairly simple: Balewa's nationalist politics was of the gentlemanly, benign, and negotiable kind, which Washington held up as a model of anticolonialism in Africa as it sought to balance its rhetorical support for decolonization with its anxieties about radical nationalist politics in Africa. In Balewa, Washington found the embodiment of a preferred, diplomatic nationalism. They saw a political partner who appreciated the political finesse of seeking independence without moving ideologically away from the West. For Americans, Balewa represented a postcolonial African elite whose politics were not driven by suspicion of Western cultures and markers of modernity but by admiration for them.

Balewa, moreover, had proved his mettle as a moderate political voice in late colonial and early independent Africa. A few months before the Washington visit, Balewa had presided over a meeting of the Monrovia Group of independent African countries in Lagos. United by their moderate and gradualist approach to African political solidarity, the Monrovia Group resolved to whittle down the unitary continental government agenda of Ghana and other members of the rival Casablanca Group. Balewa's role in crafting a moderate alternative to Kwame Nkrumah's vision of continental political unity, and in helping blunt its seemingly implacable inclination toward a complete break with colonial and Western institutions, endeared him to Washington—hence the extravagant embrace. Whatever the politics of the visit, however, it was Balewa's and other Northern Nigerian aristocrats' prior familiarity with Western modernity, politics, and cultural institutions, which came from decades of travel to Britain and interactions with British institutions and interlocutors, that facilitated the visit and made American outreach to them successful.

President Kennedy and other US leaders clearly sought to project Balewa as a model of responsible, moderate African leadership that could be relied on as a Western ally. President Kennedy's speech praising Balewa as a beacon of liberty for Nigeria and Africa, and as an epitome of a new United

States–Africa partnership, conveyed the depth of Washington's symbolic investments in Balewa. Balewa's pedigree in the conservative Muslim traditional culture of Northern Nigeria solidified his status in the minds of Washington's foreign-policy elite. In this period of ongoing nationalist struggle in Africa, the trifecta of Islamic devotion, political conservatism, and traditionalism did not invoke the specter of terrorism and anti-Western hostility that it would several decades later. Instead, it portrayed the bearer of these traits as a tolerant, restrained, and measured African, unwilling to give in to the politics of radical absolutes and anti-Western suspicion. The cultural interactions between Northern Nigerian aristocrats and British metropolitan culture in the prior decades and the relationships that developed therefrom served as platforms on which Cold War–era connections between Northern Nigerian leaders and Western governments were forged.

Balewa cleverly used the opportunity of the visit and the platforms of his address to Congress and the National Press Club to push the United States to put more pressure on European allies still holding colonies in Africa. He paid discursive homage to America's revolutionary tradition, employing flattery as a strategy for sending a powerful message about the lingering necessity for liberation in many parts of Africa. Balewa's self-positioning throughout the trip indicated his desire to be seen by his Western interlocutors as a pro-Western Muslim leader capable of reconciling the pressures of Northern Nigerian Muslim culture and those of a neocolonial Euro-American modernity. Northern Nigeria was a fertile political ground for the kind of elite culture, nationalist temperament, and governing technique Balewa embodied. The orthodox Islamic traditions of the Hausaphone and Bornuan regions of Northern Nigeria portrayed for American officialdom a calm, anticommunist, aristocratic culture treasured for its ability to put a lid on radical political and religious tendencies. The aristocratic alliance forged through Northern Nigerian elites' metropolitan travel mutated to accommodate the new relationship with America.

American interest in projecting Balewa and his brand of nationalist politics converged with Balewa's own embrace of Western affection as a bulwark against domestic political opposition. Balewa, Ahmadu Bello, and other stalwarts of the NPC saw recognition by the West as a counterweight to the oppositional politics of the NPC's rivals—Obafemi Awolowo's Action Group (AG), Nnamdi Azikiwe's National Council of Nigerian Citizens (NCNC), the United Middle Belt Congress (UMBC), and the avowedly leftist Northern Elements Progressive Union (NEPU). Balewa deftly used the platform of his Washington visit to project political inevitability and statesmanship to the world and in the process masked and diluted the tenuousness of his position at home. Not only did Washington and Balewa share a common philosophy of political restraint and a concomitant suspicion of those advocating radical, revolutionary change, but they also enjoyed the fortuitous convergence of their interests. Balewa's domestic political anxieties receded as the West showered him with praise and recognition for his skillful integration of modernity into a traditional Muslim cultural formation. This caused his rivals to accept his legitimacy, however grudgingly. Washington, for its part, used the visit to communicate a key, disputed foreign policy message: that it was friendly to African nationalism and self-determination. It was the intersection of these two priorities that made the visit into a historical event.

At that time, the familiar, sensationalized anxieties about Northern Nigeria's vulnerability to radical Islam and antimodern, anti-Western sentiment were fifty years away, as was concern about symbiotic connections between some Northern Nigerian Islamic figures and the bastions of political Islam in the Middle East, namely Iran and Saudi Arabia. As a result, and in the context of an escalating cold war, the embryonic political and religious culture of Islamic Northern Nigeria that Balewa embodied held a special appeal for American and other Western governments. American (and Canadian) officials had identified this locus of anticommunist political counterculture in Northern Nigeria several years before Nigeria's political independence in 1960, before Balewa became prime minister and before he visited the United States in his official capacity as the leader of Africa's most populous independent nation. Tafawa Balewa's visit was, in fact, the culmination of several official and unofficial embraces extended to members of Northern Nigeria's political elite, whose conservative political ideology and openness to capitalist modernity made them candidates for diplomatic courtship by the United States. Balewa himself had visited the United States in 1956 as a guest of the US government, which was keen to display its affinity for the proindependence movement in Africa even as critics claimed it was too lenient on its NATO European colonizer allies.

The congruence of American political aristocracy and the dominant aristocratic political tendency in Northern Nigeria was not as odd and unexpected as it might seem today. Northern Nigerian political leaders saw in the United States a model for meshing nationalist instincts with a conservative political disposition that was civil and restrained yet progressive and modern. This admiration for American political values was far from naive or uncritical; Northern Nigerian political tourists to the United States did not hesitate to highlight the imperfections of their host nation just as they had done when visiting Britain in earlier years. Nonetheless, politically influential figures in the dominant NPC saw a reflection of their ideological and political temperament in American statecraft. Whether or not this was an overly idealized perception, Northern Nigerian Muslim officials looked to America and other members of the Western Cold War alliance for what they saw as the right mix of secular political culture, modernity, reverence for divinity and providence, and political restraint in the pursuit of the common good. In the run-up to the 1959 independence elections in Nigeria, Tafawa Balewa, flanked by his political mentor, Alhaji Ahmadu Bello, the sardauna of Sokoto, declared proudly that he was heartened by the American interest in Nigeria's political affairs and hoped the interest would increase and be sustained.[43] The emotional investment was mutual; the US television network CBS favorably portrayed the leading political figures of the North—Balewa, Ahmadu Bello, and Maitama Sule— in its coverage of the elections.[44]

The two political formations converged on their common distrust of radical politics, belief in gradualism as a less disruptive vision of change, suspicion of socialism as an overly secular political ideology, and belief in the material cultures and infrastructures of modernity. These convergences made Northern Nigerian politicians preferred candidates for US governmental outreach in the form of invited and sponsored official visits. It also made the United States a politically safe destination for Northern Nigerian politicians. Those who were eager to embrace Western modernity but did not want the liability of being accused of excessive dalliance with British colonial oppressors—as Britain was often described in the anticolonial rhetoric of Nigerian nationalists—thronged to America.

Most of the political travelers to North America reveled in the hospitality extended to them, but it is also clear that they were personally curious, making extensive mental and written notes that would constitute the crux of their subsequent narratives on their experiences. Half sociopolitical travelogues, half commentary, the travel accounts of these travelers reveal as much about their unique lenses into their host societies as they do about how their own domestic politics of status and patronage inflected the content of the writings and the audience they imagined. The travelers were mostly politicians, but a few politically connected Northern Nigerian intellectuals outside the world of politics were courted by American institutions as part of the broader outreach to moderate molders of political opinion in African states on the verge of independence.[45] This trans-Atlantic traffic between Nigeria and the broader Western world continued and intensified in correspondence with the push and pull of the Cold War and as regional postcolonial elites traversed and expanded the routes of tourism, adventure, and exploration opened by earlier generations of aristocrats and privileged subalterns.

Notes

1. Ja'afar Ja'afar, "Another Word for the Emir," *Daily Nigerian*, April 16, 2017, https://dailynigerian.com/another-word-for-emir-sanusi-by-jaafar-jaafar/.
2. Ja'afar, "Another Word for the Emir."
3. Ranger, "The Invention of Tradition in Colonial Africa."
4. British National Archives, CO 583/243/5, Memorial to H.M King George V at Kano.
5. CO 583/243/5, Memorial to H.M King George V at Kano, Enclosed tablet design.
6. British National Archives, CO 583/243/16, Memorial to H.M. King George V at Gumel and Hadejia (Acting Resident, Kano Province, to The Crown Agents for the Colonies, London).
7. CO 583/243/16, Memorial to H.M. King George V at Gumel and Hadejia.
8. See Ranger, "The Invention of Tradition in Colonial Africa."
9. British National Archives, CO 583/243/12, Commemorative Tablet to Lord Lugard in Katsina.
10. CO 583/243/12, Commemorative Tablet to Lord Lugard in Katsina.
11. CO 583/243/12, Commemorative Tablet to Lord Lugard in Katsina.
12. CO 583/243/12, Commemorative Tablet to Lord Lugard in Katsina, Frederick Lugard to Emir Dikko.
13. CO 583/243/12, Commemorative Tablet to Lord Lugard in Katsina, Frederick Lugard to Emir Dikko.
14. Brian Larkin, *Signal and Noise: Media, Infrastructure, and Urban Culture in Nigeria* (Durham, NC: Duke University Press, 2008), chap. 1.
15. Hajiya Dadasare Abdullahi, *Mama Hajia*, unpublished memoir, Rhodes House, Oxford, MSS. Afr. s. 1832, 16.
16. Ibid., 17.
17. Ibid.
18. Ibid., 18.
19. Ibid., 18.
20. Ibid., 20.
21. Ibid.
22. Ibid., 21.

23. See Fanon, *The Wretched of the Earth*; *Black Skin, White Masks*, translated by C. L. Markman (New York: Grove, 1952).
24. Bernault, *Colonial Transactions*.
25. Abdullahi, *Mama Hajia*, 22.
26. Abdullahi, *Mama Hajia*, 21.
27. Abdullahi, *Mama Hajia*, 27.
28. Abdullahi, *Mama Hajia*, 23.
29. Rhodes House, MSS. Afr. s. 1838, "H. P. Elliot's Reminiscences of Nigeria; Graham Furniss, "On Engendering Liberal Values in the Nigerian Colonial State: The Idea behind the Gaskiya Corporation," *Journal of Imperial and Commonwealth History* 39, no. 1 (March 2011): 95–119.
30. Abdullahi, *Mama Hajia*, 23.
31. Abdullahi, *Mama Hajia*, 27.
32. Abdullahi, *Mama Hajia*, 27.
33. Abdullahi, *Mama Hajia*, 30.
34. Abdullahi, *Mama Hajia*, 28.
35. Dadasare had attempted suicide two weeks prior to her death and had hinted to her household help her intention to commit suicide a day before she was found drowned in a well at her home in Zaria. See Aliyah Adamu Ahmad, "Dadasare: A Woman of Substance in Colonial Northern Nigeria," unpublished paper cited with author's permission, 13.
36. Some of my informants believe that Dadasare died of heartbreak and the unresolved psychic injury of being betrayed and jilted by the one colonial official she had trusted and loved in the forlorn hope of using him as a crutch to heal from her childhood trauma. In a personal communication (October 19, 2017), Dr. Mairo Mandara stated that Dadasare's rumored suicide stemmed from this unaddressed trauma that she carried from childhood and that intensified when her romantic relationship with Rupert East ended.
37. For a broader study of the ways that instruments of mobility—the use of automobiles and, particularly, commercial aviation—facilitated movement within and between nodes in the British Empire, see Chandra D. Bhimull, *Empire in the Air: Airline Travel and the African Diaspora* (New York: New York University Press, 2017).
38. Jean Herskovits, "In Nigeria, Boko Haram Is Not the Problem," *New York Times*, January 2, 2012.
39. See Elisha P. Renne, *The Politics of Polio in Northern Nigeria* (Bloomington: Indiana University Press, 2010).
40. Samuel P. Huttington, *The Clash of Civilizations and the Remaking of World Order* (New York: Simon and Schuster, 1998).
41. Jonathan Reynolds, *The Time of Politics (Zamanin Siyasa): Islam and the Politics of Legitimacy in Northern Nigeria, 1956–1966*, 2nd ed. (Lanham, MD: University Press of America, 1999); Billy Dudley, *Parties and Politics in Northern Nigeria* (London: Frank Cass, 1968); Kane, *Muslim Modernity in Postcolonial Nigeria*.
42. John F. Kennedy Presidential Library and Museum, *America Welcomes Prime Minister Abubakar Balewa of Nigeria Balewa, July 1961: 25–28*, https://www.jfklibrary.org/asset-viewer/archives/USG/USG-01-H/USG-01-H.
43. "Freedom Explosion 2," A CBS Report on the 1963 Nigerian National Elections, December 13, 2011, YouTube video, 6:02, http://www.youtube.com/watch?v=y7wJfQ3_wJw&feature=related.

44. "Freedom Explosion 2."

45. Members of the Northern Nigerian elite traveled to the United States in the late 1950s and early 1960s, documenting their observasions in Northern Nigeria's English language newspaper, *The Nigerian Citizen*. See for instance, J. H. Cindo, "My Impressions of America (3): Some Facts and Figures about the Island of Puerto Rico," *Nigerian Citizen*, November 18, 1959; and "A Northerner's Impressions of America: Hospitable but Curious, Colour Discrimination Still Exists as Told to Philip Ohiare, *Citizen* Staff Reporter in Kano," *Nigerian Citizen*, September 3, 1960.

BIBLIOGRAPHY

Archives (Nigeria and Britain)

Arewa House Archive, 1/37/291.
  Confidential Report on the Visit of the Sultan of Sokoto and the Emirs of Gwandu and Kano to England, November 26, 1934.
British National Archives, CO 583/243/5. Memorial to H.M. King George V at Kano.
British National Archives, CO 583/243/16. Memorial to H.M. King George V at Gumel and Hadejia.
British National Archives, CO 583/223/1. Visit of the Emir of Katsina 1937.
British National Archives, FO 141/699/5. From the Residency in Cairo, "Visit of the Emir of Katsina."
British National Archives, FO 141/699/5. From H.E. the Governor of the Sudan, dispatch # 69 (18-3-1933), Pilgrimage of the Emir of Katsina (of Nigeria) via Sudan.
British National Archives, CO 383/187/11. Emir of Katsina, Proposed Pigrimage to Mecca and Visit to England.
British National Archives, CO 583/243/21. Visits of Native Chiefs.
British National Archives, FO 141/699/5. Katsina (Emir of).
British National Archives, CO 583/243/12. Commemmorative Tablet to Lord Lugard in Katsina.
British National Archives, CO 583/223/1. Visit of the Emir of Katsina.
British National Archives, CO 583/174/3. Pilgrimage to Mecca and Visit to England by Attach [sic] of Igbirra.
Lugard, Frederick. *Collected Annual Reports of Northern Nigeria, 1900–1911*. Lagos, Nigeria: His Majesty's Stationary Office.
NAK/AGNN 1005/Vol. I.
NAK/AGNN 1005/Vol. II.
  CDN. B.G.
NAK/AS TO/British Council Tours 1959–1964.
NAK/DDN/CDN/6/15/KADMIN/Ministry of Education, Visit of Hausa Women to UK (1952).
  Correspondence Number 266/S.1/10.
  Correspondence Number 38796/S.7/74, Ministry of Education and Social Welfare, Northern Region, to the financial secretary, Nigerian Secretariat, Lagos, Kaduna, September 20, 1954.
  Circular Number 38796/S.17/40.
  Confidential Circular Number 51057/7/1952.
NAK/Kanoprof/BCC/5.
NAK/Katprof.
  Lecture by Wakilin Gona, Daura, September 5, 1952.
  Circular 38796/s.3/5.

NAK/Katprof 110/Vol. I.
> Number 14827/5.
> Correspondence Number 14827/30.
> Number 68.
> Number 14827/50.
> Number 235 (L667/667/405).
> Number 171.
> Memo Ref FED/M. No. 4.
> Memo Number 74/146.

NAK/Katprof 110/Vol. II.
> Number 177.
> Number 180.
> Number 151.

NAK/Katprof 496/Vol. II. Emir of Katsina—General Correspondence 1941-52. Circular Number 496/540.

NAK/KatProf 1951. Diary of Journey to England and Mecca 1921. *Dikko's Journal*.

NAK/Katprof 3381/14/178-5, Emir of Katsina's visit to India.

NAK/KatProf/HIS/37. A History of Katsina Polo Club 1925-39.

NAK/Lokoprof Memo 251/1925/Vol. II/93. Memo on Visit to England by Attah of Igbirra by Resident, Kabba Province, Mr. H. B. James.

NAK/Lokoprof, File 251/1925/Vol. I. Memo 1143/83.

NAK/Prem. ASI/387/Vol. II.

NAK/ZariaProf 4427/S.
> 1: British Council Visits to UK (2), Study Course (3) Summer School, 1947-57.
> Correspondence Number 4427/29.
> Memo Number 38796/s.3/156.
> Circular Number 266/1949; 38796/s.5.
> Circular Number 38796/s.3/213. From secretary, Northern Provinces to the Resident, Zaria Province, "Short Visits to the United Kingdom 1949, Sponsored by the British Council."
> Circular Number 38796/s.3/228.
> Circular Number 38796/S.9/12.
> Circular Number 7084/24.
> File 5158, "Visit to the UK by the Emir of Ilorin"
> Circular Number 46103/51, October 2, 1951), from the secretary, Northern Provinces to the Residents of multiple provinces.

NAK/ZariaProf 4427/S.1.
> British Council Report Number NIG/331/58, November, 1955, "Visit of Mr. Ogiri Oko, Paramount Chief of Idoma and Mr. Ogo Oko, his Secretary."
> Memo Number NAK/Zariaprof 25323/3
> Correspondence Number 266/S.1/117A.
> Correspondence Number 5337/74, the Provincial Office, Maiduguri to the civil secretary, Northern Region, Kaduna, June 1, 1955, "Visit of Emir of Dikwa to the United Kingdom."
> Correspondence Number R. 658/247, from the civil secretary, Northern Provinces, to J. A. Reynolds Esq., c/o Division Office, Dikwa Division, Bama, June 1, 1955, "Visit of Emir of Dikwa to the United Kingdom."

Correspondence Number 4427/68, Daga Babban Bature D. O Zaria zuwa ga Sarkin Kagoro "Tafiya Ingila."
NAK/ZariaProf 4427/19.
Memo Number 25323/3.
M. T. Safana Archival Collection, Katsina, Nigeria.
KSHCB R.532 (Government Service: Promotion of Africans, Northernisation, Etc.).
Rhodes House, MSS. Afr. s. 597. Rupert East to Sir Arthur Richards.
Rhodes House, MSS Afr. s. 1403, Fol. 1. A Weekend in Paris, 1951.
Rhodes House, Oxford, MSS. Afr. s. 1832, 16. Hajia Dada Sare Abdullahi, *Mama Hajia*, unpublished memoir.
Rhodes House, MSS. Afr. s. 1838. "H. P. Elliot's Reminiscences of Nigeria."
Rhodes House, MSS. Afr. s. 1933, Bashir Tukur, "Britain as I Saw It," *Barewa* (June 1960): 9–11.
Rhodes House Archives, MSS. Afr. s. 8839. Hans Vischer to E. L. Mort, August 27, 1943.

American Archives and Press

Central Broadcasting Station (CBS)
New York Times
Special Collections Research Center, Henry Madden Library, California State University, Fresno.
John F. Kennedy Presidential Library and Museum. *America Welcomes Prime Minister Abubakar Balewa of Nigeria Balewa, July 1961: 25-28.* https://www.jfklibrary.org/asset-viewer/archives/USG/USG-01-H/USG-01-H.

British Newspapers, Magazines, and Press

Aberdeen Evening Express
Aberdeen Press and Journal
Birmingham Gazette
Birmingham Mail
Bristol Mirror
County Gazette
Courier and Advertiser
Daily Record and Mail
Diss Express and Norfolk and Suffolk Journal
Dundee Courier
Dundee Evening Telegraph
Edinburgh Evening News
Eton College Chronicle
Gloucestershire Echo
Hampshire Telegraph
Illustrated London News
Illustrated Sporting and Dramatic News
Lancashire Daily Post
Lancashire Evening Post
Leeds Intelligencer
Leeds Mercury

Liverpool Echo
Merthyr Express
Montrose Standard
Newscastle Daily Chronicle
Northern Whig and Belfast Post
Portsmouth Evening News
Scotsman
Sheffield Daily
The Sphere
Sunderland Echo and Shipping Gazette
Surrey Advertizer
Tatler
Taunton Courier: Bristol and Exeter Journal and Western Advertiser
Taunton Gazette
Western Daily Press
Western Mail
Western Morning News and Daily Gazette
Yorkshire Post

Nigerian Newspapers, Magazines, and Press

Barewa Magazine
Daily Comet
Daily Nigerian
Gamji.com
Gaskiya ta fi Kwabo
Nigerian Citizen

Videos

British Pathe News Agency. "The King with African Delegates to Conference (1948)." April 13, 2014. YouTube video, 1:23. https://www.youtube.com/watch?v=WeCMcxSCpjA.
John F. Kennedy Presidential Library and Museum. "America Welcomes Prime Minister Abubakar Balewa of Nigeria Balewa, July 25–28 1961." https://www.jfklibrary.org/asset-viewer/archives/USG/USG-01-H/USG-01-H.
"Freedom Explosion 2," A CBS Report on the 1963 Nigerian National Elections. December 13, 2011. YouTube video, 6:02, http://www.youtube.com/watch?v=y7wJfQ3_wJw&feature=related.

Interviews and Personal Communication

Binta, Hajiya, at Jibia, November 6, 2015.
Idris, Alhaji, grandson of Nagogo, fifty-four years, at Filin Sami Quarters, Katsina, December 29, 2015.
Jibril, Musa A., May 11, 2020.
Mandara, Mairo, October 19, 2017.
Mustapha, Munir, September 3, 2015.

Rakiya, Hajiya, Dikko's granddaughter, April 17, 2015.
Titi, Binta hajiya, Dikko's granddaughter, ninety-one years, April 16, 2015.
Usman, Dan Madamin Katsina, district head of Daddara, grandson of Dikko, fifty-five years, December 27, 2015.
Usman, Kabir Hassan, great-grandson of Emir Dikko, forty-four years, at Kofar Soro, Emir's Palace, April 18, 2015.
'Yan Turai, Hajiya Hassatu, Nagogo's daughter, at Katsina, April 17, 2015.
Yarkawu, Hajiya Mairo, wife of late Sarkin Maska Shehu II and granddaughter of Dikko, eighty-four years, at Kaduna, April 8, 2015.

Published Primary Sources

Burton, Richard. *Lake Regions of Central Africa: A Picture of Exploration*. Vols. 1 and 2. London: Longman, Green, Longman, and Roberts, 1860.
Denham, F.R.N., Hugh Clapperton, and Walter Oudney. *Narratives of Travels and Discoveries in Northern and Central Africa in the Years 1822, 1823, and 1824*. 3rd ed. London: John Murray, 1831.
Herskovits, Jean. "In Nigeria, Boko Haram Is Not the Problem," *New York Times*, January 2, 2012.
Imam, Abubakar. *Ruwan Bagaja*. Zaria, Nigeria: NORLA, 1935, 1957.
———. *Tafiya Mabudin Ilimi* [Travel is the gateway to knowledge]. Zaria, Nigeria: Gaskiya Corporation, 1944.
Kagara, Malam Bello. *Sarkin Katsina Alhaji Muhammadu Dikko, C.B.E., 1865–1944*. Zaria, Nigeria: Northern Nigerian Publishing Company, 1951.
Kingsley, May H. *Travels in West Africa: Congo Francais, Corisco, and Cameroons*. London: MacMillan, 1897.
Laird, MacGreggor, and R.A.K. Oldfield. *Narrative of an Expedition into the Interior of Africa by the River Niger in the Steam-Vessels Quorra and Alburka in 1832, 1833, and 1834*. London: Richard Bentley, 1837.
Lander, Richard. *Records of Captain Clapperton's Last Expedition to Africa*. Vol. 2. London: Henry Colburn and Richard Bentley, 1830.
Livingstone, David. *The Last Journals of David Livingstone, in Central Africa, from Eighteen Hundred and Sixty-Five to His Death, Continued by a Narrative of His Last Moments and Sufferings, Obtained from His Faithful Servants, Chuma and Susi, by Horace Waller, F.R.G.S., Rector of Twywell, Northampton*. New York: Harper and Brothers, 1875.
Longmore, Robert. *Notes on My Time in Northern Nigeria*. http://www.britishempire.co.uk/article/notesonmytimeinnorthernnigeria.htm. Accessed June 8, 2020.
Lugard, Frederick. *The Dual Mandate in British Tropical Africa*. Oxford: Frank Cass, 1922.
Ndayako, Muhammadu. *Tafiyan Etsu Nupe Ingila* [Etsu Nupe's travel to England]. Zaria, Nigeria: Gaskiya Corporation, 1954.
Odidi, Isah, and Baba Adam, "Sir Alhaji Ahmadu Bello, the Sardauna of Sokoto: The Seasons of a Man's Life," *Gamji.com*: http://www.gamji.com/article5000/NEWS5668.htm. Accessed July 16, 2018.
Palmer, H. R. Preface to *Sarkin Katsina Muhammadu Dikko, C.B.E., 1865–1944*, by Bello Kagara. Zaria, Nigeria: Gaskiya Corporation, 1951.
Reis, João, and Armando Pedro Muiuane, *Datas e documentos da história da FRELIMO*. Lourenço Marques, Mozambique: Imprensa Nacional de Moçambique, 1975.

Speke, John. *Journal of the Discovery of the Source of the Nile.* New York: Harper and Brothers, 1964.

Stanley, Henry Morton. *In Darkest Africa.* Vols. 1 and 2. New York: Charles Scribner's Sons, 1890.

Temple, Charles. *Native Races and Their Rulers: Sketches and Studies of Official Life and Administrative Problems in Nigeria.* Cape Town, South Africa: Argus, 1918.

Secondary Sources

Adamu, Abadallah Uba. "Divergent Similarities: Culture, Globalization and Hausa Creative and Performing Arts." A lead paper presented at the International Conference on Literature in Northern Nigeria, Department of English and French, Bayero University, Kano, December 5–6, 2005.

Adi, Hakim. *West Africans in Britain 1900–1960: Nationalism, Pan-Africanism and Communism.* London: Lawrence and Wishart, 1998.

Adorno, Theodor. *Minima Moralia: Reflections from a Damaged Life.* London: Verso, 1978.

Afeadie, Philip. *Brokering Colonial Rule: Political Agents in Northern Nigeria, 1886–1914.* Saarbrücken, Germany: VDM Verlag Dr. Müller, 2008.

Ahmad, Aliyah Adamu. "Dada Sare: A Woman of Substance in Colonial Northern Nigeria." Unpublished paper. Cited with author's permission.

Ajala, Olabisi. *An African Abroad.* London: Jarrolds, 1963.

Alam, Muzaffar, and Sanjay Subrahmanyam. *Indo-Persian Travels in the Age of Discoveries, 1400–1800.* Cambridge: Cambridge University Press, 2007.

Anderson, Benedict. *Imagined Communities: Reflections on the Origin and Spread of Nationalism.* London: Verso, 2003.

Appadurai, Arjun, ed. *The Social Life of Things: Commodities in Cultural Perspective.* Cambridge: Cambridge University Press, 1988.

Apter, Andrew. "On Imperial Spectacle: The Dialectics of Seeing in Colonial Nigeria." *Comparative Studies in Society and History* 44, no. 3 (2002): 564–96.

Arnold, David. *Everyday Technology: Machines and the Making of India's Modernity.* Chicago: University of Chicago Press, 2013.

Austen, Ralph. "Colonialism from the Middle: African Clerks as Historical Actors and Discursive Subjects." *History in Africa* 38 (2011): 21–33.

——. "Who Was Wangrin and Why Does It Matter?" *Mande Studies* 9 (1997): 149–64.

Ayandele, Emmanuel Ayankanmi. *Missionary Impact on Modern Nigeria, 1842–1914: A Political and Social Analysis.* London: Longman, 1966.

Bassnett-McGuire, Susan. *Translation Studies.* London: Routledge, 1991.

Bassnett-McGuire, Susan, and Andre Lefevere. *Constructing Cultures: Essays on Literary Translation.* Clevedon, UK: Multilingual Matters, 1998.

Bello, Ahmadu. *My Life.* Cambridge: Cambridge University Press, 1962.

Bernault, Florence. *Colonial Transactions: Imaginaries, Bodies, and Histories in Gabon.* Durham, NC: Duke University Press, 2019.

Bhabba, Homi. "Of Mimicry and Man: The Ambivalence of Colonial Discourse." *October,* Discipleship: A Special Issue on Psychoanalysis 28 (spring 1984): 125–33.

Bhimull, Chandra D. *Empire in the Air: Airline Travel and the African Diaspora.* New York: New York University Press, 2017.

Blackstock, Allan, and Frank O'Gorman, eds. *Loyalism and the Formation of the British World, 1775–1914.* Suffolk, UK: Boydell, 2014.

Branch, Daniel. "The Enemy Within: Loyalists and the War against Mau Mau in Kenya." *Journal of African History* 48 (2007): 291–315.

Breckenridge, Keith. *The Biometric State: The Global Politics of Identification and Surveillance, 1850 to the Present.* Cambridge: Cambridge University Press, 2014.

Boyd, Jean. *Collected Works of Nana Asma'u, Daughter of Usman 'dan Fodiyo (1793 to 1864).* African Historical Studies 9. East Lansing: Michigan State University Press, 1997.

Buckner, Philip. "The Royal Tour of 1901 and the Construction of Imperial Identity in South Africa." *South African Historical Journal* 41, no. 1 (1999): 324–48.

Cannadine, David. *Ornamentalism: How the British Saw Their Empire.* Oxford: Oxford University Press, 2001.

Chakrabarty, Dipesh. "Postcoloniality and the Artifice of Hsitory: Who Speaks for 'Indian' Pasts?" *Representations* 37, Special Issue: Imperial Fantasies and Postcolonial Histories (winter 1992): 1–26.

Chanock, Martin. *Law, Custom, and Social Order: The Colonial Experience in Malawi and Zambia.* Cambridge: Cambridge University Press, 1985.

Clark, Trevor. *A Right Honourable Gentleman: Abubakar from the Black Rock.* London: Edward Arnold, 1991.

Clendinning, Anne. "On the British Empire Exhibition, 1924–25." Branchcollective.org: http://www.branchcollective.org/?ps_articles=anne-clendinning-on-the-british-empire-exhibition-1924-25. Accessed March 18, 2019.

Cole, Juan. "Invisible Occidentalism: Eighteenth-Century Indo-Persian Constructions of the West." *Iranian Studies* 25, no. 3/4 (1992): 3–16.

Cowen, Mike. "Early Years of the Colonial Development Corporation: British State Enterprise Overseas during Late Colonialism." *African Affairs* 83, no. 330 (1984): 63–75.

Crampton, E.P.T. *Christianity in Northern Nigeria.* London: Chapman, 1979.

Daston, Loraine, and Katherine Park. *Wonders and the Order of Nature, 1150–1750.* New York: Zone Books, 1997.

Dawson, Graham. *Soldier Heroes: British Adventure, Empire, and the Imagining of Masculinities.* London: Routledge, 1994.

Diouf, Sylviane. *Servants of Allah: African Muslims Enslaved in the Americas.* New York: New York University Press, 2013.

Dlamini, Jacob. *Native Nostalgia.* Auckland Park, South Africa: Jacana Media, 2009.

Donaldson, Frances. *The British Council: The First Fifty Years.* London: J. Cape, 1984.

Dudley, Billy. *Parties and Politics in Northern Nigeria.* London: Frank Cass, 1968.

East, Rupert. "A First Essay in Imaginative African Literature." *Africa* 9 (1936): 350–57.

———. "An Experiment in Colonial Journalism." *African Affairs* 45 (1946): 80–87.

Fanon, Frantz. *Black Skin, White Masks*, translated by C. L. Markman. New York: Grove, 1952.

———. *The Wretched of the Earth*, translated by C. Farrington. New York: Grove, 1963.

Foucault, Michel. *Order of Things: An Archaeology of the Human Sciences.* London: Routledge, 1979.

Furniss, Graham. "Hausa Popular Literature and Video Film: The Rapid Rise of Cultural Productions in Times of Economic Decline." Working paper 27, Institut fur ethnologie und Afrikastudien, Johannes Gutenberg-Universitat, Mainz, Germany, 2003.

———. "On Engendering Liberal Values in the Nigerian Colonial State: The Idea behind the Gaskiya Corporation." *Journal of Imperial and Commonwealth History* 39, no. 1 (March 2011): 95–119.

———. "On Engendering Liberal Values in the Nigerian Colonial State: The Idea behind the Gaskiya Corporation." Paper presented at the School of Oriental and African Studies, Commonwealth History Seminar, October 19, 2007. Housed in Rhodes House Archives, MSS. Afr. s. 8839.

Gikandi, Simon. Introduction to *Uganda's Katikiro in England*, edited by Ham Mukasa. Manchester, UK: University of Manchester Press, 1998.

———. *Maps of Englishness: Writing Identity in the Culture of Colonialism*. New York: Columbia University Press, 1996.

Gjerso, Jonas Fossli. "The Scramble for East Africa: British Motives Reconsidered, 1884–95." *Journal of Imperial and Commonwealth History* 43, no. 5 (2015): 831–60.

Gluckman, Max. *Custom and Conflict in Africa*. London: The Free Press, 1955.

Gomez, Michael A. *Black Crescent: The Experience and Legacy of African Muslims in the Americas*. Cambridge: Cambridge University Press, 2005.

Goodfellow, David M. *Principles of Economic Sociology: The Economics of Primitive Life as Illustrated by the Bantu Peoples of South and East Africa*. London: G. Routledge & Sons, 1939.

Green, Nile. "Among the Dissenters: Reciprocal Ethnography in Nineteenth Century Inglistan." *Journal of Global History* 4, no. 2 (2009): 293–315.

Gumi, Sheikh Abubakar, with Ismaila Abubakar Tsiga, *Where I Stand*. Ibadan, Nigeria: Spectrum Books, 1992.

Hall, Catherine. *Civilizing Subjects: Metropole and Colony in the English Imagination 1830–1867*. Chicago: University of Chicago Press, 2002.

Hampate Ba, Amadou. *The Fortunes of Wangrin*. Bloomington: Indiana University Press, 1999.

Hodgkins, Thomas. *Nationalism in Colonial Africa*. New York: New York University Press, 1957.

Hogben, S. J., and A.H.M. Kirk-Greene. *The Emirates of Northern Nigeria*. Oxford: Oxford University Press, 1966.

Hubbard, James Patrick. *Education Under Colonial Rule: A History of Katsina College, 1921–42*. Lanham, MD: University Press of America, 2000.

Hulme, Peter, and Tim Youngs, eds. *The Cambridge Companion to Travel Writing*. Cambridge: Cambridge University Press, 2002.

Huttington, Samuel P. *The Clash of Civilizations and the Remaking of World Order*. New York: Simon and Schuster, 1998.

Ibhawoh, Bonny. *Imperial Justice: Africans in Empire's Court*. New York: Oxford University Press, 2013.

Imam, Kamarudeen, and Dahiru Coomasie. *Usman Nagogo: A Biography of the Emir of Katsina, Sir Usman Nagogo*. Kaduna, Nigeria: Today Communications, 1995.

Jones, Danell. *An African in Imperial London: The Indomitable Life of A.B.C. Merriman-Labor*. London: Hurst, 2018.

Kane, Ousmane. *Muslim Modernity in Postcolonial Nigeria: A Study of the Society for the Removal of Innovation and Reinstatement of Tradition*. Leiden: Brill, 2003.

Killingray, David, ed. *Africans in Britain*. London: Frank Cass, 1994.

Kolapo, Femi, and Kwabena Akurang-Parry, eds. *African Agency and European Colonialism: Latitudes of Negotiation*. Lanham, MD: University Press of America, 2007.

Kumar, Deepa. *Islamophobia and the Politics of Empire*. Chicago: Haymarket Books, 2012.
Kwanashie, George Amale. *The Making of the North in Nigeria, 1900–1960*. Kaduna, Nigeria: Arewa House, Ahmadu Bello University, 2002.
Kwarteng, Kwasi. *Ghosts of Empire: Britain's Legacies in the Modern World*. New York: Public Affairs, 2011.
Larkin, Brian. *Signal and Noise: Media, Infrastructure, and Urban Culture in Nigeria*. Durham, NC: Duke University Press, 2008.
Lawrance, Benjamin Nicholas, Emily Osborne, and Richard Roberts, eds. *Intermediaries, Interpreters, and Clerks: African Employees in the Making of Colonial Africa*. Madison: University of Wisconsin Press, 2006.
Lee, Christopher J. *Unreasonable Histories: Nativism, Multiracial Lives, and the Genealogical Imagination in British Africa*. Durham, NC: Duke University Press, 2014.
Levi-Strauss, Claude. *Tristes Tropiques*. Translated into English by John Russell. London: Hutchinson, 1961.
Lewis, Bernard. *The Muslim Discovery of Europe*. Cambridge: Cambridge University Press, 1957.
Logams, P. Chunung. *The Middle Belt Movement in Nigerian Political Development: A Study of Political Identity 1949–1967*. PhD dissertation, University of Keele, 1985.
MacCannell, Dean. *The Ethics of Sightseeing*. Berkeley: University of California Press, 2011.
———. *The Tourist: A New Theory of the Leisure Class*. Berkeley: University of California Press, 2013.
Magid, Alvin. *Men in the Middle: Leadership and Role Conflict in a Nigerian Society*. Teaneck, NJ: Holmes and Meier, 1976.
Mark, Beverly. *Hausa Women Sing: Hausa Popular Song*. Bloomington: Indiana University Press, 2004.
Marx, Karl. *Capital*. Vol. 1. Moscow: Progress, 1965.
M'bayo, Tamba E. "African Interpreters, Mediation, and the Production of Knowledge in Colonial Senegal: The Low Land Middle Senegal Valley, ca. 1850s to ca. 1920s." PhD dissertation, Michigan State University, 2009.
Mitchell, J. Clyde, Elizabeth Colson, and Max Gluckman, eds. *Human Problems in British Central Africa: The Rhodes-Livingstone Journal* 19 (1955).
Mitchell, Timothy. "Orientalism and the Exhibitionary Order." In *Colonialism and Culture*, edited by Nicholas Dirks, 289–318. Ann Arbor: University of Michigan Press, 1992.
Mora, Abdulrahman. *Abubakar Imam Memoirs*. Zaria, Nigeria: Northern Nigerian Publishing Company, 1989.
Mukasa, Ham. *Uganda's Katikiro in England: Being the Official Account of His Visit to the Coronation of His Majesty King Edward VII*. London: Hutchinson, 1904.
Northrup, David. *Africa's Discovery of Europe, 1450–1850*. Oxford: Oxford University Press, 2002.
Ochonu, Moses. "Colonial Itineraries: Muhammadu Dikko's Metropolitan Adventures." *Journal of African History* 61, no. 2 (2020): 179–200.
———. *Colonialism by Proxy: Hausa Imperial Agents and Middle Belt Consciousness in Nigeria*. Bloomington: Indiana University Press, 2014.
———. "The Idoma Hope Rising Union and the Politics of Patriarchy and Ethnic Honor." *International Journal of African Historical Studies* 46, no. 2 (2013): 229–54.
———. *Northern Nigeria in the Great Depression*. Athens: Ohio University Press, 2009.
———. "Protection by Proxy: The Hausa-Fulani as Agents of British Colonial Rule in Northern Nigeria." In *Protection and Empire: A Global History*, edited by Lauren

Benton, Adam Clulow, and Bain Attwood, 228–44. Cambridge: Cambridge University Press, 2017.

Osborn, Emily Lynn. "'Circle of Iron': African Colonial Employees and the Interpretation of Colonial Rule in French West Africa." *Journal of African History* 44, no. 1 (2003): 29–50.

Ozigi, Albert, and Lawrence Ocho. *Education in Northern Nigeria*. London: Allen and Unwin, 1981.

Paden, John. *Ahmadu Bello, Sardauna of Sokoto: Values and Leadership in Nigeria*. London: Hodder and Stoughton, 1986.

Parsons, Neil. *King Khama, Emperor Joe and the Great White Queen: Victorian Britain through African Eyes*. Chicago: University of Chicago Press, 1998.

Peel, J.D.Y. "Two Northerners Contrasted in Their Visions of Nigerian Unity." *Canadian Journal of African Studies* 22, no. 1 (1988): 144–48.

Pernau, Margrit. "Emotions and Modernity in Colonial India." Seminar paper, Vanderbilt History Seminar, Vanderbilt University, February 13, 2017.

Poynting, Scott, and Victoria Mason. "The Resistible Rise of Islamophobia: Anti-Muslim Racism in the UK and Australia Before 11 September 2001." *Journal of Sociology* 43, no. 1 (2013): 61–86.

Pratt, Mary Luise. *Imperial Eyes: Travel Writing and Transculturation*. London: Routledge, 1992.

Rabe, Dahiru. "The British Colonial Occupation and the Christian Missionary Activities in Katsina Emirate C. 1903–1936." Seminar paper, History Department, Ahmadu Bello University, Zaria, Nigeria, 2011.

Ranger, Terrence. "The Invention of Tradition in Colonial Africa." In *The Invention of Tradition*, 11th ed., edited by Eric Hobsbawn and Terence Ranger, 211–62. Cambridge: Cambridge University Press, 1983.

Reed, Charles V. *Royal Tourists, Colonial Subjects, and the Making of a British World, 1860–1911*. Manchester, UK: Manchester University Press, 2017.

Remmington, Janet, and Nickals Hallen. "Africa Travels, Africa Writes: Notes on African Intellectual Mobilities." Africa in Words, February 26, 2015. https://africainwords.com/2015/02/26/africa-travels-africa-writes-notes-on-african-intellectual-mobilities/.

Renne, Elisha P. *The Politics of Polio in Northern Nigeria*. Bloomington: Indiana University Press, 2010.

Reynolds, Jonathan. *The Time of Politics (Zamanin Siyasa): Islam and the Politics of Legitimacy in Northern Nigeria, 1956–1966*. 2nd ed. Lanham, MD: University Press of America, 1999.

Said, Edward. *Culture and Imperialism*. New York: Vintage Books, 1993.

———. *Orientalism*. New York: Vintage Books, 1979.

Sani, Habibu Angulu. *Has History Been Fair to the Atta?: Biography of a Powerful Ruler South of the Sahara*. Okene, Nigeria: Desmond Tutu Publishers, 1997.

Sapire, Hilary. "African Loyalism and Its Discontents: The Royal Tour of South Africa, 1947." *Historical Journal* 54, no. 1 (2011): 215–40.

———. "Ambiguities of Loyalism: The Prince of Wales in India and Africa, 1921–22 and 25." *History Workshop Journal* 73, no. 1 (2012): 37–65.

Schumaker, Lyn. *Africanizing Anthropology: Fieldwork, Networks, and the Making of Cultural Knowledge in Central Africa*. Durham, NC: Duke University Press, 2001.

Schumaker, Lynette. "'A Tent with a View': Colonial Officers, Anthropologists, and the Making of the Field in Northern Rhodesia, 1937–1960." *Osiris* 11, 2nd series (1996): 237–58.

Stavans, Ilan, and Joshua Ellison. *Reclaiming Travel.* Durham, NC: Duke University Press, 2015.

Stoler, Ann Laura. *Along the Archival Grain: Epistemic Anxieties and Colonial Common Sense.* Princeton, NJ: Princeton University Press, 2009.

Sulaiman, Ibraheem. *The African Caliphate: The Life, Works, and Teaching of Shaykh Usman dan Fodio.* Norwich, UK: Diwan, 1999.

Thompson, Leonard. *A History of South Africa.* New Haven, CT: Yale University Press, 2014.

Tymowski, Michal. "African Perceptions of Europeans in the Early Period of Portuguese Expeditions to West Africa." *Itinerario* 39, no. 2 (2015): 221–46.

Ubah, C. N. "Problems of Christian Missionaries in the Muslim Emirates of Nigeria." *Journal of African Studies* 3 (1967): 351–71.

Umar, Mohammed Sani. *Islam and Colonialism: Intellectual Responses of Muslims of Northern Nigeria to British Colonial Rule.* Leiden: Brill, 2006.

White, Luise. "Cars Out of Place: Vampires, Technology, and Labor in East and Central Africa." *Representations* 43 (1993): 27–50.

Wicker, E. R. "The Colonial Development Corporation." *Review of Economic Studies* 23, no. 3 (1955–56): 213–28.

Yakubu, A. M. *Sa'adu Zungur: An Anthology of the Social and Political Writings of a Nigerian Nationalist.* Kaduna, Nigeria: Nigerian Defense Academy, 1999.

INDEX

Note: Page numbers in *italics* indicate a figure.

Abbas, Muhammad, 314
Abdulmalik, Alhaji, 295
Abdul Naiz Ibn Fa'ad (king), Dikko visit with, 186
Abubakar Gumi (sheikh), 22, 47n49
Action Group (AC), 337
Adi, Hakim, 4
Ado Bayero, Alhaji, 152, 178n58
adult education, culture of literacy with, 51; NORLA impact on, 9, 65–69, 89n44, 91; resources for, 68–69; with volunteers, 67–68; for women, 68–69
adventures, 304–5; exploration and, 13; metropolitan, of Dikko, 91–96, 214–19, 231n121; Otherness and, 120–26, *121*, *122*; travel-writing craft with, 87; vernacular aesthetic of, 9–11
African Abroad, An (Ajala), 13–14
African cultural authenticity assault story, 314
African immigrant, perspectives of, 4–5
African in Imperial London, An (Jones), 4
African migrants, to Britain, 5
African mobilities, 14
African Muslims, 2, 5, 23
African oral corpus importance, 17
African social clubs, 239–40
agricultural institution visits, 162
agricultural modernity, 254, 296
agriculture engineering school, Ndayako on, 265
"Agriculture in Britain," 282
agriculture technologies, modernization of, 97, 224
Ajala, Olabisi, 13–14, 46n32
Ajami, 51–52, 53
ambivalent gaze, 332–34
American Cold War cultural and political evangelism, 334

American courtship, Balewa visit and, 334–40
Aminu Kano. *See* Kano, emir of
Anderson, Benedict, 10, 199
Anglo-imperial culture through lens, of travel writing, 269
Anglophone West African troops, Nagogo visit with, 222
anthropology, 7
anti-Western rhetoric, 3, 332–34
Arc de Triomphe, 284–85
aristocratic culture, colonial kinship and, 31–33
aristocratic institutions, in Northern Nigeria, 317
aristocratic self-fashioning, 315–16
aristocratic solidarity, 11
aristocratic subaltern, 321; adventure and exploration understood by, 13; courting of, 11–14, 23; marginalization of, 4, 44n2; mobility of, 3; modernity of, 2, 10; Nagogo as, 222–23; representational perspectives of, 15–16; travel of, 1–3, 11–14, 25–28; travelogues of, 4, 8, 15
aristocrats: modern, 1–8, 10, 11–14, 25–28. *See also specific aristocrats*
artifacts, of British and Northern Nigerian connections, 314
Atta of Ebira. *See* Ibrahim, Onoruoiza
audiovisual instruments, 198–99
Austin Motor Company, 286
Awan, Gwamna, 294
Azikiwe, Dr., 84

Balewa, Tafawa: Bello and, 337, 339; Kennedy with, *335*, 335–36; platform of, 338; politics of, 336; self-positioning of, 337; in United States, 335–40

355

Bank of British West Africa, 182–83
Bank of England, Dikko at, 110
Barewa College, 301
Barewa magazine, 235, 237
Barmo, Mallam, 102, 103, 111
Bath, 286
Bathoen (king), 19
Bauchi Discussion Circle. See Taron Tattauna Al'Amurun Bauchi
Bawa, Ahmadu, 294
Bayero, Abdullahi, 316
Bedde, emir of, 287
Beddington, E. H., 197
"Behavior of the British" (Nuhu), 258
Bello, Ahmadu, 31, 43, 243, 255–56, 277, 294–95; Balewa and, 337, 339; cultural exchange relating to, 299–301; on English family life, 259–60; as fives player, 299–301; in NPC, 281; on rural and urban Britons, 260; "There Are no Idlers in England" by, 259
Berliner Illustrirte Zeitung, 190
Bertram Mills Circus, 195–96
Bida, emir of, 286, 289
Birmingham, 76, 78–79, 286
Birmingham, Ibrahim in: on driving tour, 142; at Dunlop factory, 142; at Hercules Cycle and Motor Company, 141, 142; at Morris Commercial Car Company, 142; with photo session, 141–42; at Wolseley Motor Works, 141; with Woodhouse, 141–42
Branch, Daniel, 33, 34
Bristol, 286
Britain, 43; beholding and buying of, 138–41; cathedrals in, 75; consuming of, 152–54, 178nn60–61; critique of, 24–25; Islamophobic policies in, 23; Kaggwa in, 17–18; katikiro effect in, 17–20; modernity of, 174; Ndayako on, 24–25; Oko in, 290–93; quasi-imperial seduction of, 332; as recreational escape, 195–98; students of, 234–38; Tswana kings in, 5, 19; Victorian, 4, 23. *See also* emirs, in Britain
Britain, Ibrahim in: at Handley-Page Works, 140–41; with high-end metropolitan goods, 138–40; at London Zoological Garden, 139; at Tower of London, 140; at Windsor Castle, 139
"Britain and the British People," 280
"Britain as I Saw It" (Tukur), 235
"Britain-its Life and People," 280
Britain reenacted in Nigeria, 202–4
British accounts, of colonial travel, 166–67
British agriculture, Daura on, 275
"British Agriculture," 294
British and Nigerian clothing, Inuwa on, 237
British and Nigerian differences, Tukur on, 235–36
British and Nigerian eye contact, Inuwa on, 237
British and Northern Nigerian connections, artifacts of, 314
British Broadcasting Corporation, 253–54
British character, Ndayako on, 268
British children in public, Inuwa on, 238
British colonial patronage, of Muslim Hausa rulers, 147–48
British colonial social group, of Dadasare, 326–28
British colonizers, in Northern Nigeria, 1, 32
"British Commonwealth of Nations, The," 280
British connection. *See* Dikko-Nagogo British connection
British Council, 70, 81, 266, 277–79, 282–85, 287, 295
British embassy, in Paris, 285
British Empire Exhibition. *See* Wembly British Empire Exhibition
British expatriate personnel, 298, 301–2
British formality, Inuwa on, 237
British imperial overseas travel, 8
British Imperial realm, 200
British metropolitan life, 200
British modernity, 174, 200–202, 296
British Naval Dockyard, 157
British Paramount News, 199
British Parliament, 77, 242, 264
"British People Today, The," 294
British police, Nuhu on, 257
British relationship, with Dikko, 92–96
British views, of subaltern societies, 11
"British Way of Life," 290
British wireless broadcasts, 253–54

Bromley (admiral), 150
Bromsgrove Guild Limited, 316
Browne, G. S., 182, 185, 187, 194, 195–97, 210, 217–18
Buckingham Palace, 152, 185, 224; medal of honor given at, 112; meeting with king at, 93, 111–13, 146, 158–59, 195, 212–13; Ndayako at, 267; tour of, 111–13
Bugunda, 17, 19–20
bureaucracies, 97, 210, 296, 298. *See also* colonial bureaucracy, mechanics of travel and

Calico Printers Association, 143
caliphate goes to England, *149*; culture shock relating to, 151; at Hyde Park Hotel, 150; in Morris cars, 150; tours and activities for, 151–52; welcome party for, 148–50
Cambridge, 280
Cameron, Donald, 183, 203–4, 218
canonical polemics, of decolonization, 4
Carey, H. D. Tupper, 148, 160
car manufacturing plant, 106, 108
car-racing event, 120
cataract surgery, of Dikko, 210, 212
CBE. *See* Commander of the British Empire
center of colonial secular education, Katsina as, 97–99
certified nurse training, of Dadasare, 329
Champs-Élysées, 284
Changing of the Guard ceremony, 195
Chaytor (commander), 155
Church Missionary Society (CMS) Mission Hospital, 328
cinema, 106–7, 206
circus: Bertram Mills Circus, 195–96; Ndayako on, 262–63
Clark, Trevor, 239
Clifford, Hugh, 98–99, 103, 108, 111, 112
CMS. *See* Church Missionary Society Mission Hospital
codification, of colonial bureaucracy and mechanics of travel, 276
College of Pharmacy of University of Edinburgh, 304
colonial adventures, postcolonial metropolitan tourism and, 304–5

colonial associational leverage and modernization, 96–101, 224
colonial bureaucracy, mechanics of travel and: codification of, 276; Colonial Office role with, 276–77; for colonial pedagogical projects, 277, 280; funding relating to, 275–76, 277–79; groundwork for, 275; group guidelines relating to, 277; host homes relating to, 279; for immersive metropolitan experiences, 276; itineraries and programs relating to, 275, 279–81; Native Authorities impacted by, 276, 277, 278–79, 288, 289; Native Treasury funds relating to, 278; in 1947, 277; in 1948, 277–78; in 1949, 279–80; for Northern Nigerian elites, 276; problems relating to, 277–78; religious services relating to, 279; for reward to Nigerian aristocratic partners, 276; for study tours, 280; visitor salaries relating to, 277–78; volunteers relating to, 276–77, 306n7
colonial culture, 21, 73
colonial discourses, 85
colonial domination, 27, 36, 50
colonial ideational space, 248–49. *See also* literacy, narrative, and colonial ideational space
colonial infrastructure, 319
colonialism, 21, 325
colonial kinship, 31–33; and colonial victimhood, of Dadasare, 321–26, 330; limits and possibilities of, 329–30; with metropolitan entertainment, 155–58; mobile, 80–83, 90n73, 90nn76–77; with personal connections, 155; politics and poetics of, 155–59; across racial divide, 321; with touring fatigue, 157
colonially mediated public sphere of discussion, 238
colonial mediation, 21–23
colonial medical tourism, 214; at Buckingham Palace, 212–13; bureaucratic practices and processes relating to, 210; with cataract surgery, 210, 212; itinerary for, 211; meeting requests relating to, 210–12; with polo tournaments, 212, 231n111
colonial middlemen, 22

colonial mobility, 2
colonial modernity, 2, 20, 35, 47n48, 52, 72, 324
colonial occupation, 36
Colonial Office, 158, 276–77, 286; Dikko visit and, 75, 109, 119–20, 124–26, 183–84, 185; Ibrahim visit and, 136; weekend in Paris relating to, 283; Yahaya visit and, 146
colonial pedagogical projects, 277, 280
colonial relationships, affective economy of, 321
Colonial Secretary, 281
colonial stimulus and unlikely affections, 326–28
colonial subalternity and Muslim identity, of Dikko, 116–17
colonial sublime, 319–21
colonial touring, 42–43; evolution of, 273–74
colonial touristic imagination, 27
colonial travel as pedagogy: British accounts relating to, 166–67; emirs posttravel narratives relating to, 167–68; secretive Muslim culture impact on, 168–69
colonial victimhood and colonial kinship, of Dadasare, 321–26, 330
Colonial Welfare and Development Fund, 62–63
colonial whiteness, 325
colonization: brutality of, 31; freedoms controlled with, 11–12, 45n26, 45n28; ideational space of, 57; Lugard on, 32–33; sociopolitical bedrocks of, 11–12
colonizers, 25–28; African aristocratic subalterns relationship with, 321
Commander of the British Empire (CBE), 213
commemorative tray, 207, 207–8, 230n98
communication, with imperial travel, 165
community of readers, to community of writers: African social clubs impact on, 239–40; Bauchi Discussion Circle impact on, 239–40; emergence of colonially mediated public sphere of discussion and debate impact on, 238; intellectual activism relating to, 239; intellectual restlessness of Western-educated youth impact on, 238; with Taron Tattauna Al'Amuran Bauchi, 239, 254

complicated imperial explorations in late colonialism, 281–82
conceptual concept, 14–16
condescension and mockery, of Dikko, 118–19
conservative wing, NPC as, 281
consuming Britain, 152–54, 178nn60–61
County Gazette, 292
courtship, 11–14, 23
court system, modernization of, 97
Cowdrey Polo Ground, 304–5
credibility and facticity, with forging imperial community, 252
cross-racial fraternities, with polo, 100
Crown, 16; admiration of, 23–25, 34; seductive power of, 34–35
Croydon Aerodrome, 163, *163*, 194, *194*, 199, 214
cultivation, of official bureaucracies and technocratic ties, 296
cultural center, Katsina as, 99–101
cultural exchange, Bello relating to, 299–301
cultural space, 37
culture, 39, 68, 269, 314, 334; colonial kinship and aristocratic, 31–33; of mediation, 21. *See also specific culture*
culture of literacy, with adult education, 9, 51, 65–69, 89n44, 91
culture shock, in England, 151
Cunliff-Lister, Philip, 158, 183
curiosities, with ethnographic minutia, 247–52

Dadasare Abdullahi, Maimunatu Hajiya, 43–44, 61–64, 313; biography of, 322, 330; with British colonial social group, 326–28; certified nurse training of, 329; colonial victimhood and colonial kinship of, 321–26, 330; death of, 329–30, 341nn35–36; with East, 326–30; escape effort of, 323; European colonial officer abduction of, 322–26; Fulani family background of, 322; literacy campaign of, 328–29; pregnancy of, 323–24; socialization of, 323–24; transformation of, 324; violence relating to, 322–26, 330; in Zaria, 326–29
Daily Comet newspaper, 281

Daily Nigerian, 313
Dan Buran, Abdullahi, 294
Dan Fodio, Othman, ruling family, 52, 76
dan Sulayman, Umar, 287
Dapp, F. S., 206–7
Daura, Ihas: on British agriculture, 275; on impressions, 275; metropolitan travel lectures by, 275; metropolitan travel written primer by, 274–75; on public service, 275
death, of Dadasare, 329–30, 341nn35–36
decolonization, canonical polemics of, 4
Derby Cattle Show, Dikko on, 105–6, 108
Dewar, K., 210
dialogic culture, with newspaper travel narratives, 240
dialogue techniques, of *Gaskiya ta fi Kwabo*, 240–41
Dikko, Muhammadu: British evaluation by, 200–202; Colonial Office visit with, 75, 109, 119–20, 124–26, 183–84, 185; His Majesty King George photograph and, 207; Lugard memorial by, 317–19; Lugard visits with, 94, 120, 163–64, *164*, 213–14; metropolitan engagements of, 226, 232n154; metropolitan modernity narrative of, 204–6; metropolitan visibility impacted by, 223–24; modernization projects of, 223–24. *See also* Katsina, emir of
Dikko final metropolitan adventure: with George VI visit, 214; goodwill message broadcast, 214, *217*, 231n121; at races, 216–17, *218*; at Royal Agricultural Show, 219; Royal Society for the Prevention of Cruelty to Animals award, 214; at White City greyhound races, 216–17
Dikko memorabilia of metropolitan travel: commemorative tray, *207*, 207–8, 230n98; Dikko and His Majesty King George photograph, 207; Hajiya Binta relating to, 208; itinerary of, *214*; at Katsina Emirate, 208, *209*; UAC relating to, 206–8
Dikko-Nagogo British connection: afterlives of Katsina metropolitan outreach, 223–26; Britain as recreational escape, 195–98; colonial medical tourism, 210–14;

memorabilia of metropolitan travel, 206–9; Nagogo the modernizer, 221–23; polo and modernization in age of Nagogo, 220–21; trip planning as colonial regimen, 184–86
Dikko returns to England: audiovisual instruments during, 198–99; at Croydon Aerodrome, 194, *194*; with family, 183, 186–90, *188–89*, *191–94*; itinerary of, *187*; journalists coverage of, *187–88*, 187–95, *191–93*; king visit with, 187, 195; at Portsmouth, 194, *195*, 206
Dikwa, emir of, 293–95
Diss Express, 113, 115, 118
Dual Mandate, The (Lugard), 32–33
Dundee Courier, 110
Dundee Evening Telegraph, 112, 113
Dunlop Factory, 142

East, Rupert, 88n23, 238; Dadasare with, 326–30; on Imam, 57–58; publishing house relating to, 62–63; reading culture impact of, 54–58, 60, 61–62
Edinburgh Evening News, 94
education, 58, 97–99; crisis with, 302; culture literacy and adult, 9, 51, 65–69, 89n44, 91; Nuhu on, 257; Western-educated class, 53–57, 60–61, 254
educationally handicapped, Northern Nigerian students as, 299
educational socialization, 255
educational visits and sight-seeing tours, of women's tour, 288–99
"Education and Schools," 294
Edwardian Britain, 4
Eiffel Tower, 285
Elder Dempster Lines, 154, 165, 203
electricity company, Dikko at, 120
electricity-generating plants, Ndayako on, 266
Elizabethan Britain, 4
Elizabeth II (queen), 236, 263–64, 267, 287, 314
Ellison, Joshua, 16
Ely, Frederick, 197
emirate. *See* Katsina Emirate
emirate and palace tradition abandonment story, 313–15

Emir of Katsina locomotive, 92
emirs. *See specific emirs*
emirs, in Britain, 24, 133; afterlives of imperial courtship, 169–71; beholding Britain, buying Britain, 138–41; Birmingham, 141–42; caliphate goes to England, 148–52; colonial travel as pedagogy, 166–69; complex logistics of imperial travel, 164–65; conclusion to, 174–76; consuming Britain, 152–54; emir, traveler, narrator, 171–74; London in vernacular, 146–48; At London Zoological Garden, 139; Mecca-London itinerary, of Atta Ibrahim, 7, 134–38, *137*, 145; metropolitan explorations, 143–46; personalities and power, 159–64; politics and poetics of colonial kinship, 155–59; posttravel narratives of, 167–68; science of flight and aerodynamics as interest of, 162–63, *163*
empire, 11; Wembly British Empire Exhibition, 120, *122*, 122–25, 185. *See also* empire, persistent and evolving fraternities of
empire, persistent and evolving fraternities of, 313–18; ambivalent gaze, 332–34; American courtship and Balewa visit, 334–40; colonial stimulus and unlikely affections, 326–28; Dadasare, colonial victimhood, and colonial kinship, 321–26, 330; limits and possibilities of colonial kinship, 329–30; metropolitan explorations in late colonial and postcolonial periods, 331–32; metropolitan travel and colonial sublime, 319–21; subaltern privilege and colonial connections, 328–29
empire loyalism, metropolitan travel and, 33–35
empirical element, of ethnographic minutia and subaltern gaze, 247
England: caliphate goes to, 148–52. *See also* Dikko returns to England; Imam, Abubakar, in England
England trip narratives, 70–74, *71*, 76, 80
"English Concept of Democracy, The," 294
English Crown Jewels, 242

English family life, Bello on, 259–60
English granite mining, 249–50
English hospitality narrative, of Nuhu, 256–57
"English Language," 280
English-language lecture at Zaria Middle School, by Kafin Madaki, 274
English-language literacy, 10
English-language travel narratives, 3
English monarchy, 3, 242. *See also* Crown
English sheepherding culture, 250–51
"English Social Behavior, The," 294
epistemological engagements, 34
ethnographic commentary, of Dikko, 104–8, 202
ethnographic minutia, subaltern gaze and: curiosities with, 247–52; empirical elements of, 247; with English sheepherding culture, 250–51; ethnography and observation in colonial ideational space, 248–49; in *Gaskiya ta fi Kwabo*, 246–52; informational transactional economy relating to, 248; narrative genre and colonial traveler writings impacted by, 249; novelty and exotic character of, 247; processes, industries, material objects as, 249–50; rehabilitative effect of distance impacted by, 247; symbiotic partnership relating to, 251; trivia, fascination of, 247
ethnographic travel inquiries, 7
ethnography, 6, 9; and observation, in colonial ideational space, 248–49; of Other, 7, 8. *See also* subaltern, as colonial explorer and reverse ethnographer
Eton College, 160, 265, 286, 300–301
Eton College Chronicle, 300
Etsu Nupe's travel to England. *See Tafiyan Etsu Nupe Ingila*
Etsu Nupe testament, 261–68
Euro-American modernity, 334
European actors, 52
European colonial officer abduction, of Dadasare, 322–26
European colonial traveler-ethnographers, 8; Occidentalism relating to, 7; Orientalism relating to, 6; writings of, 6–7

"European Ships," 250
European social clubs, 240, 270n20
exoticizing, of Dikko, 118–19
expatriate British personnel, 298
explorations, 13, 40–41, 43, 118, 331–32. *See also* imperial exploration, imagining the postcolony with; metropolitan explorations, of Ibrahim extra-metropolitan world, 11

factories, Ndayako on, 266
Fanon, Frantz, 324–25
feedback, from tours, 297
Fenton Colliery, Dikko at, 117
Fletcher, D. C., 210
"Forestry in England," 248
forging imperial community, 256–61; credibility and facticity with, 252; with educational socialization, 255; with imperial cultural economy, 253; with opinionating, 253; with prescriptive punditry, 253; with returnees, 254; writers and readers, dependent relationship between, 252
freedoms, 11–12, 45n26, 45n28
Fulani family background, of Dadasare, 322
funding: for colonial bureaucracy and mechanics of travel, 275–76, 277–79; of travel, 15, 16; of women's tour, 288

Galeries Lafayette, 284
gambling, 217–18
Gana, Abba: northernization impact on, 298; student admissions goals of, 298–99; technocratic and technological assistance courted by, 297–98
Ganduje, Dr. Umar, 313
Gaskiya Corporation, 9–10, 60–64, 68, 70, 91, 239, 261
Gaskiya ta fi Kwabo, 9–10, 38, 42, 63–64, 69–70, 86–87, 268; Dadasare op-ed in, 61–62; dialogue techniques of, 240–41; English granite mining in, 249–50; growing library of, 242; imperial communal imagination with, 252–54; literary and intellectual imaginary built by, 62; Nagogo travelogue in, 218, 219;

paradigmatic shift in, 60, 61; as platform of public thought, 61; popularity of, 241–42; as propaganda instrument, 60; reporters from, 243; scarce commodities inquiries to, 242; student travel narratives to, 243–44; Yahaya in, 146
Geary, William Nevill M., 212
genres, 36–37, 70, 240, 249
George V (king): emir of Gwandu visit with, 146; memorial plaque for, 316–17
George VI (king), 223
Gikandi, Simon, 4, 20, 154
Gloucestershire Echo, 148
Goldsmith, H. S., 182, 185, 198
Gombe, emir of, 283
goodwill message broadcast, of Dikko, 214, 217, 231n121
Gordon-Marshall, W. T., 300
governor: of Medina, 186; of Northern Nigeria, Lugard as, 32–33, 51–52
Gowers, William, 108, 111, 112
gratitude letters, by Dikko, 203–4
Greer, P. A., 283–85
group guidelines, for colonial bureaucracy and, 277
Guildford, 286
Guy Buses, 287
Gwandu, emir of, 40, 148, 155, 170, 178n45; colonial culture of, 147; George V visit with, 146; in London, 146–47, 173–74; personalities and powers relating to, 159–64, *163*, *164*; privileged background of, 172; travelogues of, 20–21, 41, 133, 146, 171–74; Yahaya, 146, 173, 178n45; in Zungeru, 172

Hajiya Binta, 208
Hamilton (lord), 111
Hampshire Telegraph, 198
Handley-Page Works, 140–41
Harcourt, R. J. R., 295
Harrods, 111, 155
Hausa: British colonial patronage of Muslim, 147–48; British Empire Exhibition with Mendi, Fulani, and, 123–24; cultures of, 2, 19–20, 52, 73–74, 86–87; and Fulani women readers, 63; literature of, 51–53; Romanized Hausa fiction and travel

writer, Imam as, 57–60, 63; Romanized Hausa-language readers, 55–56, 59, 62, 63, 67, 70, 253; Romanized Hausa storytelling, 9–10, 52, 58–60, 86–87, 88n21
Hausa-and English-language travel narratives, 3
Hausa-Fulani aristocrats, 32–33
Hausa-Fulani Muslim ruling classes, 163
Hausa-language lecture at Zaria City Reading Room, by Kafin Madaki, 274
Hausa-language material, 55, 61, 243
Hausaphone Muslim males, 275
Hausa-speaking audience, 15, 70
Heart of England, The, 295
Hendon Aerodrome, Dikko at, 115–16
Hercules Cycle and Motor Company, 141, 142
Hermon Hodge, Harry B., 210–12
heroism, 36, 37
hierarchies, of class, 1, 11, 21, 37, 85, 159
Hogben, S. J., 299
Holy Land, Dikko in, 116
homogenization, 36
Hopkinson, Harry, 266
horse-racing events, Dikko at, 109, 110, 111
host homes, for travel, 279
Hotel Great Central, 210
hotels: Dikko accommodations at, 104; Ibrahim accommodations at, 146–47. *See also specific hotels*
Hotel St. Petersbourg, 283–84
House of Commons, 116, 286
House of Parliament, 185, 295, 297
humor, with sensation and narration, 83–85
Hurst Park horse races, 218
Hyde Park Hotel, 150, 187, 203

Ibn Haliru, Usman, 146, 155, 156
Ibrahim, Onoruoiza: as Atta of Ebira, 175, 176n2; in Birmingham, 141–42; in Britain, 138–41; at Colonial Office, 136; Mecca-London itinerary of, 7, 134–38, *137*, 145; metropolitan explorations of, 143–47, 197; as Muslim, 134; wealth of, 134
ideational space. *See* literacy, narrative, and colonial ideational space
ideational space of colonization, 57
Idomaland, 293

Ilford Photograph Company, 199
Illustrated London News, 122, 190, 197, 200
Ilorin, emir of, 261, 286, 289
Imam, Abubakar, 1, 40, 50–51, 54, 241, 245, 281; East on, 57–58; genre pioneered by, 70; legacy of, 86; literary technique of similitude to communicate parallels of, 75–76, 89n56; Lugard visit with, 80–83; as Romanized Hausa fiction and travel writer, 57–60, 63
Imam, Abubakar, in England: in Birmingham, 76, 78–79; at British Parliament, 77; guided tours of, 75–78; at London Bridge, 76–77; on metropolitan technology, 78; at Oxford, 79–80; *Tafiya Mabudin Ilimi* account of, 40, 64, 70–74, *71*, 76, 80, 83–86, 244; travel narrative of, 72–74, 83–86; on urban planning, 79
immersive metropolitan experiences, 276
imperial aristocratic connection, 290
imperial communal imagination, 252–54
imperial community, forging of, 252–61
imperial courtship, afterlives of, 169–71
imperial culture, 26, 253, 269
imperial epistemological space, 17
imperial evidence, ethnography of wonder and, 6–9
imperial exploration, imagining the postcolony with: colonial adventures and postcolonial metropolitan tourism, 304–5; colonial bureaucracy and mechanics of travel, 275–81; colonial touring evolution, 273–74; complicated imperial explorations in late colonialism, 281–82; conclusion to, 305–6; evolving metropolitan itineraries, 285–88; institutionalizing metropolitan travel, 274–75; late-colonial allure of metropole, 293–95; metropolitan touring as colonial validation, 289–93; from personal to official, 295–98; political independence in shadow of metropolitan courtship, 298–301; postcolonial anxieties and metropolitan outreach, 301–4; as routine travel, 273; touristic pilgrimages relating to, 273; travel memoirs and lectures relating to, 273; United Kingdom travel,

as rite of passage, 273; weekend in Paris, 283–85; women's tour, 288–89
imperial hospitality, 320
Imperial Institute, 286
imperial loyalism, 33
imperial modernity translation, 74–78
imperial overseas travel, 8
imperial pilgrimage, of Dikko, *102*, 102–4, *103*
imperial system, specialization into, 221
imperial transatlantic kinship, 296
imperial travel, complex logistics of, 164; with communication, 165; with Elder Dempster Lines, 165; with expectations, 165; with expenses, 165
imperial travel-writing genre, 36–37
indigenous reading public, 56
informational transactional economy, 248
infrastructure: for literary culture, 51; publishing, 58
intellectual activism, 239
intellectual culture, 39, 52–53
intellectualism, of students, 237
intellectual power, of African traveler, 37
intellectual space consolidation, 62; with Gaskiya Corporation, 63–64; with newspapers, 63–65; for travel narratives, 64–65; for women readers, 63
intermediaries, travel impact of, 21
International Commercial Show, 287
intersecting informational sources, universe of, 254
Inuwa, Magaji: on British and Nigerian clothing, 237; on British and Nigerian eye contact, 237; on British children in public, 238; on British formality, 237; semi-didactic pontifications of, 238; "Some Ways of Foreigners Which Seem Strange to Me" by, 237
invention of tradition, with colonial histories, symbols, relationships, 317
Islamic Cultural Center, 286
Islamic culture of gender segregation and purdah, 68
Islamic identity, of Dikko, 113
Islamic intellectual heritage, precolonial, 51–52, 88n4
Islamist radicalization and anti-Western rhetoric, of Northern Nigeria, 3
Islamophobic policies, in Britain, 23
itineraries and programs, for travel, 275, 279–81

Ja'afar, Ja'afar, newspaper story by: about African cultural authenticity assault, 314; about emirate and palace tradition abandonment, 313–15; about Kano palace, 314–16; about Sanusi financial recklessness, 313–15; about Soron Ingila demolition, 314–16, *315*; aristocratic self-fashioning, 315–16; in *Daily Nigerian*, 313; Sanusi II financial recklessness in, 313
Jakadiyya, 63–64
James, H. B., 135
James, W. M., 194
Jauro, Mallam, 283–85
Jeddah, 136, 183, 184, 185, 186
John Holt and Company, 300
Jones, Danell, 4
journalists coverage, of Dikko in England, *187–88*, 187–95, *191–93*

Kafin Madaki, Garba, 244, 255, 273, 279; English-language lecture at Zaria Middle School of, 274; Hausa-language lecture at Zaria City Reading Room of, 274
Kagara, Bello, 91, 110
Kaggwa, Apollo: in Britain, 17–18; as Katikiro of Bugunda kingdom, 17–19; Mukasa writings about, 17–18
Kaita, Isa, 301–3
Kano, emir of, 40, 148, 152, 155, 174, 178n58; Abbas as, 314; Aminu Kano as, 56, 239, 254, 281; Bayero as, 316; personalities and powers relating to, 159–64, *163*, *164*; Sanusi as, 313
Kano palace, 314–16
katikiro effect: in Britain, 17–20; Kaggwa relating to, 17–19; Mukasa writings about, 17–20; religion relating to, 19
Katsina, 181; as center of colonial secular education, 97–99; as cultural center, 99–101; palace renovation in, 224, *225*; polo and cultural identity of, 99–101

Katsina, emir of, Muhammadu Dikko as, 31, 42, 175; British relationship with, 92–96; at Buckingham Palace, 93, 111–13; colonial associational leverage and modernization, 96–99; Colonial Office and, 75, 109, 119–20, 124–26; colonial subalternity and Muslim identity of, 116–17; imperial pilgrimage, 102, 102–4, 103; King's Medal for African Chiefs for, 112, 113, 213; London allure, 108–11; metropolitan adventures of, 91–96; in metropolitan circles, 95; metropolitan encounters of, 113–19; subaltern ethnographic notebook, 104–8; wives of, 113–14, 119
Katsina College, 54–55, 57, 80, 98–99, 235, 270n1, 299
Katsina Emirate, 41, 208, 209, 219, 227
Katsina Games Club, 101
Katsina metropolitan outreach, afterlives of, 223–26
Katsina Native Authority, 96, 97, 209
Katsina Native Authority Police, 219–20
Katsina Polo Club, 31, 41, 100–101
Katsina Provincial School, 100–101
Kempton Park Jubilee race, 197
Kennedy, John F., 335, 335–36
Kew Royal Botanical Gardens, Dikko at, 115
Khama (king), 19
Killingray, David, 4
King George VI Coronation Medal, 213
King Khama (Parsons), 5
kings, 19, 174, 255; Dikko letter to, 203–4; Tswana kings, 5, 19; visits with, 93, 111–13, 146, 158–59, 187, 195. See also specific kings
kingships, of subaltern societies, 11
King's Medal: for African Chiefs, for Dikko, 112, 113, 213; for Oko, 292
kinships: imperial transatlantic kinship, 296; transactional and aristocratic, 321. See also colonial kinship
Kirtlington Polo Club, 221

Lady Lever Art Gallery, 198
Lagos, 136
Laing, E. H. B., 196–97, 218
Lambda, Yusuf, 100, 101
Lamido of Adamawa, 283–85

Lancashire Daily Post, 216–17
Larkin, Brian, 319–20
late-colonial allure of metropole: for emir of Dikwa, 293–95; with 1955 tours, 293–95; with 1956 tours, 294–95; with Reynolds, 294
Lead Intelligencer, 195
Leeds Mercury, 112, 115–16, 120–22
legacy, of Imam, 86
Letter of Credit, 183
leveraging, of metropole travel in age of modernity, 2–3
Lever Brothers soap factory, 197, 286
Leverhulme (lord), 118, 197–98, 203
Liberty's, 29, 160
"Life in an English City," 280
"Linen Manufacture in England," 249
literacy: campaign for, 9; experiential, travel writing as, 69–74; investments in, 52; mass, 9, 57, 63, 65, 67, 86; modernity and, 66; Romanized, 9–11, 39, 50, 53; vernacular aesthetic of adventure and, 9–11; writing, reading, and sharing with, 10
literacy, mass audience creation and: colonial message dissemination relating to, 65; *Jaki da Jahilci*, 66; propaganda relating to, 65–67; for rural population, 66–67
literacy, narrative, and colonial ideational space, 50–53; adult education and culture of literacy, 9, 51, 67–69, 89n44, 91; conclusion to, 86–87; Gaskiya Corporation and new public sphere, 60–62; imperial modernity translation, 74–78; intellectual space consolidation, 62–65; mobile colonial kinship, 80–83, 90n73, 90nn76–77; reading culture, forging of, 54–58, 60–62; sensation and narration, 83–86; translation as pedagogy, 78–80; travel writing as experiential literacy, 69–74
literacy culture, 50, 86
literary and intellectual imaginary, 62
literary culture, 50, 53, 56, 233–34; adult literacy relating to, 51; colonial, 9; Hausa, 52; infrastructure for, 51; school culture relating to, 51

literary self-expression, 57
literary standard, of *Tafiya Mabudin Ilimi*, 244
literary technique of similitude to communicate parallels, 75–76, 89n56
literature, 22–23, 51–53
Liverpool: Ibrahim in, 143–45; port of, 250
Liverpool Echo, 144
Local Government, 294
"Local Government," 280
"Local Governments in Transition," 280
logistical plans, for Dikko trip, 182–83
London, emir of Gwandu in, 146–47, 173–74
London allure, of Dikko, 108; at Bank of England, 110; at Harrods, 111; at London Zoological Gardens, 109, *109*, 111, 114, 120, *193*, 195; at Lord Mayor reception, 109, *110*; at Royal Mint, 110; at Russian ballet, 111
London Boat Race, 251
London Bridge, 76–77
London cars, Ndayako on, 264
London County Council, 302, 303
London County Council Housing Estate, 286
London in vernacular, 146–48
London Mosque, 286
London Museum, Ndayako on, 264
London Zoological Garden: Dikko at, 109, *109*, 111, 114, 120, *193*, 195; emirs at, 286; Ibrahim at, 139
Long, A. C. E., 291–92
Longmore, Robert, 304–5
Lord Mayor reception, Dikko at, 109, *110*
loyal imperial aristocratic ally, Nagogo as, 222–23
Lugard, Frederick: Dikko visits with, 94, 120, 163–64, *164*, 213–14; as governor of Northern Nigeria, 32–33, 51–52; Imam visit with, 80–83; memorial for, 317–19; Soron Ingila office of, 314–16, *315*; Yahaya and, 173

MacDonald, Malcom, 216, 318–19
Madame Tussaud Wax Museum, 120
Magana Jari Ce (Imam), 58–59
Maiden, R. L. B., 91–92, 93, 221
Manchester, Ibrahim in, 143, 146

Maple's, 160
marginalization, of aristocratic subaltern, 4, 44n2
Marseille, 136, 137
Marxian commodity fetishism, 30
mass audience creation, literacy and, 65–67
mass literacy, 9, 57, 63, 65, 67, 86
mass touristic travel and guided tours, 7–8
McIntosh, Marjorie, 303
Mecca direction, 284
Mecca-London itinerary, of Ibrahim, *137*; with Messrs. Horsefield, 135; with network of guides, 136; with own wealth, 134; in Paris, 136, 137–38; at Prince Albert Hotel, 138; with Thomas Cook travel agency, 7, 135, 137, 145; travel party with, 135
mechanization, Dikko on, 201
mediation, 21–23
Medina, 136, 186
memorabilia, of metropolitan travel, 206–9
memorials, 316–19
"Merchant Marine Training in England," 251
Merriman-Labor, A. B. C., 4
Merthyr Express, 199–200
Messrs. Horsefield, 135
metropole, 20, 118; colony and, 37; Dikko on, 104–8; as familiar and unknown, Tukur on, 236; as playground, 195. *See also* late-colonial allure of metropole
metropole travel in age of modernity: leveraging of, 2–3; modern aristocrats relating to, 1–8, 10, 11–14, 25–28; possibilities with, 3; subaltern metropolitan travel as colonial translation, 20–23
metropolitan, educational, medical, and agricultural institutions visits, 162
metropolitan Britain, 43
metropolitan circles, Dikko in, 95
metropolitan colonial racism, 4
metropolitan connections, 298
metropolitan conventions, travel writing about, 269
metropolitan courtship, 298–301
metropolitan culture, 35
metropolitan encounters, of Dikko, 91–96, 214–19, 231n121; as inaugural exploration

of metropole, 118; newspaper accounts of, 113–19; with tours and sightseeing, 113–16
metropolitan engagements: of Dikko, 226, 232n154; of Nagogo, 226
metropolitan entertainment, 155–58
metropolitan explorations, in late colonial and postcolonial periods, 331–32
metropolitan explorations, of Ibrahim: at Calico Printers Association, 143; with hotel accommodations, 146–47; in Liverpool, 143–45; in Manchester, 143, 146; with racism, 145–46; with shopping, 144; with technology, 144; at Unilever industrial complex, 143, 197
metropolitan goods, 138–40, 153
metropolitan institutions, Northern Nigerian relationship to, 15
metropolitan itineraries evolution, 285; with homogenization, 288; with personal sightseeing tours, 286–87; with unregimented programs, 286
metropolitan modernity, 18–19, 20, 29–31, 144–45, 204–6, 261
metropolitan outreach, 299–301
metropolitan society, mythology of, 26
metropolitan technology, 78, 144
metropolitan touring as colonial validation, 291–93; to deepen imperial aristocratic connection, 290; with Native Authority staff, 290; with 1954 delegation, 290; as social self-fortification, 290; with study tours, 289
metropolitan tours evolution, 296
metropolitan travel, 10, 13, 20–23; colonial sublime and, 319–21; connections with, 319; of Dikko, 206, *207*, 209, *209*, *214*, 230n98; empire loyalism and, 33–35
metropolitan travel, utilitarian legacy and: community of readers to community of writers, 238–40; conclusion to, 268–70; ethnographic minutia and subaltern gaze, 246–52; Etsu Nupe testament, 261–68; forging imperial community, 252–61; newspaper travel narratives and ways of knowing metropole, 240–45; other colonial Other, 245–46, 249, 251; students of Britain, 234–38; with travel-animated literary form, 233–34

metropolitan travel institutionalization: Daura written primer and lectures relating to, 274–75; Kafin Madaki lectures relating to, 274
metropolitan travelogue, *Tafiya Mabudin Ilimi* as, 40, 64
metropolitan travel writing genre, 240
metropolitan visibility, Dikko impact on, 223–24
Miacke (colonel), 110
Middlesex Hospital, 286
military industrialization, 201
military parade, Ndayako on, 263
minting and printing facility, Ndayako on, 262
Mitchell, Timothy, 123
M'Kee, W. Cevil, 297
mobile colonial kinship: encounters relating to, 80–83, 90nn76–77; habits, eccentricity, predilections, and nicknames with, 81, 90n73; narratives about, 80–83
mobilities, 28; accelerated, 14; African, 14; of aristocratic subaltern, 3; colonial, 2; travel, colonial aristocratic courtship, and, 11–14, 23
modernity, 166, 253, 325; of aristocratic subaltern, 2, 10; of Britain, 174, 200–202, 296; colonial, 2, 20, 35, 47n48, 52, 72, 324; Euro-American, 334; imperial modernity translation, 74–78; literacy and, 66; metropolitan, 18–19, 20, 29–31, 144–45, 261; travel in age of, 1–10; *zamani*, 34. *See also* metropole travel in age of modernity
modernization, 78, 201, 220–21, 299, 300–301, 306; Dikko projects for, 223–24; symbiotic relationship of development and, 296
modernization, colonial associational leverage and, 96; of agriculture technologies, 97, 224; of court system, 97; of Katsina as center of colonial secular education, 97–99; of Katsina as cultural center, 99–101; of treasury bureaucracy, 97
monarchy. *See* English monarchy
Mondlane, Eduardo, 26–27
Monrovia Group, 336
Montrose Standard, 189, 199
Moore, R. Foster, 210

morality, 50
Morris Motor company, 142, 150, 157, 203, 209
Mukasa, Ham, writings of, 17–20
"Municipal Transport Service," 294
Muslim aristocrats, in colonial Northern Nigeria, 1, 2, 5, 23
Muslim Bornu, 52
Muslim culture, colonial travel impacted by, 168–69
Muslim Hausa rulers, British colonial patronage of, 147–48
Muslim pilgrimage, to Mecca, 102, 181–82
Muslims, 40, 147–48; African, 2, 5, 23; attire of, 292–93; Dikko as, 116–17; Hausa-Fulani Muslim ruling classes, 163; Hausa Muslim cultures, 2, 19–20; Hausaphone Muslim males, 275; Hausa-speaking, Muslim audience, for travelogues, 15; Ibrahim as, 134; Qadiriyya Muslim orthodoxy, 159; Tijaniyya Muslim brotherhood, 159

de Naeyer, Jacqueline, 329
Nagogo, Usman, 112, 115, 304–5; Anglophone West African troops visit with, 222; Dikko-Nagogo British connection, 181–232; in *Gaskiya ta fi Kwabo*, 218, 219; in his father's path, 219–20; Katsina palace renovation by, 224, 225; as loyal imperial aristocratic ally, 222–23; as modernizer, 221–23; Ndayako visit with, 266; polo played by, 30–31, 100, 212, 214, *216*, 227; as son and successor of Dikko, 41–42, 175; travels of, 102, 105, 114, 210
narrative genre, colonial traveler writings and, 249
narratives: of Dikko, 204–6; of emirs, posttravel, 167–68; from returned travelers, 241; of travel, to metropole, 25–26. *See also* literacy, narrative, and colonial ideational space; newspaper travel narratives and ways of knowing metropole; *specific narratives*
National Council of Nigerian Citizens (NCNC), 337
Native Authorities, 276, 277, 278–79, 288, 289
native imperial propagandists, 15

Native Treasury funds, 278
NCNC. *See* National Council of Nigerian Citizens
Ndayako, Alhaji Muhammadu (Etsu Nupe), 24–25, 64; at agriculture engineering school, 265; at Buckingham Palace, 267; on circus, 262–63; at electricity-generating plants, 266; at factories, 266; itinerary of, 262; on London cars, 264; at London Museum, 264; on military parade, 263; on minting and printing facility, 262; on public housing project, 264; on queen's birthday celebration, 263–64; at Royal Air Force Museum, 265; at Taunton, 266; on tea with queen, 267; Usman Nagogo visit with, 266; on Windsor Castle, 263–65
neo-Christian customs, of metropole, 20
NEPU. *See* Northern Elements Progressive Union
NEPU-affiliated Northern radical intellectuals, 22
New Councilor, The, 294
newspapers, 56–57, 63–65; condescension and mockery of Dikko by, 118–19; exoticizing of Dikko by, 118–19; Ja'afar newspaper story, 313–16, *315*; metropolitan encounters of Dikko covered by, 113–19. *See also specific newspapers*
newspaper travel narratives and ways of knowing metropole, 245; dialogic culture relating to, 240; with English monarchy interest, 242; inquiries and requests impact on, 241–42; in installments, 240; with narratives from returned travelers, 241; with second- or third-person narrative pronouns, 244; storytelling style with, 240; with travel notes and diaries, 243
Nigerian aristocratic partners reward, 276
Nigerian Colonial Service, 210
Nigerian Pavilion, 122–23
1947 travel, 277
1948 travel, 277–78
1949 travel, 279–80
1950s travel, 282
1955 tours, 293–95
1956 tours, 294–95

Nkrumah, Kwame, 336
Norfolk and Suffolk Journal, 113, 115, 118
NORLA. *See* Northern Nigerian Literature Agency
Northern Elements Progressive Union (NEPU), 337; Amino Kano in, 281; opposition of, 281–82; as radical wing, 281; Zungur in, 281
northernization, 43, 297–99, 310n92
Northern Nigeria, 28, 202–4; anti-Western attitude of, 332–34; aristocratic institutions in, 317; British connections with, 235–37, 314; colonial literary scene in, 9; colonial modernity in, 2; Islamist radicalization and anti-Western rhetoric of, 3; Lugard as governor of, 32–33, 51–52; metropolitan institutions relationship with, 15; Muslim aristocrats in, 1, 2, 5, 23; political elites of, 333; School of Pharmacy in, 304; society in, 25; traveling aristocrats in, 1–3, 17; Western modernity viewed by, 334
Northern Nigeria aristocratic exploration of Britain (1930s), 40–41
Northern Nigeria Civil Service, 303
Northern Nigeria Colonial Service, 54, 83
Northern Nigerian aristocrats, 1, 2; curiosity of, 8, 37, 38; explorations of metropolitan Britain analysis, 43; travels of, 3–8
Northern Nigerian elites, 274, 276, 293
Northern Nigerian Eton fives team, 300–301
Northern Nigerian Literature Agency (NORLA), 9, 65–66, 67–69, 89n44, 91
Northern Nigerian Literature Bureau, 54, 55, 58, 60
Northern Nigerian metropolitan travelers, 10
Northern Nigerian modernistic imagination, 72
Northern Nigerian readers, Romanized, 38, 243, 275
Northern Nigerian students: as educationally handicapped, 299; Gana as advocate for, 298–99; special admission considerations for, 298–99
Northern People's Congress (NPC), 334; Bello in, 281; as conservative wing, 281; Imam in, 281

Northern Tanning Company, 286
Northern Whig and Belfast Post, 297
novelty and exotic character, of ethnographic minutia and subaltern gaze, 247
NPC. *See* Northern People's Congress
Nueilly, 285
Nuffield (lord), 150
Nuhu, Bayaro, 244–45, 259; "Behavior of the British" by, 258; British police, 257; on education, 257; English hospitality narrative of, 256–57; "Winter in England" by, 251–52

Occidentalism, 7
Och'Idoma Ogiri Oko, 29
Oko, Ogiri, in Britain: with King's Medal, 292; Muslim attire of, 292–93; as Och'Idoma, 290–91; packaged tour for, 290–91; regal artifacts taken back by, 293; Scotland visit of, 292
Orientalism, 6
Orientalism (Said), 6
Other, 7, 8, 27, 36, 72, 200, 325
other Colonial Other, with colonizer and colonized, 245–46, 249, 251
Otherness, adventures and, 120–26, *121*, *122*
"Our Visit to England," 243
Overlanders, The, 294
Oxford, 79–80, 286

packaged tour, for Oko, 290–91
Palace of Versailles, 285
Palmer, H. R., 91, 96
paradigmatic shift, in *Gaskiya ta fi Kwabo*, 60, 61
Paris, 136, 137–38, 283–85
Paris Casino, 284
Parisian perfumes, 283, 284
Parsons, Neil, 5
patronage and courtesies, 31, 35
pedagogical content, of women's tour, 289
perambulators, 153–54, 178nn60–61
personal connections, with colonial kinship, 155
personalities, powers and: divergence of itineraries with, 160, 162–63; with emir

of Gwandu, 159–64, *163*, *164*; with emir of Kano, 159–64, *163*, *164*; with metropolitan, educational, medical, and agricultural institutions, 162; religious and political superiority with, 159; with science of flight and aerodynamics, 162–63, *163*; of Sokoto Caliphate hierarchy, 159; with sultan of Sokoto, 159, 161–64, *163*, *164*; unanimity with, 160
personal sightseeing tours, 286–87
personal to official, 296–98; Abdulmalik as commissioner in Britain, 295; Bello as premier, 295; negotiations on independence, 295
photographic technology, 199
Place de la Concorde, 284
political independence in shadow of metropolitan courtship: Bello impact on, 299–300; cultural path of exchanges request, 299; Gana impact on, 298–99; metropolitan connections relating to, 298; northernization relating to, 298; technical assistance for project modernization request, 299, 300–301
polo: Katsina cultural identity and, 99–101; Nagogo with, 30–31, 100, 212, 214, *216*, 220–21, 227
polo tournaments, 212, 231n111
popular legitimacy, 13
"Port of Liverpool, The," 250
Port of London, 251
Portsmouth, 194, 195, 206, 286
Port Sunlight, 198
postcolonial anxieties, metropolitan outreach and: British expats relating to, 301–2; with educational crisis, 302; with inadequate instructional personnel, 301; Kaita relating to, 301–3; with Scotland and Northern Ireland, 303; with staffing problems, 301–4; with teacher recruitment, 302–3
postcolonial aristocracies, 317
postcolonial metropolitan tourism, 304–5
postcolonial periods, 331–32
postcolony. *See* imperial exploration, imagining the postcolony with
praise, for Dikko, 91–92

Pratt, Mary, 36
pregnancy, of Dadasare, 323–24
prescriptive punditry, 253
"Present Day Britain and Its System of Local Government," 294
prestige, 280
Prince Albert Hotel, 138
privileged background, of emir of Gwandu, 172
processes, industries, material objects, ethnographic minutia of, 249–50
professional women's tour, 288–89
progressive reforms, Dikko impact on, 96
propaganda, 15, 60, 65–67
"Public Cleansing," 294
public housing project, Ndayako on, 264
publishing house, East relating to, 62–63
publishing infrastructure, 58

Qadiriyya Muslim orthodoxy, 159
Queen Elizabeth, 250
Queen Mary, 250

racecourses, 76
"Races in Residence" exhibit, 122
racial and religious humiliation, of Muslim aristocrats, 1
racial-evolutionary hierarchies, 85
racism, 4, 100, 124–25, 145–46, 175, 217, 321
radical wing, NEPU as, 281
"Ranch in the Rockies," 287
Rankin, Mr., 210
reactionary politics, 4
reading culture, forging of: East impact on, 54–58, 60, 61–62; for indigenous reading public, 56; Katsina College relating to, 54–55, 57, 80, 98–99; in Romanized script, 55; Translation Bureau relating to, 55
Reclaiming Travel (Stavans and Ellison), 16
recreational and conservationist habituation of wildlife, Tukur on, 236
Reddington, F. H. I., 161
regal artifacts, for Oko, 293
Regent Palace Hotel, 291
rehabilitative effect of distance, ethnographic minutia impact on, 247
religion, morality and, 50

religious and political superiority, of emirs, 159
religious pilgrimages, 15
religious services, during travel, 279
repeat excursion, of Dikko, 119–20
reporters, from *Gaskiya ta fi Kwabo*, 243
representational perspectives, of aristocratic subaltern, 15–16
Reynolds, J. A., 294
Richards, Arthur, 57, 63
Richmond Hill Hotel, 265
Richmond Royal Horse Show, 282, 286
Roman Baths, 286
Romanized Hausa fiction and travel writer, Imam as, 57–60, 63
Romanized Hausa-language readers, 55–56, 59, 62, 63, 67, 70, 253
Romanized Hausa storytelling, 9–10, 52, 58–60, 86–87, 88n21
Romanized literacy, 9–11, 39, 50, 53
Romanized literary culture, 52–53
Romanized literature, 53
Romanized Northern Nigerian readers, 38
Romanized script, 55
Roman-literate Northern Nigerians, 243, 275
Rowntree, Seebohm, 161–62
Royal Agricultural Show, 219
Royal Air Force Museum, Ndayako on, 265
Royal Air Force Station, Dikko at, 116
Royal Mint, 110, 286
Royal Society for the Prevention of Cruelty to Animals award, to Dikko, 214
Royal Tournament, 282
rural populations, 66
Russian ballet, Dikko at, 111
Ruwan Bagaja (Imam), 58

Said, Edward, 6
Saint-Germain-en-Laye, 285
"Sanitary Administration and Control," 294
Sanusi, Muhammadu, II, 313
Sanusi financial recklessness story, 313–15
Sarkin Katsina Dikko (Dikko), 125
Saunders, L. G. A., 302–3
schools: culture of, 51; magazines of, 235; Ndayako on, 263, 265. *See also specific schools*

Scotland and Northern Ireland, outreach to, 303
Scotland visit, of Oko, 292
Scotsman, 190
scribal specialization, 69, 85
Sebele (king), 19
self-fashioning, 274–93, 315–16, 318
semi-didactic pontifications, of Inuwa, 238
semi-diplomatic tours, 296
sensation, narration and: in colonial discourses, 85; humor with, 83–85; in *Tafiya*, 83–86
Shakespeare, William, 142
"Sheep in England," 250
shopping expeditions, 29–30, 144, 153, 283–84, 332
Shuaybu, Abdulkadir, 261, 262
sightseeing, 1, 6, 13, 20–21, 27–29, 297
Signal and Noise (Larkin), 319–20
situational relationships, 321
Smith, Masterton, 218
socialization, of Dadasare, 323–24
sociopolitical bedrocks, of colonialization, 11–12
Sokoto. *See* sultan, of Sokoto
Sokoto Caliphate, 13, 22–23, 32, 51–52, 82, 146, 158–59
solidarity, aristocratic, 11
"Some Ways of Foreigners Which Seem Strange to Me" (Inuwa), 237
Soron Ingila demolition story, 314–16, *315*
Southampton, 286
Southern Nigerian bureaucratic labor, 298
Speaker's Corner, 236
special admission considerations, for Northern Nigerian students, 298–99
sponsorship, of travel, 15
staffing problems, 301–4
Stavans, Ilan, 16
Stockholm syndrome, 324
storytelling style, with newspaper travel narratives, 240
students: admission goals of, 298–99; Northern Nigerian, 298–99; travel narratives of, 234–38, 243–44
students, of Britain: intellectualism of, 237; in school magazines, 235; testimonial

narratives of, 234–35. *See also* Inuwa, Magaji; Tukur, Bashir
study tours, 280
subaltern. *See* aristocratic subaltern
subaltern, as colonial explorer and reverse ethnographer, 35; colony and metropole relating to, 37; distinctions with, 36–37; intellectual power relating to, 37; Other relating to, 36; Pratt on, 36; problems with, 36
subaltern ethnographic notebook, of Dikko: on car manufacturing plant, 106, 108; on Derby Cattle Show, 105–6, 108; on metropole, 104–8; on Tropical School of Medicine, 105
subaltern gaze. *See* ethnographic minutia, subaltern gaze and
subaltern metropolitan travel, as colonial translation, 20–23
subaltern privilege, colonial connections and, 328–29
subaltern societies, kingships of, 11
subaltern travel writing and weight of minutia, 38–39
submarines, 206
Sudan, 184
Sudan Railways, 185
sultan, of Sokoto, 40, 148, 155–56, 171, 222; personalities and powers relating to, 159, 161–64, *163*, *164*
Surrey Advertiser, 196–97
symbiotic partnership, of ethnographic minutia and subaltern gaze, 251

Tafiya Mabudin Ilimi (Imam): England trip narratives, 70–74, *71*, 76, 80; literary standard set by, 244; as metropolitan travelogue, 40, 64; sensation and narration relating to, 83–86
Tafiyan Etsu Nupe Ingila (Etsu Nupe's travel to England), 261
Tafiyan Etsu Nupe Ingila (Ndayako), 64
Taron Tattauna Al'Amurun Bauchi (Bauchi Discussion Circle), 239–40, 254
Tatler, 200
Taunton, Ndayako at, 266
Tay, V. M. C., 294

teacher recruitment, 302–3
tea with queen, Ndayako with, 267
technical assistance for project modernization request, 299, 300–301
technical interactions, 29
technocratic and technological assistance, Gana courting of, 297–98
technology and modernization, Dikko on, 201
telephone exchange visit, Dikko on, 106
testimonial narratives, of students, 234–35
Thames, 206
"There Are no Idlers in England" (Bello), 259
Thomas Cook Travel agency, 7, 135, 137, 145
Tijani, Ahmadu, 294
Tijaniyya Muslim brotherhood, 159
Tion, Peter Akpeto, 294
touristic imagination, staged authenticity and, 28–29
touristic pilgrimages, 273
tours, as structured quasi-diplomatic exercises, 297
Tower of London, 140
traffic lights, 205–6
transculturation, 76
transformation, of Dadasare, 324
translation, as pedagogy, 78–80
Translation Bureau, 55
transracial connections, 321, 325
transracial relationships, 322
travel: in age of modernity, 1–10; of aristocratics, 1–8; conceptual context of, 11–14; ethnography and, 7; freedom of, 12; funding of, 15, 16; intermediaries impact on, 21; mobility, colonial aristocratic courtship, and, 11–14, 23; of Nagogo, 102, 105, 114, 210; sponsorship of, 15; theorizations of, 14
travel-animated literary form, 233–34
traveler ethnographers, 6–8
traveler salaries, 277–78
travel memoirs and lectures, on imperial exploration, 273
travel narratives, 3, 6, 16, 64–65; of emir of Gwandu, 20–21, 41, 133, 146, 171–74; of Imam, 72–74, 83–86; of students, 234–38, 243–44; of Tukur, 235–37

travelogues, 4, 8, 15–16, 40, 64; of emir of Gwandu, 20–21, 41, 133, 146, 171–74; of Nagogo, 218, 219
travel writing, 38–39, 274–75; about metropolitan conventions, 269; Anglo-imperial culture through lens of, 269; appeal of, 269–70; of Imam, 57–60, 63
travel writing, as experiential literacy, 70–74; scribal specialization relating to, 69, 85
treasury bureaucracy, modernization of, 97
Trenchard, Hugh, 115
trip planning as colonial regimen: to Buckingham Palace, 185; to Houses of Parliament, 185; with regimen, control, and detail, 184–86; with Sudan Railways, 185; with visit to governor of Medina, 186; with visit to King Abdul Naiz Ibn Fa'ad, 186
trivia, fascination of, 247
Trooping of the Colour on the birthday of His Majesty the King, 282
Tropical School of Medicine, Dikko on, 105
Tswana kings, 5, 19
Tukur, Bashir, 233; "Britain as I Saw It" by, 235; on British and Nigerian differences, 235–36; Elizabeth II meeting with, 236; on familiar and unknown metropole, 236; on recreational and conservationist habituation of wildlife, 236; travel narratives of, 235–37

UAC. See United Africa Company
Uganda's Katikiro in England (Mukasa), 17–20
UMBC. See United Middle Belt Congress
Unilever House, 160–61, 206
Unilever industrial complex, 143, 197
United Africa Company (UAC), 160, 197, 206–8
United Kingdom travel, as rite of passage, 273
United Middle Belt Congress (UMBC), 337
United States, Balewa in, 334–40
University of Liverpool, 299

vernacular world, of writing, reading, and experiential sharing, 10

Victorian Britain, 4, 23
violence, Dadasare relating to, 322–26
Vischer, Hans, 51, 80–81
visual programmes, for Oko, 291
volunteers: for adult education and culture of literacy, 67–68; for colonial bureaucracy and mechanics of travel, 276–77, 306n7

Wales, Prince of, 187, 195
Waterfield, Mr., 80–81
Watt, James, 78–79
weekend in Paris, 283–85
Wembly British Empire Exhibition, 120, 122, 185; Hausa, Mendi, Fulani people at, 123–24; Nigerian Pavilion at, 122–23; "Races in Residence" exhibit at, 122; racism relating to, 124–25; "West African Walled Compound" at, 122–25
West African Pilot, 56
"West African Walled Compound," 122–25
West Country Journey, 295
Western-educated class, 53–57, 60–61, 238, 254
Western modernity, 334
Western Morning News, 165
Whipsnade Zoo, 218
White City greyhound races, 196, 216–17
white colonizers, 325
white man, image of, 26–27
Wilma (lord), 110
Windsor Castle, 139, 160, 263–65, 286
"Winter in England" (Nuhu), 251–52
wives, of Dikko, 113–14, 119
Wolseley Motor Works, 141
women, 63, 68–69
"Women in Britain," 294
women's tour: of educational visits and sight-seeing tours, 288–99; logistics and pedagogical content of, 289; Native Authorities funding of, 288; of professional women, 288–89
wonder: of ethnography, 6–9; materiality of, 8
Woodhouse, C. A., 136–38, 141–42, 145
World War II, 60
Wright, Robert, 289

writers, 10; audience interaction with, 16; community of, 238–40; readers and, 252
Wyfold (lord), 114–15

Yaki da Jailci, 66
Yakubu, A. M., 239

Yankee at the Court of King Arthur, A, 107, 114
Yorkshire Post, 195

Zungeru, 172
Zungur, Sa'adu, 56, 239, 281
Zuru, Abdullahi, 294

MOSES E. OCHONU is Professor of African History at Vanderbilt University. He is author of *Africa in Fragments: Essays on Nigeria, Africa, and Global Africanity*; *Colonialism by Proxy: Hausa Imperial Agents and Middle Belt Consciousness in Nigeria* (IUP), which was named finalist for the Herskovits Prize; and *Colonial Meltdown: Northern Nigeria in the Great Depression*. He is editor of *Entrepreneurship in Africa: A Historical Approach* (IUP).

CPSIA information can be obtained
at www.ICGtesting.com
Printed in the USA
JSHW011803051022
31347JS00001B/42